# MANCHESTER UNITED

## OFFICIAL YEARBOOK 2005

**Contributors:**
David Gill
Sir Alex Ferguson

**Thanks to:**
Cliff Butler, David Taylor, Jon Crampin, Emma Howcutt, Cheryl Francis, Caroline Hunt, Steve Morgan, Paul Davies, Rob Wightman, Ian McLeish, Cormac Bourne, David Meek, Lisa Irving, Phil Townsend.

Thanks also to all the clubs who kindly granted permission in allowing their official club crests to be reproduced in this publication.

**Photographs:**
John and Matthew Peters/Manchester United FC, Action Images, Empics

**Design and Editorial:**
Haymarket Customer Publishing

First published in 2005

10 9 8 7 6 5 4 3 2 1

Manufactured and distributed by
Carlton Books Limited
20 Mortimer Street
London W1T 3JW



A CIP catalogue record for this book is available from the British Library.

ISBN 0 233 00155 7

Printed and bound in Great Britain

# CONTENTS

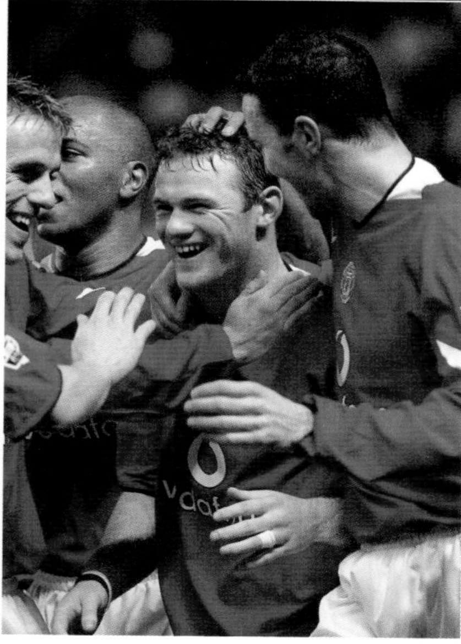

**David Gill** 5
**Sir Alex Ferguson** 6

PREMIERSHIP
Match-by-match coverage of the 2004/05 league
**August** 12
**September** 22
**October** 30
**November** 40
**December** 50
**January** 62
**February** 72
**March** 82
**April** 88
**May** 98

UEFA CHAMPIONS LEAGUE
On the road in Europe... from Dinamo to the San Siro
**Opening rounds** 110
**Knockout stage** 126

FA CUP
All the action from the Cup trail to Cardiff
**Opening rounds** 134
**Closing stages** 142

CARLING CUP 152
Search for silverware on the fourth front

**Focus on the pre-season** 160
**Other events at Old Trafford** 168
**Results and statistics** 170

PLAYER PROFILES 176
How the Reds performed
**Snapshots of the season** 192

Reserves and Academy
The young guns silverware-winning season
**Premier Reserves** 202
**Pontin's Reserves** 204
**Under-18s** 206
**Reserves profile** 208
**Transfers and Loans** 213

SUPPORTERS' CLUB INFORMATION
**Membership and travel** 214
**Supporters' information** 216

Manchester United PLC
Chairman Sir Roy Gardner
Chief executive David Gill
Group finance director Nick Humby
Commercial director Andy Anson
Non-executive directors Ian Much, Maurice Watkins, Philip Yea

Manchester United FC
Directors Michael Edelson, Sir Bobby Charlton CBE, Les Olive, Maurice Watkins, David Gill, Nick Humby
Manager Sir Alex Ferguson CBE
Secretary Ken Merrett
President Martin Edwards

# Manchester United Football Club PLC

**HONOURS**

**European Champions Clubs' Cup - winners**
1968, 1999

**European Cup Winners' Cup - winners**
1991

**FA Premier League - champions**
1993, 1994, 1996, 1997, 1999, 2000, 2001, 2003

**Football League Division One - champions**
1908, 1911, 1952, 1956, 1957, 1965, 1967

**FA Challenge Cup - winners**
1909, 1948, 1963, 1977, 1983, 1985, 1990, 1994, 1996, 1999, 2004

**Football League Cup - winners**
1992

**Inter-Continental Cup - winners**
1999

**UEFA Super Cup - winners**
1991

**FA Charity/Community Shield - winners**
1908, 1911, 1952, 1956, 1957, 1983, 1993, 1994, 1996, 1997, 2003
**Joint holders**
1965, 1967, 1977, 1990

## CLUB TELEPHONE NUMBERS

**Website** www.manutd.com
**Ticket and match info line** +44 (0) 870 442 1968
**Main switchboard** +44 (0) 161 868 8000
**Ticket sales** +44 (0) 870 442 1999
**Match hospitality, Museum and Tour centre, Ticketing Services inquiries & Membership Services** +44 (0) 870 442 1994
**Conference & Catering and Events Team** +44 (0) 870 442 1994
**Megastore** +44 (0) 161 868 8567
**Mail Order** +44 (0) 870 111 8107
**Red Café** +44 (0) 161 868 8303
**Development Association** +44 (0) 161 868 8600
**United in the Community** +44 (0) 161 708 9451
**United Radio** +44 (0) 161 868 8888
**MUTV** +44 (0) 870 848 6888
**United Review Subscriptions** +44 (0) 845 677 7801
**MU Finance** +44 (0) 870 442 2001
**Textphone for deaf/impaired hearing** +44 (0) 161 868 8668

**Welcome to** the Official One United Yearbook for the 2004/05 season.

Once again, there have been some memorable moments in a campaign that ended in shootout misery at the Millennium Stadium. After playing so well in the FA Cup final, the players did not deserve to suffer the agony of losing in the biggest lottery the game offers.

But that performance has left everyone at the club feeling optimistic about next season.

Last summer saw the squad strengthened with the arrival of Alan Smith, Gabriel Heinze and of course, shortly after the season started, we added the outstanding talents of Wayne Rooney. Who can forget that fantastic debut hat-trick against Fenerbahçe – one of the highlights of the year.

The club also celebrated Sir Alex Ferguson's 1,000th game in charge of the team – a landmark unlikely to be passed at the top level in the modern game. It is a remarkable achievement over a period of unprecedented success at Manchester United.

As we embark on a new season, the aim remains the same as ever – to challenge for the top honours. I am confident we are in good shape to do just that.

David Gill
**Chief executive**

# SIR ALEX FERGUSON

## Although the campaign ended on a low note in Cardiff, there are plenty of positives for the boss to take from the season

**I guess the FA** Cup final just about summed up our whole season.

There we were, pulverising Arsenal but we just couldn't stick the ball in the net. It must have been one of the most one-sided finals in Cup history, certainly between two top teams, and I could only sympathise with the players afterwards as well as with you the supporters.

You must have been as frustrated as I was, and probably just as mystified as to why we weren't able to turn our so superior possession and chance-making into a goal or two.

I give credit to Jens Lehmann who made some super saves and though people will say that when Freddie Ljungberg headed off the line that was what he was there for, it was yet another unbelievable escape for the Gunners.

And when you take into account hitting the bar and the post, the fact that we had a dozen corners to Arsenal's one, and all the other near misses, the result beggars belief.

I never expected to see Arsenal of all teams playing for a penalty shootout, except to say that, given the charmed life their goal enjoyed, it made some sort of sense! In extra time they didn't even attempt to get into our box.

I just feared at the end of normal time that it simply wasn't our scoring day and so it proved with Paul Scholes the luckless one to find Lehmann saving his spot-kick. Never for one moment, though, did any of us point a finger at Paul. He has done too much for United over the years to make him a scapegoat. The players know that the real reason for not winning the Cup was missing all those chances.

And what's more, although many people have said we were just plain unlucky, we know we must carry the responsibility for what at the end of the day was poor finishing.

This was not just in evidence at Cardiff for the final, we have only ourselves to blame in the League as well. This was not an isolated instance. It's the story of our season: we missed too many chances in the Premiership, especially against teams in the lower half of the table.

We threw away an awful lot of points to trail behind Chelsea, and just when we thought that the FA Cup offered us the opportunity to salvage the season, our extravagance with chances cost us dearly at Cardiff, too.

As I say, it was the story of our whole season, and I can assure you that it is a problem we are working hard to solve. As we always do in a close season, we take careful stock of the previous season as we lay our plans for the next. And I have got to stress that it's not totally a tale of woe, even if we let ourselves down in the League and then had our noses rubbed in it at Cardiff.

Certainly we have a lot of work ahead of us but I believe we have the basis to move forward again. The performance in the Cup final tells you that in terms of movement, penetration and creating chances we are as good as anyone and better than most.

Cardiff underlined that we have a bunch of exciting young players coming through fast. There was no doubting the fantastic potential of Wayne Rooney – deservedly voted Man of the Match – Cristiano Ronaldo and Darren Fletcher.

Rooney and Ronaldo are great players already but they are going to be even better. Fletcher is learning fast and he's another key part of a young squad I have been putting together over the last 18 months or so.

Defensively, we are a good mix of ages. Gary Neville is 30, Phil Neville 28 and Mikael Silvestre and Gabriel Heinze are 27, but remember that Rio Ferdinand is still 26, Wes Brown 25 and John

8

vodafone

ROO

O'Shea just 24. We have a solid foundation at the back and we can build on that.

I also think any manager would count his blessings to have four strikers like Ruud van Nistelrooy, Alan Smith, Louis Saha and, of course, Rooney who is very much part of the youthful thrust, along with Cristiano Ronaldo, that we have up front.

Darren Fletcher gives us great youthful potential in midfield as well, and though Scholes and Ryan Giggs have moved into the 30-year-old bracket, they have a lot more football in them.

Used sensibly so has Roy Keane, who, I admit, is going to be difficult to replace. We are working on it, though, and as always I don't rule out a signing this summer. One or two of the young reserves may also be ready to play a more prominent part in the squad next season, too.

So, despite the disappointment on missing out on the big prizes, I believe we have the basis for a stronger challenge next winter. We had real problems at the start of the last campaign with Rio Ferdinand missing to serve a long suspension, and our preparations were also hampered by having to fly some of our internationals to join us on tour, after originally planning to give them a rest. We had other key players missing with injury and all told we got off on the wrong foot.

You live and learn, though, and my plans are already drawn up for pre-season. All the players will report back for training on 27 June, the earliest we have ever got together for a new season. This time we are going to be ready to hit the ground running. Chelsea raised the bar with their sustained consistency of performance to win the championship and I am determined that neither they, nor anyone else, is going to pull away like that next time.

We are under a new ownership now, of course, following Malcolm Glazer's takeover. I know a lot of supporters are finding it difficult to come to terms with a family from another sporting culture moving in on what we consider to be our club and a squad of players who lie so close to our hearts.

All I can say as manager is that I shall continue to work for what at the end of the day is the really important thing, and that is Manchester United, the club we all love, and that you our fans will also stay true to the team and our glorious heritage.

*Alex Ferguson*

VIEIRA
4
RONALDO
7

# PREMIERSHIP

# August

## Sir Alex looked to rally United's depleted troops as Jose Mourinho and Rafael Benitez said hello to the Premiership

**As the latest** Premiership soap opera hit our screens yet again, the Greatest Show on Earth introduced a new star eager for top billing: outgoing Porto boss (and, lest we forget, new European champion) Jose Mourinho. The fixture computer handed the Chelsea manager a baptism of fire, with the Reds his first visitors to Stamford Bridge on 15 August. A depleted United side – missing injured trio Ruud van Nistelrooy, Louis Saha and Darren Fletcher, with Cristiano Ronaldo and new signing Gabriel Heinze still on Olympic duty, and Rio Ferdinand suspended – lost the season's curtain-raiser and continued to struggle throughout August, only narrowly beating promoted Norwich and dropping four Bank Holiday points with draws against Blackburn and Everton. Chelsea, on the other hand, set the early pace by winning all four matches, Roman Abramovich's army ending the month already seven points clear of United.

Champions Arsenal matched Chelsea stride for stride in August, winning four out of four and banging in 16 goals. Bolton continued to impress and ended the month in third place after recording an early win against Rafael Benitez's Liverpool. Teams propping up the table included new kids Crystal Palace and Norwich, but the early-season form of Blackburn and Newcastle was causing concern for managers Graeme Souness and Sir Bobby Robson. For Sir Bobby it was the end of an era, as he became the second Premiership managerial casualty of the season on 30 August, following the exit of Southampton's Paul Sturrock who left St Mary's after just two games.

**PREMIERSHIP FIXTURES THIS MONTH**

| | | |
|---|---|---|
| SUN 15 | CHELSEA | AWAY |
| SAT 21 | NORWICH CITY | HOME |
| SAT 28 | BLACKBURN ROVERS | AWAY |
| MON 30 | EVERTON | HOME |

**IN THE PREMIERSHIP THIS MONTH**

**203,583** watched United play 4 games

**3** goals were scored

**482** miles were travelled by United going to and from games

United fielded **20** players

**3** goals were conceded

### FOCUS ON ALAN SMITH

Given how quickly he settled in at Old Trafford, it's hard to believe that Alan Smith was, for many Reds, the ultimate arch nemesis. Leeds born and bred he had a habit of scoring important goals for the Whites against the Reds and boy, did he enjoy those moments. His £7million move across the Pennines in May 2004 was a genuine transfer shock with some diehard United fans suspicious from the off, but Smiffy was determined to prove the doubters wrong. He scored his first goal for his new club against Celtic on the summer US tour and was handed the responsibility of leading the line as the season kicked off. He scored a cracker against Arsenal in the Community Shield, then netted a beauty against Norwich on his OT debut, a double against Dinamo Bucharest and a vital injury-time equaliser at Blackburn. Almost like he'd been here for years...

# Chelsea 1

Gudjohnsen 15

# Manchester United 0

Clash of the Titans: captain Roy Keane slugs it out against Chelsea's Russian midfielder Alexei Smertin

**United's first** opening day defeat in nine years was undoubtedly a blow, but with so many first team stars injured, suspended or chasing gold at the Olympics in Athens, travelling Reds were disappointed but not too despondent on referee Graham Poll's final whistle. Sir Alex's side enjoyed the bulk of the possession but couldn't break down a stuffy Chelsea side determined to hold on to their early advantage.

The Londoners may have triumphed, but Roman Abramovich is entitled to expect rather more entertainment from his side after investing £200 million in 12 months. The "fun" Jose Mourinho had promised Chelsea fans in his programme notes was certainly nowhere to be seen; his players were effective, but defensive, and finished the game with every player behind the ball.

With a quarter of an hour gone Quinton Fortune misjudged the flight of the ball inside the Chelsea half, opening up a mass of unguarded space for Geremi to exploit. The Cameroon international advanced to the United box and picked out Didier Drogba, who headed the ball down for Eidur Gudjohnsen, the Icelandic striker

Sunday 15 August 2004
**Stamford Bridge**
Attendance 41,813
**Referee: Graham Poll**

coolly lifting the ball over Tim Howard into the United net.

For the next 75 minutes the home side demonstrated little interest in adding to their lead. Instead, they sat back and invited United to break them down. The Reds showed plenty of spirit and willingness, but sadly not enough penetration to trouble the Blues. The nearest United came to grasping a point was when Ryan Giggs narrowly headed wide from an Alan Smith cross in the final 10 minutes. Diego Forlan also had a promising chance when he controlled a lofted pass inside the Chelsea penalty area, but fired high and wide.

"I said to Mr Ferguson after the match that they did not deserve to leave Stamford Bridge with nothing," revealed Jose Mourinho. "I don't need anyone to tell me about that," said Sir Alex, though the pair did share a conciliatory glass of wine after the game. "I can make my own judgement about that.

"I hoped for more from our possession, which we dominated, although our crosses were a bit scrappy and over-hit. We worked really hard, we can consider ourselves a bit unlucky. But I'm confident in the ability of the team. I was before the match and I've no reason to think any differently after it."

## MAN OF THE MATCH

**PAUL SCHOLES**

In a typically tough trip to west London one Red really stood out: the newly retired England international looked energised as he beavered tirelessly away in the centre of midfield. With Chelsea's two lines of defence proving to be a very tough nut to crack, Scholes came as close as anyone to creating an opening. He also went close in the first-half with a powerful free-kick.

## MATCH FACTS

**CHELSEA**

Cech; Ferreira, Gallas, Terry, Bridge; Makele; Geremi (Carvalho 89) Lampard, Smertin; Drogba (Kezman 70) Gudjohnsen (Parker 82)
**Subs not used** Cudicini, Mutu

**MANCHESTER UNITED**

Howard; G Neville, Keane, Silvestre, Fortune (Bellion 84); Miller (Richardson 84), Djemba-Djemba (Forlan 73), O'Shea, Giggs, Scholes; Smith
**Subs not used** Ricardo, P Neville

| Man Utd | | Chelsea |
|---|---|---|
| 59% | POSSESSION | 41% |
| 1 | SHOTS ON TARGET | 3 |
| 9 | SHOTS OFF TARGET | 4 |
| 3 | CORNERS | 2 |
| 9 | FOULS | 19 |
| 2 | OFFSIDES | 4 |

### PREMIERSHIP RESULTS
WEEKEND BEGINNING 14/8/04

| | | |
|---|---|---|
| Aston Villa | 2-0 | Southampton |
| Blackburn | 1-1 | West Brom |
| Bolton | 4-1 | Charlton |
| Everton | 1-4 | Arsenal |
| Manchester City | 1-1 | Fulham |
| Middlesbrough | 2-2 | Newcastle |
| Norwich | 1-1 | Crystal Palace |
| Portsmouth | 1-1 | Birmingham |
| Tottenham | 1-1 | Liverpool |

### PREMIERSHIP TABLE
AT END OF 15/08/04

| | P | PTS |
|---|---|---|
| 1. Bolton Wanderers | 1 | 3 |
| 2. Arsenal | 1 | 3 |
| 3. Aston Villa | 1 | 3 |
| 4. Chelsea | 1 | 3 |
| 5. Middlesbrough | 1 | 1 |
| 6. Newcastle United | 1 | 1 |
| 7. Birmingham City | 1 | 1 |
| 8. Portsmouth | 1 | 1 |
| 9. Blackburn Rovers | 1 | 1 |
| 10. Tottenham Hotspur | 1 | 1 |
| 11. West Bromwich Albion | 1 | 1 |
| 12. Liverpool | 1 | 1 |
| 13. Manchester City | 1 | 1 |
| 14. Norwich City | 1 | 1 |
| 15. Crystal Palace | 1 | 1 |
| 16. Fulham | 1 | 1 |
| 17. Manchester United | 1 | 0 |
| 18. Southampton | 1 | 0 |
| 19. Everton | 1 | 0 |
| 20. Charlton Athletic | 1 | 0 |

# Manchester United 2

Bellion 32, Smith 50

# Norwich City 1

McVeigh 75

**Old Trafford's** Premiership curtain-raiser had a slightly surreal air about it, with the Reds kicking off the match bottom of the table; a strange 5.15pm kick-off time; and Alan Smith lining up at Old Trafford wearing the red of Manchester United. But by the time referee Neale Barry had blown his final whistle, just after 7pm, the Reds' first points of the season had been registered and that new striker had gone a long way towards winning over a whole new set of supporters with a cracking winner.

Newly-promoted Norwich arrived in Manchester with a raucous travelling support making the trip to M16 for the first time in a decade, and with their own new signing eager to make an impression. Manager Nigel Worthington had secured the services of Arsenal's highly-rated David Bentley on loan for a year, and in the opening half hour he almost delighted his employers in both Norwich and north London with a vicious 30-yard volley that beat Tim Howard and rattled the crossbar.

This simply spurred the Reds into action, however, and seconds later United took the lead. Ryan Giggs went on a marauding sprint up the left flank and whipped a deep cross into the Canaries'

**Flying start:** one assist and a spectacular volleyed goal made home debutant Alan Smith an instant hit with the Old Trafford faithful

Saturday 21 August 2004
**Old Trafford**
Attendance 67,812
**Referee: Neale Barry**

box. Alan Smith headed the ball towards the back post and David Bellion was on hand to stroke the ball home. Having got the taste for goal, minutes later the young Frenchman forced England Under-21 keeper Robert Green into a fingertip save in front of the Stretford End, but it was the second half before United made it two. Five minutes in Gary Neville crossed, Giggs headed the ball into the path of Smith, and the striker chested the ball down and volleyed an unstoppable shot over his shoulder and into the net.

United deserved the two-goal lead and should have comfortably closed the game out, but Norwich had no intention of playing the role of top-flight whipping boys, ex-City striker Darren Huckerby, as usual, proving a real nuisance. And with 15 minutes to go, substitute Paul McVeigh struck a powerful shot past Howard to get Delia out of her directors' box seat and give the Canaries hope. As the clock ticked down another sub, Leon McKenzie, almost equalised when he outmuscled Roy Keane, but his shot hit the side netting. And there was further good news for the Reds – Cristiano Ronaldo made a late substitute appearance, his first of the new season following a busy international summer.

## MAN OF THE MATCH

**ALAN SMITH**
After the match Sir Alex Ferguson compared Smith with Mark Hughes, saying, "Alan's a similar player to Mark, a brilliant leader of the line, tough and resilient. That was a Mark Hughes goal he scored in this match." High praise indeed, but if United's new front man continues to turn in performances of this quality - lively throughout and with a spectacular strike to boot - this probably won't be the last time he is compared with Sparky.

## MATCH FACTS

**MANCHESTER UNITED**
Howard; G Neville (P Neville 73), Silvestre, Keane, O'Shea; Bellion (Richardson 74), Miller (Ronaldo 85), Djemba-Djemba, Giggs; Scholes (Richardson 74), Smith
**Subs not used** Carroll, Eagles

**NORWICH CITY**
Green; Helveg, Fleming, Charlton, Drury; Bentley (McKenzie 76), Francis, Holt, Jonson (McVeigh 45); Huckerby, Svensson (Doherty 69)
**Subs not used** Ward, Edworthy
**Booked** Helveg

| Man Utd | | Norwich |
|---|---|---|
| 66% | POSSESSION | 34% |
| 8 | SHOTS ON TARGET | 1 |
| 6 | SHOTS OFF TARGET | 4 |
| 11 | CORNERS | 5 |
| 12 | FOULS | 24 |
| 1 | OFFSIDES | 4 |

**PREMIERSHIP RESULTS**
WEEKEND BEGINNING 21/8/04

| Home | Score | Away |
|---|---|---|
| Arsenal | 5-3 | Middlesbrough |
| Birmingham | 0-1 | Chelsea |
| Charlton | 2-1 | Portsmouth |
| Crystal Palace | 1-3 | Everton |
| Fulham | 2-0 | Bolton |
| Liverpool | 2-1 | Manchester City |
| Newcastle | 0-1 | Tottenham |
| Southampton | 3-2 | Blackburn |
| West Brom | 1-1 | Aston Villa |

**PREMIERSHIP TABLE**
AT END OF 22/08/04

| | P | PTS |
|---|---|---|
| 1. Arsenal | 2 | 6 |
| 2. Chelsea | 2 | 6 |
| 3. Aston Villa | 2 | 4 |
| 4. Fulham | 2 | 4 |
| 5. Liverpool | 2 | 4 |
| 6. Tottenham Hotspur | 2 | 4 |
| 7. Bolton Wanderers | 2 | 3 |
| 8. Manchester United | 2 | 3 |
| 9. Everton | 2 | 3 |
| 10. Southampton | 2 | 3 |
| 11. Charlton Athletic | 2 | 3 |
| 12. West Bromwich Albion | 2 | 2 |
| 13. Blackburn Rovers | 2 | 1 |
| 14. Portsmouth | 2 | 1 |
| 15. Newcastle United | 2 | 1 |
| 16. Manchester City | 2 | 1 |
| 17. Norwich City | 2 | 1 |
| 18. Birmingham City | 2 | 1 |
| 19. Middlesbrough | 2 | 1 |
| 20. Crystal Palace | 2 | 1 |

# Blackburn Rovers 1

Dickov 17

# Manchester United 1

Smith 90

**It says much** for the impressive start to the season by Arsenal and Chelsea that the Reds' draw at Blackburn felt more like a defeat. With the two London clubs starting faster than the British Olympic 4x100 metre relay team, it was vital United kept up with the early pacesetters and avoided a stumble like that on the opening day at Stamford Bridge. A 1-1 draw, even after an injury-time equaliser, proved to be another setback.

The game had started well for the Reds and the early signs were that it might be a comfortable afternoon in mid-Lancashire. United's passing game starved Rovers of possession and Cristiano Ronaldo looked capable of going past Lucas Neill at will. But domination is little use without goals, and sadly it was Blackburn who struck first, almost completely against the run of play.

In the 17th minute Morten Pedersen's long throw found its way to the diminutive, but ever-feisty, Paul Dickov. The former Manchester City man controlled the ball, turned, brushing aside Mikael Silvestre in the process, before unleashing a shot across Tim Howard into the far corner from the tightest of angles. It was a sloppy goal to concede, not that the majority of fans in Ewood Park cared.

The introduction of a fit-again Louis Saha for the second half increased the pressure on Brad Friedel's goal– and on Lorenzo Amoruso, the Italian seeing red in the 70th-minute for a professional foul on the Frenchman. Chance after chance was created, but a combination of wayward finishing, and some fine goalkeeping from Blackburn's American stopper, kept the lead intact. On another day Saha could have been climbing aboard the team coach after the game with the match ball tucked under his arm, and Kleberson, Scholes and Ronaldo could also have been reflecting on their contribution to the 'goals for' column.

In the end it took a late – very late – strike from the hard-working Alan Smith to finally beat Friedel. In the fourth minute of injury time a long ball was played into the Blackburn penalty area towards Saha. The striker appeared to control it with his arm, something missed by referee Alan Wiley, and when the ball ran loose Smith was on hand to thump it high into the net.

Salvaging a point with his fifth goal in seven games came as scant consolation for Smith, who admitted: "It feels like a defeat. We created enough chances to win three games."

Saturday 28 August 2004
**Ewood Park**
Attendance 26,155
**Referee: Alan Wiley**

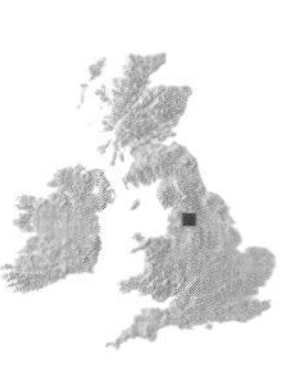

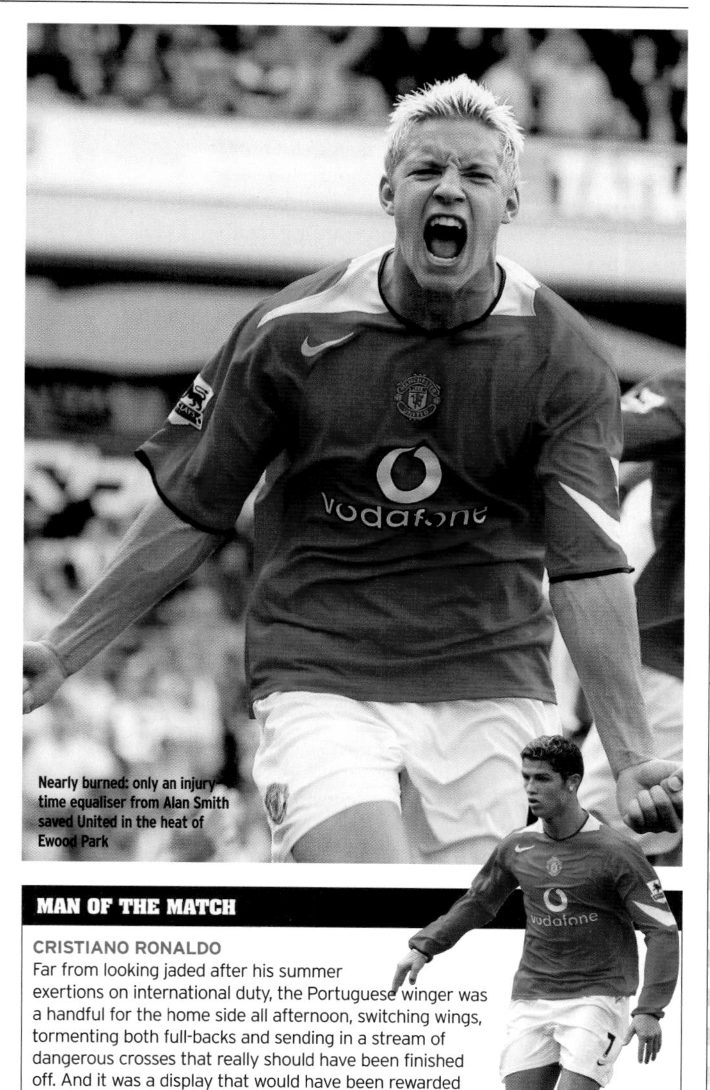

Nearly burned: only an injury time equaliser from Alan Smith saved United in the heat of Ewood Park

## MAN OF THE MATCH

**CRISTIANO RONALDO**

Far from looking jaded after his summer exertions on international duty, the Portuguese winger was a handful for the home side all afternoon, switching wings, tormenting both full-backs and sending in a stream of dangerous crosses that really should have been finished off. And it was a display that would have been rewarded with the goal it deserved but for a brilliant point-blank save from Brad Friedel in the second half.

## MATCH FACTS

**BLACKBURN ROVERS**
Friedel; Neill, Short, Matteo, Amoruso; Thompson (Emerton 17), Ferguson, Pedersen; Tugay, Stead (Yorke 64), Dickov (Johansson 71) Subs not used De Pedro, Enckelman
**Booked** Stead, Amoruso, Tugay
**Sent off** Amoruso

**MANCHESTER UNITED**
Howard; G Neville, O'Shea, Silvestre, Spector (Miller 75); Ronaldo, Djemba-Djemba (Bellion 80), Kleberson (Saha 45), Giggs, Scholes; Smith
**Subs not used** Carroll, P Neville
**Booked** Kleberson

| Manchester United | | Blackburn Rovers |
|---|---|---|
| 60% | POSSESSION | 40% |
| 9 | SHOTS ON TARGET | 2 |
| 10 | SHOTS OFF TARGET | 4 |
| 13 | CORNERS | 4 |
| 18 | FOULS | 26 |
| 4 | OFFSIDES | 3 |

### PREMIERSHIP RESULTS
WEEKEND BEGINNING 24/8/04

| | | |
|---|---|---|
| Arsenal | 3-0 | Blackburn |
| Birmingham | 1-0 | Manchester City |
| Charlton | 3-0 | Aston Villa |
| Crystal Palace | 0-2 | Chelsea |
| Fulham | 0-2 | Middlesbrough |
| Newcastle | 2-2 | Norwich |
| Southampton | 1-2 | Bolton |
| West Brom | 1-1 | Tottenham |

### PREMIERSHIP TABLE
AT END OF 28/08/2004

| | P | PTS |
|---|---|---|
| 1. Arsenal | 4 | 12 |
| 2. Chelsea | 4 | 12 |
| 3. Tottenham Hotspur | 4 | 8 |
| 4. Middlesbrough | 4 | 7 |
| 5. Aston Villa | 4 | 7 |
| 6. Bolton Wanderers | 3 | 6 |
| 7. Everton | 3 | 6 |
| 8. Charlton Athletic | 4 | 6 |
| 9. Manchester City | 4 | 4 |
| 10. Liverpool | 2 | 4 |
| 11. Manchester United | 3 | 4 |
| 12. Fulham | 3 | 4 |
| 13. Birmingham City | 4 | 4 |
| 14. West Bromwich Albion | 4 | 3 |
| 15. Southampton | 4 | 3 |
| 16. Newcastle United | 4 | 2 |
| 17. Norwich City | 4 | 2 |
| 18. Blackburn Rovers | 4 | 2 |
| 19. Portsmouth | 2 | 1 |
| 20. Crystal Palace | 4 | 1 |

# Manchester United 0

# Everton 0

**The visit of** Everton was always likely to be overshadowed by the imminent transfer of Wayne Rooney from Merseyside to Manchester. With both sets of supporters taunting each other with chants about English football's hottest prospect, the players fought out a scoreless draw that suited Everton far more than their hosts.

The Reds had tabled a £23.5 million bid for Rooney the previous week. Yet while the deal was far from finalised, some United fans wasted little time chanting his name at the visiting supporters. "He's going to sign for City" was the rather fanciful riposte from the Blue corner.

It's possible the banter in the stands was a reflection of the lack of action on the pitch. The Reds started slowly and it was Everton who came closest to opening the scoring. Marcus Bent headed over and Leon Osman and Tim Cahill both went close. The only real plus of the opening period was the performance of American full-back Jonathan Spector, making his Premiership home debut and showing a maturity well beyond his 18 years.

As half-time approached Alan Smith put in a strong challenge on Nigel Martyn in the visitors' goal which seemed to lift both his team-mates and the crowd. A sudden urgency saw the Reds throw men forward and an unmarked Louis Saha headed wide.

The second half was more engaging, with Everton battling to stay in the game and United pushing them back into their own half. Ronaldo cut in from the left and struck Martyn's left-hand post with a right-foot drive from the edge of the area. Shortly afterwards, and from a similar position, Smith drove at the Toffees' defence and fired in a strike that came back off the opposite post. In the dying minutes the woodwork came to Everton's rescue a third time – Paul Scholes could only look on in frustration as his deflected effort crashed back off the left upright.

Many times in the past the Reds have produced a late goal to win matches at Old Trafford, but this time it wasn't to be. David Moyes' players sustained the pressure and then took the acclaim from their delighted fans at the final whistle. In contrast United fans rapidly left the ground, having seen the Reds drop two more valuable points.

Blue Monday: the visitors went away much the happier after this bank holiday stalemate, even joking about the departure of star striker Wayne Rooney

Monday 30 August 2004
**Old Trafford**
Attendance 67,803
**Referee: Andy D'Urso**

## MAN OF THE MATCH

**JONATHAN SPECTOR**

The boy from Chicago, who had been a big hit on United's summer US tour, followed up a highly promising Premiership debut at Ewood Park 48 hours earlier with another assured performance. This time he kept the lively Toffees midfielder Leon Osman firmly in check. Calm in defence and confident going forward, the right-footed left-back made light of playing in his least familiar defensive position. As they say in his homeland: "It looks like we got us a goody."

## MATCH FACTS

**MANCHESTER UNITED**
Howard; G Neville, Silvestre, O'Shea, Spector; Fletcher (Giggs 64), Scholes, Kleberson (Djemba-Djemba 64), Ronaldo (Bellion 81); Smith, Saha
**Subs not used** Carroll, P Neville

**EVERTON**
Martyn; Hibbert, Weir, Stubbs, Pistone; Osman, Watson, Carsley, Kilbane, Cahill (Naysmith 70); Bent (Ferguson 54)
**Subs not used** Wright, Campbell, McFadden
**Booked** Osman, Cahill

| Man Utd | | Everton |
|---|---|---|
| 60% | POSSESSION | 40% |
| 4 | SHOTS ON TARGET | 1 |
| 9 | SHOTS OFF TARGET | 5 |
| 8 | CORNERS | 2 |
| 9 | FOULS | 15 |
| 2 | OFFSIDES | 0 |

**PREMIERSHIP RESULTS**
WEEKEND BEGINNING 28/8/04

| Home | Score | Away |
|---|---|---|
| Aston Villa | 4-2 | Newcastle |
| Bolton | 1-0 | Liverpool |
| Chelsea | 2-1 | Southampton |
| Everton | 2-1 | West Brom |
| Manchester City | 4-0 | Charlton |
| Middlesbrough | 2-1 | Crystal Palace |
| Norwich | 1-4 | Arsenal |
| Portsmouth | 4-3 | Fulham |
| Tottenham | 1-0 | Birmingham |

**PREMIERSHIP TABLE**
AT END OF 30/08/05

| | P | PTS |
|---|---|---|
| 1. Arsenal | 4 | 12 |
| 2. Chelsea | 4 | 12 |
| 3. Bolton Wanderers | 4 | 9 |
| 4. Tottenham Hotspur | 4 | 8 |
| 5. Middlesbrough | 4 | 7 |
| 6. Aston Villa | 4 | 7 |
| 7. Everton | 4 | 7 |
| 8. Charlton Athletic | 4 | 6 |
| 9. Manchester United | 4 | 5 |
| 10. Manchester City | 4 | 4 |
| 11. Portsmouth | 3 | 4 |
| 12. Liverpool | 3 | 4 |
| 13. Fulham | 4 | 4 |
| 14. Birmingham City | 4 | 4 |
| 15. West Bromwich Albion | 4 | 3 |
| 16. Southampton | 4 | 3 |
| 17. Newcastle United | 4 | 2 |
| 18. Norwich City | 4 | 2 |
| 19. Blackburn Rovers | 4 | 2 |
| 20. Crystal Palace | 4 | 1 |

# September

## As United finally kickstarted the season with back-to-back wins, two familiar faces had to face new managerial challenges

**Two draws** at the back end of the previous month saw United reach September with just five points from the first four league games, and after an early-season international break had seen Reds scattered across Europe on international duty, a trip to Bolton failed to deliver a much-needed win. But the visit of Liverpool finally gave Reds a Premiership occasion to relish (a Mikael Silvestre double doing for Rafa Benitez's men) and another valuable three points were gleaned – courtesy of a Ruud van Nistelrooy penalty – at White Hart Lane.

Elsewhere, Arsène Wenger's 'Invincibles' were still in flying form in north London – with Jose Antonio Reyes and Thierry Henry scoring for fun – and Chelsea were starting to display the kind of defensive fortitude that would see them continue to match Arsenal's early pace. Everton – post-Rooney – were continuing to defy the odds and stay on the coat-tails of the top two, but by the end of September the capital's Reds and Blues were the top flight's only unbeaten sides.

By that point two new managerial appointments had been inked in. Newcastle's 3-0 win over Blackburn came with neither club having a permanent man at the helm; Graeme Souness leaving Ewood Park a few days earlier to take up the St James' Park post, with Mark Hughes (having worked out a short-term job-share with the Welsh FA) filling the gap left by Souness. And after a Matt Jansen goal had given Hughes a win in his first game in charge, by the end of the month the wrong end of the table had taken on an all-too-predictable look – with the three promoted sides occupying the bottom three slots.

### PREMIERSHIP FIXTURES THIS MONTH

| | | |
|---|---|---|
| SAT 11 | BOLTON WANDERERS | AWAY |
| MON 20 | LIVERPOOL | HOME |
| SAT 25 | TOTTENHAM HOTSPUR | AWAY |

### IN THE PREMIERSHIP THIS MONTH...

**131,726** watched United play 3 games

**5** goals were scored

**433** miles were travelled by United going to and from games

United fielded **17** players

**3** goals were conceded

### FOCUS ON RUUD VAN NISTELROOY

A hernia injury suffered in last summer's Vodafone Cup meant United were without van Nistelrooy for the first month of the season, but after easing back into action against Bolton at the Reebok, in his second league game, against Liverpool, the Reds' record-breaking goalscorer started to show the old sharpness - buoyed, no doubt, by a double strike in the Champions League five days earlier. The Dutchman could easily have won a first-half penalty when he was tugged back by Sami Hyypia; instead he stayed on his feet and Jerzy Dudek denied him. But his first goal of the Premiership season wasn't long in coming. Welcomed to White Hart Lane by former PSV coach Frank Arnesen, the United No.10 made himself right at home, crashing home a penalty - awarded, some felt harshly, for a shove on John O'Shea - just before the break. And only an offside flag denied van Nistelrooy a second on the hour mark.

# Bolton Wanderers 2

Nolan 52, Ferdinand 90

# Manchester United 2

Heinze 44, Bellion 90

**David Bellion's** knee – or was it his back, chest, thigh or shin? – rescued a point at the Reebok in the dying seconds of injury time. A defensive mix-up between Mikael Silvestre and Tim Howard had seen Bolton take the lead in the final minute of normal time, only for the Frenchman to bundle the ball in for a well-deserved draw.

Sir Alex Ferguson's injury headaches continued going into this game with Gary Neville's fractured kneecap sidelining him for four weeks, and Louis Saha also injuring a knee on duty with France. At least the Reds' boss had two more players to bring in. Ruud van Nistelrooy made his first competitive start of the season and Gabriel Heinze made his long-awaited debut.

Against all odds it was the Argentinian defender and not the prolific Dutch striker who scored the opening goal. In the 44th minute of a first half in which the Reds had enjoyed most of the action, Heinze volleyed in smartly from six yards after Silvestre had headed Giggs' corner back across goal. The left-back looked comfortable all afternoon and thoroughly deserved his debut goal.

After the break Bolton emerged with renewed intent. El-Hadji Diouf, on loan from Liverpool, replaced Henrik Pedersen and his willingness to take players on resulted in a 52nd minute free-kick that led to the equaliser. When the ball was squared to the lively Jay-Jay Okocha he worked himself space for a shot and Tim Howard could only parry the drive to Kevin Nolan, who headed the rebound in to put Bolton level.

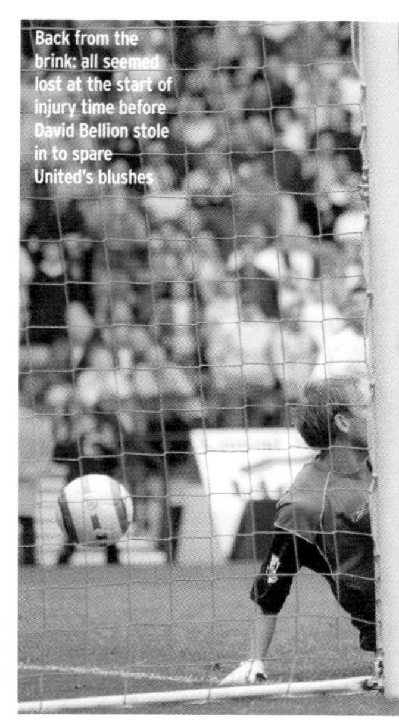

Back from the brink: all seemed lost at the start of injury time before David Bellion stole in to spare United's blushes

Saturday 11 September 2004
**Reebok Stadium**
Attendance 27,766
**Referee: Matt Messias**

Howard kept out efforts from Okocha ıd Kevin Davies but it was United who ent closest to taking the lead. Substitute ·istiano Ronaldo, on only a matter of inutes, left Ivan Campo sprawling on the ɔor and struck a fierce drive that beat ssi Jaaskelainen in the Bolton goal but ruck the crossbar and was cleared.

Then came the breathless finale. First Les ·rdinand gratefully accepted the gift from ɔward and Silvestre to tap into an empty ·t. Then, just as it looked as if United were ·aded for a first defeat at the Reebok, ıvid Bellion got on the end of an Alan nith header to nudge the ball in.

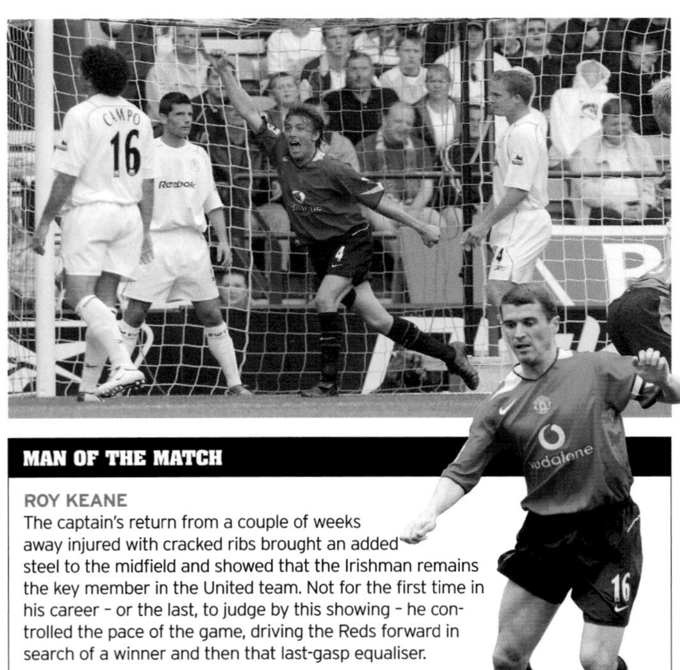

## MAN OF THE MATCH

**ROY KEANE**

The captain's return from a couple of weeks away injured with cracked ribs brought an added steel to the midfield and showed that the Irishman remains the key member in the United team. Not for the first time in his career - or the last, to judge by this showing - he controlled the pace of the game, driving the Reds forward in search of a winner and then that last-gasp equaliser.

## MATCH FACTS

**BOLTON WANDERERS**
Jaaskelainen; Hunt, N'Gotty, Jaidi, Barness; Campo; Nolan, Okocha, Speed (Hierro 87), Pedersen (Diouf 46); Davies (Ferdinand 76)
**Subs not used** Oakes, Ben Haim **Booked** Okocha

**MANCHESTER UNITED**
Howard; P Neville, Brown, Silvestre, Heinze; Kleberson (Ronaldo 65), Keane, Scholes, Giggs; Smith, van Nistelrooy (Bellion 75) **Subs not used** Carroll, Djemba-Djemba, Spector **Booked** Giggs

| | | |
|---|---|---|
| 60% | POSSESSION | 40% |
| 6 | SHOTS ON TARGET | 5 |
| 5 | SHOTS OFF TARGET | 7 |
| 7 | CORNERS | 4 |
| 18 | FOULS | 25 |
| 3 | OFFSIDES | 0 |

**PREMIERSHIP RESULTS**
WEEKEND BEGINNING 11/9/04

| | | |
|---|---|---|
| Aston Villa | 0-0 | Chelsea |
| Charlton | 0-0 | Southampton |
| Fulham | 0-3 | Arsenal |
| Liverpool | 3-0 | West Brom |
| Manchester City | 0-1 | Everton |
| Middlesbrough | 2-1 | Birmingham |
| Newcastle | 3-0 | Blackburn |
| Portsmouth | 3-1 | Crystal Palace |
| Tottenham | 0-0 | Norwich |

**PREMIERSHIP TABLE**
AT END OF 13/09/04

| | P | PTS |
|---|---|---|
| 1. Arsenal | 5 | 15 |
| 2. Chelsea | 5 | 13 |
| 3. Bolton Wanderers | 5 | 10 |
| 4. Middlesbrough | 5 | 10 |
| 5. Everton | 5 | 10 |
| 6. Tottenham Hotspur | 5 | 9 |
| 7. Aston Villa | 5 | 8 |
| 8. Liverpool | 4 | 7 |
| 9. Portsmouth | 4 | 7 |
| 10. Charlton Athletic | 5 | 7 |
| 11. Manchester United | 5 | 6 |
| 12. Newcastle United | 5 | 5 |
| 13. Manchester City | 5 | 4 |
| 14. Birmingham City | 5 | 4 |
| 15. Southampton | 5 | 4 |
| 16. Fulham | 5 | 4 |
| 17. Norwich City | 5 | 3 |
| 18. West Bromwich Albion | 5 | 3 |
| 19. Blackburn Rovers | 5 | 2 |
| 20. Crystal Palace | 5 | 1 |

# Manchester United 2

Silvestre 20, 66

# Liverpool 1

O'Shea (og) 54

French polish: a solid performance throughout from Mikael Silvestre was capped off with two well-taken headed goals

**They don't come** much bigger at OT than a clash between United and Liverpool – and this fixture had extra spice. For the Reds it was a chance to kickstart their faltering opening to the Premiership campaign, while for the new-look Liverpool it was tipped as the first real test. Throw in the return of Rio Ferdinand, pre-match rumours of a Mr Rooney warming the bench, along with fired-up fans from both sides, and you had the recipe for a big night.

After the midweek draw with Lyon, Sir Alex opted to replace Tim Howard with Roy Carroll, move John O'Shea into midfield, and bring Rio Ferdinand straight back into first-team action. But the rumour-mongers were wrong about the new No.8, who wasn't even on the bench. The changes galvanised the team and from the whistle United looked a much tighter outfit.

A vocal crowd appreciated the opening exchanges. Cristiano Ronaldo ran rings around John Arne Riise, and the Portuguese starlet almost gave United a dream start on 10 minutes, rattling Jerzy Dudek's right post from 25 yards.

Much has been made of Rafael Benitez's arrival at Anfield and his new regime, with a trio of his hotly-touted new Spanish signings hoping to impress. In fact

Monday 20 September 2004
**Old Trafford**
Attendance 67,857
**Referee: Graham Poll**

Liverpool were on the back foot throughout the first half and were lucky not to concede a penalty after Sami Hyypia pulled back Ruud van Nistelrooy, but the Dutchman stayed on his feet and forced Dudek to save with his legs.

The breakthrough wasn't long in coming. On 20 minutes United won a free-kick, Hyypia appearing to bring down Paul Scholes. From Ryan Giggs's delivery, Mikael Silvestre was allowed free rein to thunder home a header at the far post. Van Nistelrooy, Ronaldo and Gabriel Heinze all went close and, to compound matters for Benitez, the talismanic Steven Gerrard limped off with a broken metatarsal just before the interval.

In the second half Liverpool rallied and got an equaliser in the 54th minute. Xabi Alonso's free-kick found Steve Finnan, whose header rebounded off O'Shea before rolling across the line.

But United weren't about to settle for a fourth consecutive league draw, and after winning a corner, Giggs again picked out Silvestre, who headed home an almost carbon-copy winner. Liverpool went all out to grab a late equaliser but a rejuvenated United held on to claim a crucial confidence booster.

## MAN OF THE MATCH

**MIKAEL SILVESTRE**

All eyes were on the return of Rio Ferdinand, but it was his defensive colleague, Mikael Silvestre, who stole the show – along with another phenomenal performance from Cristiano Ronaldo. Mikael even managed to upstage United's top goal-getter Ruud van Nistelrooy into the bargain. After taking the flak for a defensive mistake at Bolton which gave the Trotters a last-minute goal, the Frenchman bounced back with an assured performance – and with two headed goals of which any striker would have been rightly proud.

## MATCH FACTS

**MANCHESTER UNITED**
Carroll; Brown, Ferdinand, Silvestre, Heinze; Keane, O'Shea; Ronaldo, Scholes (Smith 85), Giggs; van Nistelrooy
**Subs not used** P Neville, Kleberson, Fletcher, Ricardo
**Booked** Keane

**LIVERPOOL**
Dudek; Josemi, Carragher, Hyypia, Riise; Finnan, Alonso, Gerrard (Hamann 40), Kewell; Cisse (Baros 66), Garcia
**Subs not used** Diao, Traore, Kirkland **Booked** Josemi, Alonso

| 55% | POSSESSION | 45% |
|---|---|---|
| 8 | SHOTS ON TARGET | 1 |
| 5 | SHOTS OFF TARGET | 3 |
| 6 | CORNERS | 2 |
| 22 | FOULS | 16 |
| 2 | OFFSIDES | 5 |

### PREMIERSHIP RESULTS
WEEKEND BEGINNING 18/9/04

| | | |
|---|---|---|
| Arsenal | 2-2 | Bolton |
| Birmingham | 1-1 | Charlton |
| Blackburn | 1-0 | Portsmouth |
| Chelsea | 0-0 | Tottenham |
| Crystal Palace | 1-2 | Man City |
| Everton | 1-0 | Middlesbrough |
| Norwich | 0-0 | Aston Villa |
| Southampton | 1-2 | Newcastle |
| West Brom | 1-1 | Fulham |

### PREMIERSHIP TABLE
AT END OF 20/09/05

| | | P | PTS |
|---|---|---|---|
| 1. | Arsenal | 6 | 16 |
| 2. | Chelsea | 6 | 14 |
| 3. | Everton | 6 | 13 |
| 4. | Bolton Wanderers | 6 | 11 |
| 5. | Tottenham Hotspur | 6 | 10 |
| 6. | Middlesbrough | 6 | 10 |
| 7. | Aston Villa | 6 | 9 |
| 8. | Manchester United | 6 | 9 |
| 9. | Newcastle United | 6 | 8 |
| 10. | Charlton Athletic | 6 | 8 |
| 11. | Manchester City | 6 | 7 |
| 12. | Liverpool | 5 | 7 |
| 13. | Portsmouth | 5 | 7 |
| 14. | Birmingham City | 6 | 5 |
| 15. | Fulham | 6 | 5 |
| 16. | Blackburn Rovers | 6 | 5 |
| 17. | Southampton | 6 | 4 |
| 18. | West Bromwich Albion | 6 | 4 |
| 19. | Norwich City | 6 | 4 |
| 20. | Crystal Palace | 6 | 1 |

# Tottenham Hotspur 0

# Manchester United 1

Van Nistelrooy (pen) 42

**Before the game** Tottenham's sporting director Frank Arnesen welcomed his old PSV striker Ruud van Nistelrooy to White Hart Lane, paying tribute to his former colleague's talents in front of goal in the Spurs matchday programme. Those kind words came back to haunt Arnesen as the Dutchman's 41st-minute penalty sealed United's first league away win of the season, a welcome present on Sir Alex Ferguson's 700th League game in charge.

It was more or less as you were for United following the win over Liverpool, the only change a recall for Alan Smith in place of Paul Scholes, while Spurs coach Jacques Santini ambitiously pitched three strikers into battle: Robbie Keane roaming just behind Fredi Kanoute and Jermain Defoe.

There was early controversy when Mbulelo Mabizela tripped Gabriel Heinze in the box but referee Peter Walton allowed play to continue and the chance was lost. With half an hour gone Santini was forced to alter his game plan, Kanoute limping off to be replaced by Simon Davies. It didn't stop the home side threatening Roy Carroll's goal, the United keeper scrambling to save a long-range drive from Pedro Mendes.

As half-time approached the game turned on a decision that had Santini fuming. Spurs defender Erik Edman grabbed hold of John O'Shea's shirt, the Irishman tumbled and Walton pointed to the spot. Up stepped Ruud van Nistelrooy to rifle home his first Premiership goal of the season. The penalty incident was replayed on the big screens at half-time, the cue for roars of anger from the previously soporific home faithful.

The second half saw Spurs determined to avenge this perceived injustice, but with Rio Ferdinand again imperious and the ever-impressive Heinze not afraid to get stuck in, United were always the better side. In midfield Roy Keane drove his side on, along with his young lieutenant O'Shea (when Liam Miller replaced Ryan Giggs late on, United boasted an all-Irish central midfield trio).

Van Nistelrooy had the ball in the net after an hour when he pounced on a deep cross from Cristiano Ronaldo but was ruled offside. The Reds nearly doubled the lead again when Mikael Silvestre's drilled shot was blocked on the line by a diving Robbie Keane, and substitute David Bellion's late bullet-header, from another expert Ronaldo delivery, flew straight at Paul Robinson's chest. In the end United were happy with one goal... and three points.

Earning their Spurs: a first away win of the season made Sir Alex's day

Saturday 25 September 2004
**White Hart Lane**
Attendance 36,103
**Referee: Peter Walton**

## MAN OF THE MATCH

**ROY KEANE**
There were several contenders for outstanding Red of the day at White Hart Lane, notably Rio Ferdinand, Cristiano Ronaldo and Gabriel Heinze. But not for the first time this season the captain gets the nod. With United again starting with two wingers, the midfielders handed defensive duties were always going to be busy, but Keane was more than up to the task with a trademark no-messing display.

## MATCH FACTS

**TOTTENHAM HOTSPUR**
Robinson; Pamarot, Naybet, King, Edman; Mabizela (Jackson 67), Redknapp, Mendes, Robbie Keane; Defoe, Kanoute (Davies 30)
**Subs not used** Keller, Brown, Gardner
**Booked** Mendes

**MANCHESTER UNITED**
Carroll; Brown, Silvestre, Ferdinand, Heinze; Giggs (Miller 83), Roy Keane, O'Shea; Ronaldo; Smith, van Nistelrooy (Bellion 86)
**Subs not used** Ricardo, Kleberson, P Neville

| Man Utd | | Tottenham |
|---|---|---|
| 53% | POSSESSION | 47% |
| 5 | SHOTS ON TARGET | 5 |
| 2 | SHOTS OFF TARGET | 6 |
| 3 | CORNERS | 3 |
| 11 | FOULS | 9 |
| 6 | OFFSIDES | 2 |

### PREMIERSHIP RESULTS
WEEKEND BEGINNING 25/9/04

| | | |
|---|---|---|
| Aston Villa | 1-1 | Crystal Palace |
| Bolton | 1-1 | Birmingham |
| Charlton | 1-0 | Blackburn |
| Fulham | 1-0 | Southampton |
| Liverpool | 3-0 | Norwich |
| Manchester City | 0-1 | Arsenal |
| Middlesbrough | 0-1 | Chelsea |
| Newcastle | 3-1 | West Brom |
| Portsmouth | 0-1 | Everton |

### PREMIERSHIP TABLE
AT END OF 27/09/05

| | | P | PTS |
|---|---|---|---|
| 1. | Arsenal | 7 | 19 |
| 2. | Chelsea | 7 | 17 |
| 3. | Everton | 7 | 16 |
| 4. | Bolton Wanderers | 7 | 12 |
| 5. | Manchester United | 7 | 12 |
| 6. | Newcastle United | 7 | 11 |
| 7. | Charlton Athletic | 7 | 11 |
| 8. | Liverpool | 6 | 10 |
| 9. | Aston Villa | 7 | 10 |
| 10. | Tottenham Hotspur | 7 | 10 |
| 11. | Middlesbrough | 7 | 10 |
| 12. | Fulham | 7 | 8 |
| 13. | Manchester City | 7 | 7 |
| 14. | Portsmouth | 6 | 7 |
| 15. | Birmingham City | 7 | 6 |
| 16. | Blackburn Rovers | 7 | 5 |
| 17. | Southampton | 7 | 4 |
| 18. | West Bromwich Albion | 7 | 4 |
| 19. | Norwich City | 7 | 4 |
| 20. | Crystal Palace | 7 | 2 |

odafone

# October

## Tunnel trouble dominated the tabloids after Arsenal's visit, while the top of the Premiership table had an unfamiliar look...

**In the month** that saw Spurs legend Bill Nicholson pass away, aged 85, United dropped further off the pace following draws at home to Middlesbrough and away at Birmingham. But the Reds did at least claw back some of the deficit between them and the Gunners courtesy of a hard-fought 2-0 win at Old Trafford. That game would, of course, dominate the front and back pages for weeks afterwards as the rumours of skullduggery in the players' tunnel rumbled on. What was certain, however, was that the win ended Arsenal's record unbeaten league run, leaving them one short of 50.

United still only lay seventh, with Bolton, Liverpool and Boro among the teams above them. Steve McClaren's men, however, had to resign themselves to coping without Gaizka Mendieta in the long term after the Spaniard injured knee ligaments against Portsmouth. Rafael Benitez, meanwhile, had problems up front, Djibril Cisse breaking his leg against Blackburn.

Chelsea too, were about to lose a striker – though for very different reasons; Adrian Mutu's positive test for cocaine signalled the end of his Stamford Bridge career. And there was another departure from the Premiership at managerial level: Gary Megson's decision to tell the West Brom board he wouldn't be staying beyond the summer backfired, and he left with almost immediate effect.

In contrast, everything was still nicely on track at Goodison Park, although the pivotal figure in David Moyes's Everton machine, Thomas Gravesen, was reported to be a target for Real Madrid.

### PREMIERSHIP FIXTURES THIS MONTH

| | | |
|---|---|---|
| SUN 3 | MIDDLESBROUGH | HOME |
| SAT 16 | BIRMINGHAM CITY | AWAY |
| SUN 24 | ARSENAL | HOME |
| SAT 30 | PORTSMOUTH | AWAY |

### IN THE PREMIERSHIP THIS MONTH...

**185,261** watched United play 4 games

**3** goals were scored

**641** miles were travelled by United going to and from games

United fielded **18** players

**3** goals were conceded

### FOCUS ON RIO FERDINAND

The Reds' defensive third was always going to be a key battleground against Arsenal. After all, Arsène Wenger's side had found the net 29 times in the first nine games of the Premiership season. And after games against Middlesbrough and Birmingham where he was barely put to the test, Rio Ferdinand – still with just five games under his belt since his long-awaited return – stepped up in style against the reigning champions. In the fiery atmosphere of a fully charged Old Trafford, Ferdinand took the captain's armband in the absence of Roy Keane and played a captain's role. Assured on the ball, commanding in the air, he marshalled the Reds defence magnificently to ensure that this would be United's day. And while Ruud van Nistelrooy's penalty and Wayne Rooney's last-minute clincher earned all three points for the Reds, it was the platform provided by United's towering centre-half that made it all possible.

# Manchester United 1

Smith 81

# Middlesbrough 1

Downing 33

**Reading the morning** papers you could have been forgiven for thinking the Reds merely had to turn up to collect the three points against Boro. Rooney-mania was still in full swing following his debut hat-trick, with sections of the press wondering whether he could keep up his outstanding strike rate of a goal every 30 minutes for United. Such stats would not have fooled any supporter who had seen the Teesside club's recent visits to Old Trafford.

Steve McClaren enjoyed a two-and-a-half year apprenticeship under Sir Alex and evidently learnt much during that period, most notably how to get a result at OT. Boro had won two of their last three Premiership games in M16 against United, combining resilient defending with opportunistic finishing, and could have made it three out of four in this match.

Fielding a young side and employing tactics to deny Rooney and Ruud van Nistelrooy the space they'd exploited against Fenerbahçe, McClaren set out to frustrate the Reds. And while United had early chances, the longer the game went scoreless the more the visitors grew in confidence. Still, it was against the run of play when Boro took the lead through 20-year-old Stuart Downing, the young winger starting and finishing a flowing move in the 33rd minute to break the deadlock.

Having grabbed a lead, Boro were always likely to defend what they had. Cristiano Ronaldo was doing his utmost to break through the Gareth Southgate-inspired Boro back line, and though he failed to find an equaliser, gradually United began to build some sustained pressure with chances starting to materialise in the final half-hour. Mark Schwarzer denied Ronaldo with a sharp save, then breathed a sigh of relief as a van Nistelrooy header crashed off his crossbar.

But the momentum was now firmly with the Reds and, in the 81st minute, sub Alan Smith came to United's rescue – as he had done at Blackburn in August – with his sixth goal of the season. Inevitably it was Ronaldo who supplied the chance; almost as inevitably it was Smith, increasingly becoming a cult figure, who headed firmly past Schwarzer's despairing dive.

More pressure failed to produce a United winner and so – with Arsenal and Chelsea both registering wins – more precious ground was lost on the early Premiership pacesetters.

Pressure points: Ruud and John kept up the momentum until the equaliser

Sunday 3 October 2004
**Old Trafford**
Attendance 67,988
**Referee: Rob Styles**

## MAN OF THE MATCH

**CRISTIANO RONALDO**

The 19-year-old livewire combined his abundant skill with a prodigious work-rate and spent the afternoon tormenting Boro down both wings. The goal that his efforts deserved was not forthcoming but it was right that the young winger should play a key part in the Reds' deserved equaliser. Alan Smith provided the finish but Cristiano Ronaldo supplied the all-important cross – just as he had been doing for United all afternoon.

## MATCH FACTS

**MANCHESTER UNITED**
Carroll; G Neville, Ferdinand, Silvestre, Heinze; Ronaldo, O'Shea (Smith 69), Keane, Giggs; Rooney, van Nistelrooy **Subs not used** Ricardo, Kleberson, Djemba-Djemba, Fortune **Booked** Keane

**MIDDLESBROUGH**
Schwarzer; McMahon, Riggott, Southgate, Parnaby (Cooper 35); Morrison (Doriva 79), Mendieta, Boateng, Downing (Graham 87), Zenden; Nemeth
**Subs not used** Nash, Taylor
**Booked** Mendieta, Boateng, Nemeth

| Manchester United | | Middlesbrough |
|---|---|---|
| 52% | POSSESSION | 48% |
| 4 | SHOTS ON TARGET | 6 |
| 12 | SHOTS OFF TARGET | 4 |
| 10 | CORNERS | 2 |
| 9 | FOULS | 13 |
| 2 | OFFSIDES | 2 |

### PREMIERSHIP RESULTS
WEEKEND BEGINNING 2/10/04

| | | |
|---|---|---|
| Arsenal | 4-0 | Charlton |
| Blackburn | 2-2 | Aston Villa |
| Chelsea | 1-0 | Liverpool |
| Crystal Palace | 2-0 | Fulham |
| Everton | 0-1 | Tottenham |
| Norwich | 2-2 | Portsmouth |
| Southampton | 0-0 | Manchester City |
| West Brom | 2-1 | Bolton |
| Birmingham | 2-2 | Newcastle |

### PREMIERSHIP TABLE
AT END OF 04/10/04

| | P | PTS |
|---|---|---|
| 1. Arsenal | 8 | 22 |
| 2. Chelsea | 8 | 20 |
| 3. Everton | 8 | 16 |
| 4. Manchester United | 8 | 13 |
| 5. Tottenham Hotspur | 8 | 13 |
| 6. Newcastle United | 8 | 12 |
| 7. Bolton Wanderers | 8 | 12 |
| 8. Aston Villa | 8 | 11 |
| 9. Middlesbrough | 8 | 11 |
| 10. Charlton Athletic | 8 | 11 |
| 11. Liverpool | 7 | 10 |
| 12. Manchester City | 8 | 8 |
| 13. Portsmouth | 7 | 8 |
| 14. Fulham | 8 | 8 |
| 15. Birmingham City | 8 | 7 |
| 16. West Bromwich Albion | 8 | 7 |
| 17. Blackburn Rovers | 8 | 6 |
| 18. Southampton | 8 | 5 |
| 19. Crystal Palace | 8 | 5 |
| 20. Norwich City | 8 | 5 |

# Birmingham City 0

# Manchester United 0

**The Reds' frustrating** season continued at St Andrew's as £80 million of striking talent failed to breach Birmingham's resolute defence. Despite fielding Ruud van Nistelrooy, Alan Smith, Louis Saha and then second-half substitute Wayne Rooney, United were unable to find the goal that would almost certainly have secured three valuable league points.

A potentially difficult trip to Steve Bruce's Blues was not exactly the ideal fixture following a break for international matches. Not that it had been a break. A total of 18 United players had been away with their countries during the previous fortnight and, due to the amount of travelling some had done, Sir Alex Ferguson was forced to ring the changes. In came Quinton Fortune, Wes Brown and Louis Saha, while Rooney, Gabriel Heinze and Mikael Silvestre all dropped out.

The Reds had tended to start slowly in matches at the beginning of the season and that trend continued here. In fact, it wasn't until the second half that the match really came to life. Roy Carroll was relatively untroubled in the United goal, his defence giving him plenty of protection from ex-Red Dwight Yorke and Emile Heskey, both of whom failed to take headed opportunities. At the other end Carroll's Northern Ireland compatriot Maik Taylor in the Birmingham goal kept out efforts from van Nistelrooy and Cristiano Ronaldo to maintain the stalemate.

The second half was a better affair as both teams came out with a renewed urgency. Yet despite the increase in tempo, goals still failed to materialise. Heskey was twice denied by Carroll, and van Nistelrooy side-footed wide from a Gary Neville cross. Even after the introduction of Rooney, and the welcome sight of fellow substitute Paul Scholes back in midfield, the Reds were unable to break the deadlock. Alan Smith almost capped a fine display with an injury-time winner but his curling shot went just wide of the post. This time there was to be no fairytale ending.

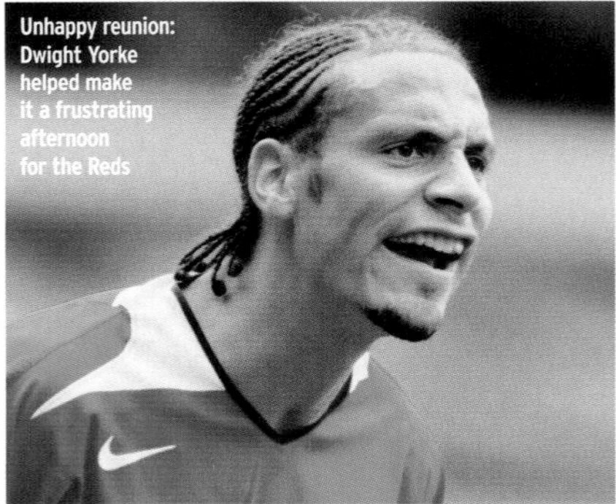

Unhappy reunion: Dwight Yorke helped make it a frustrating afternoon for the Reds

A fifth league draw for United caused a few raised eyebrows, as the Reds failed to carve out the abundance of goalscoring chances expected of a side containing such attack-minded players. Hardly the perfect preparation for the visit of Arsenal to Old Trafford.

Saturday 16 October 2004
**St Andrew's**
Attendance 29,221
**Referee: Mark Halsey**

## MAN OF THE MATCH

### ALAN SMITH

Smudger showed exactly why he's been taken to supporters' hearts, putting in another battling performance. He won almost every header, seemed to put in more tackles than the whole Birmingham midfield combined, and worked tirelessly for the Reds' cause. He deserved to be on the winning side – and was a whisker away from making it happen with a last-minute effort.

## MATCH FACTS

**BIRMINGHAM CITY**
Maik Taylor; Melchiot, Cunningham, Upson, Gray; Johnson (Tebily 90), Dunn, Savage, Gronkjaer (Anderton 45); Heskey, Yorke (Clapham 90) **Subs not used** Bennett, Martin Taylor **Booked** Savage

**MANCHESTER UNITED**
Carroll; G Neville, Ferdinand, Brown, Fortune; Smith, Kleberson (Rooney 59), Keane, Ronaldo (Scholes 77); Saha, van Nistelrooy **Subs not used** Ricardo, P Neville, O'Shea

| MANCHESTER UNITED | | BIRMINGHAM CITY |
|---|---|---|
| 54% | POSSESSION | 46% |
| 7 | SHOTS ON TARGET | 5 |
| 6 | SHOTS OFF TARGET | 8 |
| 3 | CORNERS | 3 |
| 12 | FOULS | 16 |
| 5 | OFFSIDES | 3 |

### PREMIERSHIP RESULTS
WEEKEND BEGINNING 16/10/04

| | | |
|---|---|---|
| Arsenal | 3-1 | Aston Villa |
| Blackburn | 0-4 | Middlesbrough |
| Bolton | 1-0 | Crystal Palace |
| Charlton | 1-1 | Newcastle |
| Everton | 1-0 | Southampton |
| Fulham | 2-4 | Liverpool |
| Manchester City | 1-0 | Chelsea |
| Portsmouth | 1-0 | Tottenham |
| West Brom | 0-0 | Norwich |

### PREMIERSHIP TABLE
AT END OF 18/10/04

| | P | PTS |
|---|---|---|
| 1. Arsenal | 9 | 25 |
| 2. Chelsea | 9 | 20 |
| 3. Everton | 9 | 19 |
| 4. Bolton Wanderers | 9 | 15 |
| 5. Middlesbrough | 9 | 14 |
| 6. Manchester United | 9 | 14 |
| 7. Liverpool | 8 | 13 |
| 8. Newcastle United | 9 | 13 |
| 9. Tottenham Hotspur | 9 | 13 |
| 10. Charlton Athletic | 9 | 12 |
| 11. Manchester City | 9 | 11 |
| 12. Portsmouth | 8 | 11 |
| 13. Aston Villa | 9 | 11 |
| 14. Birmingham City | 9 | 8 |
| 15. West Bromwich Albion | 9 | 8 |
| 16. Fulham | 9 | 8 |
| 17. Norwich City | 9 | 6 |
| 18. Blackburn Rovers | 9 | 6 |
| 19. Southampton | 9 | 5 |
| 20. Crystal Palace | 9 | 5 |

# Manchester United 2

Van Nistelrooy (pen) 73, Rooney 90

# Arsenal 0

**Once the dust** had settled on what had been hyped as the "biggest game of the decade", the situation was this: in winning a highly charged match 2-0, United had clawed back three points on Arsenal's League lead, put a stop to any talk of the Gunners' invincibility, and extended our own unbeaten record over the north London side in the League and FA Cup to some 20 months. But, as ever with these matches, the result was completely overshadowed by controversial incidents on, and off, the pitch.

Interviews with the Arsenal manager and squad members after the match (and for much of the following week) focused on three contentious decisions by referee Mike Riley: whether Rio Ferdinand should have been sent off for his part in the first-half collision with Freddie Ljungberg, the validity of Wayne Rooney's 73rd-minute penalty claim, and the intent in Ruud van Nistelrooy's challenge on Ashley Cole. In the heat of the moment, no doubt it was easy to forget the clear penalty denied after Cristiano Ronaldo had been felled by Cole, not to mention Kolo Toure's tumble in the United box, rightly ignored by Riley, as Arsenal chased the game.

Nerves were evident in the first half, fouls plentiful and goalmouth chances few. The visitors' one shot on target in the entire match fell late in the half to Thierry Henry, otherwise anonymous thanks to the attentions of Ferdinand. In the 73rd minute an already tense match threatened to boil over as Rooney picked up a loose ball and ran at the Arsenal defence. England colleague Sol Campbell absent-mindedly flicked a leg out and Rooney hit the deck. Under immense pressure, van Nistelrooy sent the keeper the wrong way and ran to a rapturous Stretford end, fists raised, screaming with raw emotion. Something was stirring in Manchester...

Sensing their record-breaking run was about to end, Arsenal's attacks became more frantic, but this only served to blunt their effectiveness. With Phil Neville mopping up every scrap in midfield, United looked for the goal that would finish the game, and it came courtesy of two late arrivals. In injury time subs Smith and Saha launched a counter-attack, with the Yorkshireman handing Rooney the best birthday present imaginable: the cross that set up the decisive goal.

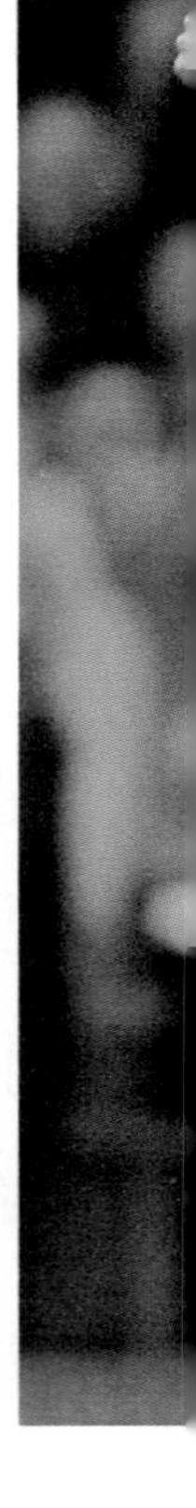

Sunday 24 October 2004
**Old Trafford**
Attendance 67,862
**Referee: Mike Riley**

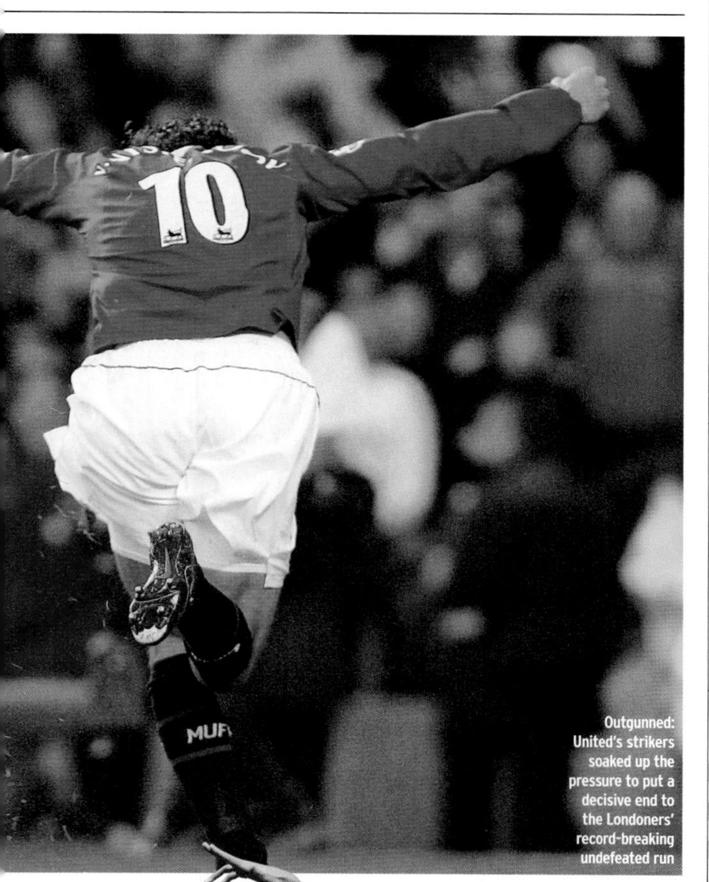

Outgunned: United's strikers soaked up the pressure to put a decisive end to the Londoners' record-breaking undefeated run

## MAN OF THE MATCH

**RIO FERDINAND**
Captain for the day, this was by far his best display in an already impressive comeback. Rio was coolness personified - all the more remarkable in the circumstances. According to author Rudyard Kipling, the mark of a man is someone who "can keep his head while all around are losing theirs". On this occasion, it applied to central defenders more than most.

## MATCH FACTS

**MANCHESTER UNITED**
Carroll; G Neville, Silvestre, Ferdinand, Heinze; Ronaldo (Smith 85), P Neville, Scholes, Giggs; Rooney, van Nistelrooy (Saha 90) **Subs not used** Howard, Brown, Miller
**Booked** G Neville, P Neville

**ARSENAL**
Lehmann; Cole, Campbell, Toure, Lauren; Edu, Vieira, Ljungberg, Bergkamp; Henry, Reyes (Pires 70) **Subs not used** Taylor, van Persie, Cygan, Fabregas
**Booked** Cole, Edu, Vieira

| Manchester United | | Arsenal |
|---|---|---|
| 48% | POSSESSION | 52% |
| 5 | SHOTS ON TARGET | 1 |
| 5 | SHOTS OFF TARGET | 7 |
| 3 | CORNERS | 3 |
| 20 | FOULS | 24 |
| 2 | OFFSIDES | 1 |

**PREMIERSHIP RESULTS**
WEEKEND BEGINNING 23/10/04

| | | |
|---|---|---|
| Aston Villa | 2-0 | Fulham |
| Crystal Palace | 3-0 | West Brom |
| Chelsea | 4-0 | Blackburn |
| Liverpool | 2-0 | Charlton |
| Norwich | 2-3 | Everton |
| Tottenham | 1-2 | Bolton |
| Middlesbrough | 1-1 | Portsmouth |
| Newcastle | 4-3 | Manchester City |
| Southampton | 0-0 | Birmingham |

**PREMIERSHIP TABLE**
AT END OF 25/10/04

| | P | PTS |
|---|---|---|
| 1. Arsenal | 10 | 25 |
| 2. Chelsea | 10 | 23 |
| 3. Everton | 10 | 22 |
| 4. Bolton Wanderers | 10 | 18 |
| 5. Manchester United | 10 | 17 |
| 6. Liverpool | 9 | 16 |
| 7. Newcastle United | 10 | 16 |
| 8. Middlesbrough | 10 | 15 |
| 9. Aston Villa | 10 | 14 |
| 10. Tottenham Hotspur | 10 | 13 |
| 11. Portsmouth | 9 | 12 |
| 12. Charlton Athletic | 10 | 12 |
| 13. Manchester City | 10 | 11 |
| 14. Birmingham City | 10 | 9 |
| 15. Crystal Palace | 10 | 8 |
| 16. West Brom wich Albion | 10 | 8 |
| 17. Fulham | 10 | 8 |
| 18. Southampton | 10 | 6 |
| 19. Norwich City | 10 | 6 |
| 20. Blackburn Rovers | 10 | 6 |

# Portsmouth 2

Unsworth (pen) 53, Yakubu 72

# Manchester United 0

**Possession may be** nine-tenths of the law, but football has a habit of ignoring the rule books. After bringing the 'invincibles' crashing back to earth, it was imperative that the trip to Fratton Park yielded maximum points. Victory – especially with Arsenal stuttering against Portsmouth's south coast neighbours Southampton – would have lent significant weight to claims that a title challenge was stirring at Old Trafford. Instead, for all the early pressure, the Reds were left to rue what might have been as the game ebbed away on the Solent tide.

United made just one change from the team that beat Arsenal – Ruud van Nistelrooy sitting out the second game of his three-match ban. And what a difference the Dutchman's predatory instincts might have made. Just 60 seconds had elapsed when Cristiano Ronaldo drove wide of Shaka Hislop's left post. Hislop made a meal of another Ronaldo effort, then had to gather shots from Paul Scholes and Alan Smith. The latter also fired over, but the goal would not come, and gradually Harry Redknapp's side began to interrupt United's swagger.

Eight minutes after the break, the deadlock was broken. Substitute Ricardo Fuller, attempting to escape the close attentions of Rio Ferdinand, was upended in the penalty area, and boyhood Red David Unsworth slammed the ball past Carroll.

United pressed harder. A header from Ronaldo hit the post but Smith, so deadeye in front of goal since his trans-Pennine

Heads you lose: United rue another missed opportunity on the south coast

Saturday 30 October 2005
**Fratton Park**
Attendance 20,190
**Referee: Neale Barry**

switch, couldn't convert the rebound, the ball striking him and clearing the bar. The din grew and Roy Keane and Louis Saha were introduced to try their luck. Then, with 18 minutes left, Hislop's long clearance was deftly taken down by Yakubu, who sidestepped Silvestre and Ferdinand before looping the ball over the falling Carroll.

In scenes similar to those from April 2004, United laid siege to the Pompey goal once more. Now, as then, it wasn't to be. "It absolutely destroyed what happened last week," said Sir Alex. "This was a bad, bad performance and an awful defeat."

## MAN OF THE MATCH

**PAUL SCHOLES**

On an afternoon when little went right in front of goal – on how many occasions will United fire off 19 shots without hitting the net? – Paul Scholes did as much as anyone to lift the gloom as United became more and more desperate to avoid a repeat of the previous season's defeat. An industrious display saw him at the heart of most of the best moves.

## MATCH FACTS

**PORTSMOUTH**
Hislop; Primus, de Zeeuw, Stefanovic, Unsworth; Quashie, Faye, Berger (Mezague 45); LuaLua, Kamara (Fuller 32), Yakubu **Subs not used** Ashdown, Griffin, Cisse

**MANCHESTER UNITED**
Carroll; G Neville (Brown 80), Ferdinand, Silvestre, Heinze; Ronaldo, P Neville (Keane 65), Scholes, Giggs; Rooney, Smith (Saha 65)
**Subs not used** Ricardo, Miller
**Booked** Rooney, Ferdinand

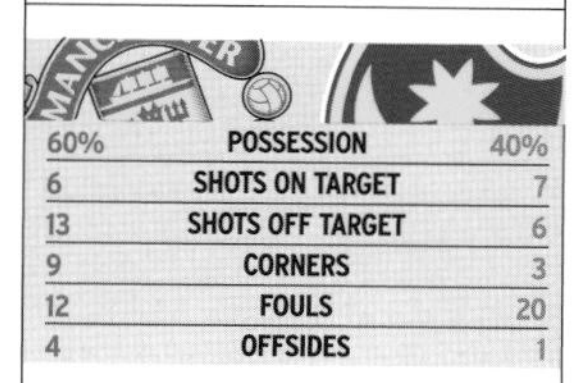

| | | |
|---|---|---|
| 60% | POSSESSION | 40% |
| 6 | SHOTS ON TARGET | 7 |
| 13 | SHOTS OFF TARGET | 6 |
| 9 | CORNERS | 3 |
| 12 | FOULS | 20 |
| 4 | OFFSIDES | 1 |

**PREMIERSHIP RESULTS**
WEEKEND BEGINNING 30/10/04

| | | |
|---|---|---|
| Arsenal | 2-2 | Southampton |
| Blackburn | 2-2 | Liverpool |
| Birmingham | 0-1 | Crystal Palace |
| Bolton | 2-1 | Newcastle |
| Charlton | 1-2 | Middlesbrough |
| Everton | 1-1 | Aston Villa |
| Fulham | 2-0 | Tottenham |
| Manchester City | 1-1 | Norwich |
| West Brom | 1-4 | Chelsea |

**PREMIERSHIP TABLE**
AT END OF 01/11/04

| | P | PTS |
|---|---|---|
| 1. Arsenal | 11 | 26 |
| 2. Chelsea | 11 | 26 |
| 3. Everton | 11 | 23 |
| 4. Bolton Wanderers | 11 | 21 |
| 5. Middlesbrough | 11 | 18 |
| 6. Liverpool | 10 | 17 |
| 7. Manchester United | 11 | 17 |
| 8. Newcastle United | 11 | 16 |
| 9. Portsmouth | 10 | 15 |
| 10. Aston Villa | 11 | 15 |
| 11. Tottenham Hotspur | 11 | 13 |
| 12. Manchester City | 11 | 12 |
| 13. Charlton Athletic | 11 | 12 |
| 14. Crystal Palace | 11 | 11 |
| 15. Fulham | 11 | 11 |
| 16. Birmingham City | 11 | 9 |
| 17. West Bromwich Albion | 11 | 8 |
| 18. Southampton | 11 | 7 |
| 19. Norwich City | 11 | 7 |
| 20. Blackburn Rovers | 11 | 7 |

# November

## City enjoyed their trip to M16, but the Red 'juggernaut' finally rolled into action as OT saluted a great Champions League Knight

**"They are not good** enough to win the championship on that display," opined Sir Alex, as November began with a damp squib of a 0-0 draw against our dear friends from across the city. And a familiar refrain it was turning out to be: plenty of possession, loads of chances – but no end product. City's unconfined joy at denying the Reds the chance to close in on Chelsea was touching – unlike the distance to Jose Mourinho's Blues, which remained nine points. Just 24 hours later, Arsène Wenger faced a charge of improper conduct from the FA for calling Ruud 'a cheat'.

November also saw a bizarre Carling Cup win over Crystal Palace, where both the teams fielded scratch sides – Sir Alex evidently saving his Sunday best for the trip to Newcastle. After Wayne Rooney scored twice in the 3-1 win at St James' Park, *The Daily Telegraph* predicted that the 'United juggernaut is rolling again'. In a vintage display, Roy Keane's personal tachometer ticked on to 300 league starts.

Bolton's late equaliser at Chelsea offered some hope, and a week later, United made the slip count with a 2-0 win over Charlton. Three nights after that, Sir Alex became the Knight of 1,000 starts, on an emotional Champions League night against Olympique Lyonnais. A fifth consecutive win, 3-0 at West Bromwich, rounded off the month in style – though Chelsea maintained their lead with a 4-0 win at Charlton. And goodbye to Portsmouth boss Harry Redknapp who picked up October's Manager of the Month – after beating the Reds – and then promptly walked out.

### PREMIERSHIP FIXTURES THIS MONTH

| | | |
|---|---|---|
| SUN 7 | MANCHESTER CITY | HOME |
| SUN 14 | NEWCASTLE UNITED | AWAY |
| SAT 20 | CHARLTON ATHLETIC | HOME |
| SAT 27 | WEST BROMWICH ALBION | AWAY |

### IN THE PREMIERSHIP THIS MONTH

**215,596** watched United play 4 games

**7** goals were scored

**459** miles were travelled by United going to and from games

United fielded **19** players

**1** goal was conceded

### FOCUS ON PAUL SCHOLES

After 231 days without a goal, two displays saw Scholes – who turned 30 this month – roll back the years, and defy a good few critics into the bargain. There's clearly something about St James' Park that brings the best out in him – remember his hat-trick in the 6-2 bashing of Sir Bobby's boys in 2002/03? Here he was back to his waspish best, escaping the shackles of his old midfield sparring partner Nicky Butt as the Reds brushed the Toon Army aside. Next stop Charlton at OT, where he capped a memorable display with a goal. And he was at it again as the month drew to a close, scoring twice in the 3-0 win over West Bromwich at The Hawthorns – first from long-range and then with his head. Still a class act.

# Manchester United 0

# Manchester City 0

Honours even: derby-day passion was not in short supply, although goals were as a dogged City left M16 clutching a precious point

**Another desperately** disappointing stalemate at Old Trafford saw United fail to capitalise on Arsenal's slip-up at Crystal Palace, as neighbours City escaped from M16 with a point following the ultimate backs-to-the-wall display. To make matters worse, Alan Smith was sent off for a second yellow card in his first Manchester derby but was given a standing ovation by the OT faithful as he left the pitch, Reds recognising the never-say-die spirit that courses through the Yorkshireman's veins.

With Ruud van Nistelrooy sitting out the last game of his three-match ban, Smith and Louis Saha got a chance to forge a partnership (Rooney handed a place on the bench for this one). And boy, did the pair have their chances. The Reds flew out of the traps and had a strong penalty shout turned down in the first 60 seconds when Mikael Silvestre looked to have been hauled back by fellow Frenchman Sylvain Distin.

United almost took the lead on four minutes, Paul Scholes's vision releasing an alert Saha in the box, but his looping shot was cleared off the line by City youngster Stephen Jordan. It was the shape of things to come. From the resultant corner the home fans screamed for another penalty when Saha was held down by Antoine

Sunday 7 November 2004
**Old Trafford**
Attendance 67,863
**Referee: Graham Poll**

Sibierski – but again referee Graham Poll waved play on. Smith's next shot was blocked on the line by Danny Mills... all this with less than 10 minutes gone.

With City on the ropes, a quick knockout seemed on the cards, but Keegan's men began to smother the Reds. Before half-time Smith nearly made the breakthrough when he shot low at David James, but the ex-England No.1 threw out a leg and the ball cannoned off his heel to safety.

At half-time Sir Alex brought on Ryan Giggs for Liam Miller and United upped the tempo. Smith's bicycle kick was cleared off the line by Steve McManaman, then Giggs curled a shot agonisingly wide. It wasn't the attacking intent that was lacking, just putting the ball in the net.

Rooney, who'd been warming up for most of the second half, finally got the nod on 77 minutes, but found the dank November evening just as frustrating as Smith and Saha. And City, who had rarely threatened, could have snatched it at the end when Shaun Wright-Phillips broke dangerously and set up McManaman, who shot wildly. At the whistle, City fans celebrated – for a point at OT, of course, but also for the body blow delivered to United in the title race.

## MAN OF THE MATCH

**GABRIEL HEINZE**

In the build-up to this match Gabriel Heinze admitted that growing up back in his native Argentina he hadn't even heard of Manchester United, never mind City. But he proved just the man for the job - quick in the tackle, always willing to bolster the attack, and there on the rare occasion when Shaun Wright-Phillips and Nicolas Anelka threatened the unthinkable.

## MATCH FACTS

**MANCHESTER UNITED**
Carroll; G Neville, Silvestre, Ferdinand, Heinze; Miller (Giggs 45), Scholes (Rooney 77), Keane, Ronaldo; Smith, Saha **Subs not used** Howard, Brown, P Neville **Booked** Keane, Smith **Sent off** Smith

**MANCHESTER CITY**
James; Mills, Dunne, Distin, Jordan; McManaman, Bosvelt, Flood, Sibierski, S Wright-Phillips; Anelka **Subs not used** B Wright-Phillips, McCarthy, Waterreus, Onuoha, Fowler **Booked** Jordan, Flood

| Man Utd | | Man City |
|---|---|---|
| 67% | POSSESSION | 33% |
| 4 | SHOTS ON TARGET | 0 |
| 8 | SHOTS OFF TARGET | 2 |
| 16 | CORNERS | 1 |
| 10 | FOULS | 10 |
| 7 | OFFSIDES | 4 |

**PREMIERSHIP RESULTS**
WEEKEND BEGINNING 06/11/04

| | | |
|---|---|---|
| Aston Villa | 3-0 | Portsmouth |
| Crystal Palace | 1-1 | Arsenal |
| Chelsea | 1-0 | Everton |
| Liverpool | 0-1 | Birmingham |
| Norwich | 1-1 | Blackburn |
| Southampton | 2-2 | West Brom |
| Tottenham | 2-3 | Charlton |
| Middlesbrough | 1-1 | Bolton |
| Newcastle | 1-4 | Fulham |

**PREMIERSHIP TABLE**
AT END OF 08/11/04

| | P | PTS |
|---|---|---|
| 1. Chelsea | 12 | 29 |
| 2. Arsenal | 12 | 27 |
| 3. Everton | 12 | 23 |
| 4. Bolton Wanderers | 12 | 22 |
| 5. Middlesbrough | 12 | 19 |
| 6. Aston Villa | 12 | 18 |
| 7. Manchester United | 12 | 18 |
| 8. Liverpool | 11 | 17 |
| 9. Newcastle United | 12 | 16 |
| 10. Portsmouth | 11 | 15 |
| 11. Charlton Athletic | 12 | 15 |
| 12. Fulham | 12 | 14 |
| 13. Manchester City | 12 | 13 |
| 14. Tottenham Hotspur | 12 | 13 |
| 15. Birmingham City | 12 | 12 |
| 16. Crystal Palace | 12 | 12 |
| 17. West Bromwich Albion | 12 | 9 |
| 18. Southampton | 12 | 8 |
| 19. Norwich City | 12 | 8 |
| 20. Blackburn Rovers | 12 | 8 |

# Newcastle United 1
Shearer 71

# Manchester United 3
Rooney 7, 90, van Nistelrooy 74

**Up to this** point in the season United had been hyped up as title favourites, written off as no-hopers, then reinstated as Premiership contenders, only to have scorn poured all over such aspirations once again. Following this victory at St James' Park, the Reds appeared to be heading in the right direction once more, with *The Daily Telegraph* reporting that the "United juggernaut is rolling again".

What this victory did do, was keep alive the possibility of a title challenge. Chelsea's 14-point advantage at the start of the day meant that anything other than a win against Graeme Souness's men would almost certainly leave the Reds already facing the prospect of competing for second place – at best.

Sir Alex Ferguson said in the build-up to this match that he wasn't concerned with what the top two sides were doing, that he wanted to concentrate on his own team finding its form and scoring more goals. So he'd have been pleased with the start his players made at St James' Park. The passing was far crisper than it had been in previous matches, the pace of play far quicker and the finishing back to the levels expected of such talented strikers. Darren Fletcher's return to the midfield, for only his second Premiership start of the season, seemed to give the Reds more control of the midfield and the three Rs (Rooney, Ronaldo and Ruud) provided more verve in attack.

It was Fletcher and Rooney who combined to give the Reds a seventh-minute lead. The Scot found Rooney in space inside the Newcastle penalty area and the 19-year-old volleyed in, first time, past Shay Given. United seemed to settle after that and although Newcastle had chances, Paul Scholes and Roy Keane controlled the tempo of the game.

There was a brief scare for the Reds when Alan Shearer equalised in the 71st minute, advancing through the middle of the United defence to shoot past Roy Carroll, but the lead was restored three minutes later. Rooney controversially capitalised on an Andy O'Brien slip to set up Scholes who was brought down for a penalty, and Ruud made no mistake for 2-1.

In injury time, the win was confirmed when Rooney slammed home from close range for his second goal and three much-needed points. A better performance and a return to goalscoring form suggested better things to come from the Reds, but the true worth of this victory would only become clear over the next few matches.

Sunday 14 November 2004
**St James' Park**
Attendance 52,320
**Referee: Mike Dean**

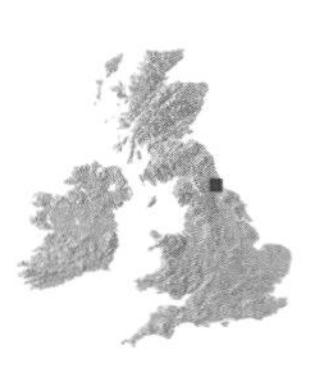

## MAN OF THE MATCH

PAUL SCHOLES

The United stalwart may have been written off up to this point as one half of a central midfield pairing past its best, but at St James', Scholes was the Reds' top man. His passing was back to its usual high standard and his vision caused problems all afternoon. He seemed to revel in the middle-of-the-park battle with ex-team-mate Nicky Butt and won the second-half penalty that turned the game back in United's favour.

## MATCH FACTS

NEWCASTLE UNITED
Given; Carr (O'Brien 18), Bramble, Johnsen, Bernard; Bowyer (Dyer 54), Butt, Jenas, Bellamy; Shearer, Kluivert (Robert 62)
**Subs not used** Harper, Ameobi
**Booked** Bramble, Johnsen

MANCHESTER UNITED
Carroll; G Neville, Ferdinand, Silvestre (Brown 57), Heinze; Fletcher (Giggs 75), Keane, Scholes, Ronaldo (Smith 83); van Nistelrooy, Rooney
**Subs not used** Howard, Saha

| Man Utd | | Newcastle |
|---|---|---|
| 55% | POSSESSION | 45% |
| 7 | SHOTS ON TARGET | 2 |
| 6 | SHOTS OFF TARGET | 5 |
| 7 | CORNERS | 2 |
| 16 | FOULS | 11 |
| 5 | OFFSIDES | 1 |

### PREMIERSHIP RESULTS
WEEKEND BEGINNING 13/11/04

| | | |
|---|---|---|
| Birmingham | 0-1 | Everton |
| Bolton | 1-2 | Aston Villa |
| Charlton | 4-0 | Norwich |
| Fulham | 1-4 | Chelsea |
| Liverpool | 3-2 | Crystal Palace |
| Manchester City | 1-1 | Blackburn |
| Southampton | 2-1 | Portsmouth |
| Tottenham | 4-5 | Arsenal |
| West Brom | 1-2 | Middlesbrough |

### PREMIERSHIP TABLE
AT END OF 15/11/04

| | P | PTS |
|---|---|---|
| 1. Chelsea | 13 | 32 |
| 2. Arsenal | 13 | 30 |
| 3. Everton | 13 | 26 |
| 4. Middlesbrough | 13 | 22 |
| 5. Bolton Wanderers | 13 | 22 |
| 6. Aston Villa | 13 | 21 |
| 7. Manchester United | 13 | 21 |
| 8. Liverpool | 12 | 20 |
| 9. Charlton Athletic | 13 | 18 |
| 10. Newcastle United | 13 | 16 |
| 11. Portsmouth | 12 | 15 |
| 12. Manchester City | 13 | 14 |
| 13. Fulham | 13 | 14 |
| 14. Tottenham Hotspur | 13 | 13 |
| 15. Birmingham City | 13 | 12 |
| 16. Crystal Palace | 13 | 12 |
| 17. Southampton | 13 | 11 |
| 18. West Bromwich Albion | 13 | 9 |
| 19. Blackburn Rovers | 13 | 9 |
| 20. Norwich City | 13 | 8 |

# Manchester United 2

Giggs 41, Scholes 50

# Charlton Athletic 0

**Game 999** will not be one that lives long in the memory of Sir Alex Ferguson or many fans, but a few hours after the final whistle, as news filtered through that the league's top two had both drawn, the three points picked up against a stuffy Charlton side looked even more welcome. The visitors came to M16 with the seemingly mandatory tactic of putting 10 men behind the ball but, unlike against Everton and Manchester City, this time the Reds found the goals to reflect their domination.

United appeared to turn the corner on a number of occasions throughout the season only to slip up in the next match. So, after half an hour, with the deadlock still not broken, murmurings were of this being "another one of those days". But such thoughts were banished shortly before half-time when Ryan Giggs registered the 124th goal of his United career. Picking the ball up on the right of midfield, he cut inside; as space opened up in front of him he fired in a shot from the edge of the penalty area that took a wicked deflection off Luke Young and looped beyond Dean Kiely.

Five minutes into the second half the Reds doubled their lead, thanks to Paul Scholes' first goal of the season. The fans hadn't had much cause to sing the Paul Scholes song up until now, as he'd not weighed in with his customary "goals galore", but this time he made no mistake with a classic strike. After a foray down the right, Darren Fletcher sent over a cross towards the far post. It was by no means an easy opportunity but Scholes leapt into the air to volley powerfully into the net. His celebration showed signs of both relief and joy at ending his barren spell.

It may have been a routine victory rather than a thriller but there were several pleasing aspects. The defence – minus regular full-backs Gary Neville and Gabriel Heinze – produced another solid display to restrict the Addicks to only three off-target shots in the entire game. And Fletcher continued to assist Scholes and Roy Keane in midfield and again impressed with his range of passing and tireless running. But most pleasing of all was recording a second straight league win and maximum points to begin the task of closing the gap with Chelsea and Arsenal at the top of the table.

Saturday 20 November 2004
**Old Trafford**
Attendance 67,704
**Referee: Rob Styles**

Fast movers: United's victory was inspired by Giggs' surges through the heart of the Addicks defence and Fletcher's forays down the flanks...

## MAN OF THE MATCH

**PAUL SCHOLES**

Fresh from celebrating his 30th birthday on the Tuesday, Scholes carried on where he'd left off at St James' Park with another improved display in midfield. He caused problems for Alan Curbishley's men all afternoon and, after getting closer and closer to ending his scoring drought over the previous weeks, capped a fine performance with a stunning second-half volley, the perfect way to mark his 300th league game and 350th start for United.

## MATCH FACTS

**MANCHESTER UNITED**
Carroll; Brown, Ferdinand, Silvestre, Fortune; Fletcher (O'Shea 84), Keane (P Neville 80), Scholes, Giggs; Rooney, van Nistelrooy (Smith 76)
**Subs not used** Howard, Ronaldo

**CHARLTON ATHLETIC**
Kiely; Young, Perry (Fortune 45), El Karkouri, Hreidarsson; Kishishev, Holland, Murphy, Thomas (Konchesky 57); Bartlett (Jeffers 75), Johansson
**Subs not used** Andersen, Euell

| Man Utd | | Charlton |
|---|---|---|
| 56% | POSSESSION | 44% |
| 8 | SHOTS ON TARGET | 0 |
| 9 | SHOTS OFF TARGET | 3 |
| 6 | CORNERS | 3 |
| 8 | FOULS | 13 |
| 7 | OFFSIDES | 2 |

**PREMIERSHIP RESULTS**
WEEKEND BEGINNING 20/11/04

| Home | Score | Away |
|---|---|---|
| Arsenal | 1-1 | West Brom |
| Aston Villa | 1-0 | Tottenham |
| Blackburn | 3-3 | Birmingham |
| Chelsea | 2-2 | Bolton |
| Crystal Palace | 0-2 | Newcastle |
| Everton | 1-0 | Fulham |
| Middlesbrough | 2-0 | Liverpool |
| Norwich | 2-1 | Southampton |
| Portsmouth | 1-3 | Manchester City |

**PREMIERSHIP TABLE**
AT END OF 22/11/04

| | P | PTS |
|---|---|---|
| 1. Chelsea | 14 | 33 |
| 2. Arsenal | 14 | 31 |
| 3. Everton | 14 | 29 |
| 4. Middlesbrough | 14 | 25 |
| 5. Aston Villa | 14 | 24 |
| 6. Manchester United | 14 | 24 |
| 7. Bolton Wanderers | 14 | 23 |
| 8. Liverpool | 13 | 20 |
| 9. Newcastle United | 14 | 19 |
| 10. Charlton Athletic | 14 | 18 |
| 11. Manchester City | 14 | 17 |
| 12. Portsmouth | 13 | 15 |
| 13. Fulham | 14 | 14 |
| 14. Birmingham City | 14 | 13 |
| 15. Tottenham Hotspur | 14 | 13 |
| 16. Crystal Palace | 14 | 12 |
| 17. Southampton | 14 | 11 |
| 18. Norwich City | 14 | 11 |
| 19. West Bromwich Albion | 14 | 10 |
| 20. Blackburn Rovers | 14 | 10 |

# West Bromwich Albion 0

# Manchester United 3

Scholes 53, 82, van Nistelrooy 72

**Throughout November** the signs were there that Paul Scholes was returning to form, and this trip to The Hawthorns underlined it using a big black marker pen. Scholes's 25-yard strike early in the second half set the Reds on course and his second in the final minutes proved he was firmly back in the goalscoring routine. In between, Ruud van Nistelrooy had notched his first goal from open play in the Premiership, as United registered a third away victory of the season.

The evidence of the first half was that it might be anything but a routine afternoon for the visitors. Baggies' boss Bryan Robson had his players pumped up for the game and, following their draw at Highbury seven days earlier, the home team set about the Reds with feverish intent. The 4-5-1 formation indicated West Brom's determination not to be beaten, and with only an off-target header from Wayne Rooney to show for the opening 45 minutes, the tactic was largely successful.

The talk among travelling Reds at half-time centred around whether this was going to be yet another of those frustrating afternoons like the ones at Blackburn, Birmingham and Bolton. But it took only eight minutes of the second half for Paul

Bye-bye Baggies: Ruud's rampaging goalscoring run continued as he put daylight between the Reds and Robbo's beleaguered side

Saturday 27 November 2004
**The Hawthorns**
Attendance 27,709
**Referee: Steve Bennett**

Scholes to provide the answer. Gabriel Heinze threaded the ball forward to Giggs, who flicked into the path of the galloping Scholes and the midfielder advanced into space before crashing a shot into the far corner of Russell Hoult's net.

With the deadlock broken, West Brom's game plan went out of the window as suddenly they were forced to push more men forward. Giggs, Rooney and Scholes were then able to exploit the resulting space and more chances were created.

The second goal finally came, and while it was less spectacular than the first, it was just as artfully crafted. A Giggs free-kick picked out Heinze at the far post, he planted a powerful header back across goal and van Nistelrooy was on hand to nod past Hoult to make it 12 goals in 14 matches.

The Reds' biggest Premiership win since the start of the campaign was confirmed in the 82nd minute when a game of head-tennis in the Baggies' six-yard box was finally ended by Scholes, who beat Hoult with a neat header. It made it a satisfying fifth successive victory in all competitions, showed that United had turned a corner and, for the first time in the season, had Messrs Mourinho and Wenger anxiously looking over their shoulders.

## MAN OF THE MATCH

**PAUL SCHOLES**

Following his brilliant volley against Charlton at Old Trafford seven days earlier, Scholes carried on in a similar vein at The Hawthorns and by the end of the afternoon had trebled his season's tally. His first was a strike from distance and his second a close-range header, but his performance was the most telling contribution of the afternoon. It hardly seems possible he was written off as a spent force at the start of the season.

## MATCH FACTS

**WEST BROMWICH ALBION**
Hoult; Scimeca, Moore (Gaardsoe 24), Purse, Clement; Greening, Sakiri (Horsfield 75), Johnson, Gera, Contra (Robinson 38); Earnshaw
**Subs not used** Kuszczak, Hulse

**MANCHESTER UNITED**
Carroll; Brown, Ferdinand, Silvestre, Heinze; Fletcher (Ronaldo 72), Keane, Scholes, Giggs; van Nistelrooy (Smith 75), Rooney
**Subs not used** Howard, O'Shea, Fortune

| Man Utd | | West Brom |
|---|---|---|
| 62% | POSSESSION | 38% |
| 4 | SHOTS ON TARGET | 2 |
| 10 | SHOTS OFF TARGET | 1 |
| 8 | CORNERS | 1 |
| 11 | FOULS | 15 |
| 4 | OFFSIDES | 1 |

**PREMIERSHIP RESULTS**
WEEKEND BEGINNING 27/11/04

| Home | Score | Away |
|---|---|---|
| Birmingham | 1-1 | Norwich |
| Bolton | 0-1 | Portsmouth |
| Charlton | 0-4 | Chelsea |
| Fulham | 0-2 | Blackburn |
| Liverpool | 2-1 | Arsenal |
| Manchester City | 2-0 | Aston Villa |
| Newcastle | 1-1 | Everton |
| Southampton | 2-2 | Crystal Palace |
| Tottenham | 2-0 | Middlesbrough |

**PREMIERSHIP TABLE**
AT END OF 29/11/04

| | P | PTS |
|---|---|---|
| 1. Chelsea | 15 | 36 |
| 2. Arsenal | 15 | 31 |
| 3. Everton | 15 | 30 |
| 4. Manchester United | 15 | 27 |
| 5. Middlesbrough | 15 | 25 |
| 6. Aston Villa | 15 | 24 |
| 7. Liverpool | 15 | 23 |
| 8. Bolton Wanderers | 15 | 23 |
| 9. Manchester City | 15 | 20 |
| 10. Newcastle United | 15 | 20 |
| 11. Portsmouth | 14 | 18 |
| 12. Charlton Athletic | 15 | 18 |
| 13. Tottenham Hotspur | 15 | 16 |
| 14. Birmingham City | 15 | 14 |
| 15. Fulham | 15 | 14 |
| 16. Crystal Palace | 15 | 13 |
| 17. Blackburn Rovers | 15 | 13 |
| 18. Southampton | 15 | 12 |
| 19. Norwich City | 15 | 12 |
| 20. West Bromwich Albion | 15 | 10 |

# December

## United enjoyed the festive season as Palace left OT with a stuffing. Only Fulham's late show and Ruud's injury threatened the party

**And so this is Christmas.** A Blue Christmas, unfortunately, in more ways than one. Despite serving up some tasty festive fare, United were still playing catch-up as Chelsea continued to slay all-comers in the Premiership. On the home front, an Achilles problem laid Ruud off for the whole month. December also brought some early Cup cheer – very early! David Bellion's Carling Cup quarter-final winner against Arsenal came after just 18.6 seconds and secured a semi-final spot before many had even taken their seats. The following Saturday's league encounter with Southampton had many out of them in excitement, Ryan Giggs inspiring a 3-0 win in which the Reds had nine shots on target, a further 17 off target, and won 16 corners.

With qualification for the Champions League second phase already assured, United's young Turks got a run-out in Istanbul, but the European hangover continued at Fulham where Papa Bouba Diop's late piledriver gave the hosts a share of the spoils. Crystal Palace paid for the profligate finishing of recent weeks, Paul Scholes continuing his goal rehabilitation with two in a 5-2 stuffing. But anything United could do, Chelsea could do as well and United tucked into their Christmas dinners in fourth, nine points adrift of the Londoners.

On Boxing Day, Bolton discovered the Theatre of Dreams isn't a term coined for their visits – slipping to a 2-0 defeat. The Reds then gained the traditional win at Villa Park – to bring the curtain down on 2004. No happy New Year for Rooney, however – he was banned for three games after a *contretemps* with Bolton's Tal Ben-Haim.

### PREMIERSHIP FIXTURES THIS MONTH

| | | |
|---|---|---|
| SUN 4 | SOUTHAMPTON | HOME |
| MON 13 | FULHAM | AWAY |
| SAT 18 | CRYSTAL PALACE | HOME |
| SUN 26 | BOLTON WANDERERS | HOME |
| TUES 28 | ASTON VILLA | AWAY |

### IN THE PREMIERSHIP THIS MONTH

**268,495** watched United play 5 games

**12** goals were scored

**566** miles were travelled by United going to and from games

United fielded **17** players

**3** goals were conceded

### FOCUS ON RYAN GIGGS

The Welshman was the last name on the scoresheet as 2004 came to a close, sliding in for the winner against Villa at our favourite other ground. Okay, so it wasn't quite as memorable a goal as *that* one against Arsenal in the 1999 FA Cup semi-final, but it was one that kept United in the chasing pack at Chelsea's shoulder. Giggs's display against the Midlanders, all strength and determination, followed hard on the heels of another corking performance in the Old Trafford victory over Bolton on Boxing Day, in which he also found the net. It seemed as if Ryan's rest in November had done him the power of good, with his inspirational displays all month fair rolling back the years. "He's in fantastic form and a tremendous threat," said Sir Alex. Amen to that. The Villa game was his 615th in all competitions for the Reds. Inching ever closer to Bill Foulkes in the hall of fame...

# Manchester United 3

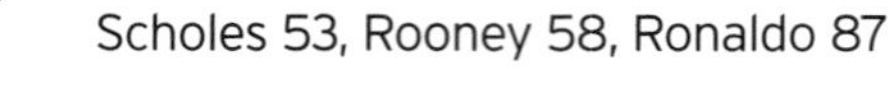

Scholes 53, Rooney 58, Ronaldo 87

# Southampton 0

**On the evidence** of this second-half display, it was not only confidence and form that was back in United's play, but also a certain swagger. After the break the Reds simply blew the Saints away. As well as goals from Paul Scholes, Wayne Rooney, and a first of the season for Cristiano Ronaldo, the Reds dominated to such a degree that the visitors could count themselves lucky to avoid a five- or six-goal mauling.

At half-time, however, you could have been forgiven for thinking that the run of improved performances and results were another false dawn. Stray passes, dogmatic build-ups and a lack of clear-cut chances encapsulated a low-key first half. But the game burst into life seven minutes after the interval. After the Saints defence had failed to clear a Ryan Giggs corner, Rio Ferdinand knocked the ball back in and the rejuvenated Scholes nodded in from six yards, his fourth goal in three games.

Shortly afterwards United were temporarily down to 10 men as Alan Smith disappeared to have stitches in a nasty head wound, but they simply moved up a gear. Suddenly Ronaldo was going past ex-Red Danny Higginbotham for fun, Rooney was looking increasingly threatening, and Giggs was enjoying his best game of the season. And it was the Welshman who provided the next moment of magic. Found in space by the excellent Gabriel Heinze, Giggs spotted Rooney making a run into the box and flighted the ball between two defenders. The teenager duly crashed the ball into the net via the underside of the crossbar.

Smith returned briefly before being substituted as United continued to create chance after chance. Amazingly it took until the 87th minute for the third goal but then, making up for an earlier missed chance, for which he was berated by team-mates, Ronaldo struck a fierce volley past Kasey Keller. His muted celebration showed his mind was still on the earlier effort.

Approaching the busy Christmas period the signs were there that the Reds were going from strength to strength. The stats from the game told their own tale: nine shots on target, 17 off target and 16 corners. All in all a performance that was a lot more like the United we all know and love.

Saturday 4 December 2004
**Old Trafford**
Attendance 67,921
**Referee: Barry Knight**

Sharp shooters: Scholes set the ball rolling while Ronaldo and Rooney provided the finishing touches

## MAN OF THE MATCH

RYAN GIGGS

On a day of several impressive individual performances – Gabriel Heinze, Cristiano Ronaldo, Paul Scholes and Wayne Rooney all staking their own claims for Man of the Match – the standout display came from the Welshman. It was his corner that resulted in the Reds' first goal and his pass played in Rooney for the second, but it was Giggs' dribbling and driving runs that caused Southampton the most problems as, just a week past his 31st birthday, the United stalwart showed no signs that those quick feet were starting to run out of steam.

## MATCH FACTS

MANCHESTER UNITED

Carroll; G Neville, Ferdinand, Silvestre, Heinze; Ronaldo, Keane, Scholes, Giggs; Rooney, Smith (Bellion 62)
**Subs not used** Howard, Brown, Miller, Fletcher

SOUTHAMPTON

Keller; Nilsson, Jakobsson, Lundekvam, Le Saux; Telfer, Delap (Fernandes 86), Higginbotham, A Svensson; Beattie (Blackstock 22), Phillips
**Subs not used** Blayney, Dodd, Crouch **Booked** Lundekvam

| Manchester United | | Southampton |
|---|---|---|
| 63% | POSSESSION | 37% |
| 9 | SHOTS ON TARGET | 1 |
| 17 | SHOTS OFF TARGET | 4 |
| 16 | CORNERS | 2 |
| 7 | FOULS | 10 |
| 4 | OFFSIDES | 0 |

### PREMIERSHIP RESULTS

WEEKEND BEGINNING 6/12/04

| | | |
|---|---|---|
| Arsenal | 3-0 | Birmingham |
| Aston Villa | 1-1 | Liverpool |
| Blackburn | 0-1 | Tottenham |
| Chelsea | 4-0 | Newcastle |
| Crystal Palace | 0-1 | Charlton |
| Everton | 3-2 | Bolton |
| Middlesbrough | 3-1 | Manchester City |
| Norwich | 0-1 | Fulham |
| Portsmouth | 3-2 | West Brom |

### PREMIERSHIP TABLE

AT END OF 6/12/04

| | P | PTS |
|---|---|---|
| 1. Chelsea | 16 | 39 |
| 2. Arsenal | 16 | 34 |
| 3. Everton | 16 | 33 |
| 4. Manchester United | 16 | 30 |
| 5. Middlesbrough | 16 | 28 |
| 6. Aston Villa | 16 | 25 |
| 7. Liverpool | 15 | 24 |
| 8. Bolton Wanderers | 16 | 23 |
| 9. Portsmouth | 15 | 21 |
| 10. Charlton Athletic | 16 | 21 |
| 11. Manchester City | 16 | 20 |
| 12. Newcastle United | 16 | 20 |
| 13. Tottenham Hotspur | 16 | 19 |
| 14. Fulham | 16 | 17 |
| 15. Birmingham City | 16 | 14 |
| 16. Crystal Palace | 16 | 13 |
| 17. Blackburn Rovers | 16 | 13 |
| 18. Southampton | 16 | 12 |
| 19. Norwich City | 16 | 12 |
| 20. West Bromwich Albion | 16 | 10 |

# Fulham 1
Diop 87

# Manchester United 1
Smith 33

London pride: Steed Malbranque shows the grit and determination that saw the Cottagers deny the Reds maximum points from this encounter

**With Arsenal** and Chelsea ending their Highbury clash in stalemate, United knew that this trip to the 'Big Smoke' was an ideal opportunity to further close the gap. Instead, it turned out to be another night of frustration, as Papa Bouba Diop's unstoppable, late equaliser cancelled out all United's earlier good work.

Despite Ruud van Nistelrooy's absence, it was still a blatantly attacking side that Sir Alex Ferguson sent out, unleashing Alan Smith, Wayne Rooney, Ryan Giggs, Cristiano Ronaldo and Paul Scholes on the Cottagers. The home team weren't short of attacking options either, and no United fan needed reminding of Andy Cole's potency in front of goal – the Fulham captain receiving a rousing tribute from the Reds in the Putney End stand.

The early signs were that United's forward-thinking policy would pay off. Edwin van der Sar's goalpost was rattled twice in the first half-hour – first by Roy Keane, convinced his long-awaited 50th United goal had arrived in style; then by Rooney. So it was no surprise when the excellent Smith broke the deadlock, winning the ball from Sylvain Legwinski

Monday 13 December 2004
**Craven Cottage**
Attendance 21,940
**Referee: Philip Dowd**

and beating young Liam Rosenior before clipping the ball home past van der Sar. And before the break the chilly air hotted up even further as the home fans barracked Ronaldo, who had gone down after feeling the full force of a series of hefty tackles.

In the second half the Reds kept trying to unlock Fulham's defence, with Scholes at the heart of most moves. But it wasn't all one-way traffic – Cole's trademark spin and shot brought the Hammersmith End woodwork into play for a third time.

Giggs, sensing the frustration emanating from the away end, tried a more direct approach and won a free-kick on the edge of the box. Gabriel Heinze stepped up, but his ambitious attempt curled just past the goal.

United's support had been bellowing the contents of the Stretford End songbook, but one festive number was conspicuous by its absence: 'Jingle Bells', which ends with the line 'oh what fun it is to see United win away'.

Without a second goal, the three points were always in the balance, and with just three minutes of the 90 left, Fulham's big Senegalese midfielder let fly with a bullet shot that whizzed through the London air to draw the match and temporarily put the brakes on United's title chase.

## MAN OF THE MATCH

**ALAN SMITH**

Raw spirit is a huge part of Alan Smith's game, but the former Leeds man is far from all blood and thunder – intelligent line-leading, subtle link-up play and an innate understanding of when help is needed at the back are all characteristics of the young man's game. Smith's eighth goal of the season, a cool finish just after the half-hour mark, looked to be the winner, and no-one was as disappointed as him when two points evaporated at the death.

## MATCH FACTS

**FULHAM**
Van der Sar; Rosenior, Pearce, Rehman, Bocanegra; Malbranque (John 83), Legwinski (Radzinski 74), Pembridge, Diop; Cole, McBride
**Subs not used** Flitney, Knight, Hammond
**Booked** Diop, Radzinski

**MANCHESTER UNITED**
Carroll; G Neville, Ferdinand, Silvestre, Heinze; Ronaldo, Keane, Scholes, Giggs; Smith, Rooney
**Subs not used** Howard, Bellion, O'Shea, Fletcher, Fortune
**Booked** Silvestre

| Man Utd | | Fulham |
|---|---|---|
| 57% | POSSESSION | 43% |
| 4 | SHOTS ON TARGET | 3 |
| 11 | SHOTS OFF TARGET | 8 |
| 7 | CORNERS | 6 |
| 14 | FOULS | 17 |
| 0 | OFFSIDES | 1 |

**PREMIERSHIP RESULTS**
WEEKEND BEGINNING 11/12/04

| | | |
|---|---|---|
| Arsenal | 2-2 | Chelsea |
| Aston Villa | 1-2 | Birmingham |
| Crystal Palace | 0-0 | Blackburn |
| Everton | 1-0 | Liverpool |
| Manchester City | 0-1 | Tottenham |
| Newcastle | 1-1 | Portsmouth |
| Norwich | 3-2 | Bolton |
| Southampton | 2-2 | Middlesbrough |
| West Brom | 0-1 | Charlton |

**PREMIERSHIP TABLE**
AT END OF 13/12/04

| | | P | PTS |
|---|---|---|---|
| 1. | Chelsea | 17 | 40 |
| 2. | Everton | 17 | 36 |
| 3. | Arsenal | 17 | 35 |
| 4. | Manchester United | 17 | 31 |
| 5. | Middlesbrough | 17 | 29 |
| 6. | Aston Villa | 17 | 25 |
| 7. | Liverpool | 16 | 24 |
| 8. | Charlton Athletic | 17 | 24 |
| 9. | Bolton Wanderers | 17 | 23 |
| 10. | Portsmouth | 16 | 22 |
| 11. | Tottenham Hotspur | 17 | 22 |
| 12. | Newcastle United | 17 | 21 |
| 13. | Manchester City | 17 | 20 |
| 14. | Fulham | 17 | 18 |
| 15. | Birmingham City | 17 | 17 |
| 16. | Norwich City | 17 | 15 |
| 17. | Crystal Palace | 17 | 14 |
| 18. | Blackburn Rovers | 17 | 14 |
| 19. | Southampton | 17 | 13 |
| 20. | West Bromwich Albion | 17 | 10 |

# Manchester United 5

Scholes 22, 49, Smith 35, Boyce og 48, O'Shea 90

# Crystal Palace 2

Granville 27, Kolkka 46

**For several weeks** United fans had been predicting that the Reds were on the verge of a goal glut, given the amount of chances being created. And against Palace, it finally happened. Two goals in the first half and three in the second were enough for United to see off a spirited Palace side who found the net twice themselves in an, at times, bewildering game.

The opening 10 minutes did little to hint at the entertainment that would follow. In fact, when Wayne Rooney saw his early penalty saved by Eagles keeper Gabor Kiraly (following a foul on Darren Fletcher), those familiar frustrations began to materialise. But any doubts were banished midway through the first half when Paul Scholes netted his fifth goal of the campaign – a fierce shot high into the far corner after a neat run and turn inside the Palace box.

Palace came back strongly and shocked OT just five minutes later, defender Danny Granville slamming in a rebound after a Gonzalo Sorondo's blocked header had dropped at his feet. But parity was short-lived, as Alan Smith rose highest at a Scholes set-piece to head powerfully into the top corner of the net.

Iain Dowie's side showed their resilience immediately after the restart. Inside 45 seconds Wayne Routledge flicked the ball to ex-City player Michael Hughes, whose cross was headed in by Joonas Kolkka. Cue yet another frenetic spell and 60 seconds later the Reds were back in front; Scholes jumped for a header but Emmerson Boyce got there first, knocking the ball goalwards and over the line to put United 3-2 up.

That became 4-2 when Scholes ran on to a Smith header and, despite losing his footing, slid the ball into the far corner for his sixth goal in five games. With the three points all but secured the Stretford End decided to find alternative entertainment, reacting to a message over the PA system for a "Mr Mystery to report to the nearest steward" by chanting his name continuously: "There's only one Mr Mystery...!" His name was then inserted into the '12 Days of Christmas' song normally reserved for the watching Eric Cantona. The festive spirit was flowing.

That was not the end of the fun though. In time added-on, substitute John O'Shea turned in a Ryan Giggs cross, and the Reds could reflect on a first five-goal haul of the Premiership season.

Saturday 18 December 2004
**Old Trafford**
Attendance 67,814
**Referee: Steve Dunn**

Five star performance: Gary Neville battles for the ball with Joonas Kolkka

## MAN OF THE MATCH

### PAUL SCHOLES

The in-form midfielder found the net twice and could have had a hat-trick if Emmerson Boyce hadn't got there first for the third goal. But it was not just Scholes' finishing that undid Iain Dowie's side; his all-round play was its usual exceptional standard and the Palace midfield were simply unable to cope with his foraging runs and clever passing.

## MATCH FACTS

### MANCHESTER UNITED

Carroll; G Neville, Ferdinand, Silvestre, Fortune (O'Shea 32); Fletcher, Scholes, Keane; Giggs, Rooney, Smith
**Subs not used** Howard, P Neville, Bellion, Miller

### CRYSTAL PALACE

Kiraly; Boyce, Sorondo, Hall, Granville; Routledge (Andrews 81), Riihilahti (Soares 69), Watson, Hughes (Lakis 69), Kolkka; Johnson
**Subs not used** Speroni, Popovic
**Booked** Granville

| 59% | POSSESSION | 41% |
|---|---|---|
| 12 | SHOTS ON TARGET | 3 |
| 4 | SHOTS OFF TARGET | 1 |
| 15 | CORNERS | 3 |
| 13 | FOULS | 10 |
| 3 | OFFSIDES | 1 |

### PREMIERSHIP RESULTS
WEEKEND BEGINNING 18/12/04

| | | |
|---|---|---|
| Birmingham | 4-0 | West Brom |
| Blackburn | 0-0 | Everton |
| Bolton | 0-1 | Manchester City |
| Charlton | 2-1 | Fulham |
| Chelsea | 4-0 | Norwich |
| Liverpool | 3-1 | Newcastle |
| Middlesbrough | 3-0 | Aston Villa |
| Portsmouth | 0-1 | Arsenal |
| Tottenham | 5-1 | Southampton |

### PREMIERSHIP TABLE
AT END OF 20/12/04

| | P | PTS |
|---|---|---|
| 1. Chelsea | 18 | 43 |
| 2. Arsenal | 18 | 38 |
| 3. Everton | 18 | 37 |
| 4. Manchester United | 18 | 34 |
| 5. Middlesbrough | 18 | 32 |
| 6. Liverpool | 18 | 28 |
| 7. Charlton Athletic | 18 | 27 |
| 8. Tottenham Hotspur | 18 | 25 |
| 9. Aston Villa | 18 | 25 |
| 10. Manchester City | 18 | 23 |
| 11. Bolton Wanderers | 18 | 23 |
| 12. Portsmouth | 18 | 23 |
| 13. Newcastle United | 18 | 21 |
| 14. Birmingham City | 18 | 20 |
| 15. Fulham | 18 | 18 |
| 16. Blackburn Rovers | 18 | 15 |
| 17. Norwich City | 18 | 15 |
| 18. Crystal Palace | 18 | 14 |
| 19. Southampton | 18 | 13 |
| 20. West Bromwich Albion | 18 | 10 |

# Manchester United 2

Giggs 10, Scholes 89

# Bolton Wanderers 0

**The Reds began** the quest for maximum points from four games in 10 days over Christmas and New Year in confident style. Bolton had won on two of their last three trips to OT, but goals from Ryan Giggs and Paul Scholes stopped them making it three out of four in this low-key local derby.

Sam Allardyce's Trotters' poor run of form going into this game suggested United might have a more comfortable afternoon than they did at the Reebok in September, when only a last-minute equaliser gave the Reds a share of the spoils. Given Chelsea's earlier victory over Aston Villa three points were essential, and any nerves were soon dispelled as Giggs put the Reds ahead on 10 minutes. Gabriel Heinze, fresh from a pre-Christmas break, put in the cross, Cristiano Ronaldo flicked on and the United stalwart acrobatically shot past Jussi Jaaskelainen from eight yards. A quiet Old Trafford crowd (too much Christmas pud?) suddenly awoke, and were soon singing the praises of the in-form Welshman.

The game's next big talking point came just before half-time. In an innocuous off-the-ball incident, Wayne Rooney pushed Tal Ben Haim in the face and the Israeli international fell to the ground as if caught by a fierce right hook. Seen by many as an over-reaction, it would nonetheless result in a three-match ban for the United youngster, deemed guilty of violent conduct.

After the break Bolton gave their all in search of an equaliser but the Reds' defence was in no mood for dishing out Christmas

Sunday 26 December 2004
**Old Trafford**
Attendance 67,867
**Referee: Dermot Gallagher**

gifts like the two Crystal Palace had received a week earlier. Roy Carroll had to make a swift intervention at the feet of Kevin Nolan but that was his only real action of the half.

In the 89th minute, sub Paul Scholes sealed the win. A Giggs dribble was only partially cleared, and Scholes fired home from 20 yards for his seventh goal in seven games. At 2-0, there was no way back for Bolton and United's fans flooded home happy that their side had kept pace with the sides above them – and, at the halfway point of the season, had kept themselves in contention for the title.

Receiving end: Rooney (left) gets the hands-on treatment from Ben Haim and Scholes seals the win

## MAN OF THE MATCH

**RYAN GIGGS**
After being rested in November, the 31-year-old enjoyed a spell of form as good as any during his 13 seasons at OT. The Reds' record medal-winner, with well over 600 games under his belt, was not only creating and scoring goals but his trademark dribbling was back to its best, and Bolton's defenders simply could not contain Giggs' goalward surges.

## MATCH FACTS

**MANCHESTER UNITED**
Carroll; O'Shea, Ferdinand, Silvestre, Heinze; Ronaldo (Scholes 69), Keane, Fletcher, Giggs; Rooney (Miller 84), Smith
**Subs not used** Howard, P Neville, Bellion

**BOLTON WANDERERS**
Jaaskelainen; Hunt, Ben Haim, Jaidi, Cesar; Diouf (Okocha 51), Campo, Nolan, Speed; Vaz Te (Giannakopoulos 69), Davies (Ferdinand 63)
**Subs not used** Oakes, N'Gotty

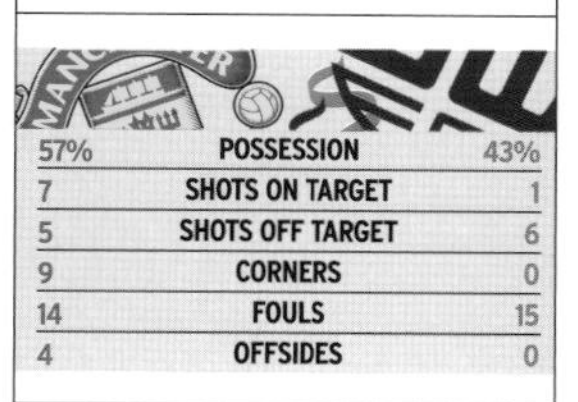

| Man Utd | | Bolton |
|---|---|---|
| 57% | POSSESSION | 43% |
| 7 | SHOTS ON TARGET | 1 |
| 5 | SHOTS OFF TARGET | 6 |
| 9 | CORNERS | 0 |
| 14 | FOULS | 15 |
| 4 | OFFSIDES | 0 |

**PREMIERSHIP RESULTS**
WEEKEND BEGINNING 25/12/04

| | | |
|---|---|---|
| Arsenal | 2-0 | Fulham |
| Birmingham | 2-0 | Middlesbrough |
| Blackburn | 2-2 | Newcastle |
| Chelsea | 1-0 | Aston Villa |
| Crystal Palace | 0-1 | Portsmouth |
| Everton | 2-1 | Manchester City |
| Norwich | 0-2 | Tottenham |
| Southampton | 0-0 | Charlton |
| West Brom | 0-5 | Liverpool |

**PREMIERSHIP TABLE**
AT END OF 27/11/04

| | P | PTS |
|---|---|---|
| 1. Chelsea | 19 | 46 |
| 2. Arsenal | 19 | 41 |
| 3. Everton | 19 | 40 |
| 4. Manchester United | 19 | 37 |
| 5. Middlesbrough | 19 | 32 |
| 6. Liverpool | 19 | 31 |
| 7. Tottenham Hotspur | 19 | 28 |
| 8. Charlton Athletic | 19 | 28 |
| 9. Portsmouth | 19 | 26 |
| 10. Aston Villa | 19 | 25 |
| 11. Manchester City | 19 | 23 |
| 12. Birmingham City | 19 | 23 |
| 13. Bolton Wanderers | 19 | 23 |
| 14. Newcastle United | 19 | 22 |
| 15. Fulham | 19 | 18 |
| 16. Blackburn Rovers | 19 | 16 |
| 17. Norwich City | 19 | 15 |
| 18. Crystal Palace | 19 | 14 |
| 19. Southampton | 19 | 14 |
| 20. West Bromwich Albion | 19 | 10 |

# Aston Villa 0

# Manchester United 1

Giggs 41

**"We showed guts** and character and we weren't going to lose," was how a contented Sir Alex Ferguson described United's battling performance at Villa Park over the Christmas holidays, with a rampant Ryan Giggs the architect of the victory – not for the first time on this big, old ground.

After brushing aside Bolton on Boxing Day, the Reds looked to continue a festive fixtures clean sweep. And it didn't take long to test keeper Thomas Sorensen, Wayne Rooney trying a shot from the edge of the area inside the first minute. But Villa were not about to roll over that easily and, despite some early Red pressure, with a quarter of an hour gone the hosts surprisingly had enjoyed the larger share of possession.

Nolberto Solano kept pressing forward on the counter-attack, troubling the Red back line with his crosses. Roy Carroll saved a Lee Hendrie shot, before Rooney found himself tackling way back in his own half to stamp out a claret-and-blue threat on the break. But then, as if spurred into life by Villa's audacity, United grabbed the game by the scruff of the neck and picked up the pace – in some style. Ryan Giggs, fresh from his Man of the Match performance at Old Trafford two days earlier, had a stinging shot deflected over the bar by Ulises de la Cruz and, from the resultant Paul Scholes corner, Darren Fletcher shot just wide.

The Giggs show then started in earnest. John O'Shea battled for a lost cause on the left before releasing the flying Welshman on another run, to the delight of the travelling Reds, who upped the volume of 'Take me Home United Road'. With Giggs, Scholes and Rooney beginning to boss the action it seemed only a matter of time before Red superiority was converted into goals. But in the 38th minute it was Villa who were a whisker away from going in front. Solano again caused the problem, firing in a cross from the left, which Liam Ridgewell headed directly at Carroll on the line.

Fresh from that let-off, United launched another attack. Giggs's deft flick out to the right wing was volleyed back into his path by O'Shea who was storming down the flank, and from the edge of the area the Welshman slammed the ball with venom into the bottom corner.

In the second half Roy Keane and Cristiano Ronaldo came on for O'Shea and Rooney in a bid to unsettle the home side and offer fresh options up front. Alan Smith did manage to hit the bar in injury time, but in the end 1-0 was enough for three vital points *en route* to the Riverside.

Tuesday 28 December 2004
**Villa Park**
Attendance 42,593
**Referee: Graham Poll**

Ball-watching: Phil Neville, Smiffy and Ronaldo keep their eye on the ball in pursuit of three more points

## MAN OF THE MATCH

**RYAN GIGGS**

There are few better sights in football than the Welshman hitting his stride and leaving defenders flailing in his wake. The winger's strength, determination and vision made sure that Villa Park again proved a happy hunting ground for the Reds, and it earned him a second Man of the Match award in three days. "Giggs is in fantastic form and a tremendous threat," said Sir Alex. And you can't argue with the boss.

## MATCH FACTS

**ASTON VILLA**
Sorensen; de la Cruz, Mellberg, Ridgewell, Barry; Solano, Hendrie (Whittingham 67), Berson (S Moore 87), Davis; Angel, Cole (L Moore 54)
**Subs not used** Drobny, Postma

**MANCHESTER UNITED**
Carroll; O'Shea (Keane 60), Ferdinand, Silvestre, Heinze; Fletcher, P Neville, Scholes, Giggs; Rooney (Ronaldo 61), Smith
**Subs not used** Bellion, Miller, Howard **Booked** Ferdinand, O'Shea, Heinze

| Man Utd | | Aston Villa |
|---|---|---|
| 50% | POSSESSION | 50% |
| 2 | SHOTS ON TARGET | 4 |
| 8 | SHOTS OFF TARGET | 2 |
| 9 | CORNERS | 6 |
| 11 | FOULS | 15 |
| 2 | OFFSIDES | 1 |

### PREMIERSHIP RESULTS
28/12/04 & 29/12/04

| | | |
|---|---|---|
| Bolton | 0-1 | Blackburn |
| Charlton | 2-0 | Everton |
| Fulham | 2-3 | Birmingham |
| Liverpool | 1-0 | Southampton |
| Manchester City | 1-1 | West Brom |
| Middlesbrough | 2-0 | Norwich |
| Newcastle | 0-1 | Arsenal |
| Portsmouth | 0-2 | Chelsea |
| Tottenham | 1-1 | Crystal Palace |

### PREMIERSHIP TABLE
AT END OF 29/12/04

| | P | PTS |
|---|---|---|
| 1. Chelsea | 20 | 49 |
| 2. Arsenal | 20 | 44 |
| 3. Manchester United | 20 | 40 |
| 4. Everton | 20 | 40 |
| 5. Middlesbrough | 20 | 35 |
| 6. Liverpool | 20 | 34 |
| 7. Charlton Athletic | 20 | 31 |
| 8. Tottenham Hotspur | 20 | 29 |
| 9. Birmingham City | 20 | 26 |
| 10. Portsmouth | 20 | 26 |
| 11. Aston Villa | 20 | 25 |
| 12. Manchester City | 20 | 24 |
| 13. Bolton Wanderers | 20 | 23 |
| 14. Newcastle United | 20 | 22 |
| 15. Blackburn Rovers | 20 | 19 |
| 16. Fulham | 20 | 18 |
| 17. Crystal Palace | 20 | 15 |
| 18. Norwich City | 20 | 15 |
| 19. Southampton | 20 | 14 |
| 20. West Bromwich Albion | 20 | 11 |

# January

## No new faces at OT, despite the transfer window, but three wins in four rekindled Reds' hopes of catching the top two...

**After a pretty** happy Christmas, United were soon enjoying a prosperous New Year, kicking off 2005 with a win at the Riverside. After a disappointing 0-0 draw at home to Spurs (which could have been worse had referee Mark Clattenburg's assistant spotted that Roy Carroll had fumbled the ball over his goalline), a 1-0 win at Anfield put the smiles back on Red faces – especially Wayne Rooney who scored the winning goal on his return to Merseyside. When Aston Villa proved the usual fall guys at OT, United found themselves within touching distance of Arsenal ahead of their trip to Highbury.

Chelsea, however, showed few signs that their considerable lead was likely to be eroded, Jose Mourinho resisted the temptation to dip into Roman Abramovich's millions during the transfer window, his one indulgence being CSKA Moscow's striker Jiri Jarosik. United fans too, saw little transfer action, though there was one departure as Eric Djemba-Djemba left Old Trafford for Villa Park. Much of the action revolved around three controversial characters, Robbie Savage, Nicolas Anelka and Craig Bellamy, who all moved on to pastures new.

Harry Redknapp revisited Portsmouth, to persuade Nigel Quashie to shuffle along the south coast, Redknapp's son Jamie also joining the Saints for the relegation battle ahead. Norwich's mid-month miracle, when two goals in injury time earned a 4-4 draw against Boro, may have done wonders for morale, but it still only earned them a point, and with West Brom picking up a first win under Bryan Robson, a battle royal was looming for the relegation places.

### PREMIERSHIP FIXTURES THIS MONTH

| | | |
|---|---|---|
| SAT 1 | MIDDLESBROUGH | AWAY |
| TUE 4 | TOTTENHAM HOTSPUR | HOME |
| SAT 15 | LIVERPOOL | AWAY |
| SAT 22 | ASTON VILLA | HOME |

### IN THE PREMIERSHIP THIS MONTH

**214,203** watched United play 4 games

**6** goals were scored

**315** miles were travelled by United going to and from games

United fielded **21** players

**1** goal was conceded

### FOCUS ON ROY KEANE

Although Roy Keane's 50th United goal continued to elude him, January saw a string of performances that hammered home - not for the first time - how important he remains to the Reds. The New Year's Day trip to the Riverside - flagged up as a potential banana skin for Sir Alex Ferguson's men - became a stroll thanks to the United skipper's drive and determination in the middle of the park. Against Spurs just three days later, Keane showed none of the fatigue that might have been expected given the onerous schedule of games, his rasping shot coming within a whisker of breaking the deadlock. And at Anfield, a crashing half-volley that might well even have eclipsed Wayne Rooney's opener, rebounded off Jerzy Dudek's crossbar. Then it was back to business as usual, steering the Reds to another vital three points, this time against Villa...

# Middlesbrough 0

# Manchester United 2

Fletcher 9, Giggs 79

Flying Scotsman: Darren Fletcher steams away from Colin Cooper and Bolo Zenden

**It was widely viewed** as the trickiest game of the festive period but a Roy Keane-inspired United banished thoughts of defeat with a comfortable win at the Riverside. Goals from Darren Fletcher – the Scotsman's first senior strike in a United shirt – and a third in three games for Ryan Giggs saw the Reds become only the second visiting Premiership side to win at Boro this season.

For the third time over the festive period Sir Alex sent out the troops knowing Chelsea and Arsenal had already registered victories. Matching their result then was the objective, and while 2,200 travelling Reds may have been concerned that Steve McClaren might again have his players primed in how to stop his former club, once Boro's defence had been breached early in the game, it was pretty straightforward.

Cristiano Ronaldo had already struck a post by the time Ryan Giggs forced a save from Mark Schwarzer in the ninth minute to set up the opening goal. The Australian was unable to hold Giggs's drive, turning the ball across the six-yard line, to where Fletcher was on hand to knock home the rebound. He'll be hoping he doesn't have

Saturday 1 January 2005
**Riverside Stadium**
Attendance 34,199
**Referee Alan Wiley**

to rack up another 53 games before the next one turns up.

United then set about taking the sting out of Boro's fightback. Keane was at his spoiling best in midfield; Rio Ferdinand dominant at the back; and there was a stream of slick passing as the Reds took control. The only threat to Roy Carroll's goal was a series of dangerous crosses from the highly-rated Stewart Downing.

As expected, the home side upped the ante after the interval, throwing more men forward and forcing a succession of corners. However, United still posed the bigger threat, looking capable of opening Boro up at will on the counter-attack.

And, just as it seemed we might be in for a nervy last 10 minutes – as against Fulham – the Reds grabbed a deserved second. Neat play on the right led to substitute Eric Djemba-Djemba playing in Giggs; the Welshman cut into the Middlesbrough penalty area, and as the ball ricocheted into his path he beat Schwarzer and Colin Cooper to the touch, prodding the ball into the corner of the net. With only 11 minutes remaining there was no way back for Boro and United had another three points safely gathered, despite the best efforts of McClaren, Downing and co.

## MAN OF THE MATCH

**ROY KEANE**

United's skipper enjoyed a similar vein of form to fellow mainstays Paul Scholes and Ryan Giggs throughout the festive period, but outshone both with a real leader's performance when it was most needed. On a night of several impressive displays by the Reds in black, Keane made everything tick, controlling the tempo of the game to frustrate Middlesbrough.

## MATCH FACTS

**MIDDLESBROUGH**
Schwarzer; Reiziger, Cooper, Southgate, Queudrue; Parlour, Zenden, Doriva (Morrison 77), Downing; Hasselbaink, Job (Nemeth 46)
**Subs not used** Nash, McMahon, Davies **Booked** Parlour

**MANCHESTER UNITED**
Carroll; P Neville, Ferdinand, Silvestre, Heinze; Fletcher, Keane, Scholes, Giggs (Bellion 82), Ronaldo (Djemba-Djemba 77); Smith
**Subs not used** Howard, G Neville, Spector

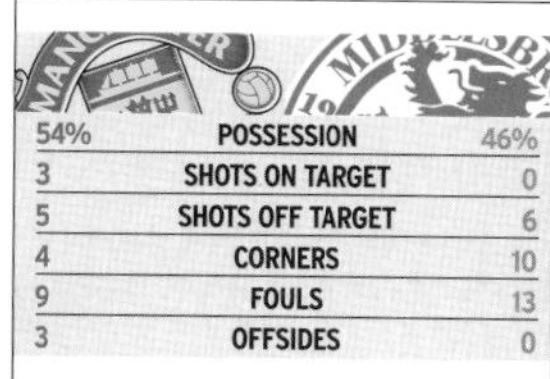

| Man Utd | | Middlesbrough |
|---|---|---|
| 54% | POSSESSION | 46% |
| 3 | SHOTS ON TARGET | 0 |
| 5 | SHOTS OFF TARGET | 6 |
| 4 | CORNERS | 10 |
| 9 | FOULS | 13 |
| 3 | OFFSIDES | 0 |

**PREMIERSHIP RESULTS**
WEEKEND BEGINNING 1/1/05

| Home | Score | Away |
|---|---|---|
| Aston Villa | 1-0 | Blackburn |
| Bolton | 1-1 | West Brom |
| Charlton | 1-3 | Arsenal |
| Fulham | 3-1 | Crystal Palace |
| Liverpool | 0-1 | Chelsea |
| Manchester City | 2-1 | Southampton |
| Newcastle | 2-1 | Birmingham |
| Portsmouth | 1-1 | Norwich |
| Tottenham | 5-2 | Everton |

**PREMIERSHIP TABLE**
AT END OF 03/01/05

| | P | PTS |
|---|---|---|
| 1. Chelsea | 21 | 52 |
| 2. Arsenal | 21 | 47 |
| 3. Manchester United | 21 | 43 |
| 4. Everton | 21 | 40 |
| 5. Liverpool | 22 | 37 |
| 6. Middlesbrough | 21 | 35 |
| 7. Tottenham Hotspur | 21 | 32 |
| 8. Charlton Athletic | 22 | 31 |
| 9. Aston Villa | 22 | 28 |
| 10. Manchester City | 21 | 27 |
| 11. Portsmouth | 21 | 27 |
| 12. Birmingham City | 21 | 26 |
| 13. Newcastle United | 22 | 26 |
| 14. Bolton Wanderers | 21 | 24 |
| 15. Blackburn Rovers | 22 | 22 |
| 16. Fulham | 21 | 21 |
| 17. Crystal Palace | 22 | 18 |
| 18. Norwich City | 22 | 16 |
| 19. Southampton | 21 | 14 |
| 20. West Bromwich Albion | 22 | 13 |

# Manchester United 0

# Tottenham Hotspur 0

**United geared up** for the festive schedule with a draw at Fulham, and a gnawing sense of frustration that dominance hadn't been rewarded with all three points. In the aftermath of the sixth game in the sequence, the Reds were lucky to escape with a draw, following the biggest talking point of an already controversial season.

The moment Roy Carroll – and assistant referee Rob Lewis – will want to forget came in the closing stages. United were chasing a win, pounding the Spurs back line with wave after wave of attack – many centred around makeshift centre-forward Rio Ferdinand. With most United players committed to attack, Carroll came haring out of his box to launch the ball back into the Spurs half. The clearance fell short, the ball was knocked back over the halfway line and, with the keeper scrambling to regain his ground, Pedro Mendes audaciously hooked the ball goalwards. By this point the Ulsterman had reached his line, but the ball struck his upper body and popped over his left shoulder, landing three feet over the line. With the linesman still sprinting back and referee Mark Clattenburg 50 yards away, Carroll hooked the ball back into play and carried on regardless. More or less everyone in the ground – not to mention millions watching on Sky Sports – knew it was in.

Sensing a let-off, United upped the ante and the foraging Ferdinand was felled on the edge of the box. Gabriel Heinze's curling free-kick was acrobatically pushed away by Paul Robinson, not his first crucial save.

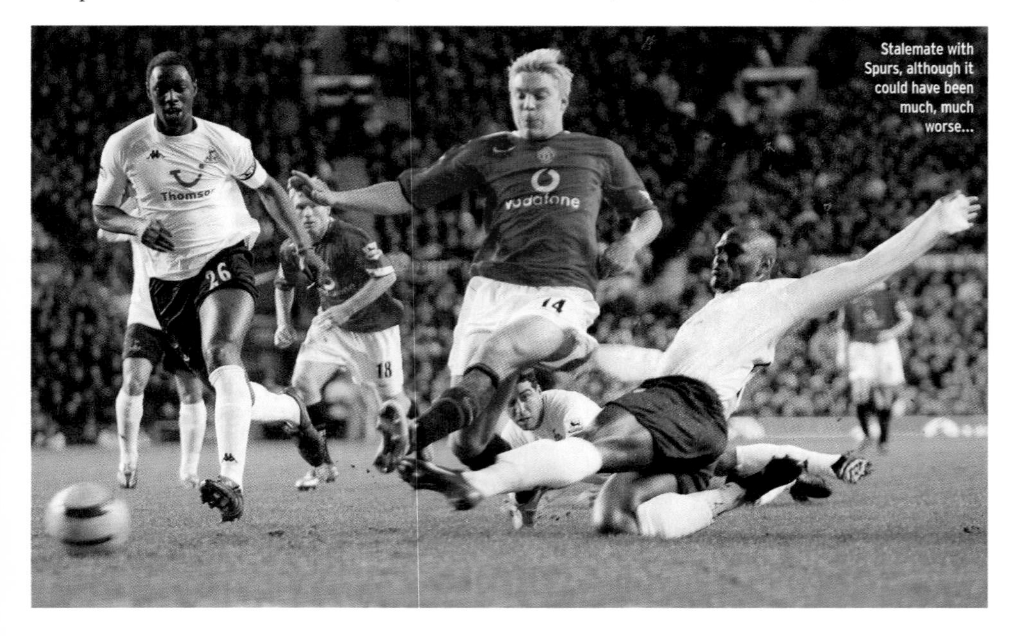


Stalemate with Spurs, although it could have been much, much worse...

Tuesday 4 January 2005
**Old Trafford**
Attendance 67,962
**Referee Mark Clattenburg**

On reflection, maybe it was destined to stay 0-0. Both teams' first-choice strike partners were injured, while the in-form Ryan Giggs departed with hamstring problems, after 37 minutes. Roy Keane went close with a rasping shot; Ronaldo headed over, and Robinson saved at the feet of ex-team-mate Alan Smith. In the second half, Noe Pamarot nearly opened the scoring for United when he knocked the ball past his own keeper, but the ball rebounded off a post. Perhaps United deserved the points, but you have to make your chances count.

## MAN OF THE MATCH

**RIO FERDINAND**
Jermain Defoe and Fredi Kanoute may have been missing, but Rio Ferdinand still had Robbie Keane and the emerging Dean Marney to deal with. Here he reinforced the boss's claim that he's the best in the game. He continually turned defence into attack and nearly obliged when called on to lead the final assault.

## MATCH FACTS

**MANCHESTER UNITED**
Carroll; P Neville, Ferdinand, Silvestre, Heinze; Fletcher (Miller 76), Roy Keane, Scholes, Ronaldo (Spector 84); Giggs (Bellion 37), Smith
**Subs not used** Ricardo, Djemba-Djemba **Booked** P Neville

**TOTTENHAM HOTSPUR**
Robinson; Pamarot, Naybet, King, Edman; Mendes, Carrick, Ricketts (Gardner 90), Ziegler; Marney; Robbie Keane
**Subs not used** Bunjevcevic, Fulop, Yeates, Ifil
**Booked** Pamarot, Marney

| Man Utd | | Spurs |
|---|---|---|
| 60% | POSSESSION | 40% |
| 10 | SHOTS ON TARGET | 1 |
| 9 | SHOTS OFF TARGET | 4 |
| 8 | CORNERS | 2 |
| 12 | FOULS | 14 |
| 10 | OFFSIDES | 1 |

**PREMIERSHIP RESULTS**
UP TO END 5/1/05

| Home | Score | Away |
|---|---|---|
| Arsenal | 1-1 | Manchester City |
| Birmingham | 1-2 | Bolton |
| Blackburn | 1-0 | Charlton |
| Chelsea | 2-0 | Middlesbrough |
| Crystal Palace | 2-0 | Aston Villa |
| Everton | 2-1 | Portsmouth |
| Norwich | 1-2 | Liverpool |
| Southampton | 3-3 | Fulham |
| West Brom | 0-0 | Newcastle |

**PREMIERSHIP TABLE**
AT END OF 09/01/05

| | P | PTS |
|---|---|---|
| 1. Chelsea | 22 | 55 |
| 2. Arsenal | 22 | 48 |
| 3. Manchester United | 22 | 44 |
| 4. Everton | 22 | 43 |
| 5. Liverpool | 22 | 37 |
| 6. Middlesbrough | 22 | 35 |
| 7. Tottenham Hotspur | 22 | 33 |
| 8. Charlton Athletic | 22 | 31 |
| 9. Manchester City | 22 | 28 |
| 10. Aston Villa | 22 | 28 |
| 11. Bolton Wanderers | 22 | 27 |
| 12. Portsmouth | 22 | 27 |
| 13. Birmingham City | 22 | 26 |
| 14. Newcastle United | 22 | 26 |
| 15. Fulham | 22 | 22 |
| 16. Blackburn Rovers | 22 | 22 |
| 17. Crystal Palace | 22 | 18 |
| 18. Norwich City | 22 | 16 |
| 19. Southampton | 22 | 15 |
| 20. West Bromwich Albion | 22 | 13 |

# Liverpool 0

# Manchester United 1

Rooney 21

**It had to be** him, didn't it? Wayne Rooney is a (young) man for the big occasion, as Fenerbahçe, Arsenal, Switzerland and Croatia will reluctantly testify. And given that the 19-year-old Evertonian from Croxteth had never experienced victory against Liverpool, never mind scored against them, he was ready. But Rooney's homecoming was almost a side issue for some in the lead-up to this clash, so excited were they by the prospect of another first – a debut goal from Fernando Morientes, recently arrived from the Bernabéu.

The Spaniard must have wondered what he'd signed up for, such was the ferocity of the opening stages; Roy Keane in particular stamping his authority on the match. Steven Gerrard, also making his presence felt, angered Paul Scholes with a late challenge. This wasn't a good move. Scholes and Keane slowly took control of midfield, shifting the balance United's way. The decisive moment arrived midway through the first half. Collecting a short pass from Cristiano Ronaldo, Rooney ran at the Liverpool defence and, suddenly, let fly with a low shot that swerved before whizzing past Jerzy Dudek. He ran towards the Kop, hands on ears, cheeks puffed out defiantly savouring the moment.

Keane nearly bagged his long-awaited 50th goal for the Reds just before the break with a vicious, dipping half-volley shot that smashed off Dudek's crossbar to safety, then it was Morientes' turn to try his luck when he was found by Gerrard, but his shot scuffed past Roy Carroll's post.

The second half was another no-nonsense affair, with the card count mounting. Wes Brown had made his way into referee Steve Bennett's book after 32 minutes, and received a second yellow after 65, following a late challenge on John Arne Riise. Ronaldo was sacrificed for John O'Shea as United looked to close out the match for a seventh successive clean sheet, but were given a scare in injury time when the home side were handed a free-kick on the edge of United's box. It was true Steven Gerrard territory and the ground held its breath as the captain approached the ball. Cleverly he side-passed the ball for Jamie Carragher to shoot, but the potential local hero blasted wide. And relax...

Saturday 15 January 2005
**Anfield**
Attendance 44,183
**Referee: Steve Bennett**

Red's letter day: Wayne Rooney had a happy return to Merseyside

## MAN OF THE MATCH

**ROY KEANE**

The United skipper had a message for the football world at the end of another pulsating victory at Anfield. "We will keep fighting for this title right until the end," he announced. "We're Manchester United. That is what we do." And never has a statement been backed up by actions so vehemently. The United captain was simply phenomenal in a fixture that still means so much to him, winning the much-hyped midfield battle with Steven Gerrard hands down.

## MATCH FACTS

**LIVERPOOL**
Dudek; Carragher, Pellegrino, Hyypia, Traore; Gerrard, Hamann (Biscan 79), Garcia, Riise (Sinama Pongolle 72); Baros, Morientes (Nuñez 75) **Subs not used** Harrison, Warnock
**Booked** Carragher, Nuñez

**MANCHESTER UNITED**
Carroll; P Neville, Silvestre, Brown, Heinze; Scholes, Fletcher, Ronaldo (O'Shea 67), Keane; Rooney (Bellion 90), Saha (Fortune 79) **Subs not used** Howard, Miller **Booked** Brown, Keane, Rooney, Fortune
**Sent off** Brown

| | | |
|---|---|---|
| 45% | POSSESSION | 55% |
| 3 | SHOTS ON TARGET | 1 |
| 9 | SHOTS OFF TARGET | 4 |
| 9 | CORNERS | 4 |
| 13 | FOULS | 28 |
| 1 | OFFSIDES | 3 |

**PREMIERSHIP RESULTS**
WEEKEND BEGINNING 15/1/05

| | | |
|---|---|---|
| Aston Villa | 3-0 | Norwich |
| Bolton | 1-0 | Arsenal |
| Charlton | 3-1 | Birmingham |
| Manchester City | 3-1 | Crystal Palace |
| Newcastle | 2-1 | Southampton |
| Portsmouth | 0-1 | Blackburn |
| Tottenham | 0-2 | Chelsea |
| Fulham | 1-0 | West Brom |
| Middlesbrough | 1-1 | Everton |

**PREMIERSHIP TABLE**
AT END OF 16/01/05

| | P | PTS |
|---|---|---|
| 1. Chelsea | 23 | 58 |
| 2. Arsenal | 23 | 48 |
| 3. Manchester United | 23 | 47 |
| 4. Everton | 23 | 44 |
| 5. Liverpool | 23 | 37 |
| 6. Middlesbrough | 23 | 36 |
| 7. Charlton Athletic | 23 | 34 |
| 8. Tottenham Hotspur | 23 | 33 |
| 9. Manchester City | 23 | 31 |
| 10. Aston Villa | 23 | 31 |
| 11. Bolton Wanderers | 23 | 30 |
| 12. Newcastle United | 23 | 29 |
| 13. Portsmouth | 23 | 27 |
| 14. Birmingham City | 23 | 26 |
| 15. Fulham | 23 | 25 |
| 16. Blackburn Rovers | 23 | 25 |
| 17. Crystal Palace | 23 | 18 |
| 18. Norwich City | 23 | 16 |
| 19. Southampton | 23 | 15 |
| 20. West Bromwich Albion | 23 | 13 |

# Manchester United 3

Ronaldo 8, Saha 69, Scholes 70

# Aston Villa 1

Barry 53

**With Arsenal** not taking on Newcastle until Sunday, United had the perfect opportunity to leapfrog the Gunners into second spot – if only for 24 hours. Sir Alex brought Gary Neville back into the fold after a virus had kept him out for five league games, and Rio Ferdinand also returned to provide further steel at the back. But it was the Reds' youthful forward line that caught the early attention, Cristiano Ronaldo, in particular, wasting no time in testing the Villa defence.

In the opening moments United's No.7 fed Wayne Rooney, whose left-foot cross to Louis Saha was headed just over. This early pressure paid dividends in the eighth minute when Saha this time became the provider, the Frenchman placing the ball into the path of the Portuguese winger, who blasted it in from the edge of the area.

United attempted to drive home the advantage – but Villa fought back. Nolberto Solano, who had caused United a major headache at Villa Park, again tried to derail the Reds' title challenge, his fierce shot from 25 yards pushed away by Roy Carroll.

Rooney, Saha and Ronaldo then produced some superb link-up play, Rooney forcing a fine save from Sorensen. And Saha, after running almost the length of the pitch, couldn't quite get enough power behind his shot after doing all the hard work. Gradually Villa fought back, almost forcing an equaliser before the break; but luckily for United, Juan Pablo Angel's poor return continued, the Colombian heading Gareth Barry's pinpoint cross at Carroll.

United missed a gilt-edged chance to double the lead at the start of the second half, after Paul Scholes played Rooney through, but the young striker lost control of the ball. At the other end Thomas Hitzlsperger's stinging long-range effort was saved by Carroll before Barry ended United's record run of eight clean sheets, slamming home after a one-two with Solano.

Cue a few anxious moments in the crowd – and for Villa – as Quinton Fortune, on for Darren Fletcher, forced a save from Sorensen. Rooney just failed to reach a Ronaldo cross in the box, but made amends minutes later, crossing for Saha, whose shot glanced off Liam Ridgewell to put United ahead. Inside a minute the Reds had a two-goal cushion. Ronaldo bamboozled and released a fierce shot; Sorensen saved, but the rebound fell nicely for Paul Scholes to head home and kill off the contest.

Saturday 22 January 2005
**Old Trafford**
Attendance 67,859
**Referee: Mark Halsey**

Shout to the top – or at least second spot. Paul Scholes toasts his goal and United's third at the Villa – and the Reds go second for 24 hours

## MATCH FACTS

**MANCHESTER UNITED**
Carroll; G Neville, Ferdinand, Silvestre, Heinze; Fletcher (Fortune 45), Scholes (O'Shea 73), Keane, Ronaldo; Rooney (Giggs 73), Saha
**Subs not used** Howard, Brown
**Booked** Keane, Ronaldo

**ASTON VILLA**
Sorensen; Delaney (De la Cruz 11), Ridgewell, Mellberg, Samuel; Solano (L Moore 74), Davis, Barry, Berson (Hitzlsperger 45), Hendrie; Angel **Subs not used** Postma, Cole **Booked** Berson, Hendrie, Ridgewell, Samuel, Solano

| Man Utd | | Aston Villa |
|---|---|---|
| 60% | POSSESSION | 40% |
| 9 | SHOTS ON TARGET | 6 |
| 6 | SHOTS OFF TARGET | 5 |
| 4 | CORNERS | 2 |
| 15 | FOULS | 24 |
| 4 | OFFSIDES | 2 |

### PREMIERSHIP RESULTS
AT END OF 24/1/05

| | | |
|---|---|---|
| Arsenal | 1-0 | Newcastle |
| Birmingham | 1-2 | Fulham |
| Blackburn | 0-1 | Bolton |
| Chelsea | 3-0 | Portsmouth |
| Crystal Palace | 3-0 | Tottenham |
| Everton | 0-1 | Charlton |
| Norwich | 4-4 | Middlesbrough |
| Southampton | 2-0 | Liverpool |
| West Brom | 2-0 | Manchester City |

### PREMIERSHIP TABLE
AT END OF 24/01/05

| | P | PTS |
|---|---|---|
| 1. Chelsea | 24 | 61 |
| 2. Arsenal | 24 | 51 |
| 3. Manchester United | 24 | 50 |
| 4. Everton | 24 | 44 |
| 5. Liverpool | 24 | 37 |
| 6. Middlesbrough | 24 | 37 |
| 7. Charlton Athletic | 24 | 37 |
| 8. Tottenham Hotspur | 24 | 33 |
| 9. Bolton Wanderers | 24 | 33 |
| 10. Manchester City | 24 | 31 |
| 11. Aston Villa | 24 | 31 |
| 12. Newcastle United | 24 | 29 |
| 13. Fulham | 24 | 28 |
| 14. Portsmouth | 24 | 27 |
| 15. Birmingham City | 24 | 26 |
| 16. Blackburn Rovers | 24 | 25 |
| 17. Crystal Palace | 24 | 21 |
| 18. Southampton | 24 | 18 |
| 19. Norwich City | 24 | 17 |
| 20. West Bromwich Albion | 24 | 16 |

## MAN OF THE MATCH

**CRISTIANO RONALDO**
Showed just how much he has matured since arriving from Sporting Lisbon. It's easy to forget he's still only 19 when he cuts through defences with such ease. He scored the first, made the third and, in between, produced a performance to give Villa defenders sleepless nights. With two goals in the last two matches, Sir Alex might have to pay out on the bet made before the season began that he wouldn't score 10.

SAHA
9
BROWN
6
FERDINAND
5
MUFC

# February

## United hit top gear in a stormy Highbury encounter, and City did us a massive favour by slowing Chelsea's title charge...

**It wasn't a** bad way to kick off the month. United's 4-2 win at Highbury, with Ryan Giggs rolling back the years and Cristiano Ronaldo – coming along nicely as the heir apparent to the Welshman – adding two to his goals tally, saw the Reds leapfrog our north London rivals to take second spot in the Premiership. And unlike October, this time there would be no slipping up. Wins at home to Birmingham and away to City swiftly followed; then, after a brief interlude for some Cup business, both home and abroad, another three points were added at the expense of the luckless Pompey.

On that sort of form United might have expected to have been breathing down Chelsea's neck. And while the Reds did creep a little closer, that was mainly due to the Blues' Carling Cup final date with Liverpool at the end of the month – though the league leaders did fail to take all three points against Manchester City. Kevin Keegan's Blues held out for 0-0 at Stamford Bridge having had the audacity to take all three points against Chelsea at Eastlands back in October.

Wins at Charlton and against Fulham suggested Liverpool might be closing in on Everton in fourth place. But David Moyes's side, after a draw at Southampton and defeat by Chelsea, made the most of their Merseyside rivals' Millennium Stadium date, putting three past Aston Villa, Leon Osman scoring twice. And the Evertonian was in good company; having made a (fleeting) full England debut a couple of weeks earlier, Crystal Palace's Andy Johnson scored two to stay in the running for the Golden Boot as the Eagles swept up three points at Birmingham.

### PREMIERSHIP FIXTURES THIS MONTH

| | | |
|---|---|---|
| TUE 1 | ARSENAL | AWAY |
| SAT 5 | BIRMINGHAM CITY | HOME |
| SUN 13 | MANCHESTER CITY | AWAY |
| SAT 26 | PORTSMOUTH | HOME |

### IN THE PREMIERSHIP THIS MONTH

**221,102** watched United play 4 games

**10** goals were scored

**394** miles were travelled by United going to and from games

United fielded **17** players

**3** goals were conceded

### FOCUS ON WAYNE ROONEY

Rooney started the month in combative mood against Arsenal - following the lead of his skipper, Roy Keane having clashed with Patrick Vieira in the Highbury tunnel - and found his way into Graham Poll's notebook before the interval. But while he failed (by a whisker) to add to his Reds goal tally that night, it was a different story in the subsequent games. The young striker made certain of the points against Birmingham, punishing a loose back pass by Kenny Cunningham. In the derby at Eastlands, he was again the man on the spot, firing home United's all-important opener midway through the second half. And when Portsmouth rolled up at Old Trafford at the end of the month, Rooney was in no mood for a rest, putting United one up early on, and then, as the clock ticked down and the spectre of a draw loomed large, firing home yet again.

# Arsenal 2

Vieira 8, Bergkamp 36

# Manchester United 4

Giggs 18, Ronaldo 54, 58, O'Shea 89

**If the Carling Cup** encounter with Chelsea had been *High Noon*, this was *The Good, the Bad and the Ugly*. After a long, hard night, 10-man United emerged victorious from another high-octane Highbury encounter, securing a league double over Arsenal for the first time in eight years.

Unbeknown to fans inside Highbury, this match kicked-off early – in the tunnel. Gunners captain Patrick Vieira approached Gary Neville, as Roy Keane put it, "shooting his mouth off". The United skipper intervened and though referee Graham Poll did his best to defuse the situation, the blue touchpaper had already been lit.

It didn't take long for the mood to manifest itself on the pitch. The match was only seconds old when Gabriel Heinze upended Fredrik Ljungberg just outside the box, earning a ticking-off from Graham Poll. Within minutes the temperature was cranked up another notch when the home side took an eighth-minute lead. From Thierry Henry's inswinging corner Vieira outjumped Heinze to nod past Roy Carroll.

The advantage lasted 10 minutes, United drawing level through Ryan Giggs's eighth goal of the season. Paul Scholes delivered a pass to Wayne Rooney on the edge of the box, who released Giggs, and the Welshman did the rest, albeit with a deflection off Ashley Cole. But again the momentum swung back in Arsenal's favour, and it wasn't long before they were back in front.

Henry was again the provider, finding Dennis Bergkamp, who advanced and lashed the ball through Carroll's legs. The match threatened to boil over when Rooney got involved in a series of heated exchanges which resulted in a booking. He had just forced a good save from Manuel Almunia but the red mist was descending. The half-time whistle couldn't come soon enough.

The second half was a different story, producing 45 minutes of football that will live long in the memory. United's second equaliser came on 55 minutes, Giggs sending Cristiano Ronaldo through on goal to rifle past Almunia. The pair combined again three minutes later. Giggs tempting the keeper out of his box, before dinking an inch-perfect cross over to leave the No.7 with the easiest of finishes.

The home side were handed a lifeline when Silvestre was sent off on 69 minutes for a headbutt on Ljungberg. Despite Arsenal's desperate attacks, the Reds remained in control, until with a minute left to play, Louis Saha found Scholes in the middle. Glancing up, he spotted John O'Shea haring into space and delivered the perfect ball. The substitute looked up and calmly chipped Almunia to neatly round off a stunning game. Arsenal 2... United 4.

Tuesday 1 February 2005
**Highbury**
Attendance 38,164
**Referee: Graham Poll**

Gunned down: Silvestre halts Robert Pires on a thrilling night in which United gained a rare double over the Londoners

## MATCH FACTS

**ARSENAL**
Almunia; Lauren (Fabregas 83), Campbell (Hoyte 79), Cygan, Cole; Ljungberg, Vieira, Flamini (Reyes 71), Pires; Bergkamp, Henry **Subs not used** Lehmann, van Persie **Booked** Pires, Reyes

**MANCHESTER UNITED**
Carroll; G Neville, Ferdinand, Silvestre, Heinze; Fletcher (O'Shea 61), Keane, Scholes, Ronaldo (Brown 71); Giggs (Saha 77); Rooney **Subs not used** Howard, P Neville **Booked** Heinze, Giggs, Rooney, Ronaldo **Sent off** Silvestre

| Manchester United | | Arsenal |
|---|---|---|
| 50% | POSSESSION | 50% |
| 7 | SHOTS ON TARGET | 9 |
| 2 | SHOTS OFF TARGET | 5 |
| 7 | CORNERS | 6 |
| 17 | FOULS | 20 |
| 3 | OFFSIDES | 3 |

### PREMIERSHIP RESULTS
WEEKEND BEGINNING 2/2/05

| | | |
|---|---|---|
| Birmingham | 2-1 | Southampton |
| Blackburn | 0-1 | Chelsea |
| Bolton | 3-1 | Tottenham |
| Charlton | 1-2 | Liverpool |
| Everton | 1-0 | Norwich |
| Fulham | 1-1 | Aston Villa |
| Manchester City | 1-1 | Newcastle |
| Portsmouth | 2-1 | Middlesbrough |
| West Brom | 2-2 | Crystal Palace |

### PREMIERSHIP TABLE
AT END OF 02/02/05

| | P | PTS |
|---|---|---|
| 1. Chelsea | 25 | 64 |
| 2. Manchester United | 25 | 53 |
| 3. Arsenal | 25 | 51 |
| 4. Everton | 25 | 47 |
| 5. Liverpool | 25 | 40 |
| 6. Middlesbrough | 25 | 37 |
| 7. Charlton Athletic | 25 | 37 |
| 8. Bolton Wanderers | 25 | 36 |
| 9. Tottenham | 25 | 33 |
| 10. Manchester City | 25 | 32 |
| 11. Aston Villa | 25 | 32 |
| 12. Newcastle United | 25 | 30 |
| 13. Portsmouth | 25 | 30 |
| 14. Birmingham City | 25 | 29 |
| 15. Fulham | 25 | 29 |
| 16. Blackburn Rovers | 25 | 25 |
| 17. Crystal Palace | 25 | 22 |
| 18. Southampton | 25 | 18 |
| 19. Norwich City | 25 | 17 |
| 20. West Bromwich Albion | 25 | 17 |

## MAN OF THE MATCH

**PAUL SCHOLES**
Choosing United's best player was a difficult task. Cristiano Ronaldo again proved he's another big-game player, while Gabriel Heinze stuck to his task despite an early booking. But the three players of excellence were Roy Keane, Ryan Giggs and Paul Scholes. Keane put in the ultimate captain's performance and didn't let the pre-match altercation affect him. Giggs was inspirational in scoring one and setting up two others, but Paul Scholes just about gets the nod. He dictated the pace of play and was everywhere - midfield, attack, and yes, even defence.

# Manchester United 2

Keane 55, Rooney 78

# Birmingham City 0

**It may have taken** more than 50 matches to finally reach this latest landmark, but Roy Keane's 50th United goal was well worth the wait. Ten minutes into the second half of an unremarkable match, the skipper rolled back the years with a trademark surging run, capping it with a 20-yard strike. It was just the breakthrough the Reds needed to follow up the midweek win at Highbury with three more points.

Most inside Old Trafford were hoping for, rather than expecting, a repeat of the second-half display that had overpowered Arsenal five days earlier. But with the visitors proving stubborn opposition, the type of onslaught that had downed the Gunners was never likely. United probed for openings, the Blues hit on the break, and both sides struck the woodwork (Wayne Rooney for United, Walter Pandiani for the Blues) in a far from memorable first half.

After 10 minutes of increased pressure following the interval, the breakthrough finally arrived. Cristiano Ronaldo played in Keane with a cute backheel, and as the space opened up in front of the Irishman, he rifled the ball past Maik Taylor from 20 yards.

With the Reds now cruising and Birmingham playing a more expansive game in search of an equaliser, a second United goal looked inevitable. In the 79th minute Rooney and Ronaldo harassed Kenny Cunningham into a loose backpass. The Portuguese winger forced keeper Taylor into another mistake and the Croxteth kid was in the right spot to lift the ball into the

Leading by example: Captain Keane is mobbed after his 50th strike, while Wayne Rooney (above) beats the Blues defence

Saturday 5 February 2005
**Old Trafford**
Attendance 67,838
**Referee: Dermot Gallagher**

unguarded net. Two-nil and game over.

"It was about time," said Keane of his goal. "It was a nice bit of skill by Cristiano to set me up, but I thought my run made it easier for him! It was a decent move and before I knew it, it was opening up for me. I just shut my eyes and went for it."

After the match Sir Alex Ferguson was in no doubt as to the catalyst of the victory. "At 33, he [Keane] is still capable of playing like he did 10 years ago," said the United manager. "In 50 or 500 years, Roy Keane will still be regarded as one of the greatest players ever at this club."

## MAN OF THE MATCH

**ROY KEANE**
Whether defending team-mates in the players' tunnel or inspiring his colleagues to greater exertions, Roy Keane remains United's most influential performer. He may not get forward like he once did, but with this performance the skipper showed there are goals in him yet – not, of course, that he needs goals to justify his inclusion in the side. As Sir Alex noted, he will be remembered as one of the all-time United greats.

## MATCH FACTS

**MANCHESTER UNITED**
Carroll; G Neville, Ferdinand, Brown, Heinze; Ronaldo, O'Shea, Keane, Giggs (P Neville 82); Rooney (Miller 82), Saha (Fortune 68)
**Subs not used** Howard, Bellion
**Booked** Heinze

**BIRMINGHAM CITY**
Maik Taylor; Melchiot, Cunningham, Martin Taylor (Tebily 81), Clapham; Pennant, Nafti (Carter 72), Johnson, Gray; Pandiani, Blake (Morrison 72)
**Subs not used** Vaesen, Kuqi
**Booked** Johnson, Nafti, Pennant

| MANCHESTER UNITED | | BIRMINGHAM CITY |
|---|---|---|
| 57% | POSSESSION | 43% |
| 7 | SHOTS ON TARGET | 0 |
| 6 | SHOTS OFF TARGET | 6 |
| 5 | CORNERS | 2 |
| 10 | FOULS | 19 |
| 3 | OFFSIDES | 1 |

### PREMIERSHIP RESULTS
WEEKEND BEGINNING 5/2/05

| | | |
|---|---|---|
| Aston Villa | 1-3 | Arsenal |
| Chelsea | 0-0 | Manchester City |
| Crystal Palace | 0-1 | Bolton |
| Liverpool | 3-1 | Fulham |
| Middlesbrough | 1-0 | Blackburn |
| Newcastle | 1-1 | Charlton |
| Norwich | 3-2 | West Brom |
| Southampton | 2-2 | Everton |
| Tottenham | 3-1 | Portsmouth |

### PREMIERSHIP TABLE
AT END OF 07/02/05

| | P | PTS |
|---|---|---|
| 1. Chelsea | 26 | 65 |
| 2. Manchester United | 26 | 56 |
| 3. Arsenal | 26 | 54 |
| 4. Everton | 26 | 48 |
| 5. Liverpool | 26 | 43 |
| 6. Middlesbrough | 26 | 40 |
| 7. Bolton Wanderers | 26 | 39 |
| 8. Charlton Athletic | 26 | 38 |
| 9. Tottenham Hotspur | 26 | 36 |
| 10. Manchester City | 26 | 33 |
| 11. Aston Villa | 26 | 32 |
| 12. Newcastle United | 26 | 31 |
| 13. Portsmouth | 26 | 30 |
| 14. Birmingham City | 26 | 29 |
| 15. Fulham | 26 | 29 |
| 16. Blackburn Rovers | 26 | 25 |
| 17. Crystal Palace | 26 | 22 |
| 18. Norwich City | 26 | 20 |
| 19. Southampton | 26 | 19 |
| 20. West Bromwich Albion | 26 | 17 |

# Manchester City 0

# Manchester United 2

Rooney 68, Dunne og 75

Dunne and dusted: Wayne Rooney's fellow former Evertonian, Richard Dunne, can't stop the Reds' striker sending City on their way to defeat

**Wayne Rooney** never tasted success in a Merseyside derby, but he didn't waste much time in savouring victory in the Mancunian version, putting City to the sword with barely disguised glee. The 19-year-old told *United Review* that derby defeat was unthinkable because "it wouldn't have been very nice for United fans going to work on Monday morning". Instead, it was the City faithful who were sporting long faces all week.

The Blue with the reddest face was the unfortunate Richard Dunne. A rock at the heart of City's defence all season, the big Irishman kept United at bay almost single-handedly when the teams met at Old Trafford in November. But that good work was undone at Eastlands with an unfortunate own goal that put the seal on United's first ever victory at the City of Manchester Stadium.

With Cristiano Ronaldo and Ryan Giggs still recovering from injury, Sir Alex Ferguson opted for a steely midfield five, adding John O'Shea and Quinton Fortune to the trio of Roy Keane, Paul Scholes and Darren Fletcher. Kevin Keegan, meanwhile, brought in Steve McManaman for the suspended Paul Bosvelt, and it was the ex-Liverpool and Real Madrid winger who got the clearest chance of the first half.

Sunday 13 February 2005
**City of Manchester Stadium**
Attendance 47,111
**Referee: Steve Bennett**

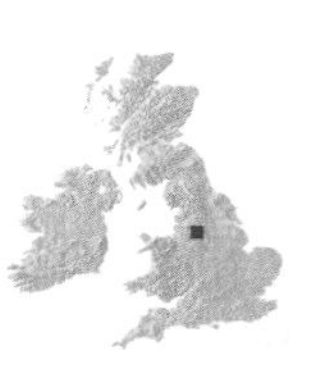

Shaun Wright-Phillips jinked past Wes Brown before firing a pinpoint cross into the path of McManaman, who lashed his shot wide from three yards. The Liverpudlian has never scored against United – he had yet to score for City – and it's unlikely he'll get a better chance.

Ronaldo made an early appearance when O'Shea came off suffering from concussion, and midway into the second half Giggs replaced the injured Fletcher. Enforced changes maybe, but they changed the pace of the game and the Reds took the lead five minutes after Giggs's introduction. The build-up was masterful: Keane was given time on the ball and used it perfectly, finally releasing Gary Neville on a run. The right-back whipped in a textbook cross that was expertly finished by Rooney, albeit with the help of a deflection off Dunne.

The match was effectively over seven minutes later with the moment Dunne will want to forget. Rooney picked the ball up on the right and ran into the box before firing the ball goalwards. Dunne intercepted and tried to put the ball in Row Z: instead he sliced wildly past David James, the ball flying into the net. After the match Rooney jokingly tried to claim both goals: if it was up to Dunne, he'd probably give them to him.

## MAN OF THE MATCH

**WAYNE ROONEY**

Rooney was just 10 when Richard Dunne signed for Everton in 1996, and the big defender remembers the precocious young kid who excited everyone at Goodison. Boy, did his past come back to haunt him at Eastlands. The first goal may not have been as jaw-droppingly spectacular as the Boro brace but it was just as crucial. And it never does a new signing any harm to score the goal that finishes off your derby rivals.

## MATCH FACTS

**MANCHESTER CITY**
James; Mills (B Wright-Phillips 83), Dunne, Distin, Thatcher; S Wright-Phillips, Barton (Macken 69), Musampa, McManaman; Sibierski; Fowler
**Subs not used** Weaver, Onuoha, Flood **Booked** Sibierski, Fowler

**MANCHESTER UNITED**
Carroll; G Neville, Ferdinand, Brown, Heinze; Fletcher (Giggs 63), O'Shea (Ronaldo 33), Scholes (P Neville 84), Keane, Fortune; Rooney
**Subs not used** Howard, Bellion
**Booked** Scholes, Keane, Rooney

| | | |
|---|---|---|
| 65% | POSSESSION | 35% |
| 5 | SHOTS ON TARGET | 3 |
| 8 | SHOTS OFF TARGET | 10 |
| 6 | CORNERS | 4 |
| 15 | FOULS | 13 |
| 6 | OFFSIDES | 1 |

**PREMIERSHIP RESULTS**
WEEKEND BEGINNING 12/2/05

| | | |
|---|---|---|
| Arsenal | 5-1 | Crystal Palace |
| Birmingham | 2-0 | Liverpool |
| Blackburn | 3-0 | Norwich |
| Bolton | 0-0 | Middlesbrough |
| Everton | 0-1 | Chelsea |
| Portsmouth | 1-2 | Aston Villa |

**PREMIERSHIP TABLE**
AT END OF 14/02/05

| | P | PTS |
|---|---|---|
| 1. Chelsea | 27 | 68 |
| 2. Manchester United | 27 | 59 |
| 3. Arsenal | 27 | 57 |
| 4. Everton | 27 | 48 |
| 5. Liverpool | 27 | 43 |
| 6. Middlesbrough | 27 | 41 |
| 7. Bolton Wanderers | 27 | 40 |
| 8. Charlton Athletic | 26 | 38 |
| 9. Tottenham Hotspur | 26 | 36 |
| 10. Aston Villa | 27 | 35 |
| 11. Manchester City | 27 | 33 |
| 12. Birmingham City | 27 | 32 |
| 13. Newcastle United | 26 | 31 |
| 14. Portsmouth | 27 | 30 |
| 15. Fulham | 26 | 29 |
| 16. Blackburn Rovers | 27 | 28 |
| 17. Crystal Palace | 27 | 22 |
| 18. Norwich City | 27 | 20 |
| 19. Southampton | 26 | 19 |
| 20. West Bromwich Albion | 26 | 17 |

# Manchester United 2

Rooney 8, 81

# Portsmouth 1

O'Neil 47

**The mobbing** by his team-mates after Wayne Rooney's sublime late winner spoke volumes. And the relief around Old Trafford was a clear sign of the palpitations that had preceded it. With the clock ticking down, the score deadlocked at 1-1, and United limbs clearly tired after the midweek exertions against Milan, the Reds needed someone to step up to the plate and make the difference against a gritty, obstinate Portsmouth, who had been well-drilled and tigerish in the tackle, if toothless in attack.

In the end, it was Rooney who provided the bite with his seventh and eighth goals in 11 games, as Pompey became the latest fall guys in the pursuit of Jose Mourinho's cashmere coat-tails. With Carling Cup final duties keeping them from fulfilling a domestic date with West Brom, the Londoners' lead was whittled down to just six points by the end of the weekend.

It was only fitting that Rooney's mesmerising piece of skill with less than 10 minutes to go settled an entertaining, if error-strewn, Saturday tea-time affair. The Croxteth kid, who had opened the scoring on eight minutes when he swept Gary Neville's cross, first time, past Kostas Chalkias, evidently has an appetite for seeing off the men from the south coast. His brace here made it four goals in five games against Pompey for United and Everton, three of them match-winners. His latest winner sent a record Premiership crowd of 67,989 home happy as the final whistle sounded at around 7pm.

Ruud van Nistelrooy, though understandably rusty on his first full return after three months out, weighted a delicious ball for Rooney to latch on to. His first touch left Dejan Stefanovic for dead, the shimmy that followed did for Chalkias, and he then simply slipped the ball to the keeper's right. And on the balance of play – especially in the first half – it was about right.

Five changes from Milan – Tim Howard making a first league start since September – had freshened things up a bit, but United lost momentum after a first half in which Cristiano Ronaldo should have doubled the lead, shooting over five minutes before half-time. Gary O'Neil's 25-yard half-volley two minutes after the break showed the England U21 skipper's credentials, but the most breathtaking display of firepower was left to England's youngest gun. "A piece of magic" purred the boss. No pulleys and wires here. Just genius at work.

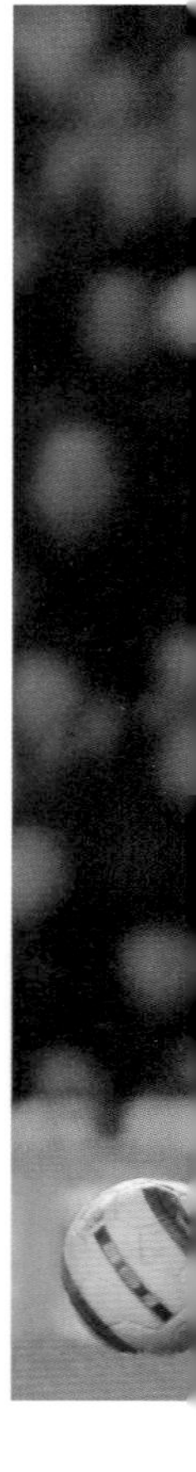

Saturday 26 February 2005
**Old Trafford**
Attendance 67,989
**Referee: Mark Halsey**

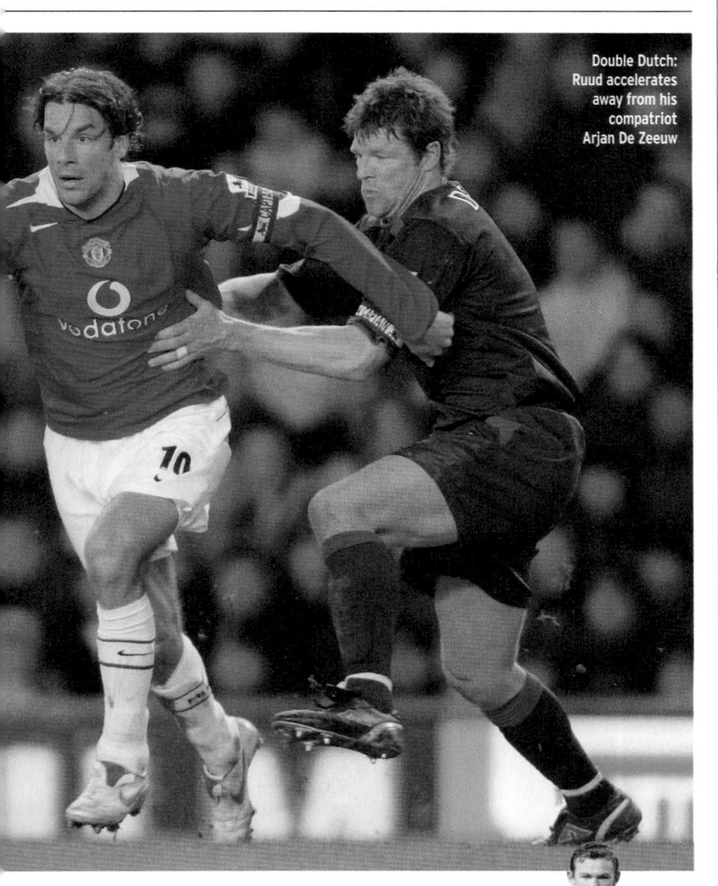

Double Dutch: Ruud accelerates away from his compatriot Arjan De Zeeuw

## MAN OF THE MATCH

**WAYNE ROONEY**

It was patently clear, as an obdurate Pompey scrapped for a point, that this game needed to be taken in hand by a special someone. And this boy – and he still is a boy, let's not forget – is so very special. This game wasn't just about the goals – they put the seal on a great all-round game in which every facet was perfect. People will always mention his price tag, but can you really put a value on this kind of ability?

## MATCH FACTS

**MANCHESTER UNITED**
Howard; G Neville (Smith 46), Brown, Silvestre, Heinze; Scholes (Giggs 65), P Neville, O'Shea; Rooney, van Nistelrooy, Ronaldo (Fortune 85)
**Subs not used** Ricardo, Saha
**Booked** P Neville

**PORTSMOUTH**
Chalkias; Griffin, de Zeeuw, Stefanovic, Taylor; O'Neil (Kamara 84), Stone, Hughes (Mezague 54), Skopelitis, LuaLua; Yakubu
**Subs not used** Hislop, Primus, Fuller **Booked** Taylor, Griffin

| Man Utd | | Portsmouth |
|---|---|---|
| 60% | POSSESSION | 40% |
| 4 | SHOTS ON TARGET | 3 |
| 7 | SHOTS OFF TARGET | 4 |
| 4 | CORNERS | 3 |
| 16 | FOULS | 18 |
| 1 | OFFSIDES | 0 |

### PREMIERSHIP RESULTS
WEEKEND BEGINNING 26/2/05

| | | |
|---|---|---|
| Aston Villa | 1–3 | Everton |
| Crystal Palace | 2–0 | Birmingham |
| Middlesbrough | 2–2 | Charlton |
| Newcastle | 2–1 | Bolton |
| Norwich | 2–3 | Manchester City |
| Southampton | 1–1 | Arsenal |
| Tottenham | 2–0 | Fulham |

### PREMIERSHIP TABLE
AT END OF 28/02/05

| | P | PTS |
|---|---|---|
| 1. Chelsea | 27 | 68 |
| 2. Manchester United | 28 | 62 |
| 3. Arsenal | 28 | 58 |
| 4. Everton | 28 | 51 |
| 5. Liverpool | 27 | 43 |
| 6. Middlesbrough | 28 | 42 |
| 7. Bolton Wanderers | 28 | 40 |
| 8. Tottenham Hotspur | 27 | 39 |
| 9. Charlton Athletic | 27 | 39 |
| 10. Manchester City | 28 | 36 |
| 11. Aston Villa | 28 | 35 |
| 12. Newcastle United | 27 | 34 |
| 13. Birmingham City | 28 | 32 |
| 14. Portsmouth | 28 | 30 |
| 15. Fulham | 27 | 29 |
| 16. Blackburn Rovers | 27 | 28 |
| 17. Crystal Palace | 28 | 25 |
| 18. Southampton | 28 | 21 |
| 19. Norwich City | 28 | 20 |
| 20. West Bromwich Albion | 27 | 18 |

CANTONA
7

# March

## The Reds lost their way at Palace, as title hopes all but disappeared, but another Ronaldo rocket finished Fulham off in style

**Beware the ides of March.** Or the 8th of March in this instance. United's preparations for the second-leg Champions League match in Milan overshadowed events at Selhurst Park – where plans for a 10th-anniversary Cantona mask party were nipped in the bud as the London club warned that no one resembling Eric would be admitted.

No teenage kicks for young Wayne in SE17 either – he was warming the bench with Paul Scholes and Cristiano Ronaldo, doubtless with the forthcoming Italian job in mind. Ruud's ring-rustiness meant two chances he'd normally snaffle were passed up and United's failure to break Palace down, even after the dismissal of Vassilis Lakis with half-an-hour to go, saw the introduction of Rooney for the last 17 minutes. It was Sir Alex's final throw of the dice to break the deadlock and cut Chelsea's lead to three points – temporarily at least. However, the Selhurst Park stalemate and the Londoners' 3-1 tea-time win away at Norwich City extended the Blues' lead to eight points with a game in hand, as the relentless game of catch-up finally appeared to catch up on United. The sense that the title had finally slipped out of United's reach left a hollow feeling at the final whistle.

Defeat in Milan brought an inevitable backlash at Southampton in the FA Cup, Roy Keane's opener in a 4-0 win putting the Reds *en route* to the last four within two minutes. The south coast scoring spree was not matched back at OT in the league against Fulham. Cristiano Ronaldo's brilliant strike the one bright spark on a frustrating afternoon, where the sense of urgency finally appeared to be waning.

### PREMIERSHIP FIXTURES THIS MONTH

| | | |
|---|---|---|
| SAT 5 | CRYSTAL PALACE | AWAY |
| SAT 19 | FULHAM | HOME |

### IN THE PREMIERSHIP THIS MONTH

**93,980** Watched United play 2 games

**1** goal was scored

**425** miles were travelled by united going to and from games

United fielded **15** players

**0** goals were conceded

### FOCUS ON CRISTIANO RONALDO

In a month where the rigours of chasing Chelsea for so long - coupled with the distractions of the Champions League and the latest round of World Cup qualifers (including England's 4-0 win over Northern Ireland at OT) - took their toll, it was good news to see Cristiano Ronaldo come to the fore once again. If February had revolved around the form of the Reds' other *wunderkind*, Wayne Rooney, March was the month in which the man from Madeira shone brightly. He got his seventh goal of the season at St Mary's in the FA Cup, finishing off a breathtaking run from Rooney for the second, but his best moment was saved for the home front against Fulham. Picking the ball up on the left flank he careered in across the edge of the box before flashing a a right-foot thunderbolt high past Edwin van der Sar.

# Crystal Palace 0

# Manchester United 0

**If ever a** draw felt like a defeat, this was it. Optimism in the United camp had been growing by the week, and at Selhurst Park the Reds had the chance to cut Chelsea's lead to just three points – if only for a couple of hours. So the failure to break down a relegation-threatened Palace, down to 10 men for most of the second half, felt like a kick in the teeth with a pair of size 11s.

Those United fans crammed into the rickety Arthur Wait Stand had left their Cantona masks at home under advice, but the sleety south London air rippled with Eric-emblazoned French flags, and the strains of 'The 12 Days Of Christmas' reflected the weather if not the date.

On the pitch, changes were afoot. With one eye on Milan, Sir Alex Ferguson rested Paul Scholes, Wayne Rooney and Cristiano Ronaldo, and Alan Smith made his first start since 4 January. Ruud van Nistelrooy was also finding his feet with only his second start in three months, but still almost gave United the lead, forcing an athletic save from Gabor Kiraly. Meanwhile ex-City man Michael Hughes soon incurred the wrath of the United faithful when he scythed down Gabriel Heinze for the first of the game's 10 yellow cards. Then, midway through the first half, Roy Keane nearly made it 51 United goals when he sprung the offside trap from a free-kick. His run from deep was perfectly timed but a late flag from the linesman provoked bemusement from the captain and fury from the manager.

After barely 10 minutes of the second half Sir Alex called Ronaldo and Scholes out of cold storage. Iain Dowie was soon forced to make his own changes after Greek international Vassilis Lakis was sent off for two quick bookings (for late tackles on Ryan Giggs and then Keane), sacrificing winger Wayne Routledge for Gary Borrowdale.

Looking to make numerical advantage pay, the United manager sent on Rooney and the Reds' stormtroopers laid siege to the Eagles' goal. Ronaldo had a shot – but failed to connect properly with a half-volley; Giggs fired just wide with a looping free-kick; Rooney created havoc by running straight through the Palace defence before losing control; van Nistelrooy had two chances he might have buried if he had been match-fit... and still Palace held out. As the four added minutes ran out, one final chance was spurned when Giggs followed up a Rooney piledriver but saw his shot loop over the bar. Advantage Chelsea...

Saturday 5 March 2004
**Selhurst Park**
Attendance 26,021
**Referee: Mark Clattenburg**

**Selhurst stalemate:** with points at a premium for both sides, United were frustrated by the Eagles' gritty rearguard action

## MAN OF THE MATCH

### RIO FERDINAND

Ferdinand missed the England-Holland game when Andy Johnson made his international debut, but he'd have needed no introduction to Palace's freescoring striker. Though the Eagles' gameplan was more about defence than attack, Rio remained alert throughout, always on hand with an assured pass or a clever run – it wasn't his fault that the game eventually finished goalless.

## MATCH FACTS

**CRYSTAL PALACE**
Kiraly; Granville, Sorondo, Boyce, Hall; Leigertwood, Hughes, Lakis, Routledge (Borrowdale 65), Soares; Johnson
**Subs not used** Speroni, Torghelle, Freedman, Kolkka
**Booked** Kiraly, Sorondo, Hughes, Lakis, Soares **Sent off** Lakis

**MANCHESTER UNITED**
Howard; Brown, Heinze, Ferdinand, Silvestre; P Neville (Ronaldo 56), Keane, Fortune (Scholes 56), Giggs; Smith (Rooney 73); van Nistelrooy
**Subs not used** Carroll, O'Shea
**Booked** Ferdinand, Heinze, Giggs, Rooney

| Man Utd | | Crystal Palace |
|---|---|---|
| 66% | POSSESSION | 34% |
| 7 | SHOTS ON TARGET | 0 |
| 12 | SHOTS OFF TARGET | 3 |
| 7 | CORNERS | 2 |
| 8 | FOULS | 12 |
| 5 | OFFSIDES | 0 |

### PREMIERSHIP RESULTS
WEEKEND BEGINNING 5/3/05

| | | |
|---|---|---|
| Arsenal | 3-0 | Portsmouth |
| Aston Villa | 2-0 | Middlesbrough |
| Everton | 0-1 | Blackburn |
| Fulham | 0-0 | Charlton |
| Manchester City | 0-1 | Bolton |
| Newcastle | 1-0 | Liverpool |
| Norwich | 1-3 | Chelsea |
| Southampton | 1-0 | Tottenham |
| West Brom | 2-0 | Birmingham |

### PREMIERSHIP TABLE
AT END OF 07/03/05

| | P | PTS |
|---|---|---|
| 1. Chelsea | 28 | 71 |
| 2. Manchester United | 29 | 63 |
| 3. Arsenal | 29 | 61 |
| 4. Everton | 29 | 51 |
| 5. Liverpool | 28 | 43 |
| 6. Bolton Wanderers | 29 | 43 |
| 7. Middlesbrough | 29 | 42 |
| 8. Charlton Athletic | 28 | 40 |
| 9. Tottenham Hotspur | 28 | 39 |
| 10. Aston Villa | 29 | 38 |
| 11. Newcastle United | 28 | 37 |
| 12. Manchester City | 29 | 36 |
| 13. Birmingham City | 29 | 32 |
| 14. Blackburn Rovers | 28 | 31 |
| 15. Fulham | 28 | 30 |
| 16. Portsmouth | 29 | 30 |
| 17. Crystal Palace | 29 | 26 |
| 18. Southampton | 29 | 24 |
| 19. West Bromwich Albion | 28 | 21 |
| 20. Norwich City | 29 | 20 |

# Manchester United 1

Ronaldo 21

# Fulham 0

Lone ranger: as Fulham's sole striker for much of the game, Andy Cole rarely found himself without a Reds defender in close attendance...

**The season may** have been far from over, but for 80 minutes of this game, it gave the impression it was. United, after starting well and taking the lead, inexplicably lost all sense of urgency and at the end were lucky to get the three points. Little wonder, then, that Sir Alex Ferguson was so critical of his players in his post-match assessment.

In the opening exchanges United looked set to considerably improve the season's goal difference. A Roy Keane effort was deflected by Zat Knight, Paul Scholes headed wide and Cristiano Ronaldo was denied by Edwin van der Sar. And in the 21st minute the Dutch keeper was left helpless. After a series of exchanges between Wayne Rooney, Scholes and Keane, Ronaldo weaved his way across the edge of the Fulham box and, when allowed half a yard of space by young Liam Rosenior, unleashed a powerful, curving, right-foot shot into the top corner. Old Trafford rose to applaud a truly great goal that left Ronaldo just two goals away from reaching double figures – and thus winning his bet with Sir Alex.

However the floodgates did not open. And while Fulham's only opportunity of a rather unambitious first half had been a somewhat

Saturday 19 March 2005
**Old Trafford**
Attendance 67,959
**Referee: Andy D'Urso**

optimistic penalty claim when Andy Cole – alone up front for all but the final 10 minutes, a far cry from his United days – went down under pressure from Mikael Silvestre, they remained resilient in defence.

After the break United seemed content to sit on the lead, just as they had back in December. Then, the Reds had dominated throughout at Craven Cottage but were punished at the death by Papa Bouba Diop's long-range screamer, and with Luis Boa Morte pushing up to join Cole, memories of that game came flooding back. Suddenly Chris Coleman's side were finding gaps. Lee Clark's effort came back off the post and Tim Howard – under fire from some sections of the press throughout the season, but instrumental in securing all three points on this occasion – kept out the rebound from Carlos Bocanegra.

United had late chances too – notably Alan Smith's audacious 60-yard effort which had a whiff of one D. Beckham about it, van der Sar frantically back-pedalling to keep the Yorkshireman's effort out. But this was a game that will not live long in the memory: two wonder goals would frankly have been rather more than it deserved.

## MAN OF THE MATCH

### CRISTIANO RONALDO

The Portuguese international not only scored the game's only goal with a brilliantly executed curling shot, he also provided all the other moments of genuine excitement. While the winger can hardly be accused of only playing well with the sun on his back, he certainly seemed to enjoy performing on what was then the warmest day of the year and was United's best performer by quite some distance. Aside from the Goal-of-the-Season contender, there was one moment of trickery down the left that might well have ended in glory, had it not been for an ungainly challenge from Papa Bouba Diop.

## MATCH FACTS

### MANCHESTER UNITED

Howard; Brown, Ferdinand, Silvestre, Heinze; Ronaldo, Scholes (P Neville 90), Keane, Fortune; van Nistelrooy (Smith 77), Rooney (O'Shea 83)
**Subs not used** Carroll, G Neville

### FULHAM

Van der Sar; Rosenior, Knight, Goma, Bocanegra; Jensen (Radzinski 89), Malbranque, Clark, Diop (Legwinski 64), Boa Morte; Cole
**Subs not used** Crossley, Volz, John
**Booked** Diop

| Man Utd | | Fulham |
|---|---|---|
| 55% | POSSESSION | 45% |
| 6 | SHOTS ON TARGET | 2 |
| 7 | SHOTS OFF TARGET | 5 |
| 18 | CORNERS | 3 |
| 9 | FOULS | 11 |
| 2 | OFFSIDES | 2 |

### PREMIERSHIP RESULTS
WEEKEND BEGINNING 19/03/05

| | | |
|---|---|---|
| Birmingham | 2-0 | Aston Villa |
| Blackburn | 0-1 | Arsenal |
| Bolton | 1-0 | Norwich |
| Charlton | 1-4 | West Brom |
| Chelsea | 4-1 | Crystal Palace |
| Liverpool | 2-1 | Everton |
| Middlesbrough | 1-3 | Southampton |
| Portsmouth | 1-1 | Newcastle |
| Tottenham | 2-1 | Manchester City |

### PREMIERSHIP TABLE
AT END OF 21/03/05

| | P | PTS |
|---|---|---|
| 1. Chelsea | 30 | 77 |
| 2. Manchester United | 30 | 66 |
| 3. Arsenal | 30 | 64 |
| 4. Everton | 30 | 51 |
| 5. Liverpool | 30 | 47 |
| 6. Bolton Wanderers | 30 | 46 |
| 7. Charlton Athletic | 30 | 43 |
| 8. Tottenham Hotspur | 30 | 42 |
| 9. Middlesbrough | 30 | 42 |
| 10. Newcastle United | 29 | 38 |
| 11. Aston Villa | 30 | 38 |
| 12. Manchester City | 30 | 36 |
| 13. Birmingham City | 30 | 35 |
| 14. Blackburn Rovers | 30 | 32 |
| 15. Portsmouth | 30 | 31 |
| 16. Fulham | 29 | 30 |
| 17. Southampton | 30 | 27 |
| 18. Crystal Palace | 30 | 26 |
| 19. West Bromwich Albion | 30 | 24 |
| 20. Norwich City | 30 | 20 |

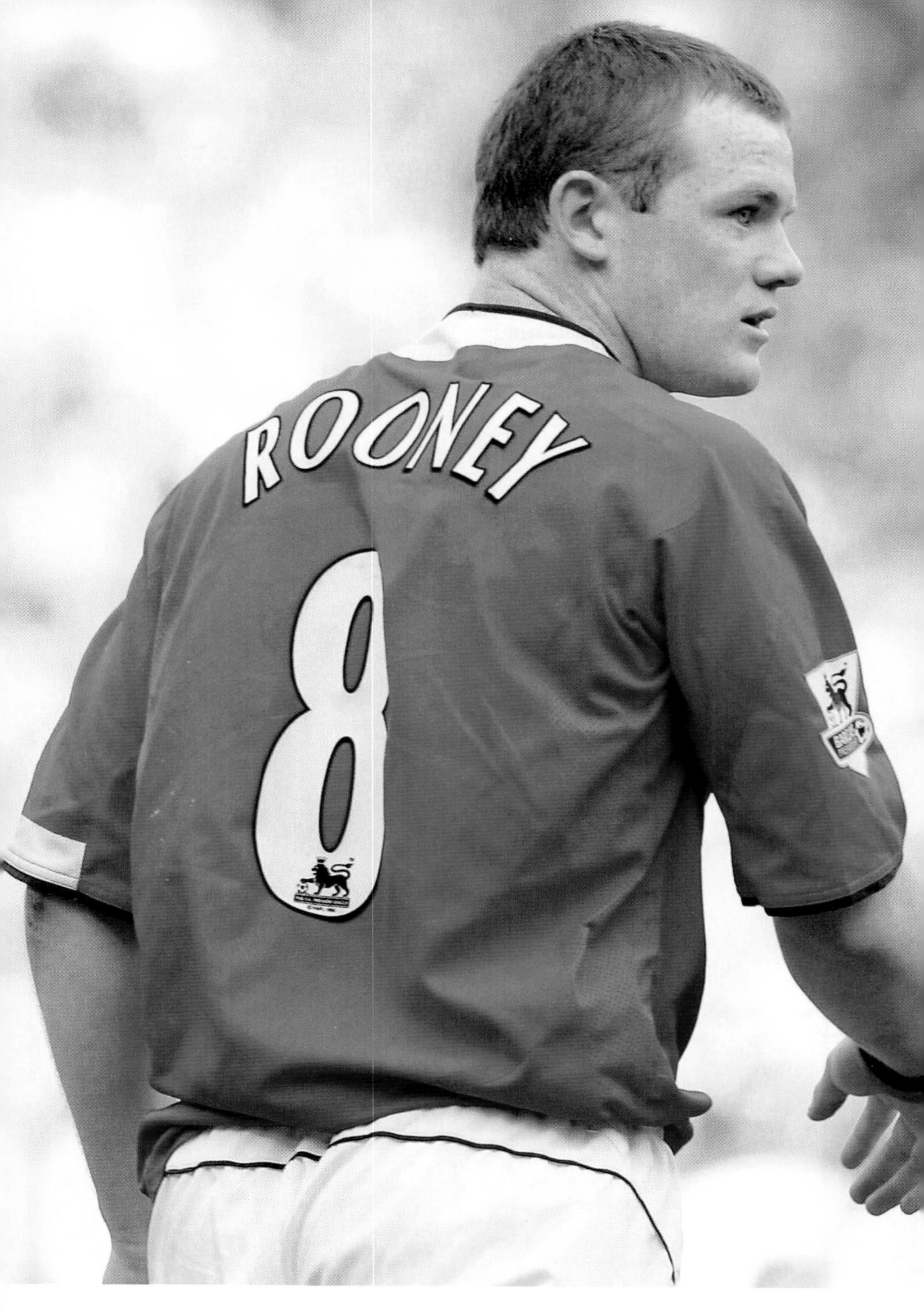
ROONEY
8

# April

## Wayne Rooney ended a forgettable month for the Reds on a high as Jose Mourinho's men marched on towards the Premiership

**April was** an eminently forgettable month for the Reds – any faint, lingering hopes of disrupting Chelsea's charge to the Premier League crown evaporating with just four points taken out of a possible 12. But the month did at least end on a high note, as Wayne Rooney's howitzer against Newcastle put United back on track. It was the best possible way to end United's mini goal drought (three league games without finding the net) and put paid to any hopes a resolute Newcastle side might have had of a famous victory at Old Trafford.

By Chelsea's stellar standards it was something of a poor month too. Only a late Didier Drogba goal rescued a point against Birmingham at Stamford Bridge and another two points were 'dropped' to the outgoing champions Arsenal. But with Frank Lampard continuing to add to his impressive goalscoring tally, wins at Southampton and then home to Fulham set the Blues up nicely for a trip to Bolton where the Premiership title was duly secured on the last day of the month.

At the opposite end of the table things remained rather less cut and dried. Norwich followed up their shock win over United by beating both Charlton and Newcastle, but then succumbed to a last-gasp winner at St Mary's to drop back behind Southampton. An Andy Johnson goal gave Crystal Palace a potentially priceless win against Liverpool (in the process seriously denting the Anfield Reds' hopes of a fourth-place finish). And West Brom, not to be outdone, eked out draws against Villa, Spurs and Blackburn after a Zoltan Gera-inspired win against Champions League-chasing Everton, to keep their survival hopes alive.

**PREMIERSHIP FIXTURES THIS MONTH**

| | | |
|---|---|---|
| SAT 2 | BLACKBURN ROVERS | HOME |
| SAT 9 | NORWICH CITY | AWAY |
| WED 20 | EVERTON | AWAY |
| SUN 24 | NEWCASTLE UNITED | HOME |

**IN THE PREMIERSHIP THIS MONTH**

**198,466** watched United play 4 games

**2** goals were scored

**460** miles were travelled by United going to and from games

United fielded **19** players

**4** goals were conceded

### FOCUS ON WES BROWN

By the start of April the Longsight-born defender had made just 12 league starts for the Reds since the season kicked off. By the end of the month he'd not only overtaken Mikael Silvestre in the pecking order, and kept the Reds in the game at Goodison with a goalline clearance from Tim Cahill, but had broken his league goalscoring duck, his 75th-minute header against Newcastle completing the recovery started by Wayne Rooney. It was a strike that Brown felt was well overdue; after Gary Neville's goal against Olympique Lyonnais, Brown had insisted that the Reds' back division should really be chipping in with a few more. It remains to be seen whether that winner against the Magpies proves to be the first of many – but Reds fans won't be too worried as long as he keeps on defending the way he's doing right now.

# Manchester United 0

# Blackburn Rovers 0

**Two years ago** Old Trafford witnessed just one goalless draw all season – and that was in the 2003 Champions League final contested by Milan and Juventus. United's failure to break down a stubborn Blackburn side resulted in the Reds' fifth 0-0 scoreline at home for the 2004/05 campaign – and the ninth in total for the season. Grim reading for Reds, and no wonder Sir Alex lamented the amount of points dropped against teams in the bottom half of the table.

The manager decided to start with his captain Roy Keane on the bench but was forced to call on his services after just six minutes when stand-in skipper Ryan Giggs was forced off with a recurrence of his hamstring problem. Still, United had plenty of attacking options on the pitch with Ruud van Nistelrooy, Wayne Rooney and Cristiano Ronaldo all starting. Rooney forced a point-blank save from Rovers' goalkeeper Brad Friedel before Tim Howard was called into action, parrying a shot into the path of Andy Todd who blasted over the bar.

Mikael Silvestre was next to bring out the best in Friedel, with a seemingly net-bound header after getting on the end of a pinpoint Paul Scholes free kick, then Rooney rattled the crossbar with a 25-yard thunderbolt. The woodwork came to Rovers' rescue once more when Keane nearly added to his two goals this season – a blocked shot from Ronaldo fell into the path of the Irishman but his snapshot cannoned off the post to safety. A breathless first half came to a close with another desperate goalline clearance from a Silvestre header, Morten Gamst Pedersen getting in the way on this occasion. The United fans headed for half-time refreshments wondering how on earth the scoreboard still read 0-0.

Unfortunately, it was to stay that way. The teams remained unchanged at the break but Blackburn had evidently taken heart from their first half great escape and continued to blunt United's attacks, which grew less and less frequent. Just after the hour mark, van Nistelrooy was replaced by Alan Smith but the fans' favourite wasn't able to give the crowd a goal and the game fizzled out.

The match ended with the news that Arsenal had hit four past Norwich City to take over second place on goal difference. And with Chelsea winning a tea-time fixture at Southampton, it all added up to a very disappointing Saturday for the Reds.

Bad hair day: Roy Keane is left scratching his head as another chance goes begging

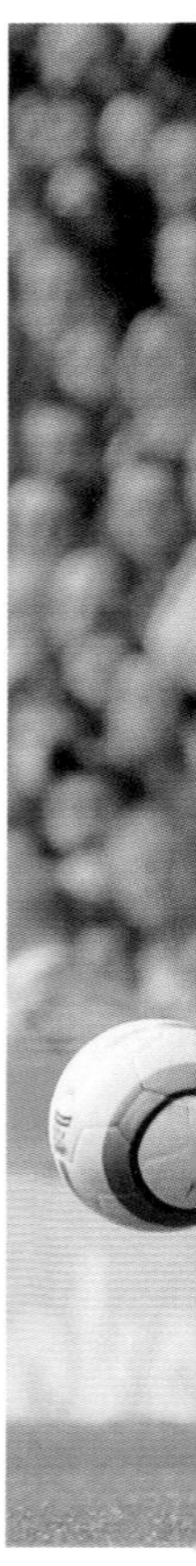

Saturday 2 April 2005
**Old Trafford**
Attendance 67,939
**Referee: Mike Riley**

## MAN OF THE MATCH

**WAYNE ROONEY**
Mikael Silvestre was unlucky not to register with two headers but it was United's favourite Merseysider who came closest to giving the Reds that all-important breakthrough. His long-range piledriver on 25 minutes looked as though it was heading in before rebounding off the woodwork. And that wasn't the only time Rooney, lively throughout, threatened the goal.

## MATCH FACTS

**MANCHESTER UNITED**
Howard; G Neville, Ferdinand, Silvestre, O'Shea; Ronaldo, Scholes, Fortune, Giggs (Keane 6); Rooney; van Nistelrooy (Smith 63)
**Subs not used** Carroll, P Neville, Brown
**Booked** G Neville, Smith, Keane

**BLACKBURN ROVERS**
Friedel: Neill, Todd, Nelsen, Matteo; Thompson, Mokoena (Emerton 68), Flitcroft, Reid, Pedersen (Gallagher 78); Stead
**Subs not used** Enckelman, Amoruso, Tugay,
**Booked** Nelsen, Stead

| | | |
|---|---|---|
| 63% | POSSESSION | 37% |
| 6 | SHOTS ON TARGET | 2 |
| 14 | SHOTS OFF TARGET | 6 |
| 9 | CORNERS | 3 |
| 21 | FOULS | 20 |
| 2 | OFFSIDES | 3 |

### PREMIERSHIP RESULTS
WEEKEND BEGINNING 2/4/05

| | | |
|---|---|---|
| Arsenal | 4-1 | Norwich City |
| Birmingham | 1-1 | Tottenham |
| Charlton | 2-2 | Manchester City |
| Crystal Palace | 0-1 | Middlesbrough |
| Fulham | 3-1 | Portsmouth |
| Liverpool | 1-0 | Bolton |
| Newcastle | 0-3 | Aston Villa |
| Southampton | 1-3 | Chelsea |
| West Brom | 1-0 | Everton |

### PREMIERSHIP TABLE
AT END OF 3/4/05

| | P | PTS |
|---|---|---|
| 1. Chelsea | 31 | 80 |
| 2. Arsenal | 31 | 67 |
| 3. Manchester United | 31 | 67 |
| 4. Everton | 31 | 51 |
| 5. Liverpool | 31 | 50 |
| 6. Bolton Wanderers | 31 | 46 |
| 7. Middlesbrough | 31 | 45 |
| 8. Charlton Athletic | 31 | 44 |
| 9. Tottenham Hotspur | 31 | 43 |
| 10. Aston Villa | 31 | 41 |
| 11. Newcastle United | 30 | 38 |
| 12. Manchester City | 31 | 37 |
| 13. Birmingham City | 31 | 36 |
| 14. Fulham | 30 | 33 |
| 15. Blackburn Rovers | 31 | 33 |
| 16. Portsmouth | 31 | 31 |
| 17. Southampton | 31 | 27 |
| 18. West Bromwich Albion | 31 | 27 |
| 19. Crystal Palace | 31 | 26 |
| 20. Norwich City | 31 | 20 |

# Norwich City 2

Ashton 55, McKenzie 66

# Manchester United 0

Off colour: Rooney failed to shine as United went down to a surprise defeat against Norwich

**United's unbeaten** league run, stretching back 20 games, caved in quite spectacularly with this Carrow Road capitulation. Even with wholesale changes to the side, few expected United to slip up against the league's bottom club, but two second-half goals punished a woefully below-par Reds.

The 2,300 away fans who travelled to East Anglia for this early evening kick-off were hoping United would put in a display like the one witnessed in the first half against Blackburn. What they ended up watching was more reminiscent of the second-half effort, lacking in both urgency and imagination. And unlike Rovers, the Canaries took full advantage.

In truth, United didn't play badly in the opening quarter of the game. The defence was untroubled and the midfield five of Paul Scholes, Quinton Fortune, Kleberson, Phil Neville and Alan Smith enjoyed plenty of possession. But ball retention, as had been demonstrated all season, is little use without an end product. United's lone striker, Louis Saha, limped out of the game

Saturday 9 April 2005
**Carrow Road**
Attendance 25,522
**Referee: Howard Webb**

after 16 minutes without a sniff of a chance, to be replaced by Cristiano Ronaldo. Alan Smith fared little better than his French team-mate when pushed further forward.

Hopes remained high that United would increase the tempo in the second half. Instead it was the home side who came out the stronger. Ten minutes after the break, second-half substitute Wayne Rooney conceded a free kick and from the ensuing dead ball, David Bentley sent over a cross which England Under-21 Dean Ashton headed powerfully past Tim Howard.

The majority of Carrow Road's record Premiership attendance erupted in delight and 11 minutes later they doubled their lead. This time Ashton was the provider, surging down Norwich's left to play in Leon McKenzie, who volleyed past Howard. Suddenly the side that had won only three games all season were on the verge of a fourth – and this without a Delia half-time rallying call.

By the end of the game United had adopted a 4-2-4 formation with a front line of Ruud van Nistelrooy, Smith, Rooney and Ronaldo, but a goal was not forthcoming, leaving the Reds with an embarrassing defeat – and handing Arsenal the advantage in the chase for second place and automatic Champions League qualification.

## MAN OF THE MATCH

**RIO FERDINAND**

On a day when no-one in a red shirt played anywhere near their full capability, Rio Ferdinand was the Reds' best performer. But for the big defender – who took several heavy knocks and limped through most of the second half – the Canaries would have taken the lead much earlier. Only Ferdinand's calmness at the back prevented an even more embarrassing defeat.

## MATCH FACTS

**NORWICH CITY**
Green; Drury, Shackell, Fleming, Francis; Stuart (Bentley 45), Safri, Helveg, Huckerby (Jonson 86); McKenzie, Ashton (Svensson 84) **Subs not used** Ward, Doherty **Booked** Bentley, McKenzie

**MANCHESTER UNITED**
Howard; G Neville, Silvestre, Ferdinand, Heinze; P Neville, Scholes, Kleberson (van Nistelrooy 63), Fortune (Rooney 45), Smith; Saha (Ronaldo 22) **Subs not used** Carroll, O'Shea **Booked** Scholes, Rooney

| Man Utd | | Norwich |
|---|---|---|
| 68% | POSSESSION | 32% |
| 4 | SHOTS ON TARGET | 3 |
| 8 | SHOTS OFF TARGET | 2 |
| 4 | CORNERS | 3 |
| 18 | FOULS | 19 |
| 1 | OFFSIDES | 1 |

### PREMIERSHIP RESULTS
WEEKEND BEGINNING 9/4/05

| Home | Score | Away |
|---|---|---|
| Aston Villa | 1-1 | West Brom |
| Blackburn | 3-0 | Southampton |
| Bolton | 3-1 | Fulham |
| Chelsea | 1-1 | Birmingham |
| Manchester City | 1-0 | Liverpool |
| Middlesbrough | 0-1 | Arsenal |
| Portsmouth | 4-2 | Blackburn |
| Tottenham | 1-0 | Newcastle |

### PREMIERSHIP TABLE
AT END OF 11/4/05

| | P | PTS |
|---|---|---|
| 1. Chelsea | 32 | 81 |
| 2. Arsenal | 32 | 70 |
| 3. Manchester United | 32 | 67 |
| 4. Everton | 32 | 54 |
| 5. Liverpool | 32 | 50 |
| 6. Bolton Wanderers | 32 | 49 |
| 7. Tottenham Hotspur | 32 | 46 |
| 8. Middlesbrough | 32 | 45 |
| 9. Charlton Athletic | 32 | 44 |
| 10. Aston Villa | 32 | 42 |
| 11. Manchester City | 32 | 40 |
| 12. Newcastle United | 31 | 38 |
| 13. Birmingham City | 32 | 37 |
| 14. Blackburn Rovers | 32 | 36 |
| 15. Portsmouth | 31 | 34 |
| 16. Fulham | 32 | 33 |
| 17. West Bromwich Albion | 32 | 28 |
| 18. Southampton | 32 | 27 |
| 19. Crystal Palace | 32 | 26 |
| 20. Norwich City | 32 | 23 |

# Everton 1

Ferguson 55

# Manchester United 0

**That big Blue** battering ram Duncan Ferguson came back to haunt United, the 33-year-old heading the only goal of a bad-tempered Goodison clash. A decade had passed since Everton last took three points from this fixture – that occasion also marked by a Ferguson winner – and it was the bruising Scot's seventh strike against the Reds. For the travelling support, his retirement can't come soon enough. And the evening went from bad to worse as Gary Neville and Paul Scholes were both sent off late on in the game, frustration obviously getting the better of the experienced pair.

Sir Alex Ferguson made just one change to the team that had brushed Newcastle aside in the FA Cup semi-final, Darren Fletcher making his first start in 15 games in place of Quinton Fortune. Wayne Rooney was making another return to his old stamping ground, which cranked the derby atmosphere up another few notches, and with both teams out to end the season on a high it was typically frenetic – though goalmouth incidents proved few and far between.

Gabriel Heinze was the first to try his luck for the Reds, his 17th-minute shot whizzing just past the intersection of post and bar. Tim Cahill then came within a whisker of giving the Toffees the lead; the Australian's shot beat Tim Howard, but Wes Brown was well placed to boot the ball off the line. Before the break Mikel Arteta and Ferguson also came close for Everton.

United's best chance came right after the interval, Rooney lobbing a perfect pass over the defence into the path of Scholes, but he shot straight at Nigel Martyn. And ten minutes after half time, Ferguson struck. Referee Phil Dowd penalised Cristiano

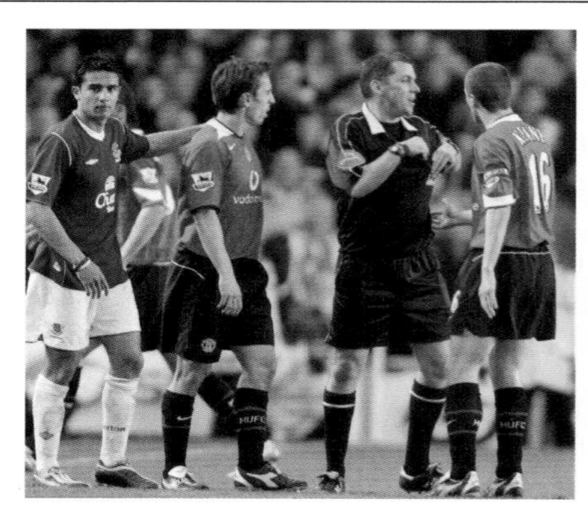

Ronaldo for a barge and an unmarked big Dunc nodded home Arteta's inswinging free kick. Rooney and Ronaldo upped the ante but Everton, roared on by the crowd, battened down the hatches.

Neville's sending off came on 72 minutes. Waiting to take a throw-in, he responded to taunts from the crowd by half-volleying the ball into the stand and Dowd flashed a straight red. Scholes, booked in the first half for a challenge on Arteta, then saw the red mist descend in injury time when he swiped at a passing Kevin Kilbane. The two managers finished the match by having what's known in their home town as a 'rammy' – but there's no doubt who went home the happier.

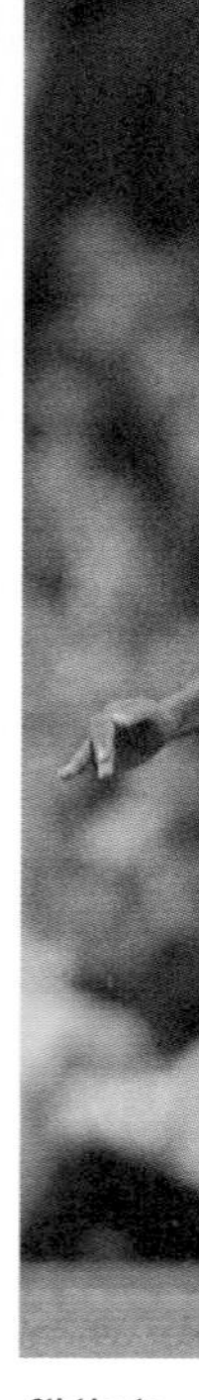

**Sticking to their task: the Toffees made it a frustrating night for the Reds...**

Wednesday 20 April 2005
**Goodison Park**
Attendance 37,160
**Referee: Phil Dowd**

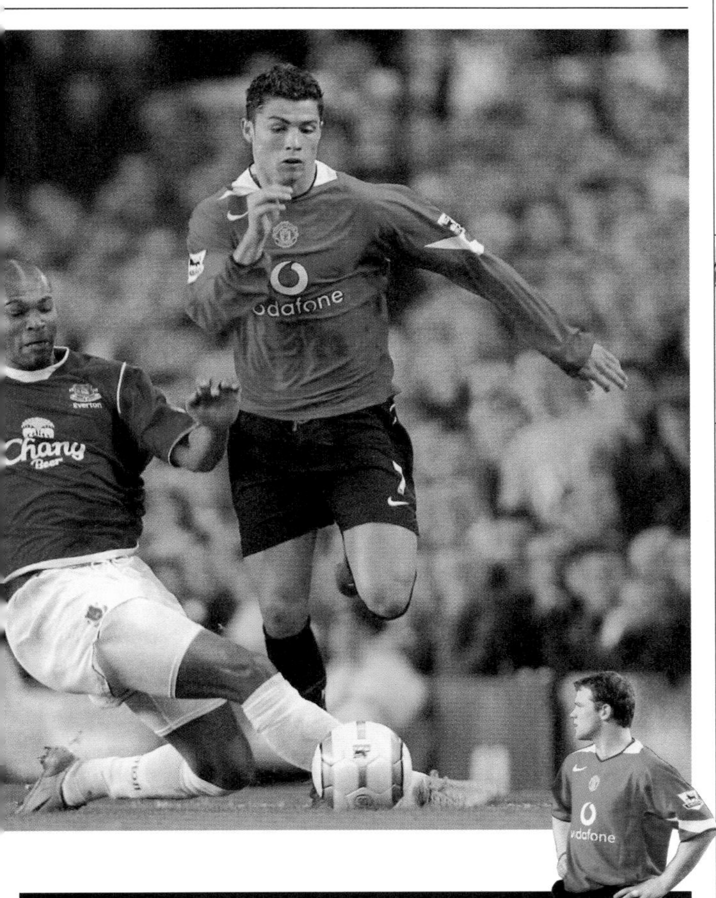


## MAN OF THE MATCH

**WAYNE ROONEY**

A night of unenviable landmarks - a first defeat in 21 games against Everton, the first time since 1992 the Reds have gone three league games without scoring, and a second successive league defeat. But none of this could be blamed on the returning Rooney, who did his best to silence the mob, and hunted high and low for the ball. His former team-mates will have been delighted to see the back of him for another season.

## MATCH FACTS

**EVERTON**
Martyn; Hibbert, Yobo, Weir, Watson; Cahill (McFadden 86), Carsley, Arteta, Kilbane; Bent (Osman 76), Ferguson (Beattie 80)
**Subs not used** Wright, Vaughan
**Booked** Arteta, Ferguson, Hibbert

**MANCHESTER UNITED**
Howard; G Neville, Ferdinand, Brown (Silvestre 72), Heinze; Fletcher (O'Shea 76), Keane, Scholes, Ronaldo; Rooney; van Nistelrooy
**Subs not used** Carroll, Smith, Fortune
**Booked** Scholes, Ronaldo
**Sent off** G Neville, Scholes

| Man Utd | | Everton |
|---|---|---|
| 65% | POSSESSION | 35% |
| 6 | SHOTS ON TARGET | 2 |
| 7 | SHOTS OFF TARGET | 5 |
| 5 | CORNERS | 4 |
| 19 | FOULS | 21 |
| 2 | OFFSIDES | 1 |

### PREMIERSHIP RESULTS
19/04/05 & 20/04/05

| | | |
|---|---|---|
| Aston Villa | 0-0 | Charlton |
| Blackburn | 1-0 | Crystal Palace |
| Bolton | 1-1 | Southampton |
| Chelsea | 0-0 | Arsenal |
| Manchester City | 3-0 | Birmingham |
| Middlesbrough | 1-1 | Fulham |
| Norwich | 2-1 | Newcastle |
| Portsmouth | 1-2 | Liverpool |
| Tottenham | 1-1 | West Brom |

### PREMIERSHIP TABLE
AT END OF 20/04/05

| | P | PTS |
|---|---|---|
| 1. Chelsea | 33 | 82 |
| 2. Arsenal | 33 | 71 |
| 3. Manchester United | 33 | 67 |
| 4. Everton | 33 | 57 |
| 5. Liverpool | 34 | 54 |
| 6. Bolton Wanderers | 34 | 53 |
| 7. Tottenham Hotspur | 34 | 48 |
| 8. Middlesbrough | 33 | 46 |
| 9. Aston Villa | 34 | 46 |
| 10. Charlton Athletic | 34 | 45 |
| 11. Manchester City | 34 | 44 |
| 12. Blackburn Rovers | 33 | 39 |
| 13. Birmingham City | 34 | 38 |
| 14. Newcastle United | 32 | 38 |
| 15. Fulham | 33 | 35 |
| 16. Portsmouth | 34 | 35 |
| 17. West Bromwich Albion | 33 | 29 |
| 18. Southampton | 34 | 28 |
| 19. Crystal Palace | 34 | 27 |
| 20. Norwich City | 34 | 27 |

# Manchester United 2

Rooney 57, Brown 75

# Newcastle United 1

Ambrose 27

Off the mark: a debut league goal from a centre-half wasn't the most likely way to get the win – but no-one was complaining...

**This game** will live long in the memory thanks to one exhilarating moment in the second half. Following a lacklustre opening 45 minutes, the Reds were struggling for inspiration and hoping for, rather than expecting, an equaliser. Then up stepped Wayne Rooney with his cannon of a right foot to score one of *the* great Old Trafford goals.

Seven days earlier the Reds had thumped Newcastle 4-1 in the FA Cup semi in Cardiff in one of the best displays of the season. But there was to be no repeat in this Premiership rematch. Even Rooney's effervescence failed to lift the Reds out of their first-half lethargy and in fact it was the Geordies who took the lead. In the 27th minute a misplaced Tim Howard clearance from a routine Phil Neville backpass fell at the feet of Darren Ambrose. The young Newcastle midfielder collected the ball, and evaded both Wes Brown and Quinton Fortune before running through unopposed to put the visitors ahead.

Such was the Reds' lethargy that the lead was rarely threatened before half-time and with 12 minutes gone in the second half, started to look like it might prove decisive. Rooney, however, had other ideas. As a headed clearance by Peter Ramage dropped

Sunday 24 April 2005
**Old Trafford**
Attendance 67,845
**Referee: Neale Barry**

in front of him, the 19-year-old advanced and struck the sweetest of swerving volleys high into the Newcastle net. Some inside Old Trafford cheered; others gasped; all looked on in awe. Yet another Goal-of-the-Season contender from a player seemingly conducting a competition all of his own.

That moment of genius proved the game's turning point. Suddenly the Reds were a different proposition. Cristiano Ronaldo (on for the injured Gabriel Heinze) turned on the trickery, Alan Smith battled for every ball as if his life depended on it, while Ryan Giggs and Rooney probed. But the winner, when it came, was from an unusual source. With 15 minutes left, Giggs swung over a corner from the left. As players jostled inside the Magpies' penalty area, Wes Brown timed his run to perfection and directed his header wide of Shay Given and into the top corner of the net. It was only his second first-team goal for United, but it secured all three points.

It was Rooney's wonder strike, however, that had provided the team and crowd with a much-needed lift and set up a victory that had looked unlikely for almost an hour. He was signed to produce moments of magic; this was most certainly one of them.

## MAN OF THE MATCH

**WAYNE ROONEY**

The young striker continued his excellent form with a tireless first-half performance as he tried to spark the Reds into life, then capped it with a Goal-of-the-Season contender after the break. All in all it was a good day for the 19-year-old, who later that evening was named PFA Young Player of the Year. Few inside Old Trafford to witness his wonder strike could disagree with his selection.

## MATCH FACTS

**MANCHESTER UNITED**
Howard; P Neville, Brown, Ferdinand, Heinze (Ronaldo 37); Fletcher (Kleberson 61), Keane (Silvestre 76), Fortune, Giggs; Rooney, Smith
**Subs not used** Carroll, O'Shea
**Booked** Rooney

**NEWCASTLE UNITED**
Given; Carr, Boumsong, O'Brien, Elliott; Milner, Ambrose, Ramage (Robert 82), N'Zogbia; Shearer (Kluivert 66), Ameobi
**Subs not used** Harper, Brittain, McClen
**Booked** Carr

| Man Utd | | Newcastle |
|---|---|---|
| 62% | POSSESSION | 38% |
| 8 | SHOTS ON TARGET | 5 |
| 8 | SHOTS OFF TARGET | 6 |
| 9 | CORNERS | 4 |
| 8 | FOULS | 21 |
| 5 | OFFSIDES | 0 |

**PREMIERSHIP RESULTS**
WEEKEND BEGINNING 23/04/05

| Home | Score | Away |
|---|---|---|
| Arsenal | 1-0 | Tottenham |
| Aston Villa | 1-1 | Bolton |
| Blackburn | 0-0 | Manchester City |
| Chelsea | 3-1 | Fulham |
| Crystal Palace | 1-0 | Liverpool |
| Everton | 1-1 | Birmingham |
| Middlesbrough | 4-0 | West Brom |
| Norwich | 1-0 | Charlton |
| Portsmouth | 4-1 | Southampton |

**PREMIERSHIP TABLE**
AT END OF 25/04/05

| | P | PTS |
|---|---|---|
| 1. Chelsea | 34 | 85 |
| 2. Arsenal | 34 | 74 |
| 3. Manchester United | 34 | 70 |
| 4. Everton | 34 | 58 |
| 5. Liverpool | 35 | 54 |
| 6. Bolton Wanderers | 35 | 54 |
| 7. Middlesbrough | 34 | 49 |
| 8. Tottenham Hotspur | 35 | 48 |
| 9. Aston Villa | 35 | 47 |
| 10. Manchester City | 35 | 45 |
| 11. Charlton Athletic | 35 | 45 |
| 12. Blackburn Rovers | 34 | 40 |
| 13. Birmingham City | 35 | 39 |
| 14. Newcastle United | 33 | 38 |
| 15. Portsmouth | 35 | 38 |
| 16. Fulham | 34 | 35 |
| 17. Crystal Palace | 35 | 30 |
| 18. Norwich City | 35 | 30 |
| 19. West Bromwich Albion | 34 | 29 |
| 20. Southampton | 35 | 28 |

vodafone
16

# May

## Though United were left with little to play for at the end of the season, May proved to be anything but a quiet month for the Reds

**It's not often** over the past few years that United have entered May with little left to aim for, but a disappointing April, FA Cup success aside, meant that as the league campaign neared its end, Arsenal had virtually confirmed their second-place finish. Still, due to the quirks of the fixture calendar, the Reds were still involved in the final shake-up at both ends of the table. West Bromwich Albion's visit to OT could have seen Bryan Robson's side relegated had results elsewhere not gone their way. As it was, some unusually wayward finishing from the Reds and a disputed penalty in Albion's favour, saw Robbo leave with a valuable point. Champions Chelsea were next up, and after the Londoners had been welcomed on to the pitch by the United players in a guard of honour, they left with a 3-1 win and several records including the most points (beating United's 92) and number of wins (29), overall.

Events elsewhere also saw United in the news as the season drew to a close, takeover plans dominating the front and back pages. Meanwhile, United played a big part in one of the tightest relegation battles of recent years. St Mary's was one of four venues around the country where fans' ears were glued to radios as Crystal Palace, Southampton, Norwich and West Brom all fought to preserve their Premiership status. While Ruud van Nistelrooy's winner ensured Southampton would join Norwich as two of the relegated three, Crystal Palace were safe with just eight minutes to go. However, a Charlton equaliser and West Brom's 2-0 win over Portsmouth meant that Robbo had pulled off one of the most dramatic escapes ever.

### PREMIERSHIP FIXTURES THIS MONTH

| | | |
|---|---|---|
| SUN 1 | CHARLTON ATHLETIC | AWAY |
| SAT 7 | WEST BROMWICH ALBION | HOME |
| TUE 10 | CHELSEA | HOME |
| SUN 15 | SOUTHAMPTON | AWAY |

### IN THE PREMIERSHIP THIS MONTH

**194,514** watched United play four games

**8** goals were scored

**874** miles were travelled by United going to and from games

United fielded **18** players

**5** goals were conceded

### FOCUS ON DARREN FLETCHER

May was a memorable month for the young Scottish midfielder, who marked his 50th start for the Reds with a goal against Charlton and followed that with a perfectly placed header against Southampton. It has been a good season all round for the 21-year-old. Hailed as one of the new generation of young Reds, Fletcher forced his way into Sir Alex Ferguson's first-team plans towards the end of the 2003/04 season, earning himself an FA Cup final place in the process, but this season saw him stake a claim in his preferred central midfield role alongside Roy Keane. Fletcher's absence through injury in March not only cost him a chance to represent Scotland against Italy, but also coincided with a dip in form for the Reds. A key player already, but at just 21, he's definitely one for the future.

# Charlton Athletic 0

# Manchester United 4

Scholes 34, Fletcher 44, Smith 62, Rooney 67

**There were** still over 20 minutes of this no-contest left when Sir Alex Ferguson declared. Deciding Charlton Athletic had suffered enough, he took off Wayne Rooney, having already substituted Roy Keane and Paul Scholes, and left Cristiano Ronaldo warming the bench. How the young winger would have loved a chance to run at the shell-shocked Addicks.

It was a painful experience for debutant keeper Stephan Andersen. The young Dane, discovered by Peter Schmeichel, kept his side in the match with a string of excellent saves before the deadlock was broken. And the architect was Rooney, who unleashed a trademark low shot from the edge of the Charlton box. The piledriver took a slight deflection and bounced off Andersen's chest straight into the path of Scholes, who had instinctively ghosted into view and finished neatly for his 12th of the season.

Number two soon followed, with Rooney and Scholes again involved, the latter teeing up Darren Fletcher, who passed the ball into the net to mark his 50th start for the Reds.

It was turning out to be a stroll in the sun for United's first team – including a returning Roy Carroll – but Rio Ferdinand may have been feeling the heat, as a section of the travelling support chose to voice their disapproval of the No.5's contract situation. After 62 minutes Ferdinand's old Leeds team-mate Alan Smith netted his first goal of 2005 when he capitalised on some slack Charlton defending. Talal El Karkouri allowed Smith to nick the ball near the

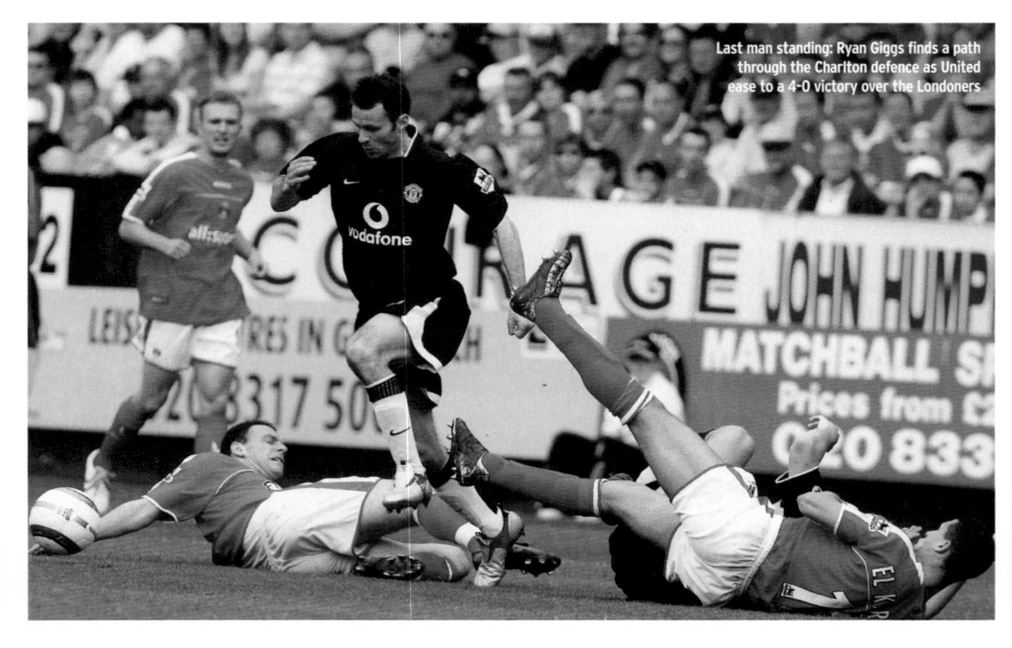


Last man standing: Ryan Giggs finds a path through the Charlton defence as United ease to a 4-0 victory over the Londoners

Sunday 1 May 2005
**The Valley**
Attendance 26,789
**Referee: Dermot Gallagher**

halfway line and the Yorkshireman advanced before curling the ball home

The last goal fell to Rooney. A slick move ended with Kleberson cleverly feeding the No.8, who lifted the ball over Andersen. Charlton's miserable afternoon was then completed when Chris Perry, only on for a matter of minutes, was sent off for hauling back Wes Brown as he advanced into the box. At the end the last man to leave the field was Ferdinand, making a point of applauding the travelling Reds who responded with a rousing chorus of "Rio..."

## MAN OF THE MATCH

**WAYNE ROONEY**
The previous Sunday had seen Rooney mark his display against Newcastle with a strike of breathtaking quality. This performance may not have grabbed the headlines, but would have given Sir Alex just as much satisfaction. Rooney could have had a hat-trick had it not been for the Charlton keeper – and The Valley woodwork on one occasion. Pundits wondered how long it would take for Rooney to fully settle into the United side. That time has come.

## MATCH FACTS

**CHARLTON ATHLETIC**
Andersen; Young, El Karkouri, Fortune, Konchesky; Rommedahl (Euell 68), Holland, Kishishev (Perry 68), Murphy, Johansson; Jeffers (Lisbie 55)
**Subs not used** Kiely, Hughes
**Sent off** Perry

**MANCHESTER UNITED**
Carroll; Brown, Silvestre, Ferdinand, O'Shea; Fletcher, Giggs, Scholes (P Neville 64), Keane (Kleberson 65); Rooney (Fortune 69); Smith
**Subs not used** Ronaldo, Howard
**Booked** Scholes, Keane

| Man Utd | | Charlton |
|---|---|---|
| 64% | POSSESSION | 36% |
| 9 | SHOTS ON TARGET | 3 |
| 7 | SHOTS OFF TARGET | 2 |
| 7 | CORNERS | 1 |
| 14 | FOULS | 8 |
| 3 | OFFSIDES | 2 |

**PREMIERSHIP RESULTS**
WEEKEND BEGINNING 30/4/05

| Home | Score | Away |
|---|---|---|
| Birmingham | 2-1 | Blackburn |
| Bolton | 0-2 | Chelsea |
| Fulham | 2-0 | Everton |
| Liverpool | 1-1 | Middlesbrough |
| Manchester City | 2-0 | Portsmouth |
| Newcastle | 0-0 | Crystal Palace |
| Southampton | 4-3 | Norwich |
| Tottenham | 5-1 | Aston Villa |
| West Brom | 0-2 | Arsenal |

**PREMIERSHIP TABLE**
AT END OF 02/5/05

| | P | PTS |
|---|---|---|
| 1. Chelsea | 35 | 88 |
| 2. Arsenal | 35 | 77 |
| 3. Manchester United | 35 | 73 |
| 4. Everton | 35 | 58 |
| 5. Liverpool | 36 | 55 |
| 6. Bolton Wanderers | 36 | 54 |
| 7. Tottenham Hotspur | 36 | 51 |
| 8. Middlesbrough | 36 | 51 |
| 9. Manchester City | 36 | 48 |
| 10. Aston Villa | 36 | 47 |
| 11. Charlton Athletic | 36 | 45 |
| 12. Birmingham City | 36 | 42 |
| 13. Blackburn Rovers | 36 | 41 |
| 14. Newcastle United | 35 | 40 |
| 15. Portsmouth | 36 | 38 |
| 16. Fulham | 35 | 38 |
| 17. Southampton | 36 | 31 |
| 18. Crystal Palace | 36 | 31 |
| 19. West Bromwich Albion | 36 | 30 |
| 20. Norwich City | 36 | 30 |

# Manchester United 1

Giggs 21

# West Bromwich Albion 1

Earnshaw 63 (pen)

**West Brom's** dreams of Premiership survival continued to the final day of the season after they secured a point at Old Trafford, to the delight of returning hero Bryan Robson. For the Reds, it was another match that promised much but ended in disappointment, almost guaranteeing a third-place finish and Champions League qualification next season.

A home win should have been secured in a first half dominated by United. Ronaldo was the first to threaten when he skipped past Ronnie Wallwork, cut into the box and fired across goal. Quinton Fortune was next to try his luck from distance and Alan Smith should have buried a point-blank header – all inside the first 15 minutes.

When Russell Hoult scrambled across goal chasing a dangerous Ronaldo cross he appeared to pull a muscle in his groin, a contributory factor in United's opener which came after 21 minutes. Thomas Gaardsoe fouled Smith on the edge of the box and captain Ryan Giggs curled a quick free kick into the net. Hoult pulled up as he scurried across his goal-line, and was replaced by Tomasz Kuszczak. The Polish keeper had only made one league appearance, but the Old Trafford arena proved to be an inspiration. A hat-trick of saves from Ronaldo and a point-blank stop from a Fortune header kept his team in it.

West Brom emerged after the break a different side, evidently inspired by Robbo's half-time battle cries. After blunting United's attacking threat they set about creating their own danger, which paid off just after the hour mark. Chasing a long ball, Geoff Horsfield tumbled while grappling with John O'Shea and referee Mark Halsey pointed to the spot. It was a generous decision to say the least, but that didn't bother Robert Earnshaw who calmly slotted past Roy Carroll.

Four minutes later, the big guns entered the fray; Scholes, Rooney and Saha replacing Phil Neville, Kleberson and Smith. The Reds chased a winner, and it nearly came with just four minutes remaining when Scholes crashed a thunderous drive against the post, but the Baggies held on.

Heads down: United threw everyone forward trying to find a breakthrough...

...but were denied all three points by the battling Baggies

Saturday 7 May 2005
**Old Trafford**
Attendance 67,827
**Referee: Mark Halsey**

## MAN OF THE MATCH

**CRISTIANO RONALDO**
Pre-match reports that a new and improved deal was on the table for the young winger were treated with some relief by the United fans. Ronaldo proved his worth in a dazzling first half display which contained the usual array of party tricks but generally backed up with an effective end product. He came agonisingly close to netting his 10th goal of the season on numerous occasions, only to be thwarted by Kuszczak.

## MATCH FACTS

**MANCHESTER UNITED**
Carroll; Brown, Ferdinand, Silvestre, O'Shea; Ronaldo, P Neville (Scholes 67), Kleberson (Rooney 67), Fortune, Giggs; Smith (Saha 67)
**Subs not used** Howard, Miller
**Booked** Smith

**WEST BROMWICH ALBION**
Hoult (Kuszczak 22); Albrechtsen, Gaardsoe, Clement, Robinson; Gera (Inamoto 83), Wallwork, Greening; Earnshaw, Campbell, Horsfield (Kanu 66)
**Subs not used** Scimeca, Moore

| Man Utd | | West Brom |
|---|---|---|
| 66% | POSSESSION | 34% |
| 12 | SHOTS ON TARGET | 1 |
| 18 | SHOTS OFF TARGET | 2 |
| 12 | CORNERS | 0 |
| 11 | FOULS | 13 |
| 1 | OFFSIDES | 3 |

### PREMIERSHIP RESULTS
WEEKEND BEGINNING 7/5/05

| | | |
|---|---|---|
| Arsenal | 3-1 | Liverpool |
| Aston Villa | 1-2 | Manchester City |
| Blackburn | 1-3 | Fulham |
| Chelsea | 1-0 | Charlton |
| Crystal Palace | 2-2 | Southampton |
| Everton | 2-0 | Newcastle |
| Middlesbrough | 1-0 | Tottenham |
| Norwich | 1-0 | Birmingham |
| Portsmouth | 1-1 | Bolton |

### PREMIERSHIP TABLE
AT END OF 8/5/05

| | P | PTS |
|---|---|---|
| 1. Chelsea | 36 | 91 |
| 2. Arsenal | 36 | 80 |
| 3. Manchester United | 36 | 74 |
| 4. Everton | 36 | 61 |
| 5. Liverpool | 37 | 55 |
| 6. Bolton Wanderers | 37 | 55 |
| 7. Middlesbrough | 37 | 54 |
| 8. Manchester City | 37 | 51 |
| 9. Tottenham | 37 | 51 |
| 10. Aston Villa | 37 | 47 |
| 11. Charlton Athletic | 37 | 45 |
| 12. Newcastle United | 37 | 43 |
| 13. Birmingham City | 37 | 42 |
| 14. Blackburn Rovers | 37 | 41 |
| 15. Fulham | 37 | 41 |
| 16. Portsmouth | 37 | 39 |
| 17. Norwich City | 37 | 33 |
| 18. Southampton | 37 | 32 |
| 19. Crystal Palace | 37 | 32 |
| 20. West Bromwich Albion | 37 | 31 |

## Manchester United 1

van Nistelrooy 7

## Chelsea 3

Tiago 17, Gudjohnsen 61, Cole 82

Blue all over: Despite Ruud's goal, United's home campaign ended on a disappointing note as Chelsea went home with three points

**Fifty years earlier** Chelsea had lifted the League trophy for the first time. United applauded them on to the Old Trafford pitch before halting the Londoners in their tracks with a face-saving 2-1 win – but there was to be no repeat half a century later.

For Reds inside OT, the visit of the newly-crowned champions turned into what could only be described as an uncomfortable night. Despite Sir Alex Ferguson praising Jose Mourinho's men as deserving champions, the expressions on the faces of the Reds players in the guard of honour showed the gesture had hurt to the core.

United, perhaps spurred on by the pain of applauding Chelsea's achievement, were the first to find their feet. With just seven minutes gone, Cristiano Ronaldo forced Carlo Cudicini into conceding a corner, from which Roy Keane picked up the loose ball and played in Paul Scholes. His shot was deflected by Robert Huth to Wayne Rooney, and the 19-year-old drilled the ball back into the box where Ruud van Nistelrooy calmly flicked the ball home.

But the lead lasted just 10 minutes as Chelsea set about producing the kind of display that had seen them win their

Tuesday 10 May 2005
**Old Trafford**
Attendance 67,832
**Referee: Graham Poll**

previous seven away games. When Claude Makelele played the ball to Tiago 30 yards out there appeared to be little danger. The Portuguese player's audacious shot appeared to be heading wide, but swung viciously, leaving Roy Carroll with no chance and clipping the intersection between post and crossbar on its way in.

The Reds rallied. A Rooney shot was headed clear and Ruud was denied a second by Ricardo Carvalho. Darren Fletcher then attempted a wonderstrike of his own only to be cruelly denied by the crossbar. Shortly after Eidur Gudjohnsen put the visitors in front, coolly chipping Carroll. Joe Cole then added a third in the dying minutes despite Reds' appeals for offside.

"The tempo was fantastic and anyone watching as a neutral would be thrilled by the football played," Sir Alex said. "I thought we played some good football, the match was very competitive and it was really a game for professionals." But it was too much for the majority inside OT to bear and at the final whistle the fans made a swift exit, eager to block out the taunts of the travelling support. If the players need to look for inspiration when the battle lines are redrawn next season they need look no further than this home defeat.

## MAN OF THE MATCH

**RUUD VAN NISTELROOY**
Two players stood out on a night that few inside OT will want to remember. Wayne Rooney hustled and bustled throughout and looked one of the few capable of spoiling the champions' party. But it was Ruud van Nistelrooy who just pipped the MOTM award. The goal was his first in the Premiership since November 27 after injury ruled him out for much of the season. How the Reds had missed him.

## MATCH FACTS

**MANCHESTER UNITED**
Carroll; G Neville, Brown, Ferdinand, Silvestre; Fletcher (Saha, 72), Keane, Scholes, Ronaldo; Rooney, van Nistelrooy
**Subs not used** Howard, Smith, O'Shea, Fortune
**Booked** Keane, van Nistelrooy

**CHELSEA**
Cudicini; Johnson (Jarosik, 72), Ricardo Carvalho, Huth, Gallas; Geremi, Tiago, Makelele, Lampard, Cole (Grant, 90); Gudjohnsen (Nuno Morais, 86)
**Subs not used** Cech, Forssell
**Booked** Makelele, Lampard, Gallas

| Man Utd | | Chelsea |
|---|---|---|
| 51% | POSSESSION | 49% |
| 2 | SHOTS ON TARGET | 5 |
| 6 | SHOTS OFF TARGET | 2 |
| 7 | CORNERS | 0 |
| 11 | FOULS | 16 |
| 4 | OFFSIDES | 0 |

**PREMIERSHIP RESULTS**
11/5/05

| Arsenal | 7-0 | Everton |
|---|---|---|

**PREMIERSHIP TABLE**
AT END OF 11/5/05

| | P | PTS |
|---|---|---|
| 1. Chelsea | 37 | 94 |
| 2. Arsenal | 37 | 83 |
| 3. Manchester United | 37 | 74 |
| 4. Everton | 37 | 61 |
| 5. Liverpool | 37 | 55 |
| 6. Bolton Wanderers | 37 | 55 |
| 7. Middlesbrough | 37 | 54 |
| 8. Manchester City | 37 | 51 |
| 9. Tottenham Hotspur | 37 | 51 |
| 10. Aston Villa | 37 | 47 |
| 11. Charlton Athletic | 37 | 45 |
| 12. Newcastle United | 37 | 43 |
| 13. Birmingham City | 37 | 42 |
| 14. Blackburn Rovers | 37 | 41 |
| 15. Fulham | 37 | 41 |
| 16. Portsmouth | 37 | 39 |
| 17. Norwich City | 37 | 33 |
| 18. Southampton | 37 | 32 |
| 19. Crystal Palace | 37 | 32 |
| 20. West Bromwich Albion | 37 | 31 |

# Southampton 1

O'Shea 10 (og)

# Manchester United 2

Fletcher 19, van Nistelrooy 63

**While the Reds** had little to fight for but pride at the end of a difficult campaign, for Southampton the prospect of dropping out of the top tier for the first time in 27 years cast a foreboding shadow over St Mary's. "It's one of those games you'd rather not have, but you've got to do your best because your reputation and pride have a lot to answer for," said Sir Alex afterwards.

A quick glance at the gaffer's teamsheet would have given some early solace to the Saints. With one eye on the FA Cup final, Paul Scholes, Cristiano Ronaldo, Roy Keane and Gary Neville took their seats on the bench. In their place Alan Smith, John O'Shea, Quinton Fortune and Ryan Giggs were all recalled. But the Reds didn't stand on ceremony and Wayne Rooney's fierce shot in the opening minutes was deflected wide, but from the corner Mikael Silvestre headed over the bar.

The home crowd started to believe that a great escape was on the cards, however, when they took the lead in the tenth minute. After Henri Camara had won a corner, Graeme Le Saux launched the ball into the box where ex-Red Danny Higginbotham knocked it past Roy Carroll. In the confusion, the ball then bounced off Nigel Quashie's chest, John O'Shea's knee and into the net. Cue wild celebrations from the red and white striped masses.

That goal only served to galvanise the Reds. O'Shea quickly made amends for his own goal, firing a cross into the area which Darren Fletcher headed home in style.

Ruud van Nistelrooy then had a goalbound effort pushed over the bar and O'Shea had a shot cleared off the line as the Reds pushed forward. At the other end only Carroll's quick reactions denied Camara. As the half time whistle sounded the sides remained level and Southampton left the field knowing that results elsewhere meant that they were on course for survival.

But just after the hour mark, there was a double whammy for Saints' fans as firstly news of West Brom taking the lead against Portsmouth filtered through to the crowd, and then van Nistelrooy put United ahead. After good work from Alan Smith on the right the ball was deflected into the path of the Dutchman who made no mistake to head home and break Saints' hearts.

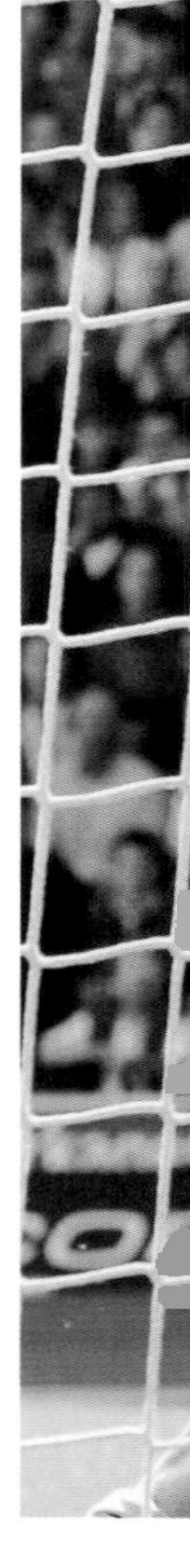

Sunday 15 May 2005
**St Mary's**
Attendance 32,066
**Referee: Steve Bennett**

Ups and downs: Ruud puts United 2-1 up – and sends Southampton down – on a day of high drama at St Mary's

## MAN OF THE MATCH

**DARREN FLETCHER**

It was a cracking display by the young Scot, who has been much admired by the manager. And with performances like this it's easy to see why Sir Alex rates him so highly. On in place of the rested captain, there were flashes of brilliance as he marauded forward that brought to mind a younger Roy Keane. Fletcher's pinpoint header to level the scores had class written all over it – and helped boost his prospects for a FA Cup final start.

## MATCH FACTS

**SOUTHAMPTON**
Niemi; Telfer, Lundekvam, Higginbotham, Bernard (Davenport, 78); Prutton (Phillips, 71), Redknapp, Quashie, Le Saux (Delap, 71); Camara Ormerod **Subs not used** Smith, Oakley **Booked** Lundekvam

**MANCHESTER UNITED**
Carroll; O'Shea, Brown, Ferdinand, Silvestre; Fortune, Fletcher, Giggs, Smith; Rooney (Saha, 74), van Nistelrooy (P Neville, 87) **Subs not used** Kleberson, Keane, Ricardo **Booked** Brown Silvestre

| | | |
|---|---|---|
| 58% | POSSESSION | 42% |
| 8 | SHOTS ON TARGET | 2 |
| 8 | SHOTS OFF TARGET | 8 |
| 3 | CORNERS | 5 |
| 13 | FOULS | 18 |
| 2 | OFFSIDES | 5 |

**PREMIERSHIP RESULTS**
15/5/05

| | | |
|---|---|---|
| Birmingham | 2-1 | Arsenal |
| Bolton | 3-2 | Everton |
| Charlton | 2-2 | Crystal Palace |
| Fulham | 6-0 | Norwich |
| Liverpool | 2-1 | Aston Villa |
| Manchester City | 1-1 | Middlesbrough |
| Newcastle | 1-1 | Chelsea |
| Tottenham | 0-0 | Blackburn |
| West Brom | 2-0 | Portsmouth |

**PREMIERSHIP TABLE**
AT END OF 15/5/05

| | P | PTS |
|---|---|---|
| 1. Chelsea | 38 | 95 |
| 2. Arsenal | 38 | 83 |
| 3. Manchester United | 38 | 77 |
| 4. Everton | 38 | 61 |
| 5. Liverpool | 38 | 58 |
| 6. Bolton Wanderers | 38 | 58 |
| 7. Middlesbrough | 38 | 55 |
| 8. Manchester City | 38 | 52 |
| 9. Tottenham Hotspur | 38 | 52 |
| 10. Aston Villa | 38 | 47 |
| 11. Charlton Athletic | 38 | 46 |
| 12. Birmingham City | 38 | 45 |
| 13. Fulham | 38 | 44 |
| 14. Newcastle United | 38 | 44 |
| 15. Blackburn Rovers | 38 | 42 |
| 16. Portsmouth | 38 | 39 |
| 17. West Bromwich Albion | 38 | 34 |
| 18. Crystal Palace | 38 | 33 |
| 19. Norwich City | 38 | 33 |
| 20. Southampton | 38 | 32 |

VIEIRA
RONALDO

# UEFA CHAMPIONS LEAGUE

vodafone

# UEFA CHAMPIONS LEAGUE
# PHASE ONE

## A third place finish meant an earlier than expected start to the campaign but the Reds were soon back on track in Europe...

After bowing out to eventual winners Porto in the knockout stage the previous season, United wasted no time getting amongst the goals in the Champions League. At times finding the net proved problematic in the Premiership but the opposite was true in Europe. In the two-legged qualifying tie with Dinamo Bucharest, the 17 times Romanian champions were easily swept aside as the Reds hit five.

Sir Alex's side weren't the only heavyweights that faced an extra qualifying hurdle. Internazionale, Juventus, Leverkusen, Liverpool, Monaco, PSV and Real Madrid all made it through to the group stages after playing qualifying matches – and all reached the last 16.

There were no real surprises in the group stage. Monaco topped Group A, despite losing 2-0 to Liverpool in the opening game, the Merseysiders booking a berth on goal difference. But Group B will be remembered for all the wrong reasons after referee Anders Frisk was struck by an object thrown from the crowd, forcing the Roma-Kyiv tie to be abandoned. Leverkusen and Real Madrid then went through.

Juventus and Bayern progressed from Group C, the latter scoring twice as many as the *Old Lady*, but beaten home and away by the Italian side. And Arsenal finished Group E unbeaten, topping the table on goal difference, PSV securing second spot. Pre-tournament favourites Milan and Barcelona went safely through from Group F, while Internazionale reached the next stage as unbeaten winners of Group G, with Bremen runners-up. Completing the picture Chelsea ran out Group H winners, and holders Porto qualified as runners-up.

### QUALIFYING ROUND & GROUP D FIXTURES

| | | |
|---|---|---|
| 11 AUG | DINAMO BUCHAREST | AWAY |
| 25 AUG | DINAMO BUCHAREST | HOME |
| 15 SEPT | OLYMPIQUE LYONNAIS | AWAY |
| 28 SEPT | FENERBAHÇE | HOME |
| 19 OCT | AC SPARTA PRAHA | AWAY |
| 3 NOV | AC SPARTA PRAHA | HOME |
| 23 NOV | OLYMPIQUE LYONNAIS | HOME |
| 8 DEC | FENERBAHÇE | AWAY |

### IN THE GROUP STAGE

**414,927**
Watched United play 8 games

**19**
goals were scored

**8,938**
miles United travelled to and from games

United fielded
**28**
players

**10**
goals were conceded

### GOAL OF THE GROUP STAGE WAYNE ROONEY v FENERBAHÇE 28/9/04

Picking the goal of the round from such an abundance of riches was hard. Ruud van Nistelrooy's impressive return in the tournament saw him score an incredible eight in five, while Wayne Rooney's stunning hat-trick on his debut against the Turkish champions was something straight from the realms of fantasy football. In the end Rooney's matchball winner against Fenerbahçe just gets the nod. All three goals were worthy winners of the honour as the teenager took just under 60 minutes to give OT a masterclass in why Sir Alex simply had to sign him. Nine minutes after the break van Nistelrooy was fouled by Fabio Luciano on the edge of the area. There were no shortage of red shirts around the ball but no one was going to stand in the on-fire youngster's way. Up he stepped and unleashed a spectacular free kick that curled up and over the five-man wall, leaving Rüstü Reçber no chance. Welcome to Old Trafford Wayne!

# Dinamo Bucharest 1

Danciulescu 10

# Manchester United 2

Giggs 38, Alistar (og) 72

## MATCH FACTS

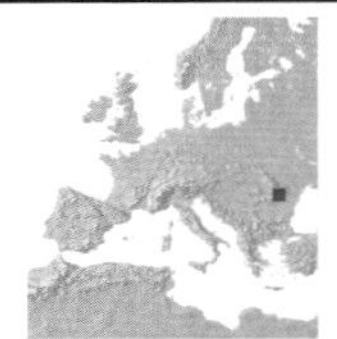

**Third qualifying round, first leg**
Wednesday 11 August 2004
**Lia Manoliu Stadium**
Attendance 58,000
**Referee: Paulo Costa**

DINAMO BUCHAREST
Gaev; Ciobotariu (Galamaz 29), Alistar, Iordache; Balan (Baltoi 79), Margaritescu (Goian 53), Tames, Semeghin, Petre; Niculescu, Danciulescu
**Subs not used** Matache, Irimia, Pacurar, V Munteanu

MANCHESTER UNITED
Howard; G Neville, Keane, Silvestre, Fortune; Fletcher (Miller 67), O'Shea, Djemba-Djemba, Giggs (P Neville 81); Scholes (Forlan 90), Smith
**Subs not used** Carroll, Eagles, Richardson, Spector
**Booked** Smith, Scholes, Silvestre, G Neville

| Manchester United | | Dinamo |
|---|---|---|
| 60% | POSSESSION | 40% |
| 2 | SHOTS ON TARGET | 3 |
| 9 | SHOTS OFF TARGET | 2 |
| 4 | CORNERS | 5 |
| 26 | FOULS | 13 |
| 6 | OFFSIDES | 5 |

## MAN OF THE MATCH

RYAN GIGGS
Showing all the experience he's gained from 90 games in European football for United, the Welshman was a constant threat on the left wing. He also scored his 21st goal in Europe with a wonderful run and calm finish to get United back in the game before half-time.

Holding firm: Scholes toughs it out in Bucharest

**After a bomb scare** at the team hotel on the morning of the game, and then falling behind to an early goal, the Reds' nerves were steady enough to to earn a win which left United on the brink of qualifying for the Champions League proper for a ninth successive season. "The last thing you want away from home in Europe is to concede an early goal," reflected Sir Alex. "The important thing is not to panic. It was very pleasing to control the second half and win the game."

It was an unfamiliar United formation that took to the field in humid conditions. Roy Keane was stationed next to Mikael Silvestre in the heart of the defence, while John O'Shea was deployed in the centre of midfield. And it was lingering pre-season rustiness that saw United fall behind. Claudiu Niculescu got to the byline, Ionel Danciulescu made an unconvincing contact with his cross at the far post, and Quinton Fortune inadvertently helped it across the line. "We didn't know what to do when we went 1-0 up," admitted Dinamo coach Ioan Andone, and that allowed United to find some composure. They were level after 38 minutes, when Paul Scholes won the ball and instantly played in Ryan Giggs, who skipped past the advancing keeper Vladimir Gaev and slid the ball into the unguarded goal.

In the second half United were much sharper, and after Alan Smith had driven a low shot against the inside of the post, the winner arrived with 18 minutes left. Liam Miller, making his United debut as a sub for Darren Fletcher, drilled the ball across goal and it diverted in off the hapless Angelo Alistar. "This result leaves us with a very low chance when we go to Manchester for the second leg," said a resigned Andone.

# Manchester United 3

Smith 47, 50, Bellion 70

# Dinamo Bucharest 0

**It was mission** accomplished as the Reds comfortably clinched that all-important place in the Champions League group stage. A brace from Alan Smith and a second in two matches for David Bellion gave a young United side a deserved 3-0 victory and a 5-1 aggregate score.

So confident was Sir Alex Ferguson that Dinamo would not deny his side that he made five changes from the team that had beaten Norwich four days earlier. In came Kleberson and Cristiano Ronaldo for their first starts of the campaign, while Chris Eagles and Jonathan Spector enjoyed full debuts.

The news that Roy Keane would be missing for up to three weeks with two fractured ribs, and that the Reds had tabled a £20 million bid for Everton's Wayne Rooney, occupied the pre-match chatter among the fans. And there was little in a low-key first half to halt the discussions though Ronaldo did his best to liven up affairs, showcasing his sublime skills as he had throughout the summer. A diving header by Alan Smith just before the interval, which was tipped over by Dinamo keeper Cristi Munteanu, was as close as United got. But United's new front man didn't have to wait much longer to get on the scoresheet.

Two minutes after the interval Kleberson sent over a free-kick, and Adrian Iordache shinned the ball into the path of the Reds' No.14 who tapped in from three yards. He then grabbed a second after a slick move down the right involving Fletcher, Eagles and Gary Neville, and Bellion rounded off proceedings, latching onto a through ball and curling a shot into the Dinamo net. The away fans did their best to rally their side, but Tim Howard remained a spectator as the Reds progressed into the Champions League draw.

Bargain buy: Smith begins to repay that £7m...

## MATCH FACTS

**Third qualifying round, second leg**
Wednesday 25 August 2004
**Old Trafford**
Attendance 61,041
**Referee: Markus Merk**

MANCHESTER UNITED
Howard; G Neville (P Neville 55), Silvestre, O'Shea, Spector; Eagles, Kleberson, Fletcher, Djemba-Djemba; Ronaldo (Richardson 64), Smith (Bellion 63)
**Subs not used** Carroll, Saha, Giggs, Scholes
**Booked** Eagles

DINAMO BUCHAREST
C Munteanu; Irimia, Iordache, Galamaz, Semeghin; Petre (Balan 67), Margaritescu, Naidin, Grigorie (Pacurar 45); Danciulescu, Niculescu (Serban 80)
**Subs not used** Gaev, Goian, Baltoi, Ciobotariu
**Booked** Galamaz

| Man Utd | | Dinamo |
|---|---|---|
| 59% | POSSESSION | 41% |
| 7 | SHOTS ON TARGET | 2 |
| 3 | SHOTS OFF TARGET | 3 |
| 7 | CORNERS | 1 |
| 20 | FOULS | 14 |
| 9 | OFFSIDES | 2 |

## MAN OF THE MATCH

ALAN SMITH
Supposedly a scorer of great goals, not a great goalscorer, Smith gave a pretty convincing impression of a predatory striker. Two clinical strikes in the space of three minutes showed he's an all-round striker - and a good one: four goals in his first five United games were proof of that.

# Olympique Lyonnais 2
Cris 35, Frau 44

# Manchester United 2
van Nistelrooy 56, 61

**Ruud van Nistelrooy's** record-breaking double saw him overhaul Denis Law's European tally and salvage a point for United, as the season's topsy-turvy form continued. Sir Alex Ferguson made three changes from the weekend's 2-2 draw with Bolton, John O'Shea, Eric Djemba-Djemba and Cristiano Ronaldo coming in for Phil Neville, Kleberson and Alan Smith. And the manager might have hoped the experience gained in the French league of Djemba-Djemba, Mikael Silvestre and Gabriel Heinze would stand the Reds in good stead. But it was the home side who got off to a flyer.

The French champions dominated the first half with the Brazilian midfielder Juninho and Sidney Govou cutting through the United defence at will. And, in a devastating nine-minute spell just before the interval, they surged into a two-goal lead. The first came after Ryan Giggs conceded a free-kick outside the United area. Juninho fired in a ball which was spilled by Tim Howard, and another Brazilian, Cris, knocked it home.

The home crowd went wild, but no-one was enjoying the evening more than former Gunner Sylvain Wiltord, who played a major part in the second goal. O'Shea lost the ball deep in Lyon territory and Wiltord raced off, mesmerising Silvestre and Wes Brown before passing to new signing Pierre-Alain Frau, who finished expertly.

The half-time whistle brought some respite for United (possibly until the manager entered the dressing room), and the second half saw an almost immediate turnaround. Just 11 minutes into the second half, Cristiano Ronaldo jabbed a fine cross into the Lyon box right on the goalline, and van Nistelrooy, the ball almost beyond him, somehow arched his back to head past Grégory Coupet. Fists clenched, he screamed with delight and relief, but somehow you knew his work wasn't done. Five minutes later, with Ronaldo again the supplier, the United No.10 pounced on a misplaced pass to level the scores.

The Reds went in search of a winner, but it was Lyon who almost snatched it at the death when Juninho hit the post. Not the result the boss had in mind perhaps, but an away point in Europe against a skilful Lyon side was far from a disaster either.

Lethal combination: Ronaldo found his range in the second half to set up Ruud's historic double

**UEFA Champions League Group D**
Wednesday 15 September 2004
**Stade Municipal de Gerland**
Attendance 40,000
**Referee: Wolfgang Stark**

## MAN OF THE MATCH

### RUUD VAN NISTELROOY

How the Dutchman loves this competition. In only his second match back after injury, Ruud van Nistelrooy passed the Lawman's European total, putting himself only nine goals behind the all-time UEFA Champions League goalscoring record of Real Madrid's Raul – but having played just half the number of games the Spaniard had. It's surely only a matter of time before that record is his too...

## MATCH FACTS

**OLYMPIQUE LYONNAIS**
Coupet; Réveillère, Cris, Caçapa, Abidal; Wiltord (Clément 88), Essien, Juninho, Malouda; Govou (Ben Arfa 75), Frau (Nilmar 65)
**Subs not used** Puydebois, Diatta, Bergougnoux, Berthod
**Booked** Cris

**MANCHESTER UNITED**
Howard; O'Shea (P Neville 83), Brown, Silvestre, Heinze; Ronaldo, Keane, Djemba-Djemba, Giggs; Scholes, van Nistelrooy (Smith 79)
**Subs not used** Carroll, Bellion, Kleberson, Richardson, Fletcher
**Booked** Heinze

| Manchester United | | Olympique Lyonnais |
|---|---|---|
| 50% | POSSESSION | 50% |
| 3 | SHOTS ON TARGET | 5 |
| 3 | SHOTS OFF TARGET | 11 |
| 3 | CORNERS | 6 |
| 20 | FOULS | 14 |
| 1 | OFFSIDES | 2 |

### UEFA CHAMPIONS LEAGUE GROUP STAGE
RESULTS 14/09/04 & 15/09/04

| | | |
|---|---|---|
| **GROUP A** | | |
| Deportivo | 0-0 | Olympiakos |
| Liverpool | 2-0 | Monaco |
| **GROUP B** | | |
| Leverkusen | 3-0 | Real Madrid |
| Roma | 0-3(f) | Dynamo Kyiv |
| **GROUP C** | | |
| Ajax | 0-1 | Juventus |
| Maccabi Tel Aviv | 0-1 | Bayern |
| **GROUP D** | | |
| Fenerbahçe | 1-0 | Sparta |
| **GROUP E** | | |
| Arsenal | 1-0 | PSV |
| Panathinaikos | 2-1 | Rosenborg |
| **GROUP F** | | |
| Celtic | 1-3 | Barcelona |
| Shakhtar | 0-1 | Milan |
| **GROUP G** | | |
| Internazionale | 2-0 | Bremen |
| Valencia | 2-0 | Anderlecht |
| **GROUP H** | | |
| Porto | 0-0 | CSKA Moskva |
| PSG | 0-3 | Chelsea |

(f) game forfeited

### GROUP D TABLE
After Matchday 1

| | P | PTS |
|---|---|---|
| 1. Fenerbahçe | 1 | 3 |
| 2. Olympique Lyonnais | 1 | 1 |
| 3. Manchester United | 1 | 1 |
| 4. Sparta Praha | 1 | 0 |

# Manchester United 6

Giggs 7, Rooney 17, 28, 54, van Nistelrooy 78, Bellion 81

# Fenerbahçe SK 2

Marcio Nobre 47, Sanli 60

Dream debut: The Croxteth kid salutes Old Trafford after announcing his arrival in style

**Has there ever** been a better Old Trafford debut? In fact, has there ever been a better debut anywhere? Wayne Rooney's first match for the Reds had been much anticipated but nobody, not even the hyperconfident player himself, could have predicted an impact quite like that. The 18-year-old was simply awesome.

At the pre-match press conference Sir Alex Ferguson had admitted he needed to "mull over" whether to give the youngster his first start against Fenerbahçe or name him as a sub. Clearly he'd been mulling over much more than that. Out went Roy Keane, Cristiano Ronaldo, John O'Shea, Wes Brown and Alan Smith from the weekend's line-up against Spurs. In came Kleberson, Eric Djemba-Djemba, David Bellion, Gary Neville and Rooney.

Some fans may have felt apprehensive at the number of rested players, but their fears were allayed when Ryan Giggs gave United a seventh-minute lead with a header from a Kleberson cross. And 10 minutes later, the 'Wayne Rooney Show' got up and running. Having already threatened twice, the star of Euro 2004 raced onto a Ruud van Nistelrooy through-ball and, from the edge of the area, fired a first-time, left-foot shot high into Rüstü Reçber's net. It was the debut goal Old

League Group D
Tuesday 28 September 2004
Old Trafford
Attendance 67,128
Referee: Frank de Bleeckere

Trafford had been longing for; but even then, few could have imagined quite what was to follow.

Eleven minutes later he did it again. Combining with Giggs this time, Rooney skipped past a defender and drove a low, 20-yard, right-foot shot into the far corner. The home fans didn't so much cheer as gasp in astonishment.

United's 3-0 lead at the break lasted for only 60 seconds of the second half – thanks to a Marcio Nobre close-range effort – but that strike was soon overshadowed. The young Liverpudlian was determined to claim his first match ball in top-flight football and on 54 minutes made no mistake with a curling free kick from the edge of the box. Having lifted the ball over the wall and beyond Reçber he ran to the corner flag in celebration. Few inside Old Trafford would have blamed him had he continued his run right up the players' tunnel, into the car park outside and all the way home.

Fenerbahçe then scored again through Tuncay Sanli before van Nistelrooy's 31st European strike was followed by a sixth from Bellion. But there was only one name on Reds' lips as they flooded home: Wayne Rooney. What a night... what a player.

## MAN OF THE MATCH

**WAYNE ROONEY**

Who else? Ryan Giggs gave a lively display on the left, Rio was calmness personified at the back, but the teenage sensation – the Liverpudlian one, not Ronaldo – was simply outstanding. Not since Charlie Sagar scored three on his debut in September 1905 has a United player enjoyed such a start. Few, if any, will remember Sagar's achievement; few inside Old Trafford will ever forget Rooney's.

## MATCH FACTS

**MANCHESTER UNITED**
Carroll; G Neville, Heinze (P Neville 81), Ferdinand, Silvestre; Bellion, Djemba-Djemba, Kleberson, Giggs (Fletcher 62); Rooney, van Nistelrooy (Miller 81)
**Subs not used** Ricardo, Ronaldo, Smith, O'Shea **Booked** Heinze

**FENERBAHÇE SK**
Reçber; Baris, Luciano, Özat, Akyel (Akin 61); Balci, Aurelio, Marcio Nobre; Sanli; Alex; van Hooijdonk
**Subs not used** Demirel, Fabiano, Yozgatli, Hacioglu, Turaci, Sahin
**Booked** Aurelio, Balci

| | | |
|---|---|---|
| 48% | POSSESSION | 52% |
| 8 | SHOTS ON TARGET | 5 |
| 4 | SHOTS OFF TARGET | 5 |
| 1 | CORNERS | 6 |
| 21 | FOULS | 19 |
| 2 | OFFSIDES | 1 |

**UEFA CHAMPIONS LEAGUE GROUP STAGE**
RESULTS 28/09/04 & 29/09/04

| | | |
|---|---|---|
| **GROUP A** | | |
| Monaco | 2-0 | Deportivo |
| Olympiakos | 1-0 | Liverpool |
| **GROUP B** | | |
| Dynamo Kyiv | 4-2 | Leverkusen |
| Real Madrid | 4-2 | Roma |
| **GROUP C** | | |
| Bayern | 4-0 | Ajax |
| Juventus | 1-0 | Maccabi Tel Aviv |
| **GROUP D** | | |
| Sparta | 1-2 | Lyon |
| **GROUP E** | | |
| PSV | 1-0 | Panathinaikos |
| Rosenberg | 1-1 | Arsenal |
| **GROUP F** | | |
| Barcelona | 3-0 | Shaktar |
| Milan | 3-1 | Celtic |
| **GROUP G** | | |
| Anderlecht | 1-3 | Internazionale |
| Bremen | 2-1 | Valencia |
| **GROUP H** | | |
| Chelsea | 3-1 | Porto |
| CSKA Moskva | 2-0 | PSG |

**GROUP D TABLE**
After Matchday 2

| | P | PTS |
|---|---|---|
| 1. Manchester United | 2 | 4 |
| 2. Olympique Lyonnais | 2 | 4 |
| 3. Fenerbahçe | 2 | 3 |
| 4. Sparta Praha | 2 | 0 |

# AC Sparta Praha 0

# Manchester United 0

**Visitors to this beautiful** old city have a host of attractions of which to take advantage, be they cultural, historical or liquid-based: and the latter proved a welcome distraction for the travelling supporters as they watched United fight out a third goalless draw of the season so far.

The point gained against a side battling for their Champions League future edged United that little bit closer to the knockout stages, but this was the first time in 13 European matches that the Reds had failed to score, symptomatic of United's performances in the Premiership.

Forced to leave lynchpins Roy Keane and Rio Ferdinand behind, Sir Alex restored Mikael Silvestre to central defence, with Irishmen Liam Miller and John O'Shea taking their places in midfield alongside Paul Scholes and Ryan Giggs. The latter, stand-in captain for the evening, started brightly and nearly handed United an early lead when he bamboozled the Sparta defence and fired in a dangerous low cross that was scrambled behind to safety.

Wayne Rooney, while surely not expecting to continue where he left off against Fenerbahçe, twice went close in the first half, but the Czechs were well aware of their own need to get something out of the game and were able to break with ease. Karel Poborsky, in particular, was giving Gabriel Heinze one of his toughest outings yet in a Red shirt and the United old boy forced a fine save from Roy Carroll, with Jiri Homola heading against the crossbar from the resulting corner.

It was a similar story in the second half. Poborsky almost caught Carroll out after the restart, while United came the closest to breaking the deadlock on the hour mark. Wayne Rooney found the goal-line and placed a fine ball to John O'Shea, who poked a shot onto the roof of the net, leaving United fans wondering what might have happened had the roles been reversed.

Marked men: Rooney and Ruud try to keep ahead of the game

Carroll pulled off a number of instinctive saves as Sparta chased the game, but United could have won it at the death, when Ruud van Nistelrooy swung in a wicked cross that was too quick even for the sharp footballing brain of substitute Cristiano Ronaldo. Following the customary wait after the final whistle, the well-oiled United supporters were singing heartily as they wound their way into the Prague night, content at seeing the Reds maintain this season's unbeaten record in Europe, and still in a prime position to qualify from Group D.

**League Group D**
Tuesday 19 October 2004
**Toyota Arena**
Attendance 20,654
**Referee: Massimo de Santis**

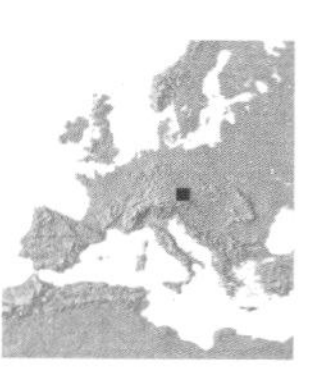

## MAN OF THE MATCH

**ROY CARROLL**

Carroll had been restored to the Northern Ireland side the week before and the big Ulsterman showed why international boss Lawrie Sanchez and Sir Alex Ferguson kept faith in him with a string of excellent saves. On the touchline Sparta coach Frantisek Straka looked on in disbelief as Carroll continually thwarted his attackers to keep a clean sheet and earn an important point for the Reds.

## MATCH FACTS

**AC SPARTA PRAHA**
Blazek; Pergl, Kovac, Homola, Petras (Cech 81); Poborsky, Sivok, Zelenka (Simak 81), Urbanek; Jun (Meduna 74), Vorisek
**Subs not used** Bicik, Michalik, Koubsky, Pacanda **Booked** Kovac

**MANCHESTER UNITED**
Carroll; G Neville, Brown, Silvestre, Heinze; Miller, Scholes, O'Shea, Giggs (Ronaldo 78); Rooney (Saha 78), van Nistelrooy
**Subs not used** Ricardo, P Neville, Smith, Kleberson, Djemba-Djemba
**Booked** Miller, Scholes

| Manchester United | | AC Sparta Praha |
|---|---|---|
| 50% | POSSESSION | 50% |
| 1 | SHOTS ON TARGET | 4 |
| 4 | SHOTS OFF TARGET | 3 |
| 9 | CORNERS | 8 |
| 17 | FOULS | 17 |
| 1 | OFFSIDES | 1 |

### UEFA CHAMPIONS LEAGUE GROUP STAGE
RESULTS 19/10/04 & 20/10/04

| | | |
|---|---|---|
| **GROUP A** | | |
| Liverpool | 0-0 | Deportivo |
| Monaco | 2-1 | Olympiakos |
| **GROUP B** | | |
| Leverkusen | 3-1 | Roma |
| Real Madrid | 1-0 | Dynamo Kyiv |
| **GROUP C** | | |
| Ajax | 3-0 | Maccabi Tel Aviv |
| Juventus | 1-0 | Bayern |
| **GROUP D** | | |
| Fenerbahçe | 1-3 | Lyon |
| **GROUP E** | | |
| Pananthinaikos | 2-2 | Arsenal |
| Rosenberg | 1-2 | PSV |
| **GROUP F** | | |
| Milan | 1-0 | Barcelona |
| Shakhtar | 3-0 | Celtic |
| **GROUP G** | | |
| Anderlecht | 1-2 | Bremen |
| Valencia | 1-5 | Internazionale |
| **GROUP H** | | |
| Chelsea | 2-0 | CSKA Moskva |
| PSG | 2-0 | Porto |

### GROUP D TABLE
After Matchday 3

| | P | PTS |
|---|---|---|
| 1. Olympique Lyonnais | 3 | 7 |
| 2. Manchester United | 3 | 5 |
| 3. Fenerbahçe | 3 | 3 |
| 4. Sparta Praha | 3 | 1 |

# Manchester United 4

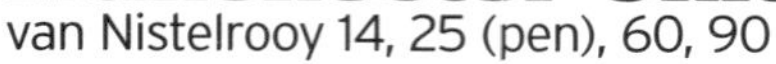

van Nistelrooy 14, 25 (pen), 60, 90

# AC Sparta Praha 1

Zelenka 53

**Ruud van Nistelrooy** became the first United player since Denis Law to score four goals in a European match, taking his UEFA Champions League scoring record to an incredible 35 goals in 36 matches. The Dutchman struck twice in each half to help the Reds see off the spirited challenge of Czech champions Sparta Praha and move one step closer to qualification for the knockout stage.

The signs of this match being full of goals were there right from the start. Tomás Sivok drove a powerful shot just over Roy Carroll's bar inside two minutes, then Gabriel Heinze thumped an Exocet of his own against the Sparta woodwork two minutes later. The biggest surprise was that it took until the 14th minute for the deadlock to be broken.

The scorer was somewhat less surprising. The Reds' number 10 capitalised on a Jiri Homola aberration – one of the worst back passes you are likely to see – and rounded Prague keeper Jaromír Blazek to stroke the ball into the empty net from 12 yards.

Just 11 minutes later the Dutchman made Sparta pay for their defensive errors again, this time from the penalty spot, after Paul Scholes had been upended by Martin Petras. Van Nistelrooy confidently stepped up to send Blazek the wrong way.

Sparta rallied after the break and pulled one back through Lukás Zelenka to give themselves hope, but the two-goal margin was soon restored. A long ball from Heinze bounced over Radoslav Kovác for Ruud to run through and loop the ball over the keeper. Amazingly, given his superb scoring

Flying Dutchman: Ruud receives a pat on the back from Ronaldo after matching the King's four goal haul

**League Group D**
Wednesday 3 November 2004
**Old Trafford**
Attendance 66,706
**Referee: Alain Hamer**

record, this was his first hat-trick in Europe for Manchester United.

The game's next major talking point was the sending off of Karel Poborsky. He never established himself as a regular during his two years at OT, but received a standing ovation from the crowd as he left the pitch. In injury time van Nistelrooy added another – this time a tap-in from two yards – to become the first player since the Lawman to net four goals in a European match. And just as Waterford had bemoaned the presence of Law on the pitch that night in 1968, so the Sparta players must have been sick of the sight of Ruud van Nistelrooy.

## MAN OF THE MATCH

**RUUD VAN NISTELROOY**

Did you really need to ask? The Dutchman's sixth hat-trick for the Reds showed he was back to his prolific best. No wonder Sir Alex likened him to the great European finishers of all-time like Johan Cruyff, Gerd Müller and Alfredo Di Stefano. Pre-match the manager had bemoaned United's early season lack of firepower and even threatened to pick himself. But after Ruud singlehandedly sunk Sparta, Sir Alex opted to keep his old striking boots in the cupboard.

## MATCH FACTS

**MANCHESTER UNITED**

Carroll; G Neville, Ferdinand, Brown, Heinze; Miller, Keane, Scholes (P Neville 70), Ronaldo (Kleberson 70); Rooney, van Nistelrooy
**Subs not used** Howard, Saha, Giggs, Smith, Djemba-Djemba
**Booked** Brown, Miller

**AC SPARTA PRAHA**

Blazek; Pergl, Homola, Kovac, Petrás; Sivok, Vorísek (Meduna 72), Poborsky, Zelenka; Urbánek (Simák 82), Jun (Pacanda 81)
**Subs not used** Bicík, Michalik, Cech, Koubsky **Booked** Poborsky, Homola **Sent off** Poborsky

| Man Utd | | Sparta |
|---|---|---|
| 61% | POSSESSION | 39% |
| 9 | SHOTS ON TARGET | 7 |
| 6 | SHOTS OFF TARGET | 10 |
| 6 | CORNERS | 7 |
| 18 | FOULS | 22 |
| 3 | OFFSIDES | 1 |

**UEFA CHAMPIONS LEAGUE GROUP STAGE**
RESULTS 2/11/04 & 3/11/04

| | | |
|---|---|---|
| **GROUP A** | | |
| Deportivo | 0-1 | Liverpool |
| Olympiakos | 1-0 | Monaco |
| **GROUP B** | | |
| Dynamo Kyiv | 2-2 | Real Madrid |
| Roma | 1-1 | Leverkusen |
| **GROUP C** | | |
| Bayern | 0-1 | Juventus |
| Maccabi Tel Aviv | 2-1 | Ajax |
| **GROUP D** | | |
| Lyon | 4-2 | Fenerbahçe |
| **GROUP E** | | |
| Arsenal | 1-1 | Panathinaikos |
| PSV | 1-0 | Rosenberg |
| **GROUP F** | | |
| Barcelona | 2-1 | Milan |
| Celtic | 1-0 | Shakhtar |
| **GROUP G** | | |
| Bremen | 5-1 | Anderlecht |
| Internazionale | 0-0 | Valencia |
| **GROUP H** | | |
| CSKA Moskva | 0-1 | Chelsea |
| Porto | 0-0 | PSG |

**GROUP D TABLE**
After Matchday 4

| | P | PTS |
|---|---|---|
| 1. Olympique Lyonnais | 4 | 10 |
| 2. Manchester United | 4 | 8 |
| 3. Fenerbahçe | 4 | 3 |
| 4. Sparta Praha | 4 | 1 |

# Manchester United 2

G Neville 19, van Nistelrooy 53

# Olympique Lyonnais 1

Diarra 40

**The game may have** been about Champions League qualification and maintaining a run of good form, but the occasion focused on one man; Sir Alex Ferguson.

Such has been the success he's enjoyed, and the entertainment his players have produced over the past 18 years, anything other than victory on his big night would have been unthinkable. Yet, despite the ballyhoo surrounding his landmark 1,000th match, Sir Alex was not taking victory for granted. The Group D leaders, undefeated so far in the competition, arrived at OT determined to play the party poopers.

It soon became clear the Reds were in no mood to let them. In the 12th minute Wayne Rooney posted a message of intent with a low drive from 20 yards that beat Lyon keeper Nicolas Puydebois, only to thump against the post and bounce clear. Then, seven minutes later, Gary Neville – a doubt before the game with a virus – began and ended a move that gave the Reds a deserved lead. As Wes Brown limbered up to replace him, the full back took a quick free kick and played a one-two with Ronaldo. When Lyon failed to clear Alan Smith's cross, the ball dropped to Neville and he made no mistake from six yards.

The goal stung Lyon into life but their slick football created only one real effort and the Reds looked set for a half-time lead. But then disaster struck for Roy Carroll. The Ulsterman looked to have a long-range effort from Mahamadou Diarra well covered, only to let the ball slip over his left shoulder and into the net. Lyon were level.

The United at the start of the season may have struggled to recover from such a blow but not the rejuvenated Reds. Seven minutes after the break Rio Ferdinand took the ball inside the Lyon box, skipped around a defender, then chipped to the far post. With Ruud van Nistelrooy on the end of the cross – the man Sir Alex says is the best finisher he's ever managed – there was only ever going to be one result. He headed into the corner for a 2-1 lead.

The Dutchman hit a post soon after, following a superb pass from the lively Rooney, as United threatened a third. When the goal didn't materialise the final stages became a little nervy but the rearguard held out to provide Sir Alex with the perfect present on his big night; safe passage to the Champions League knockout stage.

French lieutenants: on a night to remember for Sir Alex, everyone played his part

League Group D
Tuesday 23 November 2004
Old Trafford
Attendance 66,398
Referee: Kim Milton Nielsen

## MAN OF THE MATCH

**ROY KEANE**
Maintained his run of impressive form with a supremely controlled display that offered both protection to his defence and direction to the attack. He'll be the first to admit he can no longer cover every blade of grass, but he remains the heartbeat of the team and an inspiration to his younger team-mates. The Reds' skipper revelled in having Scholes, Smith, Rooney and Ronaldo alongside him.

## MATCH FACTS

**MANCHESTER UNITED**
Carroll; G Neville (Brown 45), Ferdinand, Silvestre, Heinze; Smith, Keane (Fortune 90), Scholes, Ronaldo; Rooney, van Nistelrooy (Fletcher 71)
**Subs not used** Howard, Bellion, Djemba-Djemba, O'Shea
**Booked** Keane

**OLYMPIQUE LYONNAIS**
Puydebois; Réveillère, Diatta, Cris, Berthold; Govou (Wiltord 60), Essien, Diarra, Juninho, Frau (Bergougnoux 72); Nilmar (Malouda 72) **Subs not used** Jaccard, Clément, Gomez, Hima

| Man Utd | | Lyon |
|---|---|---|
| 51% | POSSESSION | 49% |
| 3 | SHOTS ON TARGET | 2 |
| 10 | SHOTS OFF TARGET | 8 |
| 5 | CORNERS | 6 |
| 13 | FOULS | 16 |
| 3 | OFFSIDES | 2 |

### UEFA CHAMPIONS LEAGUE GROUP STAGE
RESULTS 23/11/04 & 24/11/04

| | | |
|---|---|---|
| **GROUP A** | | |
| Monaco | 1-0 | Liverpool |
| Olympiakos | 1-0 | Deportivo |
| **GROUP B** | | |
| Dynamo Kyiv | 2-0 | Roma |
| Real Madrid | 1-1 | Leverkusen |
| **GROUP C** | | |
| Bayern | 5-1 | Maccabi Tel Aviv |
| Juventus | 1-0 | Ajax |
| **GROUP D** | | |
| Sparta | 0-1 | Fenerbahçe |
| **GROUP E** | | |
| PSV | 1-1 | Arsenal |
| Rosenborg | 2-2 | Panathinaikos |
| **GROUP F** | | |
| Barcelona | 1-1 | Celtic |
| Milan | 4-0 | Shakhtar |
| **GROUP G** | | |
| Anderlecht | 1-2 | Valencia |
| Bremen | 1-1 | Internazionale |
| **GROUP H** | | |
| Chelsea | 0-0 | PSG |
| CSKA Moskva | 0-1 | Porto |

### GROUP D TABLE
After Matchday 5

| | P | PTS |
|---|---|---|
| 1 Manchester United | 5 | 11 |
| 2. Olympique Lyonnais | 5 | 10 |
| 3. Fenerbahçe | 5 | 6 |
| 4. Sparta Praha | 5 | 1 |

# Fenerbahçe SK 3

Tuncay 46, 62, 90

# Manchester United 0

**Anyone casting** a glance at the squad that boarded the plane for Istanbul could have been forgiven for thinking the Carling Cup had reconvened in Turkey. But, as the Reds were already assured of a berth in the next round of the Champions League, Sir Alex opted to gift his young charges an early Christmas present: a runout in Europe.

Cristiano Ronaldo was the sole survivor from the team that brushed Southampton aside four days earlier, although Eric Djemba-Djemba and David Bellion played in the corresponding fixture at Old Trafford in September. "It's not my recognised first team, but there'll be nine internationals starting," said Sir Alex. "I have 25 players and I must give them match practice."

A practice match was not what the Turkish league leaders had in mind. Fenerbahçe were also without key men, most notably Pierre van Hooijdonk. Yet the hosts, despite already qualifying for the UEFA Cup, were in no mood to make up the numbers. Revenge for the 6-2 drubbing in Manchester was on the menu and Sanli Tuncay served it up with a well taken hat-trick in front of a very vocal crowd.

In the first half the youngsters held their own, Ronaldo starting brightly and Bellion and Kieran Richardson trying their luck from distance. However, Fener kept on the offensive, forcing United to concede a rash of free kicks. Indeed, the Brazilian Alex seemed to spend much of the first half practising his dead-ball technique. Two minutes after the restart Tuncay acrobatically opened his account, his overhead kick from Umit Ozat's cross giving Tim Howard no chance as it crashed in off the underside of the bar. The Reds could have grabbed an early equaliser but some neat passing between Darren Fletcher, Ronaldo, Bellion and Richardson fizzled out on the edge of the area.

Youth opportunity: with qualification assured, Sir Alex opted for a young United side in the Turkish capital

Fener went on the counter-attack and minutes later Richardson gave away a free kick just outside the box. Tuncay nodded home his second from Alex's perfect delivery. He completed his hat-trick at the death after the Reds were caught on the break. The scoreline could have been worse but substitute Gerard Piqué, in his second senior game, cleared off the line to spare United any further blushes.

It might have been a night to delight the Turks, but for a young United team, with an average age just 23, it was another important step along the learning curve.

**League Group D**
Wednesday 8 December 2004
**Sükrü Saraçoglu**
Attendance 35,000
**Referee: Arturo Dauden Ibañez**

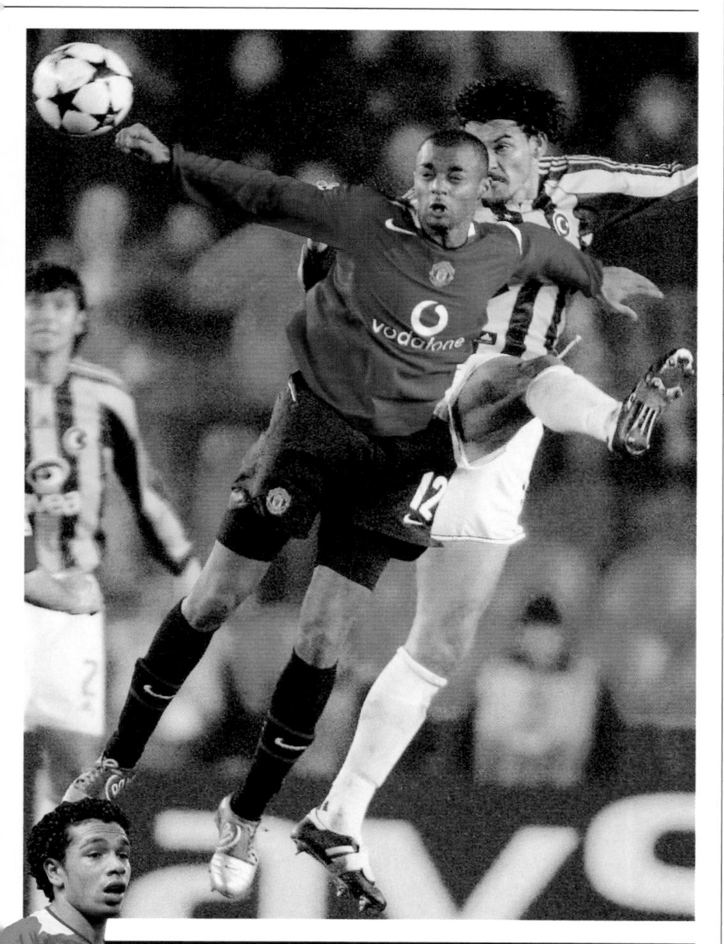


## MAN OF THE MATCH

### KIERAN RICHARDSON

There were some plus points to bring back from defeat on the banks of the Bosphorus. Tim Howard had a good first half, keeping the Reds in the match with some fine saves, and Phil Neville threw himself into every tackle. But among United's young guard Richardson stood out, particularly in the first half, where his battling performance showed that the commitment was there, even if the goals weren't.

## MATCH FACTS

### FENERBAHÇE SK

Rüstu; Turaci, Luciano, Cetin, Ozat; Balci (Yozgatli 71), Sahin, Aurelio, Tuncay (Fabiano 90); Alex, Marcio Nobre (Akin 90) **Subs not used** Rodriguez, Hacioglu, Erdogdu, Sergen **Booked** Aurelio

### MANCHESTER UNITED

Howard; P Neville, Brown (Piqué 66), O'Shea, Fortune; Ronaldo, Djemba-Djemba, Fletcher, Richardson (Spector 68), Miller (Eagles 77); Bellion **Subs not used** Ricardo, Jones, McShane, Ebanks-Blake **Booked** Djemba- Djemba

| Man Utd | | Fenerbahçe |
|---|---|---|
| 52% | POSSESSION | 48% |
| 2 | SHOTS ON TARGET | 6 |
| 2 | SHOTS OFF TARGET | 4 |
| 2 | CORNERS | 3 |
| 19 | FOULS | 19 |
| 4 | OFFSIDES | 1 |

### UEFA CHAMPIONS LEAGUE GROUP STAGE

RESULTS 7/12/04 & 8/12/04

| | | |
|---|---|---|
| **GROUP A** | | |
| Deportivo | 0-5 | Monaco |
| Liverpool | 3-1 | Olympiakos |
| **GROUP B** | | |
| Leverkusen | 3-0 | Dynamo Kyiv |
| Roma | 0-3 | Real Madrid |
| **GROUP C** | | |
| Ajax | 2-2 | Bayern |
| Maccabi Tel Aviv | 1-1 | Juventus |
| **GROUP D** | | |
| Lyon | 5-0 | Sparta |
| **GROUP E** | | |
| Arsenal | 5-1 | Rosenborg |
| Panathinaikos | 4-1 | PSV |
| **GROUP F** | | |
| Celtic | 0-0 | Milan |
| Shakhtar | 2-0 | Barcelona |
| **GROUP G** | | |
| Internazionale | 3-0 | Anderlecht |
| Valencia | 0-2 | Bremen |
| **GROUP H** | | |
| Porto | 2-1 | Chelsea |
| PSG | 1-3 | CSKA Moskva |

### GROUP D TABLE

After Matchday 6

| | P | PTS |
|---|---|---|
| 1. Olympique Lyonnais | 6 | 13 |
| 2. Manchester United | 6 | 11 |
| 3. Fenerbahçe | 6 | 9 |
| 4. Sparta Praha | 6 | 1 |

vodafone

# UEFA CHAMPIONS LEAGUE KNOCKOUT PHASE

## While Old Trafford welcomed the mighty Milan, Europe's finest were locking horns in a bid to win a coveted quarter-final slot...

**Against a** Milan side full of world-class performers, United were always going to need a top-drawer performance to give themselves a fighting chance for the second leg. And despite not firing on all cylinders they were looking good to at least deny Milan an away goal. All that changed, of course, when Hernan Crespo lashed the ball home after Roy Carroll's failure to hold Clarence Seedorf's shot. Milan didn't have things all their own way in the return at the Giuseppe Meazza, and had Ryan Giggs's first-half shot gone in off the post rather than spun away to safety, it would have been game on. Instead, sadly, it was Crespo who again proved the man for the big occasion and Milan who went marching on.

It was better news for two other English clubs in the competition. Chelsea went down 2-1 to Barcelona in the Nou Camp, but then won 4-2 in an astonishing game at Stamford Bridge: the Blues went 3-0 up inside 20 minutes but Barça, inspired by some Ronaldinho magic, roared back and looked set for the quarter-finals until John Terry headed a fourth for Chelsea 14 minutes from time. Liverpool, meanwhile, made light of a late Leverkusen goal at Anfield, winning 3-1 in Germany to take the tie 6-2 on aggregate. Like United, Arsenal went out, after a 3-2 aggregate defeat to Bayern Munich.

Qualification was achieved with no real dramas for PSV Eindhoven, Internazionale and Juventus (the latter despatching Real Madrid's *galacticos*); but Lyon's 10-2 aggregate win over Werder Bremen was more redolent of a qualifying-round score than the knockout stages.

### ROUND OF 16 FIXTURES

| | | |
|---|---|---|
| 23 FEBRUARY | AC MILAN | HOME |
| 8 MARCH | AC MILAN | AWAY |

### MANCHESTER UNITED IN THE KNOCKOUT PHASE...

**146,119** watched United play 2 games

**0** goals were scored

**1,514** miles were travelled by United going to and from Milan

United fielded **16** players

**2** goals were conceded

### PLAYER OF THE ROUND RIO FERDINAND

While Milan's progress to the Champions League quarter-finals was relatively smooth, it was never easy. And much of that was down to the efforts of the Reds' No.5. In the first leg, the talents of Rui Costa, Kaka and Hernan Crespo largely came to nothing against a defence marshalled supremely by the England centre half. In the return at the Giuseppe Meazza, it was more of the same. It took a sublime header by Crespo to break the deadlock as Ferdinand's intuitive reading of the game snuffed out the home side's attacking initiatives time after time. A stunning last-ditch tackle had already denied Crespo as Milan tried to take advantage of being a man up (Ryan Giggs having left the field for treatment) and Rio's defensive heroics stopped United's European dream being extinguished far earlier than it might otherwise have been.

# Manchester United 0

# Milan 1

Crespo 78

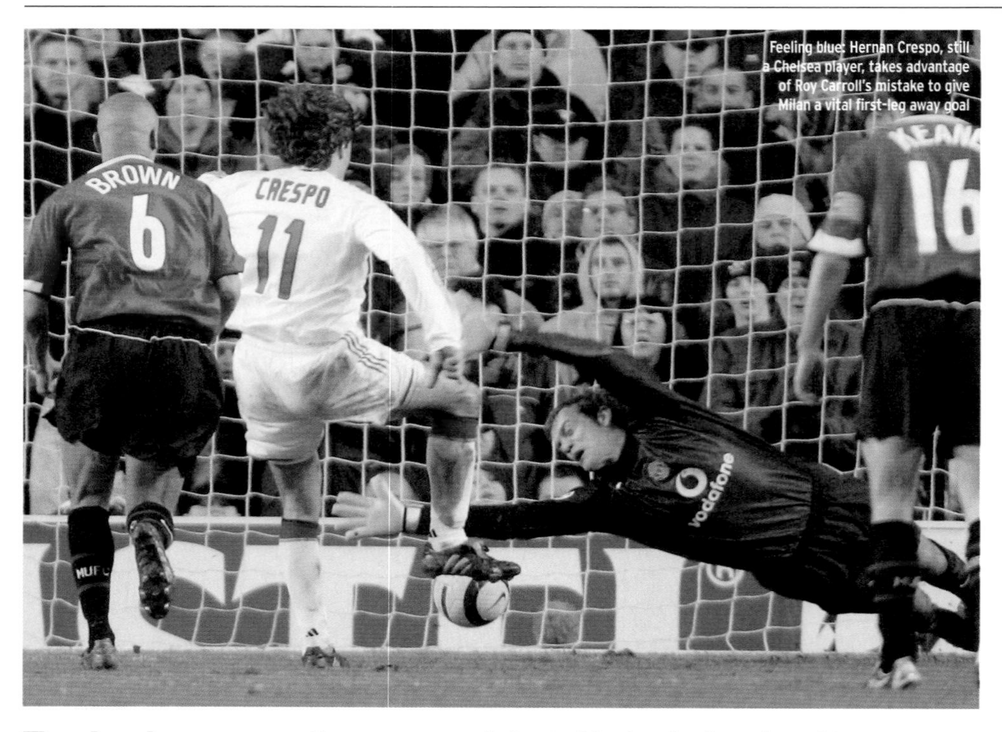


Feeling blue: Hernan Crespo, still a Chelsea player, takes advantage of Roy Carroll's mistake to give Milan a vital first-leg away goal

**There have been** some great European nights at Old Trafford down the years, but this was not one of them. Before the game, optimism was high that the Reds' excellent form – just two defeats in 27 matches – would see Sir Alex's charges take a lead to the San Siro. Milan had other ideas.

In the past decade Juventus, Fiorentina and Internazionale have all been seen off at Old Trafford. And for all their illustrious history, Milan's failure to have won a European match on English soil before seemed a promising omen. However, one look at the visitors' line-up – even without Jaap Stam, injured in the warm-up, and the missing Andriy Shevchenko – showed it was going to be a difficult night.

Sir Alex had predicted an open game, and he was spot on. Paul Scholes went close for United – blazing wide from 12 yards when you'd put your mortgage on him to score – and Clarence Seedorf's rifled free kick clipped the top of the crossbar.

Gradually Milan took control of midfield, with Gattuso and Pirlo keeping possession brilliantly, restricting United to the counter-attack. Cristiano Ronaldo looked the Reds' most likely outlet for a goal, and he nearly created one eight minutes before half-time. After a weaving run he found Quinton

**First knockout round, first leg**
Wednesday 23 February 2005
**Old Trafford**
Attendance 67, 162
**Referee: Manuel González**

Fortune with a superb pass through the middle. The South African, at full stretch, chipped the ball goalwards over Milan stopper Dida. But his effort drifted agonisingly wide of the right post.

The second half was as open as the first, but still United struggled to find top form. Scholes, Roy Keane and Ryan Giggs – who had all produced star performances in the run up to this match – were unable to impose themselves and Milan increased the tempo. Midway through the half Rui Costa created a chance for Crespo but the striker, on loan from Chelsea, blazed his shot high into the crowd. However, he was to prove far more clinical a few moments later.

Just 12 minutes from time Roy Carroll spilt a 20-yard strike from Seedorf, after the Dutchman had been given too much time and space to tee up his shot. As the ball cannoned off Carroll's chest, the Argentinian pounced to thump the ball into the empty United net. Old Trafford fell instantly silent. Stunned.

Despite the introduction of Ruud van Nistelrooy (who saw one header fly just wide of the post) with just under half an hour left, United didn't really look like regaining parity. Milan headed home to the Giuseppe Meazza with a crucial advantage.

## MAN OF THE MATCH

**GABRIEL HEINZE**

Fortune and Keane battled manfully and Brown put in a strong performance, but Heinze was United's star performer. He contained Cafu's attacking intent and made several timely clearances in the second half when Milan were most threatening. It wasn't his best game, but he never stopped trying. A fine quality that Reds have grown accustomed to.

## MATCH FACTS

**MANCHESTER UNITED**
Carroll; G Neville (Silvestre 80), Ferdinand, Brown, Heinze; Ronaldo (van Nistelrooy 62), Scholes, Keane, Fortune (Saha 80); Giggs, Rooney
**Subs not used** Howard, P Neville, Smith, O'Shea
**Booked** Fortune

**MILAN**
Dida; Cafu (Costacurta 86), Nesta, Maldini, Kaladze; Gattuso, Pirlo (Ambrosini 84), Seedorf, Rui Costa, Kaka (Serginho 90); Crespo
**Subs not used** Abbiati, Tomasson, Dhorasoo **Booked** Nesta

| Man Utd | | Milan |
|---|---|---|
| 51% | POSSESSION | 49% |
| 1 | SHOTS ON TARGET | 3 |
| 7 | SHOTS OFF TARGET | 7 |
| 3 | CORNERS | 7 |
| 12 | FOULS | 20 |
| 1 | OFFSIDES | 1 |

**UEFA CHAMPIONS LEAGUE FIRST KNOCKOUT ROUND FIRST LEG**
RESULTS 22/2/05 & 23/2/05

| | | |
|---|---|---|
| Barcelona | 2-1 | Chelsea |
| Bayern | 3-1 | Arsenal |
| FC Porto | 1-1 | Inter Milan |
| Liverpool | 3-1 | Leverkusen |
| PSV | 1-0 | Monaco |
| Real Madrid | 1-0 | Juventus |
| Werder Bremen | 0-3 | Lyon |

*"It was a match of high quality. They played an open game, which suggests they thought their best chance was here. If we'd gone in front we'd have had less work to do, but the opportunities we had in the first half were rushed and we failed to take advantage."*
**SIR ALEX FERGUSON**

# Milan 1

Crespo 61

# Manchester United 0

**It was always going** to be an uphill struggle. Statistics ominously revealed no English team had beaten Milan in their own backyard in nine attempts and the Giuseppe Meazza was packed to the rafters in hope of a perfect 10; a sell-out for the first time in the Champions League, too. And, roared on by their passionate support, the Italians gave a lesson in how to defend a one-goal advantage.

For the first time since October's 2-0 win over Arsenal, Sir Alex Ferguson fielded Ruud van Nistelrooy with Wayne Rooney, Ryan Giggs, Paul Scholes and Cristiano Ronaldo in support. Despite this mouthwatering line-up, the *rossoneri* showed their pedigree from the start, snaffling out any threat of attack. Roy Keane had an early shot from distance, but whenever the Reds got the slightest sniff of possession, two players in red and black were soon in close attendance.

Sir Alex had hinted beforehand that he'd have been happy if the tie was goalless with 20 minutes left, hoping Milan's ageing backline might creak under pressure, but it wasn't to be. Paolo Maldini might have cemented a place in Milan's first team when Wayne Rooney was still in nappies, but experience won out against enthusiasm.

Just before the half-hour mark, however, it looked for one tantalising moment that it might be the Reds' night after all. In United's first, and only, real clear-cut chance, van Nistelrooy fed the perfect pass to Giggs on the left, and for once the world's best defence was breached. Giggs looked to have done everything right as his shot evaded the diving Dida – but it glanced agonisingly off the post and rebounded to safety. And with the Welshman forced from the field with just over half an hour remaining, his nose bloodied after a clash with Gennaro Gattuso, there was no chance of a repeat showing.

With Maldini, Jaap Stam, Alessandro Nesta and Cafu producing a team performance that saw Milan installed as favourites for the trophy, it was going to need something very special to claw a goal back. And when Hernan Crespo looped a perfectly weighted header over Tim Howard from a Cafu cross just past the hour mark, that hill started to look more like a mountain.

On another day, a fully match-fit Dutch striker might have converted the slim chances that came his way in either half, but Milan were well worth their win. On this kind of form, it would take a very brave man to back against them reaching a second final in three years.

**First knockout round, second leg**
Tuesday 8 March 2005
**Giuseppe Meazza Stadium**
Attendance 78,957
**Referee: Herbert Fandel**

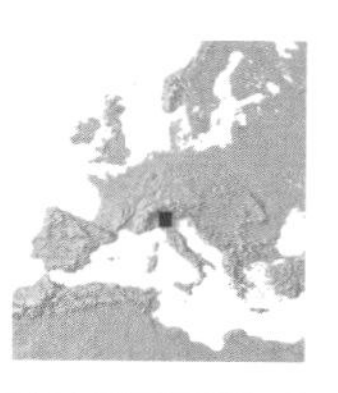

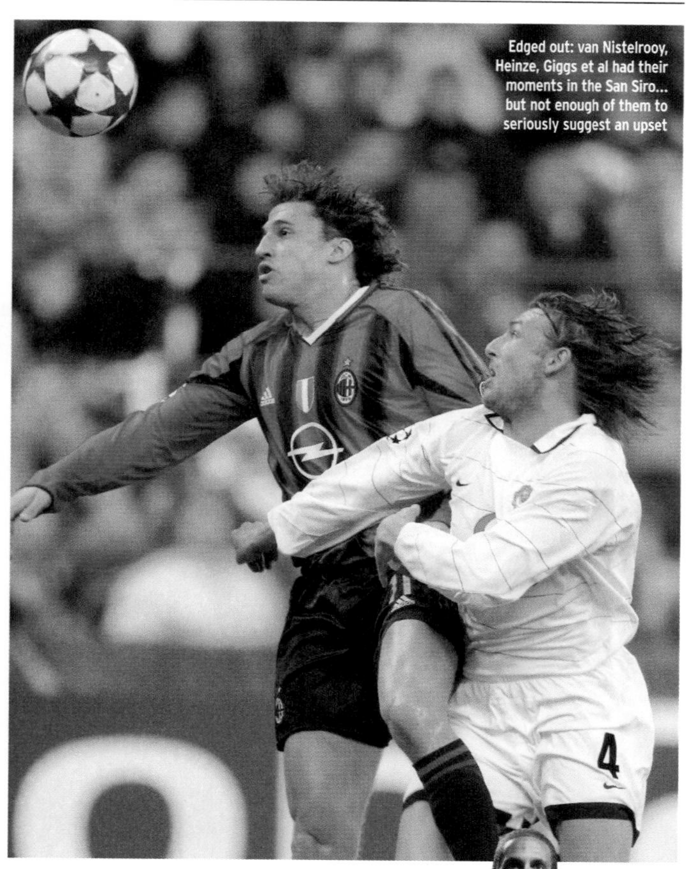

Edged out: van Nistelrooy, Heinze, Giggs et al had their moments in the San Siro... but not enough of them to seriously suggest an upset

## MAN OF THE MATCH

**RIO FERDINAND**

Even in comparison with the jewel-encrusted Milan backline, the performance of our own unruffled No.5 in the San Siro cauldron drew more than its share of plaudits. Relaxed and in control throughout, Rio was instrumental in preventing a bigger winning margin, and his telling tackles were every bit as classy as the reception United fans gave Jaap Stam at the end.

## MATCH FACTS

**MILAN**
Dida; Cafu, Nesta, Stam, Maldini; Gattuso (Costacurta 89), Pirlo, Seedorf, Rui Costa (Dhorasoo 85); Kaka, Crespo (Ambrosini 78)
**Subs not used** Abbiati, Inzaghi, Tomasson, Serginho

**MANCHESTER UNITED**
Howard; Brown (Smith 85), Ferdinand, Silvestre, Heinze; Ronaldo, Keane, Scholes, Giggs (Fortune 57); Rooney, van Nistelrooy
**Subs not used** Carroll, P Neville, Bellion, Miller, O'Shea
**Booked** Fortune

| Man Utd | | Milan |
|---|---|---|
| 53% | POSSESSION | 47% |
| 0 | SHOTS ON TARGET | 3 |
| 9 | SHOTS OFF TARGET | 8 |
| 3 | CORNERS | 3 |
| 16 | FOULS | 14 |
| 2 | OFFSIDES | 9 |

**UEFA CHAMPIONS LEAGUE FIRST KNOCKOUT ROUND, SECOND LEG**
08/03/05, 09/03/05 & 15/03/05

| | | |
|---|---|---|
| Arsenal | 1-0 | Bayern |
| Chelsea | 4-2 | Barcelona |
| Internazionale | 3-1 | Porto |
| Juventus | 2-0 | Real Madrid |
| Leverkusen | 1-3 | Liverpool |
| Lyon | 7-2 | Bremen |
| Monaco | 0-2 | PSV |

*“If you look at the two games [against Milan] we had six good chances and we didn't take any of them. That is what has decided the tie overall. I have no complaints about the way my team played... we just didn't get the goal that could have changed the game.”*

**SIR ALEX FERGUSON**

VIEIRA
4
RONALDO
7

# FA CUP

ARAGE
Co-operative Group
778
co.uk
PRODUCTION
20
7
Ba
rcard
0 1 2
7 1 1 1 7

# FA CUP OPENING ROUNDS

## Non-league opposition at OT should have been a formality, but plucky Exeter showed the Cup hasn't lost its capacity for shocks

**When the third** round draw saw Conference side Exeter City drawn away at OT, few gave them a prayer. Sir Alex fielded an inexperienced line-up, and was left ruing his decision as the West Country side earned themselves a second shot at the Cup holders with a 0-0 draw.

The Reds fielded a much stronger line-up for the replay in Devon, but despite Cristiano Ronaldo's early strike, the expected goal avalanche never materialised, and the non-league side gave United some tense moments before Wayne Rooney sealed a 2-0 win with just three minutes remaining. Overall, the third round provided few genuine shocks, though Manchester City went down 1-0 in a local derby with Oldham, and Rafael Benitez's team selection backfired as Liverpool lost by the same scoreline at Burnley.

There was to be no similar mistake in round four, when Steve McLaren's Middlesbrough were the visitors. Boro have often been a thorn in United's side in the Premiership, but a goal from John O'Shea in the tenth minute settled any early nerves and a spectacular double strike from Wayne Rooney gave the Reds a comfortable 3-0 win.

Rooney was the focus of attention again when the draw for the fifth round gave him the opportunity of a quick return to Everton, the team he had left just five months earlier. Amid much hype, and more than a little hostility from the Toffees fans who once idolised him, United calmly negotiated a tricky tie, goals from Quinton Fortune and Ronaldo sealing a place in the last eight. Elsewhere, Chelsea's bid for four trophies finished, as Patrick Kluivert gave Newcastle a 1-0 win.

### FA CUP FIXTURES

| | | |
|---|---|---|
| 8 JAN | EXETER CITY | HOME |
| 19 JAN | EXETER CITY | AWAY |
| 29 JAN | MIDDLESBROUGH | HOME |
| 19 FEB | EVERTON | AWAY |

### IN THE FA CUP 3RD, 4TH AND 5TH ROUNDS

**182,499** Watched United play 4 games

**7** goals were scored

**540** miles were travelled by United going to and from games

United fielded **27** players

**0** goals were conceded

### GOAL OF THE FA CUP WAYNE ROONEY v MIDDLESBROUGH 29/1/05

Spectacular though his debut against Fenerbahçe back in September was, Wayne Rooney had struggled to hit those heights since. By the time Middlesbrough arrived at OT for the fourth round Cup tie, Rooney was in need of something to remind the Reds faithful just what he was capable of, and boy, what a reminder! In an outstanding second half display, Rooney caused problems for Boro throughout, and the goal his performance deserved eventually arrived in the 67th minute. As United broke, Rooney collected Gary Neville's through ball and, spotting Boro keeper Mark Schwarzer off his line, chipped him from 30 yards. Point proven? Not quite. There was still time for an even better strike. In the 82nd minute, Louis Saha flicked a long ball towards Rooney, who smashed a spectacular first-time volley into the net.

## MATCH FACTS

**The FA Cup**
Saturday 8 January 2005
**Old Trafford**
Attendance 67,551
**Referee: Phil Dowd**

MANCHESTER UNITED
Howard; P Neville, Brown, Piqué, Spector; Eagles (Ronaldo 63), Djemba-Djemba, Jones, Miller (Scholes 63); Bellion (Smith 76), Richardson
**Subs not used** Heinze, Ricardo

EXETER CITY
Jones; Hiley, Sawyer, Gaia, Jeannin; Martin, Clay (Ampadu 66), Taylor (Edwards 89), Moxey; Devine, Flack (Afful 74)
**Subs not used** Rice, Sheldon

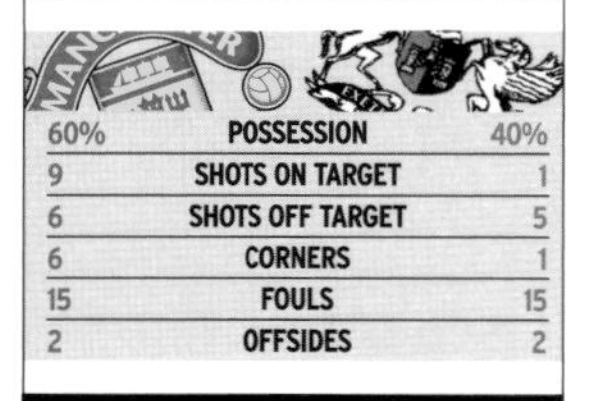

| 60% | POSSESSION | 40% |
|---|---|---|
| 9 | SHOTS ON TARGET | 1 |
| 6 | SHOTS OFF TARGET | 5 |
| 6 | CORNERS | 1 |
| 15 | FOULS | 15 |
| 2 | OFFSIDES | 2 |

## MAN OF THE MATCH

DAVID JONES
The 20-year-old, making his first start for the Reds, grew in confidence as the game progressed and was one of the few players to come out of the game with significant credit. His neat and tidy football overshadowed that of his senior midfield partners and having been involved in much of the good play United produced, can be pleased with his full debut, if not the result.

# Manchester United 0

# Exeter City 0

Man-marked: Kieran Richardson gets close attention from Exeter

**"I apologise to the fans.** They did not deserve that," said Sir Alex after seeing his side held by Nationwide Conference side Exeter City. "In my 18 years at this club, that was the worst performance ever in the FA Cup." The boss had felt confident enough in his young reserves to make 10 changes from the side held 0-0 by Spurs four days earlier. It was not a case of underestimating Exeter, merely showing faith in a group of emerging players and reserves he believed to be more than capable of the task... but it didn't work out as he'd hoped.

United made the livelier start but half-chances for lone striker David Bellion were easily saved by Exeter keeper Paul Jones and without the expected early onslaught, the visitors slowly grew in confidence. Former United youngster Andy Taylor went close to a fairytale goal, hitting the side netting with a free kick. Then Dean Moxey almost gave the visitors a shock lead on the stroke of half-time.

While the 9,000 travelling Exeter fans were enjoying what they were seeing, the rest of OT expected an improvement after the break. But it was only when internationals Paul Scholes, Cristiano Ronaldo and Alan Smith were introduced that the Reds actually threatened a goal. Even the senior stars, however, could not conjure a late winner.

Exeter boss Alex Inglethorpe watched in pride as his players held out for a deserved replay; then the whole Exeter squad joined in an on-pitch celebration that lasted long after the final whistle. Sir Alex did not quite see it that way. Having apologised to the fans, the Reds boss promised a stronger side – and a better performance – in the replay.

# Exeter City 0

# Manchester United 2

Ronaldo 9, Rooney 87

**They say the underdogs** only have one chance of causing a Cup upset against the big guns. And while Cristiano Ronaldo's early goal made it a tall order for Exeter, the Conference side ignored the early setback, raised their game once more and made United battle all the way, before Wayne Rooney's 87th-minute strike finally settled the tie.

The 8,000 Grecians were thrilled and not a little fearful when the team-sheets were read out. Gone were Piqué, Spector, Eagles, Jones and Richardson, replaced by Gary Neville, Paul Scholes, Ryan Giggs, Ronaldo and Rooney. When Ronaldo gave United the lead in the ninth minute, manager Alex Inglethorpe must have feared the worst. The winger cut in from the left and passed to Scholes, who returned the favour for Ronaldo who slipped the ball through keeper Paul Jones's legs. Cue for floodgates to open? Not exactly. United threatened but failed to apply the finishing touch. Ronaldo, Rooney and Scholes all had chances to put the game beyond Exeter, but the home side nearly grabbed an equaliser in first-half injury time but Sean Devine fired wide.

Exeter came out after the break with renewed belief. Devine had another chance when a pinpoint cross from Alex Jeannin dropped for him six yards out. To United's relief, his volley was off-target. Just as the Grecians began to believe they could force extra-time, Rooney finally scored his first ever FA Cup goal, when with just three minutes to go he calmly rounded Paul Jones and slotted home. So for United a fourth-round tie with Middlesbrough, for Exeter a bank account swelled by £800,000, and 180 minutes of football they'd never forget.

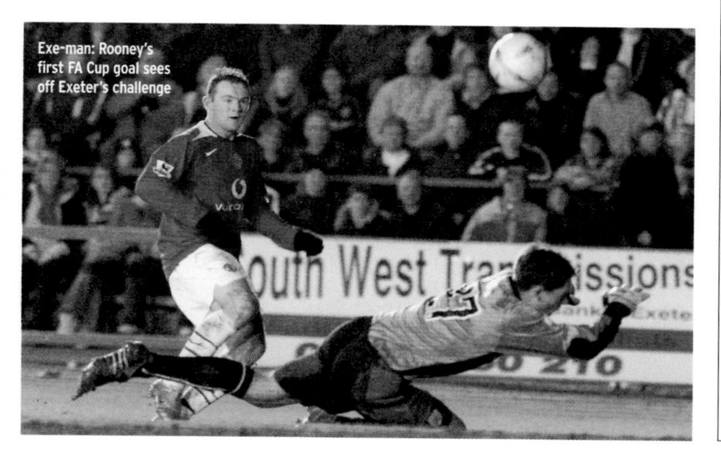

Exe-man: Rooney's first FA Cup goal sees off Exeter's challenge

## MATCH FACTS

**The FA Cup**
Wednesday 19 January 2005
**St James Park**
Attendance 9,033
**Referee: Phil Dowd**

**EXETER CITY**
Jones; Hiley, Sawyer, Gaia, Jeannin; Moxey, Taylor (Martin 89), Ampadu (Afful 69), Clay, Flack (Edwards 74), Devine
**Subs not used** Rice, Todd
**Booked** Ampadu, Clay

**MANCHESTER UNITED**
Howard; P Neville, G Neville, O'Shea, Fortune; Giggs (Saha 70), Miller (Fletcher 66), Scholes, Djemba-Djemba (Silvestre 80); Ronaldo, Rooney
**Subs not used** Ricardo, Bellion

| 57% | POSSESSION | 43% |
|---|---|---|
| 9 | SHOTS ON TARGET | 2 |
| 8 | SHOTS OFF TARGET | 4 |
| 9 | CORNERS | 1 |
| 12 | FOULS | 14 |
| 4 | OFFSIDES | 5 |

## MAN OF THE MATCH

**PAUL SCHOLES**
If there was one player to cause the Exeter fans to take a sharp intake of breath when the teams were read out, it would have been Paul Scholes. He was central to most of the Reds' attacking moves, and his pass which set up Cristiano Ronaldo for the opening goal was proof of the ultimate gulf in class between the Cup holders and the team from the Nationwide Conference.

# Manchester United 3

O'Shea 10, Rooney 67, 82

# Middlesbrough 0

**There were no prizes** for guessing which Red would be dominating the back pages of the Sunday papers after this Cup tie. Two sublime strikes from the brilliant Wayne Rooney sent Old Trafford wild and left the sports writers looking for new superlatives to describe the teenage sensation.

Some had suggested – not without justification – that the Liverpudlian has made a quiet start to his United career – his ability has been seen in glimpses rather than sustained spells during his 22 games since his debut back in September. However, this display against Steve McClaren's Middlesbrough was the closest he has come to emulating that Fenerbahçe performance.

The Reds had taken an early lead when John O'Shea had capitalised on some sloppy defending by Boro to shoot from 12 yards into the top right corner of Mark Schwarzer's goal. The Irishman's second goal of the season, coming in the 10th minute of the match, was the only one United managed in the first half – with Middlesbrough coming closest to scoring next, Roy Carroll denying Bolo Zenden with a brilliant, instinctive, one-handed save.

In the second half, however, the Wayne Rooney show began in earnest. Alternating between operating as a lone striker and occupying a deep-lying role, he began to trouble Middlesbrough more and more.

In the 67th minute he got his just rewards when, having collected a through-ball from Gary Neville, he spotted Schwarzer off his line and lifted the ball over the Australian into the unguarded net from 30 yards.

It was a finish good enough to win any match – yet better was to come. Eight minutes from the end Rooney netted again, with a strike all about power and precision rather than awareness and opportunism. Louis Saha flicked a Carroll long ball in his direction and the £27-million man leapt into the air to crash a first-time volley into Schwarzer's top corner. Old Trafford duly rose to celebrate another wonder strike from the young maestro.

Rooney's superb double will live far longer in the memory than the game itself. After this performance he must have been relishing a return to his old stamping ground when Everton came out of the hat as the Reds' fifth-round opponents...

Steady progress: the Reds' Cup run continues thanks to solid defending combined with fireworks up front...

**FA Cup fourth round**
Saturday 29 January 2005
**Old Trafford**
Attendance 67,251
**Referee: Steve Dunn**

## MAN OF THE MATCH

**WAYNE ROONEY**

Phil Neville and John O'Shea both excelled in their midfield roles but the outstanding player on the pitch was undoubtedly Wayne Rooney. Two Goal-of-the-Season contenders in one match is quite a feat, even for a man of his ability, with fans departing Old Trafford left debating which was the better. On nights like this, the England striker looks every bit the player we hoped he would be.

## MATCH FACTS

**MANCHESTER UNITED**
Carroll; G Neville, Ferdinand, Brown, Heinze (Silvestre 79); Ronaldo (Miller 72), P Neville, O'Shea, Fortune, Giggs (Saha 65); Rooney
**Subs not used** Howard, Scholes

**MIDDLESBROUGH**
Schwarzer; Reiziger, Southgate, Cooper (McMahon 79), Queudrue; Morrison, Parlour, Doriva (Job 45), Zenden, Downing; Hasselbaink (Graham 83)
**Subs not used** Nash, Parnaby

| Man Utd | | Middlesbrough |
|---|---|---|
| 58% | POSSESSION | 42% |
| 7 | SHOTS ON TARGET | 0 |
| 5 | SHOTS OFF TARGET | 1 |
| 7 | CORNERS | 1 |
| 19 | FOULS | 12 |
| 2 | OFFSIDES | 1 |

**FA CUP FOURTH ROUND**
29/01/05 TO 13/02/05

| Home | Score | Away |
|---|---|---|
| Arsenal | 2-0 | Wolves |
| Blackburn | 3-0 | Colchester |
| Burnley | 2-0 | Bournemouth |
| Charlton | 3-2 | Yeovil |
| Chelsea | 2-0 | Birmingham |
| Everton | 3-0 | Sunderland |
| Fulham | 4-2*(1-1) | Derby |
| Hartlepool | 0-1*(0-0) | Brentford |
| Newcastle | 3-1 | Coventry |
| Nottingham Forest | 1-0 | Peterborough |
| Oldham | 0-1 | Bolton |
| Reading | 1-2 | Leicester |
| Sheffield United | 1-1*(1-1)** | West Ham |
| Southampton | 2-1 | Portsmouth |
| Tottenham | 3-1*(1-1) | West Brom |

*replay (first game score)
**Sheffield United won on penalties, 3-1

*"You won't get many better goals than those two. The volley reminded me of Marco Van Basten. It was a marvellous overall performance and will do him the power of good."*
**SIR ALEX FERGUSON**

# Everton 0

# Manchester United 2

Fortune 23, Ronaldo 58

**If a week** is a long time in football, then a year must feel like a lifetime. Last February, when United played at Goodison, second-half Everton sub Wayne Rooney came on to a hero's welcome. Fast-forward to 2005: SAS bodyguards, a helicopter hovering overhead, and the promise of a Figo-style welcoming committee heralded Rooney's return. From the opening whistle the Goodison boo-boys did their best to put off their once-favourite son; the Reds, though, rose above it, producing a determined display on the pot-holed surface to progress to the next round.

Everton had the better of the earlier possession as United got used to a surface that resembled more a farmer's field than a Premiership pitch. Dangerous crosses from James McFadden kept United pegged back, and lone striker Marcus Bent had an early chance to take the lead, his goalbound header cleared by Quinton Fortune.

After soaking up the early pressure United began to dictate the game. With Everton's attentions focused on Rooney, Fortune took full advantage after 23 minutes. Gary Neville fed Cristiano Ronaldo on the right, sending the young winger on a trademark run. He skipped past Kevin Kilbane and Gary Naysmith to deliver an inch-perfect cross at the far post for Fortune to head home.

With Roy Keane and Paul Scholes bossing the midfield, and Rio Ferdinand and co calmly mopping up any stray balls, United looked to be cruising. But it could have been level at the break had it not been for the quick reactions of Roy Carroll. The keeper

Marked man: Rooney, given little room to manoeuvre on his return to Goodison, still caused his share of problems...

**FA Cup fifth round**
Saturday 19 February 2005
**Goodison Park**
Attendance 38,664
**Referee: Rob Styles**

bravely dived at Bent's feet after the striker had been fed through by Mikel Arteta.

Early in the second half Nigel Martyn dived low to save from Ronaldo, and the veteran twice denied Rooney late on. But by then, any chance of an Everton comeback had been snuffed out. Thirteen minutes into the half Ronaldo had been hacked down on the edge of the box; Scholes stepped up for the free kick. Martyn did well to parry his shot, but Ronaldo cracked home the rebound.

It was a polished performance by the Reds – but sadly the match is likely to be remembered for the missiles thrown onto the pitch rather than for the football played on it.

## MAN OF THE MATCH

**CRISTIANO RONALDO**

All eyes were on Rooney; instead, despite the cut-up pitch, it was Ronaldo who carried the United threat, his fleet-footed brilliance making the Everton defence back-pedal time after time until finally they hacked him down. And it was his pinpoint delivery that set up the first goal and his lightning-quick reactions that got him the second.

## MATCH FACTS

**EVERTON**
Martyn; Hibbert, Yobo, Stubbs, Naysmith; Osman, Carsley, Arteta (Pistone 80), Kilbane, McFadden (Weir 68); Bent
**Subs not used** Wright, Plessis, Vaughan
**Booked** Weir

**MANCHESTER UNITED**
Carroll; G Neville, Brown, Ferdinand, Heinze; Ronaldo, P Neville, Keane (Miller 81), Scholes, Fortune; Rooney
**Subs not used** Howard, Giggs, Smith, Spector
**Booked** Keane

| Man Utd | | Everton |
|---|---|---|
| 55% | POSSESSION | 45% |
| 6 | SHOTS ON TARGET | 2 |
| 3 | SHOTS OFF TARGET | 3 |
| 7 | CORNERS | 4 |
| 17 | FOULS | 11 |
| 4 | OFFSIDES | 0 |

**FA CUP FIFTH ROUND**
**19/02/05 TO 02/03/05**

| | | |
|---|---|---|
| Blackburn | 2-1*(0-0) | Burnley |
| Bolton | 1-0 | Fulham |
| Brentford | 1-3*(2-2) | Southampton |
| Charlton | 1-2 | Leicester |
| Newcastle | 1-0 | Chelsea |
| Nottingham Forest | 0-3*(1-1) | Tottenham |
| Sheffield United | 0-0*(1-1)** | Arsenal |

*replay (first game score)
**Arsenal won on penalties, 4-2

> *"It was a fantastic performance by us. In fairness I think Everton have missed a couple of players and got some young players out today, [but] we played professionally, had good discipline, good concentration on that pitch, and our possession of the ball was very good."*

**SIR ALEX FERGUSON**

vodafone
18

# FA CUP
# CLOSING STAGES

## A breeze on the south coast as the Reds see off the Saints, and the semi-final draw sets up a mouthwatering final with Arsenal

**Rarely has** the path to the FA Cup final been such a procession. Southampton, seemingly with one eye on averting their slide towards relegation, chose not to view the sixth-round clash as a distraction, and were toyed with by a United side who were out to make up for the disappointing midweek Champions League exit. With the Reds straining every sinew in a quest for a semi-final spot, Roy Keane's second-minute opener at St Mary's set the tone for the game. Goals from Cristiano Ronaldo on the stroke of half-time and Paul Scholes three minutes after it, killed off the contest. "We'll be back to send you down," taunted the clairvoyant Red Army.

Elsewhere, semi-final berths were booked by 1-0 scorelines. Arsenal saw off Bolton with a Freddie Ljungberg goal; Patrick Kluivert's early header saw Newcastle beat Tottenham, and Paul Dickov shot Blackburn into their first semi-final for 45 years against Leicester City.

Sadly for the Toon Army, their Red counterparts were determined to make amends for the abject display at Norwich City eight days earlier and spoil the Geordies' semi-final party. And so a week that started so promisingly for Nicky Butt and his Newcastle team-mates ended in disaster. Their midweek 4-1 UEFA Cup defeat by Sporting Lisbon was matched in a one-sided game in Cardiff. Ruud van Nistelrooy scored twice – his first goals since 27 November – and Scholes and Ronaldo obliged again. So United would lock horns with Arsenal on 21 May: the Gunners' 3-0 victory over Blackburn denying Mark Hughes a meeting against his old mentor on his native soil.

### FA CUP FIXTURES

| | | |
|---|---|---|
| 12 MARCH | SOUTHAMPTON | AWAY |
| 17 APRIL | NEWCASTLE UNITED | CARDIFF |
| 21 MAY | ARSENAL | CARDIFF |

### IN THE FA CUP FINAL CLOSING STAGES

**172,127** Watched United play 3 games

**8** goals were scored

**805** miles were travelled going to and from games

United fielded **18** players

**1** goal was conceded

### FOCUS ON RUUD VAN NISTELROOY

Form is temporary, class is permanent. Words oft-repeated but always worth hearing, particularly when doubting the goalscoring abilities of one Rutgerus van Nistelrooy. While his Dutch international team-mate Patrick Kluivert – born on the same day in the same year – waited 64 minutes for his slice of the action, by then Ruud had feasted twice in the Newcastle box to book a showdown at the Millennium Stadium with Arsenal. The brace was his first taste of goal action since he scored in the 3-0 rout of West Bromwich Albion at The Hawthorns back in November. His first here saw him swivel to hit Cristiano Ronaldo's dangerous cross past Shay Given on 19 minutes; his second, just before the hour mark, was a more sedate slotting home from 10 yards after some impressive counter-attacking work from the Reds. "I hope he maintains his scoring," said the boss. "When he's doing that he's unstoppable." A Ruud awakening, indeed.

# Southampton 0

# Manchester United 4

Keane 2, Ronaldo 45, Scholes 48, 87

Early doors: Keane fires home in the second minute to put the Saints on the back foot right from the off...

**Third time lucky,** as a disappointing week ended on a relative high. A tame draw at Crystal Palace had been followed by a European exit to Milan in midweek, so it was vital that United retained a grip on the FA Cup. As things turned out, two goals from Paul Scholes and one apiece from Roy Keane and Cristiano Ronaldo, comprehensively clinched a place in the semi-finals to keep alive hopes of successfully defending the trophy for the first time.

Any fears that Sir Alex Ferguson's men might slip to a third unwanted result in seven days were short-lived. With the greatest respect to the Saints, a stripey kit is about all this display had in common with the Italian champions who'd beaten the Reds four days earlier. Milan had restricted United to six goalscoring opportunities in 180 minutes; Southampton were undone inside two. Roy Keane broke into the penalty area, making the most of the space allowed to drive in a shot that flicked off Peter Crouch's head and into the top corner. The perfect start to a potentially tricky evening.

Nerves settled, the Reds slipped into cruise control. Crouch's height caused the occasional problem, as did the pace of Henri Camara, but Tim Howard was little more than a spectator for the majority of the match.

**FA Cup sixth round**
Saturday 12 March 2005
**St Mary's Stadium**
Attendance 30,971
**Referee: Howard Webb**

If there are especially good times to score, they're meant to be at the start of a game, shortly before half-time, just after the break and right at the end. United managed all four, with Ronaldo following up Keane's early opener. The inspired Wayne Rooney surged past three Saints defenders on the backline, in the manner of King Kong swatting flies, before pulling the ball back to van Nistelrooy. The Dutchman slipped the ball to Ronaldo who had time and space to tee himself up before slamming a left-foot volley past the helpless Paul Smith.

Immediately after the break it was 3-0. Van Nistelrooy brought a save from Smith, but after a series of deflections and half-clearances the ball ran loose to Scholes, who calmly drove home to scupper any lingering hopes Harry Redknapp's side may have had. And having had a hand in goals two and three, it was no surprise to see van Nistelrooy set up the fourth. With time running out he spotted Scholes lurking at the far post, and from wide on the right his deliciously weighted, pinpoint cross found the little midfielder who nodded it in.

The result set United up to face the Magpies in the semi-final, as the FA Cup became the main hope of silverware for a second successive season.

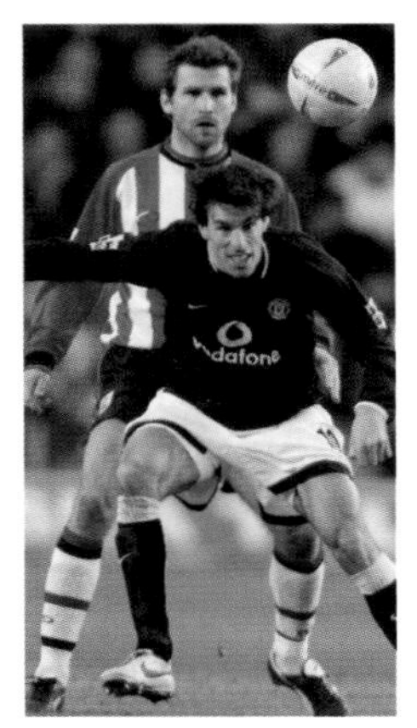

## MAN OF THE MATCH

**WAYNE ROONEY**

He may have struggled against the might of Milan's defensive giants, but the experience gained in the two Champions League knockout matches will prove invaluable, and against Southampton, Rooney was rampant. The Saints could find no answers to his powerful, driving runs, nor his incisive, subtle passing. And they had to thank their goalkeeper Paul Smith for denying him the goal he so richly deserved. One of his best United displays to date.

## MATCH FACTS

**SOUTHAMPTON**
Smith; Cranie, Lundekvam (Davenport 45), Jakobsson; Higginbotham, Telfer, Oakley, A Svensson, Bernard (McCann 62); Camara (Phillips 80), Crouch
**Subs not used** Niemi, Nilsson

**MANCHESTER UNITED**
Howard; Brown, Ferdinand, Silvestre, Heinze (O'Shea 60); Ronaldo (Smith 68), Keane (P Neville 70), Scholes, Fortune; van Nistelrooy, Rooney
**Subs not used** Carroll, Bellion
**Booked** Heinze

| Man Utd | | Southampton |
|---|---|---|
| 65% | POSSESSION | 35% |
| 9 | SHOTS ON TARGET | 5 |
| 6 | SHOTS OFF TARGET | 9 |
| 7 | CORNERS | 2 |
| 7 | FOULS | 5 |
| 4 | OFFSIDES | 4 |

**FA CUP SIXTH ROUND**
**WEEKEND BEGINNING 12/03/05**

| | | |
|---|---|---|
| Blackburn Rovers | 1-0 | Leicester City |
| Newcastle United | 1-0 | Tottenham Hotspur |
| Bolton Wanderers | 0-1 | Arsenal |

*"You could see from the support how much it means to the fans... it was unthinkable that we wouldn't win. We had a setback on Tuesday, but we have recovered and got ourselves into another semi-final"*
**SIR ALEX FERGUSON**

*"The early goal killed us. That left us with a huge task, especially with a mix and match side"*
**HARRY REDKNAPP**

# Newcastle United 1
Ameobi 59

# Manchester United 4
Van Nistelrooy 19, 58, Scholes 45, Ronaldo 76

**The Reds moved** a step closer to retaining the FA Cup with a comprehensive semi-final win over Newcastle in Cardiff. Two goals from Ruud van Nistelrooy, one from Paul Scholes and a fourth from Cristiano Ronaldo saw United put a difficult week to bed by clinching a return trip to Wales on 21 May.

Eight days earlier, the Reds had produced one of the most inept performances of Sir Alex Ferguson's reign. The Carrow Road debacle had left fans dejected and concerned, and the subsequent press attention had done little to lift the gloom, with Roy Keane calling on his team-mates to examine their contribution. Hardly the best preparation for a semi-final – but it is often said the Reds are most dangerous when up against it, and that proved to be the case again. Inside two minutes Ruud van Nistelrooy's low, curling shot was turned around the post by Shay Given and that set the tone for the game. A Newcastle side depleted by injuries and suspensions, and still reeling from their midweek exit from Europe, courtesy of a 4-1 thumping by Ronaldo's old team Sporting Lisbon, were simply no match for the rejuvenated Reds.

In the 19th minute, van Nistelrooy capped his impressive start by ending his eight-game barren spell. Swivelling on a dangerous Ronaldo cross he turned the ball past Given and into the far corner of the net. Not his best Reds goal, but his celebration – running half the length of the pitch, fists clenched – showed what it meant to him.

From that point the result was never in doubt. Scholes flashed a glancing header past Given on the stroke of half-time (from another superb Ronaldo cross) and 13 minutes after the break Ruud made it three, slotting home from 10 yards after a flowing counter-attack. Shola Ameobi briefly gave the Geordies hope straight after United's third, but those hopes died when Ronaldo rounded things off with 14 minutes remaining, slotting home a right-foot shot after another slick, passing move.

It was no less than the Reds deserved and the nature of the win, as much as the win itself, gave United fans a much-needed lift. Many hadn't been entirely looking forward to this trip to Cardiff; you can bet they were rather more excited by the prospect of a return in May. With van Nistelrooy in this form there was every reason to be optimistic of a record 12th FA Cup win.

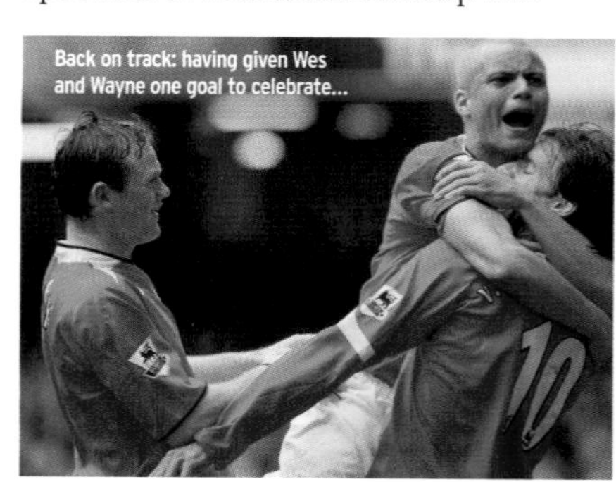

Back on track: having given Wes and Wayne one goal to celebrate...

... Ruud decides he may as well repeat the feat

**FA Cup semi-final**
Sunday 17 April 2005
**Millennium Stadium**
Attendance 69,280
**Referee: Mike Riley**

Magician at work: Cristiano Ronaldo treats Magpies defenders Steve Carr and Andy O'Brien to his full repertoire of flicks and tricks

## MAN OF THE MATCH

RUUD VAN NISTELROOY
The Dutch goal machine made a mockery of criticism in the build up to this match, with strikes in either half to clinch a Cardiff return. His opener, steered inside Given's right-hand post, ended his eight-game goal drought and he produced a similarly clinical finish after the break. Ruud appeared to be back to his best; imagine ever doubting he would be.

## MATCH FACTS

NEWCASTLE UNITED
Given; Carr, Boumsong, Taylor, Babayaro (O'Brien 45); Butt, Faye (N'Zogbia 45), Robert, Milner (Kluivert 63); Shearer, Ameobi
**Subs not used** Harper, Ambrose
**Booked** Robert, Milner

MANCHESTER UNITED
Howard; G Neville, Brown, Ferdinand, Heinze; Scholes (Fletcher 78), Keane, Ronaldo (Smith 78), Fortune; Rooney (Giggs 78), van Nistelrooy
**Subs not used** Carroll, Silvestre
**Booked** Ronaldo, Brown, Heinze

| Man Utd | | Newcastle |
|---|---|---|
| 57% | POSSESSION | 43% |
| 10 | SHOTS ON TARGET | 2 |
| 5 | SHOTS OFF TARGET | 5 |
| 7 | CORNERS | 5 |
| 26 | FOULS | 26 |
| 0 | OFFSIDES | 2 |

FA CUP SEMI-FINAL
16/04/05

| Arsenal | 3-0 | Blackburn Rovers |
|---|---|---|

*"We needed to remind everyone just what Manchester United is all about. I never had any doubt they would come back. The ability in the squad is fantastic... but you have to work in life"*

**SIR ALEX FERGUSON**

*"We played a very good United team and, given our suspensions and injuries, it was always going to be a difficult afternoon"*

**GRAEME SOUNESS**

# Arsenal 0

# Manchester United 0

**(Arsenal won 5-4 on penalties)**

Battle rejoined: Cristiano Ronaldo tussles with Lauren in Cardiff

**As the gleeful** Gunners cavorted in the Cardiff sunshine, having finally got a shot on target to triumph in the penalty shootout, Sir Alex Ferguson and Roy Keane looked on impassively, wondering where to put themselves. And if you couldn't tell how much these two old war horses were hurting, the teary eyes of young stallion Wayne Rooney, burning brightly at the sheer injustice of it, were all the evidence you required.

If you wanted one afternoon to sum up United's 2004/05, this was it. It was the season's story encapsulated in two hours: attractive, free-flowing football, bucket-loads of passion and commitment – and, ultimately, a failure to convert chances. The more philosophical Red could have been excused a wry smile at the irony of it all – a campaign that had so often threatened to explode into life had ended exactly as it had begun – with defeat by Arsenal in Cardiff.

History remembers only the winners on occasions such as this, but Sir Alex's troops – missing Gabriel Heinze and Gary Neville, the latter on the bench – performed admirably considering the off-field traumas

**FA Cup final**
Saturday 21 May 2005
**Millennium Stadium**
Attendance: 71,876
**Referee: Rob Styles**

that had cloaked the build-up to the match all week.

Rooney was his everyday superhuman self, hitting the post and smashing a volley just over; in midfield Keane remains the epitome of his surname, Cristiano Ronaldo teased and tormented Lauren, and Darren Fletcher showed an ever-growing maturity. At the back, United's rearguard stood firmly against the little that came their way, with Arsenal fielding Dennis Bergkamp as a lone striker. But, for all United's pressure, and 20 attempts on Jens Lehmann's goal, there was no way through.

And so to the penalty shootout. For the first time in 133 years the Cup winners would be decided from the spot. United had dominated the previous 120 minutes, Roy Carroll only being called into action to repel a van Persie free kick in the 93rd minute, but deep down there was a nagging feeling that it wasn't going to be United's day.

Sir Alex's mantra has always been that a successful campaign is one in which at least one trophy is captured. By the great man's logic alone, it's clear that this season was far short of vintage. The abiding memory of 2004/05 will be one of failure, illustrated here by Paul Scholes's unfortunate spot-kick miss. But the Reds will be back – you can count on that.

## MAN OF THE MATCH

**WAYNE ROONEY**
If he continues improving at this rate, his performances should soon carry a health warning. A menace from start to finish, possessing power and unpredictability that just can't be second-guessed. Hit the post, fizzed one just over, and was dead-eyed in the shootout. His penalty, with no run-up, was arguably the fiercest of the lot. Simply irresistible.

## MATCH FACTS

**ARSENAL**
Lehmann; Lauren, Senderos, Touré, Cole; Pires (Edu 105), Fabregas (Van Persie 86), Vieira, Gilberto, Reyes; Bergkamp (Ljungberg 65) **Subs not used** Almunia, Campbell **Booked** Cole, Lauren, Reyes, Vieira **Sent off** Reyes

**MANCHESTER UNITED**
Carroll; Brown, Ferdinand, Silvestre, O'Shea (Fortune 76); Rooney, Fletcher (Giggs 91), Keane, Scholes, Ronaldo; van Nistelrooy **Subs not used** Howard, G Neville, Smith **Booked:** Silvestre, Scholes

| Manchester United | | Arsenal |
|---|---|---|
| 45% | POSSESSION | 55% |
| 8 | SHOTS ON TARGET | 1 |
| 12 | SHOTS OFF TARGET | 4 |
| 12 | CORNERS | 1 |
| 23 | FOULS | 30 |
| 6 | OFFSIDES | 3 |

*"In Cup football you need a break and we didn't get it. But we've had luck in the past in Cup games, so I understand. It can happen and it happened to us."*
**SIR ALEX FERGUSON**

*"There were some times in the second half when we were a bit lucky. Of course it is bad for the team that loses on penalties but it was a very intense game."*
**ARSÈNE WENGER**

FLETCHER
24
VIEIRA
4
RONALDO
7

RICHARDSON
23
CARLING CUP

RICHARDSON
23
MUFC
19

# CARLING CUP
## COMPETITION

This season's Carling Cup final provided a pulsating end to a cracking competition in which United's youngsters came to the fore...

**From the romance** of a first encounter with Crewe Alexandra in more than a century, to a gripping two-legged semi-final against the champions-elect from the capital, United's Carling Cup campaign provided wall-to-wall entertainment. It also gave Sir Alex Ferguson a valuable opportunity to pitch his young lions into the competitive fray and see how they fared – and the answer was encouraging. Against Crewe, Crystal Palace and then the young Gunners, David Bellion, Kieran Richardson, Liam Miller and Chris Eagles all grabbed their opportunities with both hands and showed that there's plenty of young talent coming through the Old Trafford ranks.

With a few valuable lessons learnt against Exeter City in the FA Cup, however, it was a more familiar-looking United that locked horns with Chelsea, bidding for a trip to Cardiff in February. After a tight first leg at Stamford Bridge, a late Damien Duff free kick split the sides and sent the Blues on to meet Liverpool in the final.

The Anfield Reds, in need of some Cup cheer after a disastrous third-round FA Cup defeat at Burnley, had made hard work of their semi-final win over Championship-side Watford. After a 1-0 win at Anfield, the game at Vicarage Road was goalless until Steven Gerrard settled the tie with just over 10 minutes left. Sadly for the Anfield favourite, his scoring exploits in the final were rather more forgettable; Liverpool's precarious 1-0 lead disappeared when he deflected Paulo Ferreira's free kick past Jerzy Dudek with just 11 minutes left, and goals from Drogba and Kezman in extra time meant the silverware was bound for west London.

### CARLING CUP FIXTURES

| | | |
|---|---|---|
| 26 OCT | CREWE ALEXANDRA | AWAY |
| 10 NOV | CRYSTAL PALACE | HOME |
| 1 DEC | ARSENAL | HOME |
| 12 JAN | CHELSEA | AWAY |
| 26 JAN | CHELSEA | HOME |

### IN THE CARLING CUP THIS SEASON

**234,589**
watched United play 5 games

**7**
goals were scored

**470**
miles were travelled by United going to and from games

United fielded
**28**
players

**2**
goals were conceded

### GOAL OF THE CAMPAIGN DAVID BELLION

If ever there was a lesson about getting to your seat in good time, this was it. Just under 19 seconds after Mark Halsey had blown to get the quarter-final tie against Arsenal under way, Sir Alex Ferguson's young side had put themselves firmly in the box seat. Admittedly they had plenty of help from the visitors. A nervy Johan Djorou slipped as he looked to clear United's first raid of the evening, allowing a lurking David Bellion to take possession, and the young Frenchman wasn't about to stand on ceremony, almost instantly unleashing a skimming shot towards the Arsenal goal. It still could – in fact, should – have been dealt with, but as Manuel Almunia, at 27 the elder statesman of the side and skipper for the night, prepared to gather the ball, it bounced off his knee and in. Cue predictably wild celebrations from the Reds, and plenty of head-scratching from the Gunners, immediately faced with a mountain to climb.

## MATCH FACTS

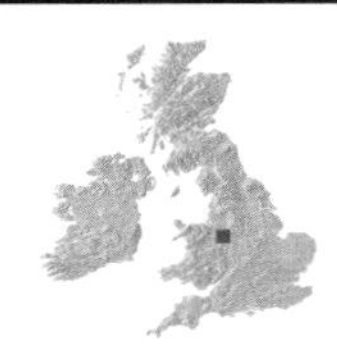

**Carling Cup third round**
Tuesday 26 October 2004
**Alexandra Stadium**
Attendance 10,103
**Referee: Matt Messias**

CREWE ALEXANDRA
Williams; Otsemobor, B Jones (Walker 85), Foster, Tonkin; Lunt, Sorvel (Rivers 63), Cochrane, Vaughan; Ashton, S Jones (White 68)
**Subs not used** Ince, Roberts

MANCHESTER UNITED
Howard; Djemba-Djemba, Brown, O'Shea (Piqué 67), Richardson; Miller, Fletcher (Eagles 78), Kleberson, Bellion (Ebanks-Blake 85); Smith, Saha
**Subs not used** Spector, Ricardo
**Booked** Smith

## MAN OF THE MATCH

ALAN SMITH
Smith further enhanced his burgeoning cult status with a goal and another wholehearted display, leaving Crewe boss Dario Gradi singing his praises: "He was the most outstanding player on the pitch."

*"Crewe gave it a real go. But there were a lot of positives from my point of view and I was pleased with how we performed."*
**SIR ALEX FERGUSON**

# Crewe Alexandra 0

# Manchester United 3

Smith 10, Miller 57, Foster og 59

Off the mark: a debut strike from Miller... and a Reds' win is assured

**United's first** competitive match against Crewe Alexandra for more than a century saw them progress comfortably into the Carling Cup fourth round. At Gresty Road in that Division Two encounter 109 years ago, Dick Smith had netted a brace for Newton Heath; this time it was Alan Smith who was instrumental in the defeat of Cheshire's Railwaymen.

Sir Alex Ferguson named a completely different starting XI from that against Arsenal two days previously, but this was still a far stronger side than many expected to see, with the Reds fielding some nine internationals. Another surprise was Kieran Richardson and Eric Djemba-Djemba filling the full-back berths. But, captained by Wes Brown and led by the fiery Smith, the Reds set about the Coca-Cola Championship side with gusto and, on 10 minutes, the talismanic Smith opened the scoring. After a Darren Fletcher shot deflected off the bar, Louis Saha played in Smith who, 18 yards out, slid a low drive beyond the reach of former United youngster Ben Williams – and cemented his position as the Reds' top scorer, with seven goals.

The returning Tim Howard was soon in the thick of things, saving well from Dean Ashton and Steve Jones, while Richardson put in a solid performance at left-back. Then, in the 57th minute, Liam Miller assured the Reds' passage to the last 16, sidefooting home Bellion's threaded pass from close range. Two minutes later a Richardson cross, turned goalwards by Bellion, was bundled into his own net by unfortunate Alex defender Stephen Foster; job done by the Reds.

# Manchester United 2

Saha 22, Richardson 39

# Crystal Palace 0

**United's fringe players** secured a place in the last eight of the Carling Cup with a comfortable victory over their Palace equivalents in front of a respectable OT crowd, first-half goals from Louis Saha and Kieran Richardson setting up a quarter-final tie with Arsenal.

Sir Alex Ferguson made 10 changes from the side that had drawn a blank against Manchester City the previous Sunday (Iain Dowie went one better, changing all 11 players that had held Arsenal at Selhurst Park), given an opportunity to several fringe players who'd featured only sporadically so far, such as Darren Fletcher and Quinton Fortune. And it was a long pass from the South African that resulted in the Reds' 22nd-minute opener. Louis Saha rose between Mark Hudson and Gary Borrowdale to chest down Fortune's flighted pass, then drilled a low shot past keeper Julian Speroni for his first goal in nine matches.

A deflected shot from Sandor Torghelle almost levelled things, but Richardson then doubled United's lead, letting fly with a left-foot shot that the hapless Speroni let slip under his body. It was Richardson's second senior goal for the Reds, his first having come in the same competition against Leicester almost exactly two years earlier.

In the second half a 20-yard effort from Kleberson was tipped around the post while Eric Djemba-Djemba had a drive headed clear. Palace's best chance fell to sub Vassilis Lakis but Wes Brown headed off the line. And with youngsters Jonathan Spector, Chris Eagles and debutant Giuseppe Rossi coming off the bench late on, the Reds coasted to the final whistle – and to that date with Arsène Wenger's young charges...

Doing their bit: a rare outing for Eric Djemba-Djemba...

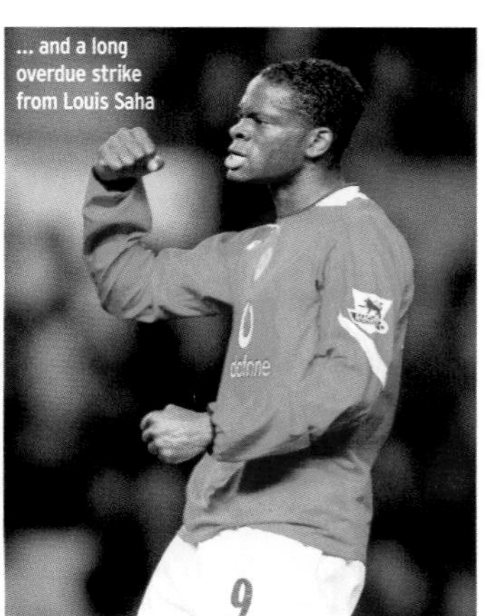

... and a long overdue strike from Louis Saha

## MATCH FACTS

**Carling Cup fourth round**
Wednesday 10 November 2004
**Old Trafford**
Attendance 48,891
**Referee: Steve Dunn**

MANCHESTER UNITED
Howard; P Neville, Brown, O'Shea, Fortune; Kleberson (Spector 79), Djemba-Djemba, Fletcher, Richardson (Eagles 79); Bellion (Rossi 86), Saha
**Subs not used** Ricardo, Ngalula

CRYSTAL PALACE
Speroni; Butterfield (Shipperley 77), Hudson, Powell, Borrowdale; Leigertwood, Soares, Danze (Lakis 45), Derry; Torghelle (Kaviedes 69), Freedman
**Subs not used** Kiraly, Boyce
**Booked** Hudson

| Man Utd | | Crystal Palace |
|---|---|---|
| 58% | POSSESSION | 42% |
| 5 | SHOTS ON TARGET | 5 |
| 6 | SHOTS OFF TARGET | 4 |
| 12 | CORNERS | 3 |
| 10 | FOULS | 14 |
| 1 | OFFSIDES | 4 |

## MAN OF THE MATCH

DARREN FLETCHER
His passing, tireless running and constant involvement made this a good night's work for the young Scot. Sir Alex admitted earlier in the week that Fletcher was suffering from "second season syndrome"; the Reds' boss will be pleased the 20-year-old showed signs here of regaining the form of the latter half of last season.

# Manchester United 1

Bellion 1

# Arsenal 0

**In the build-up** to this eagerly awaited game, Sir Alex Ferguson treated the press corps to the opening line of the Tartan Army anthem "*Flower Of Scotland*", to mark St Andrew's Day. The following day, his young troops went into battle with Arsenal and, just like in the song, sent them homeward to think again. It's almost inevitable that matches between these two teams will deliver controversy and drama, no matter what the competition. Phil Neville was the sole survivor from the infamous league meeting six weeks before, but despite the wholesale change in personnel, no quarter was asked nor, for that matter, given. And just like after that league meeting, Arsenal returned to London a beaten team.

It took just 18.6 seconds for the match to spark into life. United kicked off and moved the ball down the left wing. And before you knew it, David Bellion had capitalised on a slip by young Swiss defender Johan Djourou and let fly from outside the box. Goalkeeper and captain for the night Manuel Almunia, by six years the elder statesman of the Arsenal team, looked to have it covered but the ball bounced off his knee and into the net.

It was an incredible start and for the rest of the half the more experienced home side controlled the tempo and let the young Gunners chase the game. Quincy Owusu-Abeyie, Arturo Lupoli and Mathieu Flamini fought to showcase their undoubted talents in front of a big crowd, but couldn't create any clear chances to trouble Tim Howard in the United goal.

The young Reds were also thriving on the Old Trafford atmosphere. Chris Eagles and Kieran Richardson were both relishing rare

first-team starts, while Bellion visibly grew in confidence after netting his fifth of the season. Eagles had a fine chance to double United's lead but saw his shot-cum-cross flash across goal, while Richardson's rasping drive forced a good save from Almunia.

The visitors threatened the United goal twice in the first half, both incidents involving Howard and Jermaine Pennant. First Pennant almost capitalised on a sloppy backpass; he then forced the American keeper into his only save of the night from a threatening free kick.

The second half saw another incendiary start, but for all the wrong reasons. Again the action happened down United's left wing as Richardson tried to launch another early attack. Robin van Persie chased the ball down but seemed more interested in stopping Richardson than winning the ball. The players came together, with van Persie first throwing an elbow, then kicking out at the United youngster. Richardson reacted, players from both sides arrived en masse, and referee Mark Halsey moved in quickly to

**Carling Cup quarter-final**
Wednesday 1 December 2004
**Old Trafford**
Attendance 67,103
**Referee: Mark Halsey**

Big game players: Bellion's rapid strike put United's youngsters on course for a Carling Cup semi-final

try and stop another ugly scene. Both protagonists were booked but the temperature had been raised. For a short while tackles were flying in and van Persie looked to be heading for an early exit, but the Reds' managed to keep their heads.

Sir Alex Ferguson was afforded the opportunity of introducing Giuseppe Rossi and David Jones to the sell-out crowd as the match fizzled out and United eased into the semi-finals – earning a crack at Chelsea.

## MATCH FACTS

**MANCHESTER UNITED**
Howard; P Neville, Brown, O'Shea, Fortune; Eagles (Rossi 79), Miller, Djemba-Djemba, Richardson, Kleberson (Jones 79); Bellion
**Subs not used** Ricardo, Piqué, Ebanks-Blake
**Booked** Richardson

**ARSENAL**
Almunia; Hoyte, Senderos, Djourou, Clichy (Karbassiyoon 81); Pennant, Flamini, Larsson (Cregg 72), Owusu-Abeyie; Lupoli (Smith 68), van Persie
**Subs not used** Simek, Wright
**Booked** van Persie

| Manchester United | | Arsenal |
|---|---|---|
| 46% | POSSESSION | 54% |
| 4 | SHOTS ON TARGET | 1 |
| 3 | SHOTS OFF TARGET | 1 |
| 5 | CORNERS | 4 |
| 19 | FOULS | 12 |
| 10 | OFFSIDES | 0 |

*“We played very well in the first half but were complacent in the second half. But the outstanding feature is I think that Arsenal only had one shot, from a free kick.”*
**SIR ALEX FERGUSON**

## MAN OF THE MATCH

**CHRIS EAGLES**
United observers had been quietly confident some of Carrington's kids would soon get their moment to shine – and against Arsenal, Chris Eagles proved the man for the big occasion. The talented right-sided midfielder provided craft and guile, and could have had a goal to boot.

## MATCH FACTS

**Carling Cup semi-final, first leg**
Wednesday 12 January 2005
**Stamford Bridge**
Attendance 41,492
**Referee: Neale Barry**

**CHELSEA**
Cudicini; Ferreira, Terry, Gallas, Bridge; Lampard, Makelele, Tiago (Kezman 66), Cole (Jarosik 75); Gudjohnsen (Drogba 45), Duff
**Subs not used** Cech, Johnson
**Booked** Drogba

**MANCHESTER UNITED**
Howard; P Neville, Silvestre, O'Shea, Heinze; Ronaldo (Smith 90), Fletcher, Djemba-Djemba (Scholes 61), Fortune; Saha, Rooney
**Subs not used** Carroll, Miller, Spector
**Booked** Heinze, Ronaldo

| Manchester United | | Chelsea |
|---|---|---|
| 55% | POSSESSION | 45% |
| 3 | SHOTS ON TARGET | 2 |
| 5 | SHOTS OFF TARGET | 8 |
| 7 | CORNERS | 4 |
| 20 | FOULS | 17 |
| 6 | OFFSIDES | 4 |

## MAN OF THE MATCH

**GABRIEL HEINZE**
Another composed, rock-solid performance from the Argentinian who is fast endearing himself to his team-mates and the Red faithful. He helped snuff out every attacking wave, and his presence of mind to get on the line for that crucial clearance illustrated just how well he reads the game.

# Chelsea 0

# Manchester United 0

**In contrast to** OT's Exeter debacle four days earlier, there was no post-match apology from Sir Alex Ferguson after this determined display. Roared on by around 6,000 fans behind the goal, the fired-up Reds produced a performance that left the league leaders rattled.

Before United pitched up, Stamford Bridge had been a formidable fortress for Chelsea and this game looked a tough test for United on paper. But with the Reds' defence equally miserly in the run-up to this game, the stage was set for a fascinating double-header.

Sir Alex retained the core of the team from the quarter-final, but brought in a backbone of first-teamers. Jose Mourinho, meanwhile, without the suspended Arjen Robben, made just one other significant change to his Premiership line-up, recalling Carlo Cudicini for Petr Cech. Chelsea were quicker off the mark but United had the best chance to take the lead – Louis Saha was barged down inside the area but what seemed a legitimate penalty appeal was turned down. On the half-hour mark Eidur Gudjohnsen's 'goal' was ruled offside, and as the break approached Saha headed over from a Wayne Rooney corner before being denied by a super stop from Cudicini.

In the second half Mourinho brought on his big guns in the shape of Didier Drogba and Mateja Kezman, but a resolute Red defence retained a clean sheet. Gabriel Heinze's vision to track back saved Tim Howard's blushes, and Phil Neville also cleared off the line.

The match finished honours even, but the Reds had cause to be much the happier; they were, after all, returning to OT with the psychological boost of having held Chelsea in their own backyard...

Saha, so good: Louis came as close as anyone to a goal...

# Manchester United 1

Giggs 67

# Chelsea 2

Lampard 29, Duff 85

Close encounter: the Reds and Blues matched each other stride for stride...

**Sir Alex Ferguson** had billed this clash as *High Noon*, but it was young gunslinger Jose Mourinho who rode out of town in triumph. Both teams went with full-strength sides – Roy Keane, Rio Ferdinand and Ryan Giggs made their first League Cup appearances of the season, while Mourinho chose first-choice keeper Petr Cech in place of Carlo Cudicini. Scholes and Keane dictated the early pace as Louis Saha led the line again, and the Frenchman was first to trouble the Chelsea back line, darting through the box but then losing control under pressure from compatriot William Gallas. Gary Neville had a chance to become an unlikely hero but his snatched shot flew across goal, and for all United's possession and endeavour, Cech was still a spectator. Then, with the half-hour mark approaching. Frank Lampard released the scampering Arjen Robben, who quickly found Didier Drogba. He laid the ball to an arriving Lampard, who took one touch and fired home.

On the hour mark, Sir Alex sent for Wayne Rooney – and before long United were back in the tie. Like Lampard before him, Giggs started and finished the move, artfully lobbing the 6ft 5in Cech. But with both teams eyeing extra time, Chelsea won a free kick on the United touchline; Damien Duff swung in a vicious, curling ball that eluded defence, attack and Tim Howard to spin straight into the net.

In a frantic final few minutes Mikael Silvestre's header was cleared off the line by Wayne Bridge, and Cristiano Ronaldo's drilled shot forced a fingertip save from the Chelsea No.1. As the final whistle blew, birthday boy Mourinho – not for the first time – celebrated wildly on the OT turf.

## MATCH FACTS

**Carling Cup semi-final, second leg**
Wednesday 26 January 2005
**Old Trafford**
Attendance 67,000
**Referee: Rob Styles**

MANCHESTER UNITED
Howard; G Neville, Ferdinand, Silvestre, Heinze; Ronaldo, Keane, Scholes, Fortune (Rooney 59); Giggs, Saha
**Subs not used** Ricardo, P Neville, Brown, O'Shea
**Booked** Keane

CHELSEA
Cech; Ferreira, Gallas, Terry, Bridge; Makelele, Lampard, Tiago, Robben (Cole 90); Drogba (Gudjohnsen 68), Duff (Jarosik 87)
**Subs not used** Cudicini, Huth
**Booked** Makelele

| Man Utd | | Chelsea |
|---|---|---|
| 58% | POSSESSION | 42% |
| 5 | SHOTS ON TARGET | 5 |
| 6 | SHOTS OFF TARGET | 3 |
| 5 | CORNERS | 6 |
| 10 | FOULS | 13 |
| 4 | OFFSIDES | 3 |

## MAN OF THE MATCH

RIO FERDINAND
Up against fellow England centre-half John Terry, Rio got a big thumbs up from Paolo Maldini: "Ferdinand has played at every level and is one of the best players in the world," said the Milan legend. And so it proved, as Rio stood firm under pressure from Drogba, Duff, Robben and Gudjohnsen.

VIEIRA
4
RONALDO
7

PRE-SEASON
GATE 6

# Arsenal 3

Gilberto 49, Reyes 58, Silvestre (og) 79

# Manchester United 1

Smith 55

**"It is the** worst start we have had, no doubt about it," said Sir Alex Ferguson after he had watched his depleted side lose 3-1 to Arsenal in the Community Shield. Ten players were either absent or injured for the trip to Cardiff, forcing the boss to travel with a significantly under-strength squad. The only good news was that the list wasn't lengthened at the Millennium Stadium, and some key players enjoyed some vital match practice on the eve of the trip to Bucharest for the crucial Champions League qualifier.

Another notable absentee in Cardiff was Arsenal's Patrick Vieira, out of the game with a thigh strain and, at the time, rumoured to be heading out of Highbury for Real Madrid. But Arsène Wenger's side didn't appear to miss their skipper; they started the game with purpose and probably should have been in front before half-time. Dennis Bergkamp stumbled when through on Tim Howard's goal, while Jermaine Pennant scuffed his shot when presented with an open goal.

Arsenal were guilty of an even more glaring miss soon after the interval when winger Jose Antonio Reyes, inexplicably left out of Spain's Euro 2004 squad, sliced through the heart of the United defence and dummied Tim Howard, but with the goal at his mercy could only find the side netting.

No matter. A minute later Arsenal were ahead after more stunning play from Reyes. The youngster broke free of the United defence to run onto a pass from Dennis Bergkamp before squaring the ball for Gilberto Silva to tap into an empty net.

United's response wasn't long in coming. Alan Smith, continuing his impressive pre-season, pounced on some poor defending

by Kolo Toure and Pascal Cygan to equalise with a beautifully hit shot from the edge of the area that flew past Jens Lehmann. But United were behind again only three minutes later, the Gunners' Man of the Match, Reyes, scoring from Gilberto's pass after sloppy defending in the penalty area from United.

Arsenal continued to pour forward for a third goal, and with 11 minutes remaining, got it. Ashley Cole's burst into the box took him past Gary Neville and David Bellion, before his cross was deflected off Mikael Silvestre and past Howard.

Despite the defeat, United fans could take some heart from the fact that the Community Shield winners have not gone on to win the Premiership since the Reds did so back in the 1996/97 season.

**FA Community Shield**
Sunday 8 August 2004
**Millennium Stadium**
Attendance 63,317
**Referee: Mike Dean**

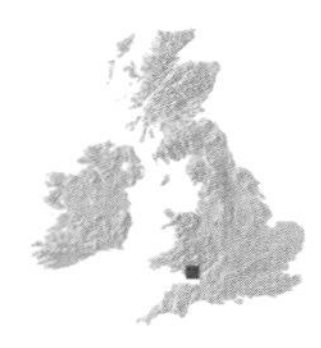

Level headed: Alan Smith puts an under-strength United back in the game

## MATCH FACTS

**ARSENAL**
Lehmann; Lauren, Toure, Cygan, Cole; Pennant, Gilberto, Fabregas (Svard 87), Reyes (Hoyte 80); Bergkamp (Aliadiere 61, Clichy 69), Henry (van Persie 45)
**Subs Not Used:** Senderos, Almunia **Booked:** Cole

**MANCHESTER UNITED**
Howard; G Neville, O'Shea (Spector 82), Silvestre, Fortune (P Neville 51); Bellion, Keane (Fletcher 51), Djemba-Djemba, Giggs (Forlan 51), Scholes (Richardson 74); Smith (Eagles 73) **Subs Not Used:** Carroll
**Booked:** P Neville, Djemba-Djemba

| Manchester United | | Arsenal |
|---|---|---|
| 60% | POSSESSION | 40% |
| 6 | SHOTS ON TARGET | 7 |
| 3 | SHOTS OFF TARGET | 6 |
| 7 | CORNERS | 5 |
| 18 | FOULS | 13 |
| 8 | OFFSIDES | 3 |

*"It was the right pace of game for us ahead of the Champions League qualifier. There was an edge and some intelligent play."*
**SIR ALEX FERGUSON**

## MAN OF THE MATCH

**ALAN SMITH**
In the absence of Ruud van Nistelrooy and Louis Saha, the former Leeds striker staked his claim for a regular place in the United attack with an impressive performance which earned comparisons with Eric Cantona from Sir Alex. He scored his first competitive goal with a powerful shot from outside the penalty box to get United briefly back on level terms.

Clockwise from top: Alan Smith gets off to a flyer against Celtic; but the Hoops battled hard; Tim Howard was a big draw; Reds soak up the sun

# US TOUR
## COMING TO AMERICA

### MANCHESTER UNITED V BAYERN MUNICH

**Manchester United 0**
**Bayern Munich 0**
*(Bayern win 4-2 on penalties)*

25 July 2004
**Soldier Field, Chicago**
Att: 58,121

A young Manchester United outfit held a strong Bayern side in a low-key match. Neither team created a genuine goalscoring opportunity, nor was it the entertainment the crowd had been hoping for, boos greeting the final whistle. A penalty shoot out was hastily arranged to determine a winner for the US public - and that was Bayern, 4-2.

**"The perfect** pre-season," said Sir Alex Ferguson after the 2003 US tour. United banged home 14 goals in four wins against top-class opposition, in front of near sell-out crowds. And, on their return home, the Reds made their best start to a Premiership campaign. No wonder the boss called it "an easy decision to come back".

But it was a different United that returned for the 10-day tour. Shorn of key players through injury, Euro 2004, Copa America and the Olympics, youngsters Chris Eagles, Phil Bardsley and Jonathan Spector were included in an 18-man squad.

Bayern Munich were first up in Chicago. Tim Howard wasn't playing, but young compatriot Jonathan Spector – born just down the road in Arlington Heights – made the headlines; "Spector won't be a spectator," read the *Chicago Sun-Times*. Spector was one of four debutants against Bayern, and the young Reds acquitted themselves admirably in a 0-0 draw.

But that was not how sections of the crowd saw it, many booing the closing stages. Though they were appeased by an impromptu penalty shoot out (Americans don't do draws), the press were less easily placated, the *Sun-Times* dubbing it a "sorry spectacle".

Not that some minded. "The standard was better than anything in MLS [Major League Soccer]," said American Red Kurt Meninger, from Kansas City.

A youthful Reds side held off their German opponents

## MANCHESTER UNITED V CELTIC

**Manchester United 1**
Smith 35

**Celtic 2**
Sutton 9 (pen), Beattie 71

28 July 2004
**Lincoln Financial Field, Philadelphia**
Att: 55,421

Celtic came out on top in a typically feisty encounter between the two British footballing giants. Alan Smith scored his first goal in the red of United, a first-half header from Chris Eagles' corner, but it wasn't enough. Smith's goal equalised Chris Sutton's ninth-minute penalty, but late in the second half Celtic sub Craig Beattie latched on to a slack back pass to net the winner for the men in green and white.

**Following** the Chicago stalemate, Sir Alex and co headed back to Philadelphia in reflective mood. "I was quite pleased with the youngsters against Bayern," said Ferguson. "But the people coming to the games are entitled to expect the best United players. I'm going to get back to as strong a side as I can in the next two matches."

And the boss was true to his word, with both his Americans in the starting line-up against Celtic. One noteable absentee was Nicky Butt, who left to complete a £3m switch to Newcastle.

Most of the noise inside the Lincoln Financial Field stadium – home to the Philadelphia Eagles American football team – came from the Celtic support. They were the ones celebrating at the end too. In a game looking destined for a draw, Craig Beattie notched a late winner to condemn the Reds to a 2-1 defeat.

Sir Alex singled out Alan Smith, scorer of United's first-half goal, for praise. "We're delighted with his performance, he could maybe have scored four tonight."

The result didn't seem to affect the 500 or so Reds, whose numbers had doubled since Philadelphia. From the 'Rocky steps' of the Philadelphia Art Museum to queues for the Liberty Bell (symbol of US independence) red shirts could be seen mingling with the green-and-white-hooped jerseys. Both parties were oblivious to the other high-profile visitor in town, Democratic presidential candidate John Kerry, in Philly for a campaign speech. "Is he United or Celtic?" quipped one fan. "I thought he played for Chelsea," said another.

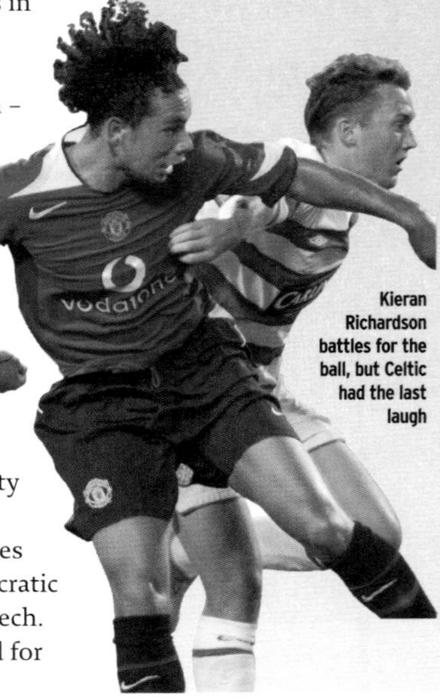


Kieran Richardson battles for the ball, but Celtic had the last laugh

## MANCHESTER UNITED V AC MILAN

**Even in America's** largest city, there were plenty of signs that 'Man U' were in town. The Nike store on Fifth Avenue was displaying United merchandise, Irish pubs advertised live coverage and replica shirts could be spotted at the Big Apple's tourist attractions. *The New York Times* carried another article on Jonathan Spector and the *Daily Post* predicted: "Man U ready to pull out all the stops".

Fears that a United side still missing big names would affect the gate proved inaccurate as 74,511 turned out, including an estimated 1,250 from the UK, to see United's most convincing display. Tim Howard, on his old stamping ground, was again the star attraction, but it was Paul Scholes, who'd flown over with Mikael Silvestre two days earlier, who induced the loudest cheer.

The midfielder latched on to a mistake from Alessandro Nesta in the first half, but Andriy Shevchenko prodded in a last-minute equaliser to usher in another shoot out, which ended 9-8 to the Italians.

But chief executive David Gill was pleased. "We got 180,000-190,000 fans at our games, more than any other club," he said. "In that respect, it was spectacular."

Paul Scholes's strike gave United the lead, until Andriy Shevchenko popped up

**Manchester United 1**
Scholes 33

**Milan 1**
Shevchenko 89

(Milan win 9-8 on penalties)

31 July 2004
**Giants Stadium, East Rutherford**
Att: 74,511

Tour reinforcement Paul Scholes gave the Reds a 33rd-minute lead, taking advantage of Alessandro Nesta's defensive slip. With time running out, that goal seemed to have secured victory, but as the minutes ticked away, Andriy Shevchenko denied the Reds with a poacher's finish from a low, deflected cross. Another session of 'PKs' followed, the Italians eventually winning 9-8.

# UNDER STARTER'S ORDERS

## The Reds warmed up for the season with the Vodafone Cup, a trip to Turf Moor, and Roy's return to the Ramblers...

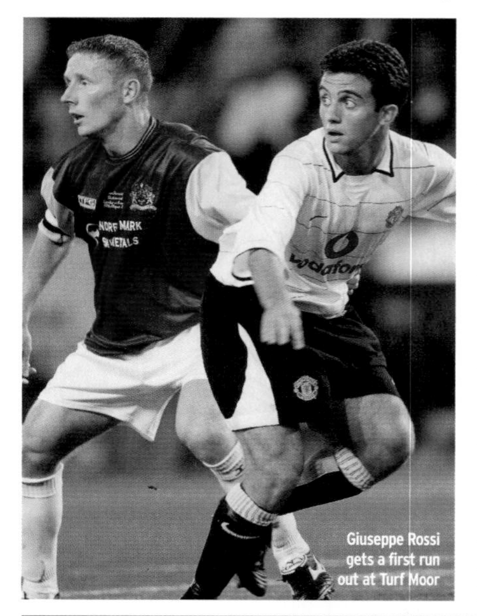

Giuseppe Rossi gets a first run out at Turf Moor

Boca Juniors won the inaugural Vodafone Cup but it was the weather that grabbed the headlines, after electric storms caused the match between Boca and PSV to be called off. Boca were winning 1-0 but after consultation between the referee and the Met Office the game was stopped. United's match with Urawa Red Diamonds was also cancelled. The previous day United had beaten PSV 1-0 thanks to a Mikael Silvestre goal and Boca had brushed aside the Diamonds 5-2.They were awarded the trophy, courtesy of a points system that gave three for a win and one for every goal. United would have needed to have trounced Urawa 6-1 to have lifted the trophy.

The month before, Sir Alex took a United team to Turf Moor to play in a testimonial match for former Burnley boss Stan Ternent. United ran out 3-1 winners thanks to Paul Scholes, Phil Neville and Chris Eagles. Also in July, Roy Keane returned to County Cork and led a young United side against Cobh Ramblers. A late Kenny Cooper strike gave the Reds a 2-1 win.

Stormy weather: A case of rain stops play for the inaugural Vodafone Cup

# ...ALSO AT OLD TRAFFORD

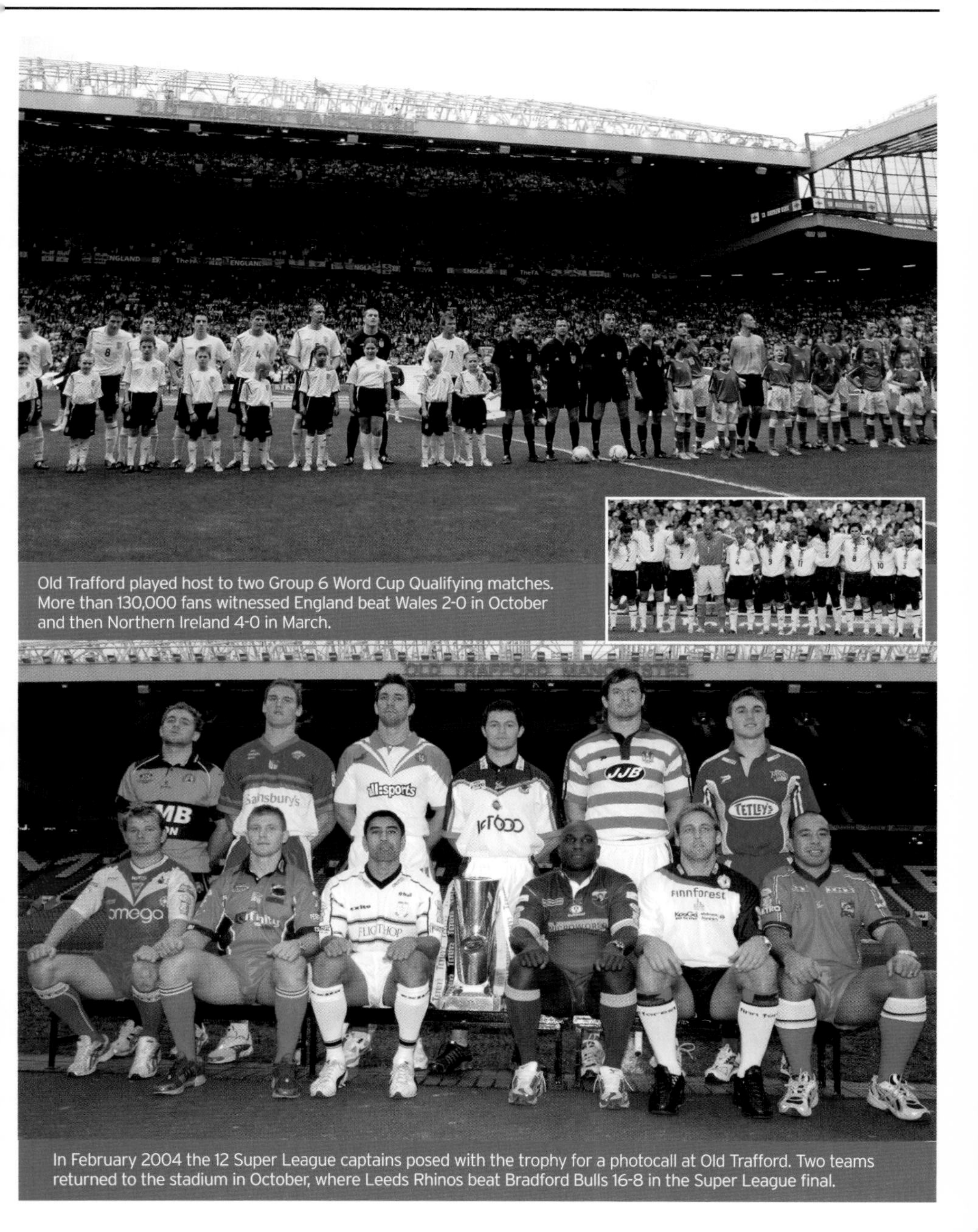


Old Trafford played host to two Group 6 Word Cup Qualifying matches. More than 130,000 fans witnessed England beat Wales 2-0 in October and then Northern Ireland 4-0 in March.

In February 2004 the 12 Super League captains posed with the trophy for a photocall at Old Trafford. Two teams returned to the stadium in October, where Leeds Rhinos beat Bradford Bulls 16-8 in the Super League final.

**Unless stated all home matches kick-off 3pm Saturday, 8pm midweek. UEFA Champions League home matches kick-off 7.45pm**

| AUGUST | RESULT | | | STARTING LINE-UP | | | | | | | |
|---|---|---|---|---|---|---|---|---|---|---|---|
| ● SUN 8 | ARSENAL | Cardiff | 1-3 | HOWARD | G NEVILLE | O'SHEA | SILVESTRE | FORTUNE | DJEMBA-DJEMBA* | BELLION | KEANE |
| ● WED 11 | DINAMO BUCHAREST | Away | 2-1X | HOWARD | G NEVILLE* | KEANE | SILVESTRE* | FORTUNE | DJEMBA-DJEMBA | O'SHEA | FLETCHE |
| ● SUN 15 | CHELSEA 4.05pm | Away | 0-1 | HOWARD | G NEVILLE | KEANE | SILVESTRE | FORTUNE | DJEMBA-DJEMBA | O'SHEA | MILLER |
| **● SAT 21** | **NORWICH CITY** 5.15pm | **Home** | 2-1 | HOWARD | G NEVILLE | KEANE | SILVESTRE | O'SHEA | DJEMBA-DJEMBA | **BELLION** | MILLER |
| **● WED 25** | **DINAMO BUCHAREST** 8.10pm | **Home** | 3-0 | HOWARD | G NEVILLE | O'SHEA | SILVESTRE | SPECTOR | DJEMBA-DJEMBA | EAGLES | FLETCHE |
| ● SAT 28 | BLACKBURN ROVERS 12.45pm | Away | 1-1 | HOWARD | G NEVILLE | O'SHEA | SILVESTRE | SPECTOR | DJEMBA-DJEMBA | RONALDO | KLEBERS |
| **● MON 30** | **EVERTON** 12pm | **Home** | 0-0 | HOWARD | G NEVILLE | O'SHEA | SILVESTRE | SPECTOR | FLETCHER | RONALDO | KLEBERS |
| **SEPTEMBER** | | | | | | | | | | | |
| ● SAT 11 | BOLTON WANDERERS | Away | 2-2 | HOWARD | P NEVILLE | BROWN | SILVESTRE | **HEINZE** | KLEBERSON | KEANE | SCHOLES |
| ● WED 15 | OLYMPIQUE LYONNAIS | Away | 2-2 | HOWARD | O'SHEA | BROWN | SILVESTRE | HEINZE* | DJEMBA-DJEMBA | RONALDO | KEANE |
| **● MON 20** | **LIVERPOOL** | **Home** | 2-1 | CARROLL | BROWN | FERDINAND | **SILVESTRE(2)** | HEINZE | O'SHEA | KEANE* | RONALD |
| ● SAT 25 | TOTTENHAM HOTSPUR | Away | 1-0 | CARROLL | BROWN | FERDINAND | SILVESTRE | HEINZE | O'SHEA | KEANE | RONALD |
| **● TUE 28** | **FENERBAHÇE SK** | **Home** | 6-2 | CARROLL | G NEVILLE | FERDINAND | SILVESTRE | HEINZE* | DJEMBA-DJEMBA | **BELLION** | KLEBERS |
| **OCTOBER** | | | | | | | | | | | |
| **● SUN 3** | **MIDDLESBROUGH** 3pm | **Home** | 1-1 | CARROLL | G NEVILLE | FERDINAND | SILVESTRE | HEINZE | RONALDO | O'SHEA | KEANE* |
| ● SAT 16 | BIRMINGHAM CITY 12.45pm | Away | 0-0 | CARROLL | G NEVILLE | FERDINAND | BROWN | FORTUNE | SMITH | KLEBERSON | KEANE |
| ● TUE 19 | AC SPARTA PRAHA | Away | 0-0 | CARROLL | G NEVILLE | BROWN | SILVESTRE | HEINZE | MILLER* | SCHOLES* | O'SHEA |
| **● SUN 24** | **ARSENAL** 4.05pm | **Home** | 2-0 | CARROLL | G NEVILLE* | FERDINAND | SILVESTRE | HEINZE | RONALDO | P NEVILLE* | SCHOLES |
| ● TUE 26 | CREWE ALEXANDRA (CC3) 7.45pm | Away | 3-0X | HOWARD | RICHARDSON | BROWN | O'SHEA | **MILLER** | DJEMBA-DJEMBA | FLETCHER | KLEBERS |
| ● SAT 30 | PORTSMOUTH | Away | 0-2 | CARROLL | G NEVILLE | FERDINAND* | SILVESTRE | HEINZE | RONALDO | P NEVILLE | SCHOLES |
| **NOVEMBER** | | | | | | | | | | | |
| **● WED 3** | **AC SPARTA PRAHA** | **Home** | 4-1 | CARROLL | G NEVILLE | FERDINAND | BROWN* | HEINZE | MILLER* | KEANE | SCHOLES |
| **● SUN 7** | **MANCHESTER CITY** 4.05pm | **Home** | 0-0 | CARROLL | G NEVILLE | FERDINAND | SILVESTRE | HEINZE | MILLER | KEANE* | SCHOLES |
| **● WED 10** | **CRYSTAL PALACE** | **Home** | 2-0 | HOWARD | P NEVILLE | BROWN | O'SHEA | FORTUNE | DJEMBA-DJEMBA | FLETCHER | KLEBERS |
| ● SUN 14 | NEWCASTLE UNITED 4.05pm | Away | 3-1 | CARROLL | G NEVILLE | FERDINAND | SILVESTRE | HEINZE | FLETCHER | KEANE | SCHOLES |
| **● SAT 20** | **CHARLTON ATHLETIC** 12.45pm | **Home** | 2-0 | CARROLL | BROWN | FERDINAND | SILVESTRE | FORTUNE | FLETCHER | KEANE | **SCHOLE** |
| **● TUE 23** | **OLYMPIQUE LYONNAIS** | **Home** | 2-1 | CARROLL | **G NEVILLE** | FERDINAND | SILVESTRE | HEINZE | SMITH | KEANE* | SCHOLES |
| ● SAT 27 | WEST BROMWICH ALBION | Away | 3-0 | CARROLL | BROWN | FERDINAND | SILVESTRE | HEINZE | FLETCHER | KEANE | **SCHOLE** |
| **DECEMBER** | | | | | | | | | | | |
| **● WED 1** | **ARSENAL** (CC4) 7.45pm | **Home** | 1-0 | HOWARD | P NEVILLE | BROWN | O'SHEA | FORTUNE | DJEMBA-DJEMBA | EAGLES | MILLER |
| **● SUN 4** | **SOUTHAMPTON** | **Home** | 3-0 | CARROLL | G NEVILLE | FERDINAND | SILVESTRE | HEINZE | **RONALDO** | KEANE | **SCHOLE** |
| ● WED 8 | FENERBAHÇE SK | Away | 0-3 | HOWARD | P NEVILLE | BROWN | O'SHEA | FORTUNE | DJEMBA-DJEMBA* | RONALDO | FLETCHE |
| ● MON 13 | FULHAM 8pm | Away | 1-1 | CARROLL | G NEVILLE | FERDINAND | SILVESTRE* | HEINZE | RONALDO | KEANE | SCHOLES |
| **● SAT 18** | **CRYSTAL PALACE** | **Home** | 5-2X | CARROLL | G NEVILLE | FERDINAND | SILVESTRE | FORTUNE | FLETCHER | **SCHOLES(2)** | KEANE |
| **● SUN 26** | **BOLTON WANDERERS** | **Home** | 2-0 | CARROLL | O'SHEA | FERDINAND | SILVESTRE | HEINZE | RONALDO | KEANE | FLETCHE |
| ● TUE 28 | ASTON VILLA | Away | 1-0 | CARROLL | O'SHEA* | FERDINAND* | SILVESTRE | HEINZE* | FLETCHER | P NEVILLE | SCHOLES |
| **JANUARY** | | | | | | | | | | | |
| ● SAT 1 | MIDDLESBROUGH 5.30pm | Away | 2-0 | CARROLL | P NEVILLE | FERDINAND | SILVESTRE | HEINZE | RONALDO | **FLETCHER** | SCHOLES |
| **● TUE 4** | **TOTTENHAM HOTSPUR** | **Home** | 0-0 | CARROLL | P NEVILLE* | FERDINAND | SILVESTRE | HEINZE | RONALDO | FLETCHER | SCHOLES |
| **● SAT 8** | **EXETER CITY** (FAC3) | **Home** | 0-0 | HOWARD | P NEVILLE | BROWN | PIQUÉ | SPECTOR | DJEMBA-DJEMBA | EAGLES | JONES |
| ● WED 12 | CHELSEA 8pm (CCSF, 1ST LEG) | Away | 0-0 | HOWARD | P NEVILLE | SILVESTRE | O'SHEA | HEINZE* | DJEMBA-DJEMBA | RONALDO* | FLETCHE |
| ● SAT 15 | LIVERPOOL 12.30pm | Away | 1-0 | CARROLL | P NEVILLE | BROWN* | SILVESTRE | HEINZE | FLETCHER | KEANE* | SCHOLES |
| ● WED 19 | EXETER CITY (FAC3R) | Away | 2-0 | HOWARD | P NEVILLE | G NEVILLE | O'SHEA | FORTUNE | DJEMBA-DJEMBA | GIGGS | MILLER |
| **● SAT 22** | **ASTON VILLA** | **Home** | 3-1 | CARROLL | G NEVILLE | FERDINAND | SILVESTRE | HEINZE | **RONALDO*** | FLETCHER | **SCHOLE** |
| **● WED 26** | **CHELSEA** (CCSF, 2ND LEG) | **Home** | 1-2 | CARROLL | G NEVILLE | FERDINAND | SILVESTRE | HEINZE | RONALDO | KEANE* | SCHOLES |
| **● SAT 29** | **MIDDLESBROUGH** (FAC4) 5.20pm | **Home** | 3-0 | CARROLL | G NEVILLE | FERDINAND | BROWN | HEINZE | RONALDO | P NEVILLE | **O'SHEA** |
| **FEBRUARY** | | | | | | | | | | | |
| ● TUE 1 | ARSENAL | Away | 4-2 | CARROLL | G NEVILLE | FERDINAND | SILVESTRE* | HEINZE* | FLETCHER | KEANE | SCHOLES |
| **● SAT 5** | **BIRMINGHAM CITY** | **Home** | 2-0 | CARROLL | G NEVILLE | FERDINAND | BROWN | HEINZE* | RONALDO | O"SHEA | **KEANE** |
| ● SUN 13 | MANCHESTER CITY 1pm | Away | 2-0X | CARROLL | G NEVILLE | FERDINAND | BROWN | HEINZE | O'SHEA | KEANE* | FORTUNE |
| ● SAT 19 | EVERTON (FAC5) 5.30pm | Away | 2-0 | CARROLL | G NEVILLE | BROWN | FERDINAND | HEINZE | **RONALDO** | P NEVILLE | KEANE* |
| **● WED 23** | **MILAN** 7.45pm (1ST KO RND, 1ST LEG) | **Home** | 0-1 | CARROLL | G NEVILLE | BROWN | FERDINAND | HEINZE | RONALDO | SCHOLES | KEANE |
| **● SAT 26** | **PORTSMOUTH** 5.15pm | **Home** | 2-1 | HOWARD | G NEVILLE | BROWN | SILVESTRE | HEINZE | RONALDO | O'SHEA | SCHOLES |
| **MARCH** | | | | | | | | | | | |
| ● SAT 5 | CRYSTAL PALACE | Away | 0-0 | HOWARD | BROWN | FERDINAND* | SILVESTRE | HEINZE* | FORTUNE | P NEVILLE | KEANE |
| ● TUE 8 | MILAN (1ST KO RND, 2ND LEG) | Away | 0-1 | HOWARD | BROWN | FERDINAND | SILVESTRE | HEINZE | RONALDO | KEANE | SCHOLES |
| ● SAT 12 | SOUTHAMPTON (FAC6) 5.15pm | Away | 4-0 | HOWARD | BROWN | FERDINAND | SILVESTRE | HEINZE* | **RONALDO** | **KEANE** | **SCHOLE** |
| **● SAT 19** | **FULHAM** | **Home** | 1-0 | HOWARD | BROWN | FERDINAND | SILVESTRE | HEINZE | **RONALDO** | SCHOLES | KEANE |
| **APRIL** | | | | | | | | | | | |
| **● SAT 2** | **BLACKBURN ROVERS** | **Home** | 0-0 | HOWARD | G NEVILLE* | FERDINAND | SILVESTRE | O'SHEA | RONALDO | SCHOLES | FORTUNE |
| ● SAT 9 | NORWICH CITY 5.15pm | Away | 0-2 | HOWARD | G NEVILLE | FERDINAND | SILVESTRE | HEINZE | KLEBERSON | SCHOLES* | P NEVILL |
| ● SUN 17 | NEWCASTLE UNITED (FAC SF) 2pm | Cardiff | 4-1 | HOWARD | G NEVILLE | FERDINAND | BROWN | HEINZE | KEANE | FORTUNE | **RONALD** |
| ● WED 20 | EVERTON | Away | 0-1 | HOWARD | G NEVILLE* | FERDINAND | BROWN | HEINZE | KEANE | FLETCHER | RONALD |
| **● SUN 24** | **NEWCASTLE UNITED** 4.05pm | **Home** | 2-1 | HOWARD | P NEVILLE | FERDINAND | **BROWN** | HEINZE | FLETCHER | KEANE | FORTUNE |
| **MAY** | | | | | | | | | | | |
| ● SUN 1 | CHARLTON ATHLETIC 4.05pm | Away | 4-0 | CARROLL | BROWN | FERDINAND | SILVESTRE | O'SHEA | GIGGS | KEANE* | **SCHOL** |
| **● SAT 7** | **WEST BROMWICH ALBION** 5.15pm | **Home** | 1-1 | CARROLL | BROWN | FERDINAND | SILVESTRE | O'SHEA | RONALDO | P NEVILLE | KLEBERS |
| **● TUE 10** | **CHELSEA** | **Home** | 1-3 | CARROLL | G NEVILLE | BROWN | FERDINAND | SILVESTRE | FLETCHER | KEANE* | SCHOLES |
| ● SUN 15 | SOUTHAMPTON | Away | 2-1 | CARROLL | O'SHEA | BROWN* | FERDINAND | SILVESTRE* | FORTUNE | **FLETCHER** | GIGGS |
| ● SAT 21 | ARSENAL (FAC FINAL) | Cardiff | 0-0▲ | CARROLL | BROWN | FERDINAND | SILVESTRE* | O'SHEA | ROONEY | FLETCHER | KEANE |

**Key:** ● Community Shield ● Barclays Premiership ● UEFA Champions League ● Carling Cup ● FA Cup **BOLD NAME** Goalscorer ● Penalty
x Own goal (15) Substitute appearance and squad no. of player replaced *After extra time *Yellow card *Red card ▲ United lost 4-5 on penalties

| | | | SUBSTITUTES | REFEREE | ATTENDANCE |
|---|---|---|---|---|---|
| OLES | GIGGS | **SMITH** | FLETCHER (16), P NEVILLE* (25), FORLAN (11), EAGLES (14), RICHARDSON (18), SPECTOR (22), CARROLL | M DEAN | 63,317 |
| OLES* | **GIGGS** | SMITH* | MILLER (24), P NEVILLE (11), FORLAN (18), CARROLL, EAGLES, SPECTOR, RICHARDSON | P COSTA | 58,000 |
| OLES | GIGGS | SMITH | FORLAN (19), BELLION (25), RICHARDSON (17), RICARDO, P NEVILLE | G POLL | 41,813 |
| OLES | GIGGS | **SMITH** | P NEVILLE (2), RICHARDSON (12), RONALDO (17), CARROLL, EAGLES | N BARRY | 67,812 |
| 3ERSON | RONALDO | **SMITH(2)** | P NEVILLE (2), **BELLION** (14), RICHARDSON (7), CARROLL, SCHOLES, SAHA, GIGGS | M MERK | 61,041 |
| OLES | GIGGS | **SMITH** | SAHA (15), MILLER (29), BELLION (19), CARROLL, P NEVILLE | A WILEY | 26,155 |
| OLES | SAHA | SMITH | GIGGS (24), DJEMBA-DJEMBA (11), BELLION (7), CARROLL, P NEVILLE | D GALLAGHER | 67,803 |
| 3S* | V NISTELROOY | SMITH | RONALDO (15), **BELLION** (10), CARROLL, DJEMBA-DJEMBA, SPECTOR | M MESSIAS | 27,766 |
| 3S | SCHOLES | **V NISTELROOY(2)** | SMITH (10), P NEVILLE (22), CARROLL, BELLION, KLEBERSON, RICHARDSON, FLETCHER | W STARK | 40,000 |
| 3S | SCHOLES | V NISTELROOY | SMITH (18), RICARDO, P NEVILLE, FLETCHER, KLEBERSON | G POLL | 67,857 |
| 3S | SMITH | **V NISTELROOY•** | MILLER (11), BELLION (10), RICARDO, P NEVILLE, KLEBERSON | P WALTON | 36,103 |
| **GS** | **ROONEY(3)** | **V NISTELROOY** | FLETCHER (11), P NEVILLE (4), MILLER (10), RICARDO, RONALDO, SMITH, O'SHEA | F D BLEECKERE | 67,128 |
| 3S | ROONEY | V NISTELROOY | **SMITH** (22), RICARDO, KLEBERSON, DJEMBA-DJEMBA, FORTUNE | R STYLES | 67,988 |
| ALDO | SAHA | V NISTELROOY | ROONEY (15), SCHOLES (7), P NEVILLE, O'SHEA, RICARDO | M HALSEY | 29,221 |
| 3S | ROONEY | V NISTELROOY | RONALDO (11), SAHA (8), RICARDO, P NEVILLE, SMITH, KLEBERSON, DJEMBA-DJEMBA | M DE SANTIS | 20,654 |
| 3S | **ROONEY** | **V NISTELROOY•** | SMITH (7), SAHA (10), HOWARD, BROWN, MILLER | M RILEY | 67,862 |
| .ION | **SMITH*** | SAHA | PIQUÉ (22), EAGLES (24), EBANKS-BLAKE (12), RICARDO, SPECTOR | M MESSIAS | 10,103 |
| 3S | ROONEY* | SMITH | BROWN (2), KEANE (3), SAHA (14), MILLER, RICARDO | N BARRY | 20,190 |
| ALDO | ROONEY | **V NISTELROOY•(4)** | P NEVILLE (18), KLEBERSON (7), HOWARD, SAHA, GIGGS, SMITH, DJEMBA-DJEMBA | A HAMER | 66,706 |
| ALDO | SAHA | SMITH* | GIGGS (17), ROONEY (18), HOWARD, PHIL NEVILLE, BROWN | G POLL | 67,863 |
| **HARDSON** | BELLION | **SAHA** | SPECTOR (15), EAGLES (23), ROSSI (12), RICARDO, NGALULA | S DUNN | 48,891 |
| ALDO | **ROONEY(2)** | **V NISTELROOY•** | BROWN (27), GIGGS (24), SMITH (7), HOWARD, SAHA | M DEAN | 52,320 |
| **GS** | ROONEY | V NISTELROOY | O'SHEA (24), P NEVILLE (16), SMITH (10), HOWARD, RONALDO | R STYLES | 67,704 |
| ALDO | ROONEY | **V NISTELROOY** | BROWN (2), FORTUNE (16), FLETCHER (10), HOWARD, BELLION, DJEMBA-DJEMBA, O'SHEA | K NIELSEN | 66,398 |
| 3S | ROONEY | **V NISTELROOY** | RONALDO (24), SMITH (10), HOWARD, O'SHEA, FORTUNE | S BENNETT | 27,709 |
| 3ERSON | RICHARDSON* | **BELLION** | ROSSI (33), JONES (15), RICARDO, PIQUÉ, EBANKS-BLAKE | M HALSEY | 67,103 |
| 3S | **ROONEY** | SMITH | BELLION (14), HOWARD, BROWN, MILLER, FLETCHER | B KNIGHT | 67,921 |
| IARDSON | MILLER | BELLION | PIQUÉ (6), SPECTOR (23), EAGLES (17) RICARDO, JONES, McSHANE, EBANKS-BLAKE | A D IBANEZ | 35,000 |
| 3S | ROONEY | **SMITH** | HOWARD, BELLION, O'SHEA, FLETCHER, FORTUNE | P DOWD | 21,940 |
| 3S | ROONEY | **SMITH** | **O'SHEA** (25), HOWARD, P NEVILLE, BELLION, MILLER | S DUNN | 67,814 |
| **GS** | ROONEY | SMITH | **SCHOLES** (7), MILLER (8), HOWARD, P NEVILLE, BELLION | D GALLAGHER | 67,867 |
| **GS** | ROONEY | SMITH | KEANE (22), RONALDO (8), HOWARD, MILLER, BELLION | G POLL | 42,593 |
| NE | **GIGGS** | SMITH | DJEMBA-DJEMBA (7), BELLION (11), HOWARD, G NEVILLE, SPECTOR | A WILEY | 34,199 |
| NE | GIGGS | SMITH | BELLION (11), MILLER (24), SPECTOR (7), RICARDO, DJEMBA-DJEMBA | M CLATTENBURG | 67,962 |
| .ER | BELLION | RICHARDSON | RONALDO (33), SCHOLES (17), SMITH (12), RICARDO, HEINZE | P DOWD | 67,551 |
| TUNE | SAHA | ROONEY | SCHOLES (19), SMITH (7), CARROLL, MILLER, SPECTOR | N BARRY | 41,492 |
| ALDO | **ROONEY*** | SAHA | O'SHEA (7), FORTUNE* (9), BELLION (8), HOWARD, MILLER | S BENNETT | 44,183 |
| OLES | **ROONEY** | **RONALDO** | FLETCHER (17), SAHA (11), SILVESTRE (19), RICARDO, BELLION | P DOWD | 9,033 |
| NE* | ROONEY | **SAHA** | FORTUNE (24), O'SHEA (18), GIGGS (8), HOWARD, BROWN | M HALSEY | 67,859 |
| TUNE | **GIGGS** | SAHA | ROONEY (25), RICARDO, BROWN, O'SHEA, P NEVILLE | R STYLES | 67,000 |
| TUNE | GIGGS | **ROONEY(2)** | SAHA (11), MILLER (7), SILVESTRE (4), HOWARD, SCHOLES | S DUNN | 67,251 |
| **GS*** | ROONEY* | **RONALDO(2)*** | **O'SHEA** (24), BROWN (7), SAHA (11), HOWARD, P NEVILLE | G POLL | 38,164 |
| S | **ROONEY** | SAHA | FORTUNE (9), P NEVILLE (11), MILLER (8), HOWARD, BELLION | D GALLAGHER | 67,838 |
| CHER | **ROONEY*** | SCHOLES* | RONALDO (22), GIGGS (24), P NEVILLE (18), HOWARD, BELLION | S BENNETT | 47,111 |
| OLES | **FORTUNE** | ROONEY | MILLER (16), HOWARD, GIGGS, SMITH, SPECTOR | R STYLES | 38,664 |
| TUNE* | GIGGS | ROONEY | V NISTELROOY (7), SILVESTRE (2), SAHA (25), HOWARD, P NEVILLE, SMITH, O'SHEA | M GONZALEZ | 67,162 |
| VILLE* | **ROONEY(2)** | V NISTELROOY | SMITH (2), GIGGS (18), FORTUNE (10), RICARDO, SAHA | M HALSEY | 67,989 |
| S* | SMITH | V NISTELROOY | SCHOLES (25), RONALDO (3), ROONEY (14), CARROLL, O'SHEA | M CLATTENBURG | 26,021 |
| 3S | ROONEY | V NISTELROOY | SMITH (6), FORTUNE* (11), CARROLL, P NEVILLE, BELLION, MILLER, O'SHEA | H FANDEL | 78,957 |
| TUNE | ROONEY | V NISTELROOY | O'SHEA (4), SMITH (7), P NEVILLE (16), CARROLL, BELLION | H WEBB | 30,971 |
| TUNE | ROONEY | V NISTELROOY | P NEVILLE (18), O'SHEA (8), SMITH (10), CARROLL, G NEVILLE | A D'URSO | 67,959 |
| 3S | ROONEY | V NISTELROOY | KEANE* (11), SMITH* (10), CARROLL, P NEVILLE, BROWN | M RILEY | 67,939 |
| TUNE | SAHA | SMITH | RONALDO (9), ROONEY* (25), V NISTELROOY (15), CARROLL, O'SHEA | H WEBB | 25,522 |
| **OLES** | ROONEY | **V NISTELROOY(2)** | GIGGS (7), SMITH (18), FLETCHER (8), CARROLL, SILVESTRE | M RILEY | 69,280 |
| OLES* | ROONEY | V NISTELROOY | SILVESTRE (6), O'SHEA (24), CARROLL, FORTUNE, SMITH | P DOWD | 37,160 |
| S | **ROONEY*** | SMITH | RONALDO (4), KLEBERSON (24), SILVESTRE (16), CARROLL, O'SHEA | N BARRY | 67,845 |
| **TCHER** | **ROONEY** | **SMITH** | KLEBERSON (16), FORTUNE (8), P NEVILLE (18), HOWARD, RONALDO | D GALLAGHER | 26,789 |
| TUNE | **GIGGS** | SMITH* | SCHOLES (3), ROONEY (15), SAHA (14), HOWARD, MILLER | M HALSEY | 67,827 |
| ALDO | ROONEY | **V NISTELROOY*** | SAHA (24), SMITH, FORTUNE, HOWARD, O'SHEA | G POLL | 67,832 |
| TH | ROONEY | **V NISTELROOY** | SAHA (8), P NEVILLE (10), KLEBERSON, KEANE, RICARDO | S BENNETT | 32,066 |
| OLES* | RONALDO | V NISTELROOY | FORTUNE (22), GIGGS (24), G NEVILLE, SMITH, HOWARD | R STYLES | 71,876 |

# Wayne Rooney... a season in stats

| | |
|---|---|
| Appearances | 29 |
| Minutes on pitch | 2,185 |
| **Goal Attempts** | |
| Goals | 11 |
| Shot on target | 46 |
| Shot off target | 49 |
| Blocked | 39 |
| **Passing** | |
| Goal assists | 2 |
| Total passes | 954 |
| Pass completion | 77% |
| **Crossing** | |
| Total crosses | 83 |
| Cross completion | 23% |
| **Dribbling** | |
| Dribbles & runs | 240 |
| Dribble completion | 56% |
| **Defending** | |
| Tackles made | 49 |
| Tackles won | 69% |
| Blocks | 2 |
| Clearances | 3 |
| Interceptions | 12 |
| **Discipline** | |
| Fouls | 40 |
| Offsides | 13 |
| Yellow card | 7 |
| Red card | 0 |

## IN THE 2004/05 SEASON...

- **United tried more shots than any other side - 536**
- **United hit the woodwork more than any team - 21 times**
- **United's passing accuracy of 82% was the best in the top flight**
- **United whipped in 997 crosses - more than any other side**
- **United's 19 clean sheets was their second best in Premiership history**
- **United never lost a game in which Wayne Rooney scored**

## UNITED DISCIPLINE

| | F | Y | R |
|---|---|---|---|
| Roy Keane | 37 | 9 | 0 |
| Alan Smith | 50 | 2 | 1 |
| Wayne Rooney | 40 | 7 | 0 |
| Paul Scholes | 44 | 3 | 1 |
| Gabriel Heinze | 43 | 4 | 0 |
| Cristiano Ronaldo | 39 | 3 | 0 |
| Mikael Silvestre | 26 | 2 | 1 |
| Ruud van Nistelrooy | 31 | 1 | 0 |
| Wes Brown | 21 | 1 | 1 |
| Ryan Giggs | 21 | 3 | 0 |
| John O'Shea | 27 | 1 | 0 |
| Gary Neville | 17 | 2 | 1 |
| Phil Neville | 20 | 3 | 0 |
| Rio Ferdinand | 18 | 3 | 0 |
| Darren Fletcher | 26 | 0 | 0 |
| Quinton Fortune | 22 | 1 | 0 |
| Louis Saha | 17 | 0 | 0 |
| Kleberson | 4 | 1 | 0 |
| Liam Miller | 3 | 0 | 0 |
| Roy Carroll | 2 | 0 | 0 |
| Jonathan Spector | 2 | 0 | 0 |
| Eric Djemba-Djemba | 2 | 0 | 0 |
| David Bellion | 2 | 0 | 0 |
| Tim Howard | 0 | 0 | 0 |
| Kieran Richardson | 0 | 0 | 0 |
| Diego Forlan | 0 | 0 | 0 |

Y = Yellow cards
R = Red cards
F = Total fouls
P = Discipline points

## APPEARANCES & GOALS 2004/05

| | LEAGUE | | FA CUP | | CARLING CUP | | EUROPE | | OTHERS | | TOTAL | |
|---|---|---|---|---|---|---|---|---|---|---|---|---|
| | A | G | A | G | A | G | A | G | A | G | A | G |
| **David Bellion** | 1(9) | 2 | 1 | 0 | 3 | 1 | 2(1) | 2 | 1 | 0 | 8(10) | 5 |
| **Wes Brown** | 18(3) | 1 | 6 | 0 | 3 | 0 | 6(1) | 0 | 0 | 0 | 33(4) | 1 |
| **Roy Carroll** | 26 | 0 | 3 | 0 | 0 | 0 | 5 | 0 | 0 | 0 | 34 | 0 |
| **Eric Djemba-Djemba** | 3(2) | 0 | 2 | 0 | 4 | 0 | 5 | 0 | 1 | 0 | 15(2) | 0 |
| **Chris Eagles** | 0 | 0 | 1 | 0 | 1(2) | 0 | 1(1) | 0 | 0(1) | 0 | 3(4) | 0 |
| **Sylvan Ebanks-Blake** | 0 | 0 | 0 | 0 | 0(1) | 0 | 0 | 0 | 0 | 0 | 0(1) | 0 |
| **Rio Ferdinand** | 31 | 0 | 5 | 0 | 1 | 0 | 5 | 0 | 0 | 0 | 42 | 0 |
| **Darren Fletcher** | 18 | 3 | 1(2) | 0 | 3 | 0 | 3(2) | 0 | 0(1) | 0 | 25(5) | 3 |
| **Diego Forlan** | 0(1) | 0 | 0 | 0 | 0 | 0 | 0(1) | 0 | 0(1) | 0 | 0(3) | 0 |
| **Quinton Fortune** | 12(5) | 0 | 5(1) | 1 | 4 | 0 | 3(2) | 0 | 1 | 0 | 25(8) | 1 |
| **Ryan Giggs** | 26(6) | 6 | 2(2) | 0 | 1 | 1 | 6 | 2 | 1 | 0 | 36(8) | 9 |
| **Gabriel Heinze** | 26 | 1 | 4 | 0 | 2 | 0 | 7 | 0 | 0 | 0 | 39 | 1 |
| **Tim Howard** | 12 | 0 | 4 | 0 | 5 | 0 | 5 | 0 | 1 | 0 | 27 | 0 |
| **David Jones** | 0 | 0 | 1 | 0 | 0(1) | 0 | 0 | 0 | 0 | 0 | 1(1) | 0 |
| **Roy Keane** | 28(3) | 1 | 4 | 1 | 1 | 0 | 6 | 0 | 1 | 0 | 40(3) | 2 |
| **Kleberson** | 6(2) | 0 | 0 | 0 | 3 | 0 | 2(1) | 0 | 0 | 0 | 11(3) | 0 |
| **Liam Miller** | 3(5) | 0 | 2(2) | 0 | 2 | 1 | 3(2) | 0 | 0 | 0 | 10(9) | 1 |
| **Gary Neville** | 22 | 0 | 4 | 0 | 1 | 0 | 7 | 1 | 1 | 0 | 35 | 1 |
| **Phil Neville** | 12(7) | 0 | 4(1) | 0 | 3 | 0 | 1(5) | 0 | 0(1) | 0 | 20(14) | 0 |
| **Ruud van Nistelrooy** | 16(1) | 6 | 3 | 2 | 0 | 0 | 6(1) | 8 | 0 | 0 | 25(2) | 16 |
| **John O'Shea** | 16(7) | 2 | 3(1) | 1 | 4 | 0 | 5 | 0 | 1 | 0 | 29(8) | 3 |
| **Gerard Piqué** | 0 | 0 | 1 | 0 | 0(1) | 0 | 0(1) | 0 | 0 | 0 | 1(2) | 0 |
| **Ricardo** | 0 | 0 | 0 | 0 | 0 | 0 | 0 | 0 | 0 | 0 | 0 | 0 |
| **Kieran Richardson** | 0(2) | 0 | 1 | 0 | 3 | 0 | 1(1) | 0 | 0(1) | 0 | 5(4) | 1 |
| **Cristiano Ronaldo** | 25(8) | 5 | 6(1) | 4 | 2 | 0 | 7(1) | 0 | 0 | 0 | 40(10) | 9 |
| **Wayne Rooney** | 24(5) | 11 | 6 | 3 | 1(1) | 0 | 6 | 3 | 0 | 0 | 37(6) | 17 |
| **Giuseppe Rossi** | 0 | 0 | 0 | 0 | 0(2) | 0 | 0 | 0 | 0 | 0 | 0(2) | 0 |
| **Louis Saha** | 7(7) | 1 | 0(2) | 0 | 4 | 1 | 0(2) | 0 | 0 | 0 | 11(11) | 2 |
| **Paul Scholes** | 29(4) | 9 | 5(1) | 3 | 1(1) | 0 | 7 | 0 | 1 | 0 | 43(6) | 12 |
| **Mikael Silvestre** | 33(2) | 2 | 2(2) | 0 | 2 | 0 | 7(1) | 0 | 1 | 0 | 45(5) | 2 |
| **Alan Smith** | 22(9) | 6 | 0(3) | 0 | 1(1) | 1 | 3(2) | 2 | 1 | 1 | 27(15) | 10 |
| **Ole Gunnar Solskjaer** | 0 | 0 | 0 | 0 | 0 | 0 | 0 | 0 | 0 | 0 | 0 | 0 |
| **Jonathan Spector** | 2(1) | 0 | 1 | 0 | 0(1) | 0 | 1(1) | 0 | 0(1) | 0 | 4(4) | 0 |

## HOW AND WHEN WE SCORED 2004/05

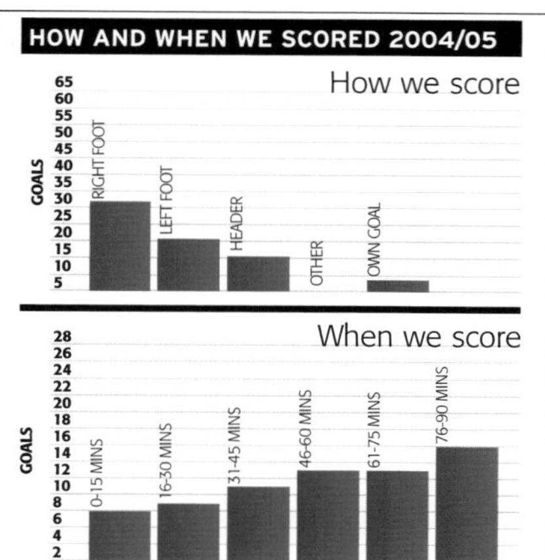


## HOW AND WHEN WE CONCEDED 2004/05

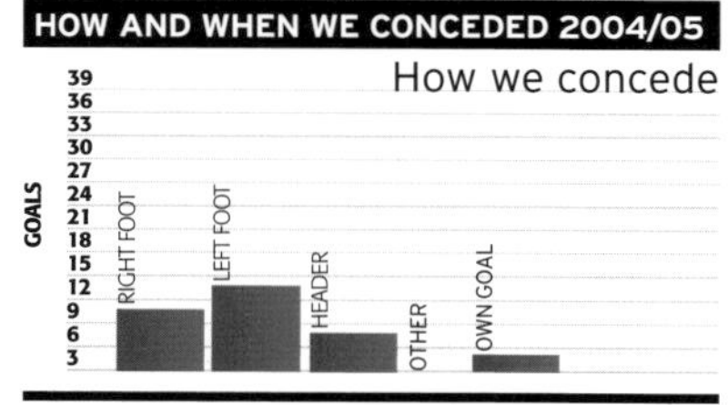


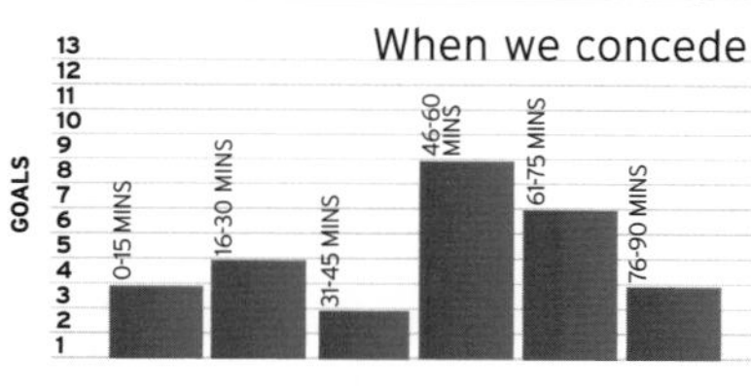


## WHERE WE SCORE AND CONCEDE

GRAPHS AND CHARTS FOR THE PREMIERSHIP ONLY

## PREMIERSHIP TABLE 2004/05

| | | P | W | D | L | F | A | GD | PTS |
|---|---|---|---|---|---|---|---|---|---|
| 1 | Chelsea | 38 | 29 | 8 | 1 | 72 | 15 | 57 | 95 |
| 2 | Arsenal | 38 | 25 | 8 | 5 | 87 | 36 | 51 | 83 |
| 3 | Manchester United | 38 | 22 | 11 | 5 | 58 | 26 | 32 | 77 |
| 4 | Everton | 38 | 18 | 7 | 13 | 45 | 46 | -1 | 61 |
| 5 | Liverpool | 38 | 17 | 7 | 14 | 52 | 41 | 11 | 58 |
| 6 | Bolton Wanderers | 38 | 16 | 10 | 12 | 49 | 44 | 5 | 58 |
| 7 | Middlesbrough | 38 | 14 | 13 | 11 | 53 | 46 | 7 | 55 |
| 8 | Manchester City | 38 | 13 | 13 | 12 | 47 | 39 | 8 | 52 |
| 9 | Tottenham Hotspur | 38 | 14 | 10 | 14 | 47 | 41 | 6 | 52 |
| 10 | Aston Villa | 38 | 12 | 11 | 15 | 45 | 52 | -7 | 47 |
| 11 | Charlton Athletic | 38 | 12 | 10 | 16 | 42 | 58 | -16 | 46 |
| 12 | Birmingham City | 38 | 11 | 12 | 15 | 40 | 46 | -6 | 45 |
| 13 | Fulham | 38 | 12 | 8 | 16 | 52 | 60 | -8 | 44 |
| 14 | Newcastle United | 38 | 10 | 14 | 14 | 47 | 57 | -10 | 44 |
| 15 | Blackburn Rovers | 38 | 9 | 15 | 14 | 32 | 43 | -11 | 42 |
| 16 | Portsmouth | 38 | 10 | 9 | 19 | 43 | 59 | -16 | 39 |
| 17 | West Bromwich Albion | 38 | 6 | 16 | 16 | 36 | 61 | -25 | 34 |
| 18 | Crystal Palace | 38 | 7 | 12 | 19 | 41 | 62 | -21 | 33 |
| 19 | Norwich City | 38 | 7 | 12 | 19 | 42 | 77 | -35 | 33 |
| 20 | Southampton | 38 | 6 | 14 | 18 | 45 | 66 | -21 | 32 |

## UNITED PLAYER CAREER STATS

| | LEAGUE | | FA CUP | | CARLING CUP | | EUROPE | | OTHERS | | TOTAL | |
|---|---|---|---|---|---|---|---|---|---|---|---|---|
| | A | G | A | G | A | G | A | G | A | G | A | G |
| **Phillip Bardsley** | 0 | 0 | 0(1) | 0 | 1 | 0 | 0 | 0 | 0 | 0 | 1(1) | 0 |
| **David Bellion** | 5(19) | 4 | 2(1) | 0 | 5 | 2 | 2(5) | 2 | 1 | 0 | 15(25) | 8 |
| **Wes Brown** | 107(14) | 1 | 15(2) | 0 | 9(1) | 0 | 31(6) | 1 | 0 | 0 | 162(23) | 2 |
| **Roy Carroll** | 46(3) | 0 | 7(1) | 0 | 5 | 0 | 10 | 0 | 0 | 0 | 68(4) | 0 |
| **Chris Eagles** | 0 | 0 | 1 | 0 | 1(4) | 0 | 1(1) | 0 | 0(1) | 0 | 3(6) | 0 |
| **Sylvan Ebanks-Blake** | 0 | 0 | 0 | 0 | 0(1) | 0 | 0 | 0 | 0 | 0 | 0(1) | 0 |
| **Rio Ferdinand** | 78(1) | 0 | 8 | 0 | 5 | 0 | 22 | 0 | 1 | 0 | 114(1) | 0 |
| **Darren Fletcher** | 35(5) | 3 | 5(3) | 0 | 5 | 0 | 8(5) | 0 | 0(1) | 0 | 53(14) | 3 |
| **Quinton Fortune** | 53(23) | 6 | 8(1) | 1 | 8 | 0 | 16(12) | 2 | 3(2) | 2 | 88(38) | 11 |
| **Ryan Giggs** | 396(51) | 92 | 46(6) | 9 | 22(5) | 7 | 91(5) | 22 | 12(1) | 0 | 567(68) | 130 |
| **Gabriel Heinze** | 26 | 1 | 4 | 0 | 2 | 0 | 7 | 0 | 0 | 0 | 39 | 1 |
| **Tim Howard** | 44 | 0 | 8 | 0 | 5 | 0 | 12 | 0 | 2 | 0 | 71 | 0 |
| **Eddie Johnson** | 0 | 0 | 0 | 0 | 0(1) | 0 | 0 | 0 | 0 | 0 | 0(1) | 0 |
| **David Jones** | 0 | 0 | 1 | 0 | 0(1) | 0 | 0 | 0 | 0 | 0 | 1(1) | 0 |
| **Roy Keane** | 305(16) | 33 | 44(2) | 2 | 12(2) | 0 | 80(1) | 14 | 12 | 2 | 453(21) | 51 |
| **Kleberson** | 16(4) | 2 | 1 | 0 | 4 | 0 | 3(2) | 0 | 0 | 0 | 24(6) | 2 |
| **Liam Miller** | 3(5) | 0 | 2(2) | 0 | 2 | 1 | 3(2) | 0 | 0 | 0 | 10(9) | 1 |
| **Gary Neville** | 301(14) | 5 | 36(2) | 0 | 11(1) | 0 | 91(5) | 2 | 8(1) | 0 | 447(23) | 7 |
| **Phil Neville** | 210(53) | 5 | 25(6) | 1 | 16(1) | 0 | 43(22) | 2 | 7(3) | 0 | 301(85) | 8 |
| **Ruud van Nistelrooy** | 109(6) | 74 | 9(3) | 14 | 4 | 1 | 37(2) | 36 | 2 | 1 | 161(11) | 126 |
| **John O'Shea** | 78(19) | 4 | 10(1) | 1 | 13 | 0 | 23(8) | 0 | 1(1) | 0 | 125(29) | 5 |
| **Gerard Piqué** | 0 | 0 | 1 | 0 | 0(1) | 0 | 0(1) | 0 | 0 | 0 | 1(2) | 0 |
| **Ricardo** | 0(1) | 0 | 0 | 0 | 0 | 0 | 3(1) | 0 | 0 | 0 | 3(2) | 0 |
| **Kieran Richardson** | 0(4) | 0 | 2(1) | 0 | 5(1) | 1 | 3(4) | 0 | 0(1) | 0 | 10(11) | 1 |
| **Cristiano Ronaldo** | 40(22) | 9 | 11(1) | 6 | 3 | 0 | 10(3) | 0 | 0 | 0 | 64(26) | 15 |
| **Wayne Rooney** | 24(5) | 11 | 6 | 3 | 1(1) | 0 | 6 | 3 | 0 | 0 | 37(6) | 17 |
| **Giuseppe Rossi** | 0 | 0 | 0 | 0 | 0(2) | 0 | 0 | 0 | 0 | 0 | 0(2) | 0 |
| **Louis Saha** | 16(10) | 8 | 0(2) | 0 | 4 | 1 | 1(3) | 0 | 0 | 0 | 21(15) | 9 |
| **Paul Scholes** | 259(62) | 87 | 23(9) | 12 | 11(5) | 8 | 74(11) | 21 | 10 | 0 | 377(87) | 128 |
| **Mikael Silvestre** | 186(13) | 4 | 13(2) | 1 | 7 | 0 | 51(7) | 2 | 7 | 1 | 264(22) | 8 |
| **Alan Smith** | 22(9) | 6 | 0(3) | 0 | 1(1) | 1 | 3(2) | 2 | 1 | 1 | 27(15) | 10 |
| **Ole Gunnar Solskjaer** | 142(71) | 84 | 10(12) | 6 | 7(3) | 6 | 34(41) | 19 | 6(3) | 0 | 199(130) | 115 |
| **Jonathan Spector** | 2(1) | 0 | 1 | 0 | 0(1) | 0 | 1(1) | 0 | 0(1) | 0 | 4(4) | 0 |
| **Paul Tierney** | 0 | 0 | 0 | 0 | 1 | 0 | 0 | 0 | 0 | 0 | 1 | 0 |
| **Mads Timm** | 0 | 0 | 0 | 0 | 0 | 0 | 0(1) | 0 | 0 | 0 | 0(1) | 0 |

# ACTION STATIONS...

**Appearances**

| | |
|---|---|
| Mikael Silvestre | 35 |
| Cristiano Ronaldo | 33 |
| Paul Scholes | 33 |
| Ryan Giggs | 32 |
| Rio Ferdinand | 31 |
| Roy Keane | 31 |
| Alan Smith | 31 |

**Shots**

| | |
|---|---|
| Cristiano Ronaldo | 98 |
| Wayne Rooney | 95 |
| Paul Scholes | 58 |
| Alan Smith | 58 |
| Ryan Giggs | 44 |

**Assists**

| | |
|---|---|
| Ryan Giggs | 9 |
| Cristiano Ronaldo | 4 |
| Alan Smith | 4 |
| Gary Neville | 3 |
| Paul Scholes | 3 |

**Crosses**

| | |
|---|---|
| Cristiano Ronaldo | 219 |
| Ryan Giggs | 170 |
| Gary Neville | 109 |
| Gabriel Heinze | 87 |
| Wayne Rooney | 61 |

**Dribbles**

| | |
|---|---|
| Cristiano Ronaldo | 458 |
| Ryan Giggs | 242 |
| Wayne Rooney | 240 |
| Roy Keane | 123 |
| Paul Scholes | 121 |

**Tackles**

| | |
|---|---|
| Roy Keane | 160 |
| Gabriel Heinze | 113 |
| Paul Scholes | 98 |
| Mikael Silvestre | 82 |
| Darren Fletcher | 80 |

**Clearances**

| | |
|---|---|
| Mikael Silvestre | 249 |
| Rio Ferdinand | 202 |
| Gabriel Heinze | 121 |
| Wes Brown | 102 |
| Gary Neville | 56 |

**Fouls won**

| | |
|---|---|
| Cristiano Ronaldo | 101 |
| Gabriel Heinze | 63 |
| Alan Smith | 63 |
| Roy Keane | 39 |
| Ryan Giggs | 37 |

**Saves**

| | |
|---|---|
| Roy Carroll | 56 |
| Tim Howard | 17 |

Vintage Reds: the men leading the charge when it came to the Opta statistics were (clockwise from top left) Mikael Silvestre, Ryan Giggs, Roy Carroll, Roy Keane and Cristiano Ronaldo

From appearances to clearances and shots to saves, these are the men who were busier than most...

opta
opta index

vodafone

# PLAYER PROFILES

# Tim Howard

**Magic moment** In a season with more downs than ups, Howard did at least spare United's blushes against Fulham. With the Reds clinging to a tenuous 1-0 lead, Lee Clark's shot hit a post and fell to Carlos Bocanegra, but Howard acrobatically clawed away the defender's effort and the three points - this time - were United's.

**Position** Goalkeeper

**Born** North Brunswick, New Jersey, USA, 3 June 1979
**Signed** New York/New Jersey Metrostars, 15 July 2003
**Senior United debut** 10 August 2003 v Arsenal, Cardiff, FA Community Shield
**United record** League: 12 games; 0 goals, FA Cup: 4 games, 0 goals; League Cup: 5 games, 0 goals; Europe: 5 games, 0 goals; Others: 1 game, 0 goals
**Total** 71 games, 0 goals
**International** 9 caps for the US

He enjoyed a thoroughly memorable first season in English football, but the big American probably won't linger long over 2004/05 before consigning it to the memory bank. Whereas 2003's Community Shield cast him as the penalty shootout hero on his debut – this season's rematch saw his goal breached three times by a rampant Arsenal attack in the regulation 90 minutes. That performance set the tone for a campaign in which the Reds' defence was too often far from watertight, and Howard regularly alternated with Roy Carroll as United's first choice.

Howard played only 12 Premiership games, and though he did find himself back in favour for the Carling Cup campaign, he failed to kick on from there, not helped by his difficulty dealing with Damien Duff's semi-final winner for Chelsea at Old Trafford. Will be hoping to experience better fortune in 2005/06.

# Gary Neville

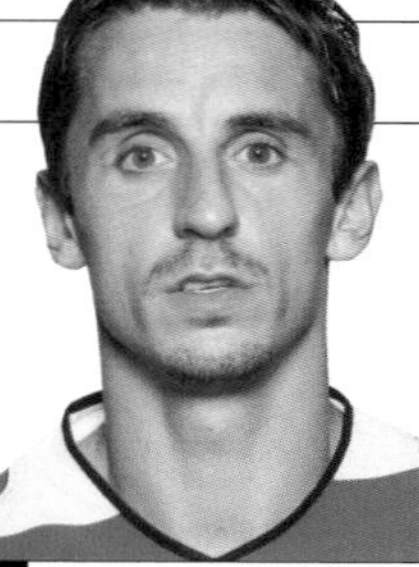

**Magic moment** When you've scored just seven times in almost 450 starts, any goal is special. It's even better when it puts your side up in a crucial Champions League game - the boss's 1,000th in charge. Neville's quick free kick caught the Olympique Lyonnais defence out, and he thumped home Alan Smith's partially-cleared cross.

**2** **Position** Defender

**Born** Bury, 18 February 1975
**Signed** Trainee, 8 July 1991
**Senior United debut** 16 September 1992 v Torpedo Moscow, home, UEFA Cup
**United record** League: 300 (14) games, 5 goals; FA Cup: 36(2) games, 0 goals; League Cup: 11 (1) games, 0 goals; Europe: 91(5) games, 2 goals; Others: 8(1) games, 0 goals
**Total** 447 (23) games, 7 goals
**International** 74 caps for England

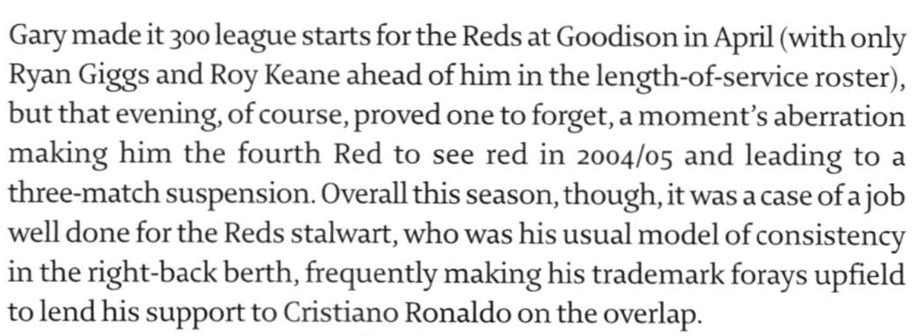

Gary made it 300 league starts for the Reds at Goodison in April (with only Ryan Giggs and Roy Keane ahead of him in the length-of-service roster), but that evening, of course, proved one to forget, a moment's aberration making him the fourth Red to see red in 2004/05 and leading to a three-match suspension. Overall this season, though, it was a case of a job well done for the Reds stalwart, who was his usual model of consistency in the right-back berth, frequently making his trademark forays upfield to lend his support to Cristiano Ronaldo on the overlap.

He was, however, denied a chance to take part in United's biggest games of the season; after limping out of United's Premiership fixture against Portsmouth in late February, he failed to make the Champions League trip to Milan 10 days later. Injury then restricted him to watching the FA Cup final from the bench.

# Phil Neville

**Magic moment** Opportunity rarely knocked, but Neville junior was always up for it when required. Never was there a better example of his willingness to aid the cause than the 2-0 victory at OT that ended Arsenal's unbeaten run. Picked in midfield, he snapped relentlessly at the Gunners' heels, mopping up any scraps.

**3** **Position** Defender/midfielder

**Born** Bury, 21 January 1977
**Signed** Trainee, 5 July 1993
**Senior United debut** 28 January 1995 v Wrexham, home, FA Cup
**United record**
League: 210(53) games, 5 goals; FA Cup: 25(6) games, 1 goal; League Cup: 16(1) games, 0 goals; Europe: 43(22) games, 2 goals; Others: 7(3) games, 0 goals
**Total** 301(85) games, 8 goals
**International** 50 caps for England

Just 12 league starts tells the story of a frustrating season for the younger Neville. With Gabriel Heinze taking a firm grip on the left-back slot, the Reds' Mr Versatility was unable to force himself into a regular place in the centre of the park, despite performing heroics there during 2003/04. Apart from a spell at the start of the year, when injury to big brother Gary saw Phil deputising on the right-hand, side of defence, he found himself mostly warming the Reds' bench.

That said, he did manage to pass one milestone – his 200th start in a league game for the Reds (he also won a 50th England cap at Euro 2004), but even in the Carling Cup, where he'd seemed a permanent fixture – as a veteran among a brigade of youthful team-mates – he found himself back in the role of substitute (and a non-playing one at that) when it came to crunch time against Chelsea in the semi-final.

# Gabriel Heinze

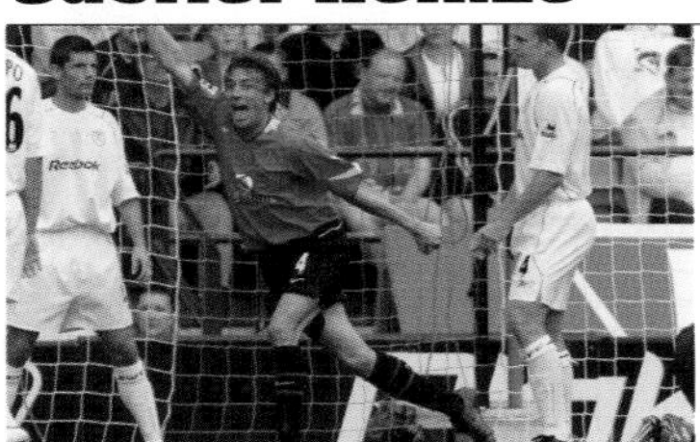

**Magic moment** Heinze had yet to demonstrate his defensive mettle when, just 44 minutes into his Reds' debut, against Bolton Wanderers at the Reebok, he popped up in the area to lash the ball home from the edge of the six-yard box. The first step to becoming a fans' favourite had been well and truly taken...

**Position** Defender

**Born** Crespo, Argentina 19 March 1978
**Signed** From Paris Saint-Germain, 11 June 2004
**Senior United debut** 11 September 2004 v Bolton Wanderers, away, Premiership
**United record** League: 26 games, 1 goal; FA Cup: 4 games, 0 goals; League Cup: 2 games, 0 goals; Europe: 7 games, 0 goals; Others: 0 games, 0 goals
**Total** 39 games, 1 goal
**International** 20 caps for Argentina

We were made to wait for a first glimpse of our Argentinian signing, but with his international duties behind him – and an Olympic winner's medal to boot – Gabriel Heinze showed he was indeed, as good as gold. He opened the scoring against Bolton Wanderers on his debut, but soon proved that he knew where his real duties lay. Terrier-like in the tackle, with a positional sense that is second to none – and a great ability in the air despite not being the tallest – he has proved a phenomenal addition to the Reds' rearguard. Having missed the start of the season, he was sadly absent for the tail-end too; an ankle injury sustained against Newcastle United ruled him out of his first showpiece final for the Reds. But if he continues the form he showed this season, he won't have too long to wait before he helps lift some silverware. A serious contender for the Matt Busby Player of the Year award.

# Rio Ferdinand

**Magic moment** Despite his exploits on the pitch, the biggest roar on Rio's behalf was reserved for the moment, in late September, when he stepped on to the Old Trafford pitch after eight months out suspended. And he responded just as Sir Alex knew he would, his calm, reassured touch to the fore in a 2-1 victory over Liverpool.

**Position**
Defender

When Rio rejoined the fray, six weeks into the season, United were still in the wrong half of the table. By the time he helped halt the record-breaking run of Arsène Wenger's 'Invincibles' in late October, the Reds were about to overhaul Bolton Wanderers and Middlesbrough and close in on Everton in third spot. It's no coincidence that in Ferdinand's first four Premiership games United's defence was breached just twice; his centre-half pairing with Mikael Silvestre providing the platform for a four-pronged assault on silverware. In that first league encounter against the Gunners, Ferdinand's towering performance was instrumental in keeping Thierry Henry and Dennis Bergkamp quiet and saw him named Man of the Match – the first of several times he was awarded the accolade marshalling a United defence that conceded just 26 league goals in total, 10 less than second-placed Arsenal.

**Born** Peckham, 11 July 1978
**Signed** from Leeds United, July 2002
**Senior United debut** 27 August 2002 v Zalaegerszeg, home, Champions League qualifier
**United record** League: 78(1) games, 0 goals; FA Cup: 8 games, 0 goals; League Cup: 5 games, 0 goals; Europe: 22 games, 0 goals; Others: 1 game, 0 goals
**Total** 114(1) games, 0 goals
**International** 36 caps for England

# Wes Brown

**Magic moment** The winner against Newcastle United in April was overshadowed by Wayne Rooney's netbuster, but it was a landmark first league goal for the centre-half, who'd stated earlier in the season that he felt United's defenders ought to be on the scoresheet more regularly.

**Position**
Defender

Sadly, not too many months go by without Wes finding himself on the treatment table – and 2004/05 was no exception. But this time round his troubles were relatively minor niggles – Achilles and calf injuries – and he got himself into Sir Alex's starting XI for the game at the Reebok against Bolton Wanderers in mid-September. With Rio Ferdinand and Mikael Silvestre playing the lion's share of the season in the centre of defence, Brown subsequently found himself in and out of the side, but he did play a pivotal role in the Carling Cup campaign, even captaining the side for the first game of the competition, a 3-0 success at Crewe Alexandra. The FA Cup also gave Wes plenty of opportunity to stretch his legs – he played in every match except the third-round replay against Exeter City, demonstrating his versatility in the final as he filled in for the injured Gary Neville on the right side of the back four.

**Born** Manchester, 13 October 1979
**Signed** Trainee, 8 July 1996
**Senior United debut** 4 May 1998 v Leeds United, home, Premiership
**United record** League: 107(14) games, 1 goal; FA Cup: 15(2) games, 0 goals; League Cup: 9(1) games, 0 goals; Europe: 31(6) games, 1 goal
**Total** 162(23) games, 2 goals
**International** 8 caps for England

# Cristiano Ronaldo

**Magic moment** The young winger's close-range finish after Nigel Martyn could only parry a Paul Scholes free kick capped a mesmerising FA Cup fifth-round display at Goodison Park in February. Running the Toffees ragged, he set up Quinton Fortune for a first-half opener and kept United on course for another trip to Cardiff.

**7**

**Position**
Forward

**Born** Madeira, Portugal, 5 February 1985
**Signed** from Sporting Lisbon, August 2003
**Senior United debut** 16 August 2003 v Bolton Wanderers, home, Premiership
**United record** League: 40(22) games, 9 goals; FA Cup: 11(1) games, 6 goals; League Cup: 3 games, 0 goals; Europe: 10(3) games, 0 goals
**Total** 64(26) games, 15 goals
**International** 18 caps for Portugal

With Euro 2004 and Olympic duties successfully behind him, Ronaldo's first taste of action came as a late substitute in the first home league game of the season against Norwich City. But from that point he was a regular starter, and while the stepover count may have been slightly down from his first, flamboyant season at Old Trafford, his skill on the ball and ability to terrify opposition defences was evident in the bulk of the 33 league games in which he figured. Scoring two of his five Premiership goals in the 4-2 defeat of Arsenal at Highbury only served to heighten his cult status among the United faithful, and his strike in another four-goal haul, against Newcastle in the FA Cup semi-final, was a just reward for an overall performance which included two whipped-in right-wing crosses that Messrs van Nistelrooy and Scholes, respectively, were only too happy to despatch. Unquestionably one of the star performers of 2004/05.

# Wayne Rooney

**Magic moment** There were some who wondered about the wisdom of pitching Rooney straight in against Fenerbahçe. But the striker made it a debut to eclipse just about any other, his hat-trick goal – a 54th-minute free-kick – arguably the most memorable moment in a performance for which no superlative seemed enough.

**Position**
Forward

**Born** Croxteth, 24 October 1985
**Signed** from Everton, August 2004
**Senior United debut** 28 September v Fenerbahçe, home, Champions League
**United record** League: 24(5) games, 11 goals; FA Cup: 6 games, 3 goals; League Cup: 1(1) games, 0 goals; Europe: 6 games, 3 goals; Others: 0 games, 0 goals
**Total** 37(6) games, 17 goals
**International** 21 caps for England

A metatarsal injury picked up against Portugal in Euro 2004 proved no stumbling block to a switch to Old Trafford in August, and almost from the second he made his debut in the glare of the Champions League, he began to repay his £27 million fee. A hat-trick against Fenerbahçe in that game – all three of them stunning strikes – could have proved a hard act to follow… but didn't. Although never in the hunt for the Golden Boot, Rooney's all-round forward play saw him a regular recipient of Man of the Match awards, and when the goals did come they were invariably spectacular. His two against Middlesbrough in the FA Cup (a 30-yard lob that left Boro keeper Mark Schwarzer flat-footed, and a technically brilliant mid-air volley) would have been hard to beat… until the crashing volley that beat Newcastle's Shay Given all ends up. Never has the Young Player of the Year been such a foregone conclusion.

# Louis Saha

**Magic moment** The winner against Aston Villa in January. The Reds needed three points to overhaul Arsenal in second spot and keep the pressure on Chelsea. After Gareth Barry had levelled Cristiano Ronaldo's early opener, the Frenchman restored the lead with 20 minutes to go, converting Wayne Rooney's cross.

An extremely disappointing second season for the former Fulham forward. His first full campaign in a red shirt was hampered by a string of injuries that made him an absentee for the bulk of the action – he was limited to just 11 starts all told – with a further 11 from the bench.

The 2004/05 campaign began badly and didn't improve – it opened with Saha nursing a medial ligament injury which ruled him out of action until the Reds made the trip to Blackburn Rovers at the end of August, where he came on in the second half. After a couple of starts and a handful of appearances from the bench, he got off the mark in the fourth round of the Carling Cup against Crystal Palace in November. But no sooner had he broken his scoring duck than he picked up an injury while on international duty for France against Poland, and didn't feature again until January. Few Reds will be happier to see the back of the season.

9

**Position**
Forward

**Born** Paris, France, 8 August, 1978
**Signed** from Fulham, January 2004
**Senior United debut** 31 January 2004 v Southampton, home, Premiership
**United record** League: 16(10) games, 8 goals; FA Cup 0(2) games, 0 goals; League Cup: 4 games, 1 goal; Europe: 1(3) games, 0 goals; Others: 0 games, 0 goals
**Total** 21(15) games, 9 goals
**International** 8 caps for France

# Ruud van Nistelrooy

**Magic moment** Surpassing Denis Law's 35-year European record goal haul. At level pegging when the Reds travelled to Lyon, the Dutchman's double took his tally to 30. "That's almost a goal-a-game," purred Sir Alex. "He's a great goalscorer and will keep on breaking records here." Amen.

Ruud was ruled out of action for the first month of the season after picking up a sportsman's hernia against former employers PSV Eindhoven in the Vodafone Cup. Back in the frame in September, four goals in five games signalled his intentions and, after helping end the Gunners' unbeaten run with a spotkick at Old Trafford in October, he upped the tempo in November with a glorious run of seven goals in five games. Along the way he single-handedly swept aside Czech Republic champs Sparta Prague with a four-goal Champions League haul.

Sadly, any hope of matching his goalscoring feats of previous league campaigns was brought to a juddering halt after picking up an Achilles injury in December. United fans had to wait until the FA Cup semi-final in Cardiff in April to see the Dutchman celebrate again. He'll be eager to get back on track and among the records in 2005/06.

**Position**
Forward

**Born** Oss, Holland, 1 July 1976
Signed from PSV Eindhoven, 1 July 2001
**Senior United debut** 12 August 2001 v Liverpool, Cardiff, FA Charity Shield
**United record** League: 109(6) games, 74 goals; FA Cup: 9(3) games, 14 goals; League Cup: 4 games, 1 goal; Europe: 37(2) games, 36 goals; Others: 2 games, 1 goal
**Total** 161(11) games, 126 goals
**International** 36 caps for Holland

# Ryan Giggs

**Magic moment** A toss-up between two Man-of-the-Match shows in three days in December, but running Aston Villa ragged on their own Villa Park turf - and getting a Christmas cracker - just gets the nod over his Boxing Day display against Bolton in which his wing wizardry fair rolled back the years. Still plenty left in the tank yet.

Got the Reds' European ball rolling with the first goal against Dinamo Bucharest in the Champions League third qualifying round, and the Welshman was an easy pick for Man of the Match after an inspired performance in the Romanian capital. Back on Premiership duty, his pinpoint crosses against Liverpool ensured that Mikael Silvestre bagged a brace for the first time in his United career and, even more importantly, that the Merseysiders left M16 without a point after taking the lot in three of their previous four Premiership visits.

Giggs's festive goalscoring flourish may have captured the headlines, but it was his rampaging runs and precision passing that made the difference throughout the year. You can't argue with the end-of-season Opta stats that confirmed Giggsy was head and shoulders above his team-mates in terms of goal assists, with nine.

**11** **Position** Forward

**Born** Cardiff, 29 November 1973
**Signed** Trainee, 9 July 1990
**Senior United debut** 2 March 1991 v Everton, home, Division One
**United record** League: 396(51) games, 92 goals; FA Cup: 46(6) games, 9 goals; League Cup: 22(5) games, 7 goals; Europe: 91(5) games, 22 goals; Others: 12(1) games, 0 goals
**Total** 567(68) games, 130 goals
**International** 49 caps for Wales

# David Bellion

**Magic moment** Easy. The early, early doors strike that knocked Arsenal out of Carling Cup. While fans were still taking their seats, the Frenchman picked up the ball on the left and shot from outside the area. Manuel Almunia looked to have it covered, but the ball bounced in off the keeper's knee Just 18.6 seconds had elapsed. Nice!

Bellion burst out of the blocks in 2004/05, scoring the opener in the Old Trafford Premiership curtain-raiser against Norwich City, when he got the crucial touch on an Alan Smith header towards the back post. But for an extra coat of paint on the woodwork, he might well have doubled his tally inside the first half.

He had only to wait until Dinamo Bucharest arrived in M16 for the Champions League qualifier four days later. Replacing his strike partner Smudger, who'd already put two past the Romanians, the Frenchman curled in a low shot to wrap up the proceedings at 3-0. Three substitute appearances followed, and it proved third-time lucky against Bolton Wanderers when he came on with 15 minutes to go to rescue a point at the Reebok. With fierce competition for places up front, Bellion finished the campaign with a respectable five goals in all competitions.

**Position** Forward

**Born** Paris, France, 27 November 1982
**Signed** From Sunderland, 1 July 2003
**Senior United debut** 27 August 2003 v Wolves, home, Premiership
**United record** League: 5(19) games, 4 goals; FA Cup: 2(1) games, 0 goals; League Cup: 5 games, 2 goals; Europe: 2(5) games, 2 goals; Others: 1 game, 0 goals
**Total** 15(25) games, 8 goals

# Roy Carroll

**Magic moment** Preferred to Tim Howard for the FA Cup final, the Irishman had been a virtual spectator – until extra-time. When Robin van Persie's free kick finally posed a threat to the United goal, Carroll proved his agility and alertness by springing smartly to his right to push the Dutchman's effort round the post.

The Northern Ireland international again shared goalkeeping duties with Tim Howard in 2004/2005. "He's always been a steady and consistent performer and will stay in the team now as long as his performances merit," Sir Alex said when selecting Carroll ahead of Tim Howard after the American appeared ill at ease in the 2-2 Champions League draw at Lyon.

However, Carroll was himself relieved of his duties between the sticks in similar circumstances following a high-profile blunder against Milan. But the Irishman ended the campaign as first choice once more, playing in the FA Cup final despite indications he would leave Old Trafford after his new-contract negotiations stalled. Understandably, Carroll is keen to steer clear of comparisons with the masterful Peter Schmeichel. "I'm a different person to Schmeichel. He was one in a million," he says. "I don't look up to him, I just do my own thing."

**Position** Goalkeeper

**Born** Enniskillen, Northern Ireland, 30 September 1977
**Signed** From Wigan, 1 July 2001
**Senior United debut** 26 September 2001 v Aston Villa, away, Premiership
**United record** League: 46(3) games, 0 goals; FA Cup: 7(1) games, 0 goals; League Cup: 5 games, 0 goals; Europe: 10 games, 0 goals; Others: 0 games, 0 goals
**Total** 68(4) games, 0 goals
**International** 16 caps for N Ireland

# Alan Smith

**Magic moment** Capped his home Premiership debut against Norwich City with one of the most spectacular goals of 2004/05. Demonstrating precise balance and technique, he turned to fire a left-foot volley past Robert Green – a strike the boss likened to one of Mark Hughes's best!

The ebullient striker's energy and commitment won him instant respect after his controversial £7 million switch from relegated Leeds United. "I'm not prepared to spend time on the bench – I want to make an impact straight away," he said on his arrival at Old Trafford.

He was as good as his word, too. His last-minute strike at Blackburn Rovers earned the Reds a point at the end of August, while a brace against Dinamo Bucharest ensured qualification for the Champions League group phase. But time on the bench and deployment in midfield reduced his goalscoring chances as the campaign wore on.

One of the season's undoubted success stories, the move has been a revelation to Smith himself. "I enjoy every minute at Manchester United and have done since the moment I came here," he said in a typically positive tone. Long may that continue.

**Position** Forward

**Born** Wakefield, 28 October 1980
**Signed** From Leeds United, 27 May 2004
**Senior United debut** 8 August 2004 v Arsenal, Millennium Stadium, FA Community Shield
**United record** League: 22(9) games, 6 goals; FA Cup: 0(3) games, 0 goals; League Cup: 1(1) games, 0 goals; Europe: 3(2) games, 2 goals; Others: 1 game, 0 goals
**Total** 27(15) games, 10 goals
**International** 12 caps for England

# Kleberson

**Magic moment** Skipping past Fenerbahçe's right-back to deliver a killer cross, which Ryan Giggs headed home with aplomb. That began a rout in which Wayne Rooney hammered a dazzling debut hat-trick. Sadly, Kleberson's early contribution that night was the one outstanding moment of a disappointing, injury-hit season.

"To play at Manchester United is a dream for me," Kleberson declared on his arrival in Manchester in summer 2003. The Brazilian could be forgiven for believing there's a jinx on his Old Trafford career. Although desperate to establish himself as a first-team regular, the World Cup winner has suffered a hellish run of frustrating injuries.

At 26, however, time is on his side and Sir Alex insists we have yet to see the best of the £6 million signing from Atletico Paranaense. "It's very difficult because I have had some long-term injuries, and when I come on I want to do everything," the midfielder revealed. "Hopefully, little by little I will be able to make my way into the first 11."

Perhaps 2005/2006 will prove a third season lucky and Kleberson will finally show the blend of steel and finesse that made him into a World Cup winner with Brazil. If only he can stay fit...

**Position** Midfielder

**Born** Uraí, Brazil, 19 June 1979
**Signed** from Atletico Paranaense, 12 August 2003
**Senior United debut** 27 August 2003 v Wolves, home, Premiership
**United record** League: 16(4) games, 2 goals; FA Cup: 1 game, 0 goals; League Cup: 4 games, 0 goals; Europe: 3(2) games, 0 goals; Others: 0 games, 0 goals
**Total** 24(6) games, 2 goals
**International** 21 caps for Brazil

# Roy Keane

**Magic moment** Keane grabbed the 50th goal of his illustrious United career in the 2-0 home defeat of Birmingham City in February, exploiting some slack defending to drill his shot past Maik Taylor. "We needed someone to open the game up and Roy did that with his goal," Sir Alex reflected. "He was unbelievable."

No stranger to defying the odds – and the critics – United's inspirational skipper continues to prove that age has not sapped his influence. But there is a difference in the role he plays these days. No longer is he the Keano who makes lung-busting surges into enemy territory then gets back to make goal-saving challenges. Now he performs the screening midfield role with control and purpose.

The Irishman's mastery of Arsenal's Patrick Vieira in the 4-2 Premiership victory at Highbury was one of the outstanding performances of the season. Sir Alex hailed Keane, who he signed from Nottingham Forest for £3 million, as one of the greatest players he has worked with. "It's not just the quality of his game, it's also his influence and great determination," said Ferguson when celebrating 18 years in the Old Trafford hot-seat. "There are a lot of parts to making a great player; he's fulfilled them all."

**Position** Midfielder

**Born** Cork, Ireland, 10 August 1971
**Signed** From Nottingham Forest, 19 July 1993
**Senior United debut** 7 August 1993 v Arsenal, Wembley, FA Charity Shield
**United record** League: 305(16) games, 33 goals; FA Cup: 44(2) games, 2 goals: League Cup: 12(2) games, 0 goals; Europe: 80(1) games, 14 goals; Others: 12 games, 2 goals
**Total** 453(21) games, 51 goals
**International** 63 caps for the Republic of Ireland

# Liam Miller

**Magic moment** Even if the Ireland international has not made the positive impact at Old Trafford he would have liked, at least he had the pleasure of chalking up his first goal in United colours. Miller was on target in the 3-0 Carling Cup victory at Crewe Alexandra's Gresty Road, neatly collecting David Bellion's pass and then finishing coolly.

**17** **Position** Midfielder

**Born** Cork, 13 February 1981
**Signed** From Celtic, January 2004
**Senior United debut** 11 August 2004 v Dinamo Bucharest, away, Champions League
**United record** League: 3(5) games, 0 goals; FA Cup: 2(2) games, 0 goals; League Cup: 2 games, 1 goal; Europe: 3(2) games, 0 goals; Others: 0 games, 0 goals
**Total** 10(9) games, 1 goal
**International** 8 caps for the Republic of Ireland

"We recognised the potential of Liam, he has had a great season at Celtic. He is very much part of our progressive thinking of developing a young team over the next few years," said Sir Alex Ferguson as he welcomed the young Irishman after his free transfer from Celtic. And the new United recruit was just as delighted at the deal. "It's very exciting to be here and playing for United is a great feeling having supported them as a boy," he declared. "All the lads are world-class players who you can learn a lot from."

The midfielder's competitive edge and accurate passing in the Premiership opener at Chelsea hinted at a bright future. Miller, however, made just 10 starts in his debut campaign – though he came off the bench on another nine occasions. But the Cork-born midfielder remains resolute in facing up to the challenge. "I knew the players United had when I signed," said Miller. "I always knew it was going to be tough because of the quality here."

# Paul Scholes

**Magic moment** Newcastle have often fallen victim to Scholes' predatory instincts, and it was the midfielder who struck United's second and ultimately decisive goal just before half-time when the sides met in the FA Cup semi-final. Ghosting into the box in typical fashion, Scholes met Ronaldo's cross with a precise header that left Shay Given helpless.

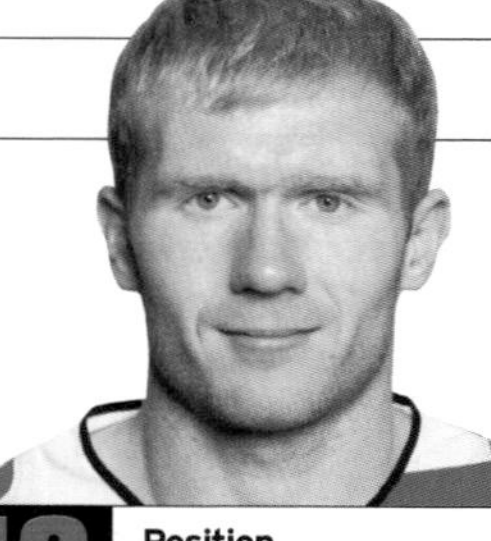

**18** **Position** Midfielder

**Born** Salford, 16 November 1974
**Signed** Trainee, 8 July 1991
**Senior United debut** 21 September 1994 v Port Vale, away, League Cup
**United record** League: 259(62) games, 87 goals; FA Cup: 23(9) games, 12 goals; League Cup: 11(5) games, 8 goals; Europe: 74(11) games, 21 goals; Others: 10 games, 0 goals
**Total** 377(87) games, 128 goals
**International** 66 caps for England

One of Fergie's original 'fledglings', Scholesy has served United with consistent excellence over the past decade. In 2004/05, his passing remained as neat as ever. Against Everton in the FA Cup, for instance, on a pitch not exactly conducive to a smooth passing game, he gave a masterclass in how to retain possession and use the ball efficiently.

The Salford-born midfielder has often been prolific on the goalscoring front, yet it took him until late November to open his account for the season. And it was a goal welcomed across the board. "I am absolutely delighted for Paul. He is a natural finisher and that goal will do him the world of good," Sir Alex Ferguson enthused after the flame-haired schemer netted in the defeat of Charlton Athletic. "I expect him to go on and reach double figures for us." Sure enough, Scholes did, adding another 11 goals to his tally before the end of the campaign. Scholes, 31 in November, may have retired from international football after Euro 2004, but he'll hope to keep delivering top-notch performances for several years to come.

# Eric Djemba-Djemba

**Magic moment** Ex-Nantes player Djemba-Djemba could revel in the part he played in United's dramatic recovery at French titleholders Olympique Lyonnais, as the Reds came from two goals down to snatch a point.

**Position** Midfielder

**Born** Douala, Cameroon, 4 May 1981
**Signed** From FC Nantes, 3 July 2003
**Senior United debut** 10 August 2003 v Arsenal, Cardiff, FA Community Shield
**United record** League: 13(7) games, 0 goals; FA Cup: 2(1) games, 0 goals; League Cup: 5 games, 1 goal; Europe: 6(3) games, 1 goal; Others: 1(1) games, 0 goals
**Total** 27(12) games, 2 goals
**International** 11 caps for Cameroon

"I want to propel myself into my United career next season and I already feel as though I have learned a lot," said Djemba-Djemba after his first season at the Theatre of Dreams. But sadly, the likeable Cameroon international found the competition for central midfield places at United beyond him, and after just three league starts he decamped to Aston Villa in the January 2005 transfer window for £1.35 million.

# Diego Forlan

**Magic moment** As Forlan played just a few minutes of football for United in 2004/05, it's best to focus on the earlier jewels the Uruguayan delivered – like *that* brace against Liverpool.

**Position** Forward

**Born** Montevideo, Uruguay, 19 May 1979
**Signed** from Independiente, 22 January 2002
**Senior United debut** 29 January 2002 v Bolton Wanderers, away, Premiership
**United record** League: 23(40) games, 10 goals; FA Cup: 2(2) games, 1 goal; League Cup: 4(2) games, 3 goals; Europe: 8(15) games, 3 goals; Others: 0(2) games, 0 goals
**Total** 37(61) games, 17 goals
**International** 11 caps for Uruguay

"As soon as I arrived at United, all the fans seemed to expect me to score two goals a game," admitted the Uruguayan striker, sold to Spanish side Villarreal early in the 2004/05 campaign. "There was a lot of pressure and it got to me." But after leaving OT last August, Forlan has bounced back with a vengeance, winning the golden boot – or *pichichi* – in *La Liga* after netting 25 times to propel the 'yellow submarine' into the Champions League.

# John O'Shea

**Magic moment** Substitute O'Shea's wonderful chip at Arsenal in February was worthy of the great Eric Cantona, his deliciously deft strike nestling in the top corner and sealing a heroic, 10-man, 4-2 victory.

**Position** Defender

**Born** Waterford, Ireland, 30 April 1981
**Signed** Trainee, 3 August 1998
**Senior United debut** 13 October 1999 v Aston Villa, away, League Cup
**United record** League: 78(19) games, 4 goals; FA Cup: 10(1) games, 1 goal; League Cup: 13 games, 0 goals; Europe: 23(8) games, 0 goals; Others: 1(1) games, 0 goals
**Total** 125(29) games, 5 goals
**International** 22 caps for the Republic of Ireland

O'Shea's season was restricted, in part, by the outstanding form of Gabriel Heinze at left-back, yet he proved a valuable member of the squad by operating in the heart of midfield and defence, as well as at full-back. A lack of regular first-team opportunities led to talk of his departure, but the Republic of Ireland man made his intentions clear, stating: "I'm definitely staying and, fingers crossed, I will be here for a long time to come."

# Kieran Richardson

**Position** Midfielder

**Magic moment** Scoring his second senior goal in the Carling Cup victory against Crystal Palace. Maybe Palace keeper Julian Speroni should have saved his 20-yard left-foot drive, but it was still an impressive strike.

Kieran made five starts and four substitute appearances for United, his best total for a season so far, but Sir Alex felt his best chance of further progress lay away from Old Trafford. So in January 2005 he linked up with ex-Red Bryan Robson at West Bromwich Albion and made an immediate impact in central midfield. He helped the Baggies avoid relegation, and earned a call-up for England scoring twice on his debut.

**Born** Greenwich, 21 October 1984
**Signed** Trainee, 2 July 2001
**Senior United debut**
23 October 2002 v Olympiakos, away, Champions League
**United record**
League: 0(4) games, 0 goals;
FA Cup: 2(1) games, 1 goals;
League Cup: 5(1) games, 1 goals;
Europe: 3(4) games, 0 goals;
Others: 0(1) games, 0 goals
**Total** 10(11) games, 2 goals
**International** 2 caps for England

# Darren Fletcher

24

**Position** Midfielder

**Magic moment** He'd waited 52 games, but nine minutes into United's 2-0 win away at Middlesbrough, he scored his first senior goal. When Mark Schwarzer spilled a Ryan Giggs shot, Fletcher was quickest to react.

Despite an injury-disrupted campaign the 21-year-old Scot played a key part in the Reds' mid season revival, revelling in his central role alongside Roy Keane and Paul Scholes. He finally broke his scoring duck against Middlesbrough in a 2-0 win at the Riverside and returned from injury to play the final month of the season. In that time he justified his manager's belief that the Reds have three, not two, young stars of the future.

**Born** Edinburgh, 1 February 1984
**Signed** Trainee 3 July 2000
Senior United debut 12 March 2003 v FC Basel, home, UEFA Champions League
**United record**
League: 35(5) games, 3 goals;
FA Cup: 5(3) games, 0 goals;
League Cup: 5 games, 0 goals;
Europe: 8(5) games, 0 goals;
Others 0(1) games, 0 goals
**Total** 53(14) games, 3 goals
**International** 12 caps for Scotland

# Quinton Fortune

25

**Position** Defender/Midfielder

**Magic moment** The South African's only goal of the season came in the FA Cup fifth round at Goodison Park, the midfielder finishing off a swift move down the right-hand side with a powerful far post header.

With Gabriel Heinze performing so well at left-back, Fortune reverted to a midfield role, alternating between left-wing and a more central role. His best displays came in the middle, chiefly when he headed the opening goal in United's FA Cup fifth-round victory at Everton. His combative style, allied with an array of tricks, saw him continue to improve and he can be pleased with his contribution in 2004/05 – his best season yet.

**Born** Cape Town, South Africa 21 May 1977
**Signed** from Atletico Madrid, 1 August 1999
**Senior United debut** 30 August 1999 v Newcastle United, home, Premiership
**United record**
League: 53(23) games, 6 goals;
FA Cup: 8(1) games; 1 goal;
League Cup: 8 games, 0 goals;
Europe: 16(12) games, 2 goals;
Others: 3(2) games, 2 goals
**Total** 88(38) games, 11 goals
**International** 44 caps for South Africa

# Mikael Silvestre

**Magic moment** The long-awaited return of Rio Ferdinand from suspension seemed to bring the best out of his defensive partner. Silvestre struck twice, both headers, to condemn Liverpool to a 2-1 defeat. The Frenchman headed home from Giggs's free kick in the 20th minute, then produced a carbon copy from Giggs's corner in the 66th minute.

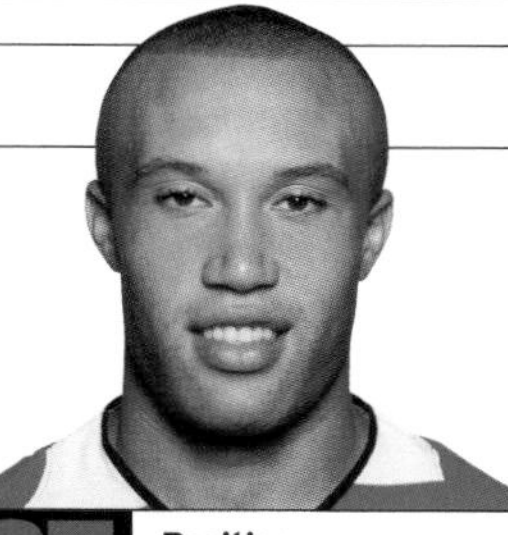

Despite an indifferent start to the season, Mikael can be pleased with his overall contribution in 2004/05. From the moment he was reunited with Rio Ferdinand at the heart of the Reds' defence his own form improved – and likewise, United's defensive stability. The pair picked up where they'd left off prior to Ferdinand's ban to help United record the second-best Premiership defensive record behind Chelsea, conceding only 26 goals.

The 27-year-old missed just three Premiership matches all season, made more starts than anyone and scored two goals, both against Liverpool as Ferdinand returned from suspension. His Man-of-the-Match performance that night demonstrated his main defensive strengths: pace,strong tackling and a good reading of the game. Although he is still prone to the occasional lapse in concentration, he was rarely punished and proved his versatility in the final weeks of the campaign by filling in for the injured Gabriel Heinze in the left-back slot.

**27**

**Position**
Defender

**Born** Chambray-les-Tours, France, 9 August 1977
**Signed** from Internazionale, 2 September 1999
**Senior United debut**
11 September 1999 v Liverpool, away, Premiership
**United record** League: 186(13) games, 4 goals; FA Cup: 13(2) games, 1 goal; League Cup: 7 games, 0 goals; Europe: 51(7) games, 2 goals; Others: 7 games, 1 goal
**Total** 264(22) games, 8 goals
**International** 33 caps for France

# Gerard Piqué

**Magic moment** The 23 minutes he played at Crewe on his debut were his best at senior level. Taking his place alongside Wes Brown in the centre of defence he looked instantly at ease, twice snuffing out the threat of Dean Ashton, and his crunching tackles had travelling United fans singing his name. His calmness and reading of the game auger well for the future.

The 18-year-old Catalan switched from his home club of Barcelona to United last summer in the hope of hastening his chances of first team football. Whilst his senior outings were limited to just one start and two substitute appearances in 2004/05, he nonetheless showed enough in those matches to justify the widespread belief at Old Trafford that he'll develop into a top class centre-half.

He made his Reds' debut in the 3-0 Carling Cup win at Crewe in October, coming on for John O'Shea in the 67th minute. He then played 28 minutes of United's 0-3 Champions League defeat to Fenerbahçe in Istanbul, and in January was selected to make his first start for United in the dire scoreless draw with Exeter City in the FA Cup third round.

Piqué was an integral part of the quadruple-winning reserve team, with observers likening his style to that of Rio Ferdinand. Although still very much a raw talent, he will be expecting to see a few more first team opportunities in 2005/06.

**Position**
Defender

**Born** Barcelona, 2 February 1987
**Signed** Trainee, 1 October 2004
**Senior United debut**
26 October 2004 v Crewe Alexandra, away, League Cup
**United record** League: 0 games, 0 goals; FA Cup: 1 game, 0 goals; League Cup: 0(1) games, 0 goals; Europe: 0(1) games, 0 goals; Others: 0 games, 0 goals
**Total** 1(2) games, 0 goals

# Jonathan Spector

**Magic moment** On a night when the headlines went to United's attackers - and in particular Alan Smith - the 18-year-old Jonathan Spector stepped out against Dinamo Bucharest at an expectant Old Trafford and played an ample part in ensuring United's progress to the Champions League group stage was never in threat.

**29** **Position** Defender

**Born** Arlington Heights, USA, 1 March 1986
**Signed** 1 September 2003
**Senior United debut** 8 August 2004 v Arsenal, Millennium Stadium, FA Community Shield
**United record** League: 2(1) games, 0 goals; FA Cup: 1 game, 0 goals; League Cup: 0(1) games, 0 goals; Europe: 1(1) game, 0 goals; Others: 0(1) games, 0 goals
**Total** 4(4) games, 0 goals

A year after arriving at Old Trafford, Jonathan Spector made his first inroads into the senior team as a late substitute in the somewhat makeshift side which took on Arsenal in the 2004 Community Shield. And while that day may not have gone the way of the young American, his subsequent showings for the Reds suggested he'll have a big part to play in the next few years. A fortnight later he got his first start, in the Champions League qualifier at home to Dinamo Bucharest, helping ease United's passage into the competition 'proper' and by the time United entertained Everton at the end of August there was no stopping him, his Man-of-the-Match performance in the left-back slot keeping the Toffees' Leon Osman firmly under wraps.

Once Rio Ferdinand and Gabriel Heinze were available, Spector's chances were limited, but in the four other games in which he figured, the fact that the opposition failed to break through speaks volumes for his contribution.

# David Jones

**Magic moment** Senior games were few and far between for former FA Youth Cup winner David Jones. But as skipper of the Reds' Premier League Reserve side, he had one big moment to savour - lifting the league trophy (in this case the Barclays Premiership Reserve League North trophy) at Old Trafford; it's a feat he plans to repeat in the senior side...

**31** **Position** Midfielder

**Born** Southport, 4 November 1984
**Signed** Trainee, 1 July 2003
**Senior United debut** 1 December 2004 v Arsenal, home, Carling Cup
**United record** FA Cup: 1 game, 0 goals; League Cup: 0(1) games, 0 goals
**Total** 1(1) game, 0 goals

David Jones may not have figured as prominently as he might have liked in the Reds' senior side in 2004/05 but the two games in which he did play a part were ones to remember. He came on as a substitute in the Carling Cup game against Arsenal in December, helping to protect the match-winning lead given to United by David Bellion in the first minute. He then got a senior start against Exeter City in the third round of the FA Cup – a game in which he was the only player to emerge with credit after the Reds just escaped with a goalless draw against the non-leaguers.

But Jones's real heroics came in the Barclays Premier Reserve League, where, having lifted the league trophy at Old Trophy, he then went on to skipper the side to victory over Charlton Athletic in the FAPRL play-off final – and got himself on to the scoresheet, scoring the second of United's four goals. The youngster has revealed that he's had the benefit of advice from his senior counterpart, Roy Keane, over the course of the season; Keane's words of wisdom have clearly been paying off.

## Chris Eagles

**33** **Position** Midfielder

**Born** Hemel Hempstead, 19 November 1985
**Signed** Trainee, 8 July 2002
**Senior United debut** 28 October 2003 v Leeds United, away, Carling Cup
**United record** FA Cup: 1 game, 0 goals; League Cup: 1(4) game, 0 goals; Others: 1(2) game, 0 goals
**Total** 3(6) games, 0 goals

**Magic moment** Eagles' debut goal may have come for his loan club Watford, but it would have made any Red proud; dribbling past a clutch of Gillingham defenders, he then calmly rolled the ball past the Gills' keeper.

Eagles followed the path trodden by fellow former Red trainee Danny Webber when he relocated from Old Trafford to Vicarage Road for a spell on loan with Championship side Watford in January. Having been a sub for most of United's Carling Cup games up until that point (coming off the bench in two of the three games), after switching to the Hornets he made 10 league starts – and notched a debut goal, against Gillingham.

## Sylvan Ebanks-Blake

**40** **Position** Forward

**Born** Cambridge, 29 March 1986
**Signed** Trainee, 8 July 2002
**Senior United debut** 26 October 2004 v Crewe Alexandra, Carling Cup
**United record** League Cup: 0(1) games, 0 goals
**Total** 0(1) games, 0 goals

**Magic moment** Ten minutes of Carling Cup action at Crewe - just a day after getting his senior squad number - had Sir Alex Ferguson flagging Ebanks-Blake as "a player with some promise".

It couldn't have been going much better for the Reserve striker. Eleven goals in 12 league starts for the Premier Reserve League side, plus another four goals in four games for Brian McClair's Pontin's League outfit, had fired the former United trainee firmly into the public eye. But any hopes of adding to his brief cameo as a sub in the Carling Cup game against Crewe vanished on 10 February when a broken leg ended the youngster's season.

## Giuseppe Rossi

**42** **Position** Forward

**Born** New Jersey, USA, 1 February 1987
**Signed** 6 July 2004
**Senior United debut** 10 November 2004 v Crystal Palace, Carling Cup
**United record** League Cup: 0(2) games, 0 goals
**Total** 0(2) games, 0 goals

**Magic moment** His tap-in against Charlton in May (to add to the two left-footed curlers he'd produced earlier in the game) completed a memorable hat-trick that ensured a Reds victory in the FAPRL play-off final.

After arriving from Parma last August, Rossi wasted little time in proving his worth to the United Reserves. He found the net 13 times in his first 19 starts for Ricky Sbragia's Premier League side (with another five goals in eight Pontin's League games), and, with two substitute appearances in the Carling Cup for the seniors under his belt, rounded things off in style with a hat-trick as the Reds beat Charlton 4-2 in the FAPRL play-off game.

# Golden goals

You beauty: Giggs nets against Bolton on Boxing Day

Welcome to OT: Al Smith announces arrival in Lan

Paul Scholes volleys home in style against Charlton for his first of the season

ebruary 2005: The
tain bags his 50th
home to Birmingham

Hat-trick hero: Ruud lobs the ball over Blazek
for his third of four against Sparta Prague

Wayne bags a brilliant
late winner against
Portsmouth...

...and helps Gary Neville
celebrate his goal against
Olympique Lyonnais

# Blood, sweat and tear

Arm combat: Gabriel Heinze clashes with Milan's Gattuso

Alan Smith came off second best in this particular argument

Heinze, Scholes and Ke
snuff out the threa
Villa's Juan Pablo An

ıinute's silence the victims of tsunami in th-east Asia

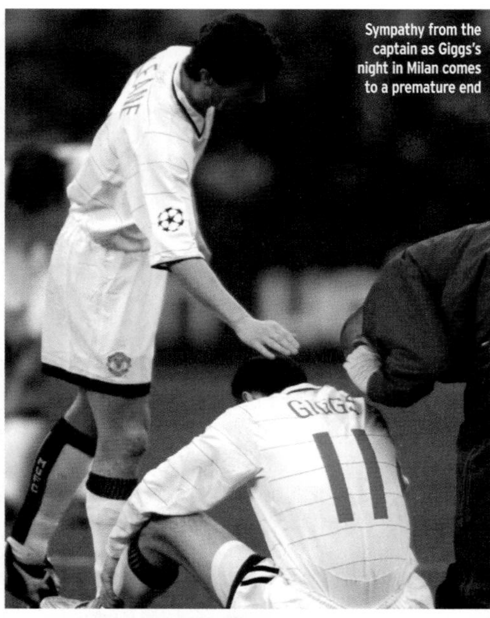


Sympathy from the captain as Giggs's night in Milan comes to a premature end

: a prayer: Cristiano ıaldo sees a nce go begging

War and pizza: tempers fray against Arsenal (again), this time in the Carling Cup

# On the bench

Sir Alex and Carlos Queiroz look for a few pointers during the game at West Brom

Coach Mike Phelan pa on Sir Alex's instruct

It's a wrap: The be enjoys the late Octo temperatures in Pra

ıchmark: United's bench can only watch as
Reds go down to a 2-0 defeat in Norwich

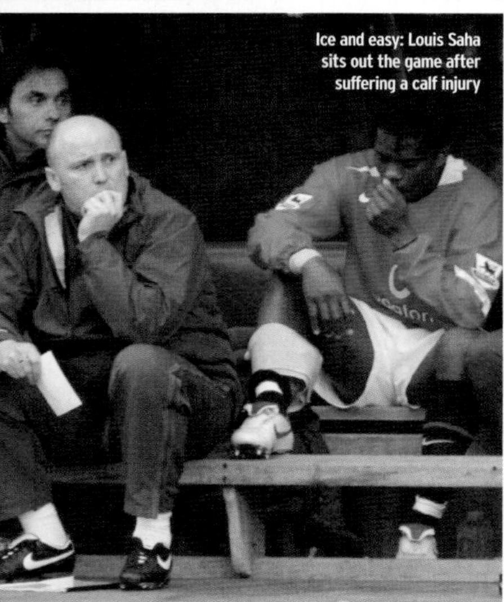
Ice and easy: Louis Saha sits out the game after suffering a calf injury

# Celebration time

Guess who's back?: Ruud shows h
much it means to be back on t
scoresheet in the FA Cup semi-fi

The eyes have it: Giggs gets the captain's vote after his equaliser at Arsenal

The late, late show: Smudger scores in the fourth minute of added time to rescue a point at Blackburn

ıds we win: Rio adds his
ıport to the Dutchman

Poacher's punch: Scholes
celebrates the first of
four at Charlton Athletic

u're not singing anymore: Rooney
ences the Red half of Merseyside

Jump for joy: Gabriel
Heinze marks his Red
bow with a goal at Bolton

vodafone
BARCLAYS
PREMIERSHIP
RESERVE LEAGUE
WINNERS

RESERVES
ACADEMY

# PREMIER RESERVES

Giuseppe Rossi puts Charlton to the sword in the play-off

The big prizes may have escaped United's grasp in a largely disappointing season, but that was far from true for those who regularly cheer on the club's other teams. Indeed, there was plenty to admire and enjoy from the Reserves' campaign, which ended with a glittering array of silverware.

Ricky Sbragia's team – a couple of blips aside – looked potential champions right from the start, building a solid foundation. There were some outstanding matches throughout the campaign, but few could compare with the eight-goal thriller against Aston Villa at Bescot Stadium, which ended with honours even. Remarkably, that match signalled the charge that took Sbragia's lads all the way to the championship – and the inaugural national title – after a Giuseppe Rossi-inspired 4-2 victory over Charlton Athletic in the end-of-season play-off at The Valley.

It was a thoroughly enjoyable season with few downsides. Injury to Sylvan Ebanks-Blake, winner of the Denzil Haroun Reserve Team Player of the Year award, and David Bellion were the major exceptions, along with a defeat against Manchester City in the Manchester Senior Cup final, which robbed the Reds of a clean sweep of the trophies.

Rossi finished the season as top scorer with 16 goals while Ebanks-Blake, who picked up his ankle injury in early February, was next with 11.

**BARCLAYS PREMIERSHIP RESERVE LEAGUE NORTH**

**THURSDAY 12 AUGUST 2004**
NOTTINGHAM FOREST (Home, Moss Lane, Altrincham)
W 2-0 (Cooper, Jones D)
Carroll, Picken, Eckersley, Howard, McShane, Fox, Heath, Jones D, Cooper, Ebanks-Blake, Djordjic
Substitutes: Poole (Heath), Heaton, Timm (Ebanks-Blake), Collett (Djordjic), Jones R

**TUESDAY 24 AUGUST**
WOLVERHAMPTON WANDERERS (Away)
W 1-0 (Poole)
Heaton, Picken, Lawrence, Howard, McShane, Fox, Poole, Jones D, Calliste, Timm, Djordjic
Substitutes: Ngalula (Jones D), Lee, Jones R, Neumayr, Collett (Timm)

**THURSDAY 9 SEPTEMBER**
ASTON VILLA (Home, Moss Lane)
D 0-0
Steele, Picken, Tierney, Howard, McShane, Fox, Poole, Jones D, Heath, Rossi, Djordjic
Substitutes: Crockett, Ngalula, Collett, Calliste (Djordjic)

**MONDAY 13 SEPTEMBER**
BOLTON WANDERERS (Away, Lancashire FA County Ground, Leyland)
W 3-0 (Ebanks-Blake, Eagles, Rossi)
Heaton, Picken, Tierney, Howard, McShane, Fox, Eagles, Jones D, Ebanks-Blake, Rossi, Djordjic
Substitutes: Collett, Crockett, Jones R., Ngalula, Poole (Eagles)

**MONDAY 27 SEPTEMBER**
MIDDLESBROUGH (Away, Riverside Stadium)
D 3-3 (McShane, Ebanks-Blake 2)
Heaton, Spector, Tierney, Howard, McShane, Fox, Eagles, Jones D, Ebanks-Blake, Rossi, Richardson
Substitutes: Picken (Tierney), Crockett, Heath, Poole, Collett

**THURSDAY 7 OCTOBER**
BIRMINGHAM CITY (Home, Moss Lane)
L 2-3 (Eagles, Bellion)
Ricardo, Ngalula, Spector, Howard, McShane, Djordjic, Eagles, Jones D, Bellion, Saha, Richardson
Substitutes: Piqué, Crockett, Picken (Djordjic), Poole (Spector), Rossi (Saha)

**TUESDAY 12 OCTOBER**
MANCHESTER CITY (Away, Regional Athletics Arena, Sportcity)
L 1-2 (Jones D)
Ricardo, Brown, Spector, Howard, McShane, Djordjic, Eagles, Jones D, Saha, Bellion, Richardson
Substitutes: Rossi, Heaton, Ebanks-Blake (Djordjic), Ngalula, Picken

**THURSDAY 21 OCTOBER**
LIVERPOOL (Home, Moss Lane)
W 5-2 (Richardson 2, Ebanks-Blake, Eagles, Heath)
Heaton, Picken, Lawrence, Piqué, Spector, Fletcher, Eagles, Jones D, Ebanks-Blake, Rossi, Richardson
Substitutes: Heath (Eagles), Crockett, Poole (Richardson), Ngalula, Howard

**WEDNESDAY 27 OCTOBER**
BLACKBURN ROVERS (Away, Christie Park, Morecambe)
D 2-2 (Poole 2)
Heaton, Picken, Lawrence, Piqué, Spector, Ngalula, Eagles, Jones D, Ebanks-Blake, Poole, Heath
Substitutes: Collett, Crockett, Hogg, Jones R, Howard

**MONDAY 1 NOVEMBER**
WEST BROMWICH ALBION (Away, Aggborough Stadium, Kidderminster)
D 1-1 (Jones D)
Heaton, Picken, Lawrence, Spector, McShane, Jones D, Eagles, Ngalula, Ebanks-Blake, Poole, Heath
Substitutes: Jones R, Crockett, Howard, Rossi (Heath), Collett

**THURSDAY 11 NOVEMBER**
SUNDERLAND (Home, Moss Lane)
W 4-1 (Ebanks-Blake 3, Piqué)
Ricardo, Picken, Lawrence, Piqué, McShane, Ngalula, Eagles, Jones D, Ebanks-Blake, Rossi, Heath
Substitutes: Poole (Ebanks-Blake), Heaton, Collett (Heath), Jones R. (Lawrence), Howard

**MONDAY 15 NOVEMBER**
NEWCASTLE UNITED (Away, Kingston Park, Kenton)
W 3-0 (Jones D, Heath, Rossi)
Heaton, Picken, Lawrence, Piqué, McShane, Ngalula, Heath, Jones D, Ebanks-Blake, Rossi, Richardson
Substitutes: Poole (Ngalula), Crockett, Collett (Ebanks-Blake), Howard, Hogg (Richardson)

**THURSDAY 25 NOVEMBER**
EVERTON (Home, Moss Lane)
W 3-1 (Eagles, Poole, Bosnar og)
Heaton, Picken, Lawrence, Howard, Spector, Heath, Eagles, Jones D, Ebanks-Blake, Poole, Richardson
Substitutes: Collett (Richardson), Crockett, Hogg, Timm (Heath), Calliste

**TUESDAY 7 DECEMBER**
NOTTINGHAM FOREST (Away)
L 0-1
Heaton, Picken, Lawrence, Tierney, Howard, Neumayr, Marsh, Fox, Calliste, Timm, Collett
Substitutes: Eckersley (Collett), Crockett (Calliste), Hogg, Shawcross, Mullan (Marsh)

**THURSDAY 13 JANUARY 2005**
ASTON VILLA (Away, Bescot Stadium, Walsall)
D 4-4 (Ebanks-Blake, Richardson 2, Rossi)
Heaton, Picken, Eckersley, Lawrence, Ngalula, Fox, Eagles, Jones D., Ebanks-Blake, Rossi, Richardson
Substitutes: Poole (Richardson), Crockett, Cooper (Ebanks-Blake), Collett, Hogg (Eckersley)

**THURSDAY 27 JANUARY**
LEEDS UNITED (Away, Atlantic Solutions Stadium, Wakefield)
W 4-0 (Ebanks-Blake 2, Jones D., Rossi)
Heaton, Picken, Eckersley, Spector, Hogg, Ngalula, Poole, Jones D, Ebanks-Blake, Rossi, Richardson
Substitutes: Martin (Ebanks-Blake), Crockett, Jones R, Collett, Calliste (Rossi)

**THURSDAY 10 FEBRUARY**
MIDDLESBROUGH (Home, Moss Lane)
W 2-0 (Rossi pen, Ebanks-Blake)
Heaton, Picken, Eckersley, Piqué, Spector, Fox, Calliste, Ngalula, Ebanks-Blake, Rossi, Poole
Substitutes: Gray (Ngalula), Crockett, Martin (Ebanks-Blake), Howard M, Jones R (Calliste)

**MONDAY 14 FEBRUARY**
BIRMINGHAM CITY (Away)
W 3-0 (Poole, Heath, Ngalula)
Heaton, Picken, Eckersley, Piqué, Spector, Fox, Heath, Ngalula, Poole, Rossi, Martin
Substitutes: Timm (Fox), Crockett, Howard M, Neumayr (Martin), Jones R (Heath)

**THURSDAY 17 FEBRUARY**
LEEDS UNITED (Home, Moss Lane)
W 3-0 (Rossi 2, Fox)
Heaton, Picken, Eckersley, Piqué, Spector, Fox, Heath, Ngalula, Poole, Rossi, Martin
Substitutes: Jones D (Ngalula), Crockett, Howard M, Calliste (Rossi), Timm (Heath)

**TUESDAY 1 MARCH**
LIVERPOOL (Away, Racecourse Ground, Wrexham)
W 1-0 (Miller)
Ricardo, Picken, Eckersley, Piqué, Spector, Miller, Heath, Jones D, Bellion, Rossi, Martin
Substitutes: Ngalula, Heaton, Timm (Bellion), Calliste, McShane

**THURSDAY 10 MARCH**
BLACKBURN ROVERS (Home, Moss Lane)
W 2-1 (Rossi 2)
Ricardo, Picken, Eckersley, Piqué, Spector, Miller, Heath, Jones D, Bellion, Rossi, Martin
Substitutes: McShane (Eckersley), Heaton, Jones R, Poole (Bellion), Marsh (Heath)

**WEDNESDAY 16 MARCH**
SUNDERLAND (Away, Archibalds Stadium, Durham)
W 4-0 (Bellion, Martin, Poole, Marsh)
Ricardo, Picken, Eckersley, Piqué, Spector, Miller, Bellion, Jones D, Poole, Rossi, Martin
Substitutes: Heath (Bellion), Lee T, McShane, Marsh (Martin), Fox (Miller)

**THURSDAY 24 MARCH**
WEST BROMWICH ALBION (Home, Moss Lane)
W 2-0 (Rossi, Kleberson)
Ricardo, Picken, Eckersley, Piqué, Spector, Fox, Kleberson, Jones D, Bellion, Rossi, Martin
Substitutes: Heath (Kleberson), Cooper (Martin), Lawrence (Picken), Neumayr

**THURSDAY 31 MARCH**
NEWCASTLE UNITED (Home, Moss Lane)
D 1-1 (Bellion pen)
Heaton, McShane, Lawrence, Piqué, Spector, Fox, Bellion, Jones D, Heath, Poole, Martin
Substitutes: Rossi (Martin), Lee T, Marsh (Poole), Jones R (Heath), Picken

**MONDAY 4 MARCH**
EVERTON (Away, Haig Avenue, Southport)
W 1-0 (Rossi pen)
Carroll, McShane, Eckersley, Piqué, Spector, Miller, Bellion, Neville P, Smith, Rossi, Kleberson
Substitutes: Jones D (McShane), Lee T, Fox, Heath, Lawrence

**THURSDAY 14 APRIL**
BOLTON WANDERERS (Home, Moss Lane)
W 5-0 (Martin 3, Heath, Rossi)
Heaton, McShane, Eckersley, Piqué, Spector, Fox, Jones R, Jones D, Heath, Rossi, Martin
Substitutes: Picken (Spector), Lee T, Marsh (Jones R), Bardsley (McShane), Lawrence

**MONDAY 18 APRIL**
WOLVERHAMPTON WANDERERS (Home, Old Trafford)
W 3-0 (Bellion 2, Jones D)
Heaton, Picken, Lawrence, Evans J, McShane, Miller, Bellion, Jones D, Heath, Rossi, Martin
Substitutes: Fox (Miller), Lee T, Marsh (Martin), Jones R, Bardsley (Evans J)

**THURSDAY 28 APRIL**
MANCHESTER CITY (Home, Old Trafford)
W 3-1 (Bellion, Rossi pen, Miller)
Carroll, Picken, Ngalula, Piqué, Bardsley, Miller, Heath, Jones D, Bellion, Rossi, Martin
Substitutes: Fox (Jones D), Heaton, Eagles (Martin), Marsh (Heath), Shawcross

## NATIONAL PLAY-OFF

**THURSDAY 12 MAY**
CHARLTON ATHLETIC (Away, The Valley)
W 4-2 (Rossi 3, Jones D)
Heaton, Picken, Tierney, Piqué, McShane, Fox, Eagles, Jones D, Bellion, Rossi, Martin
Substitutes: Bardsley, Crockett, Ngalula, Jones R, Campbell (Bellion)

## MANCHESTER SENIOR CUP - 2004/05

**TUESDAY 14 DECEMBER 2004**
OLDHAM ATHLETIC (Home, Moss Lane)
W 5-1 (Ebanks-Blake 2, Spector, Timm, Richardson)
Heaton, Picken, Tierney, Spector, McShane, Neumayr, Eagles, Jones D, Ebanks-Blake, Timm, Richardson
Substitutes: Howard M, Poole (Neumayr), Hogg (McShane), Collett, Calliste (Timm)

**TUESDAY 21 DECEMBER**
BURY (Away)
W 2-0 (Calliste, Poole)
Crockett, Picken, Eckersley, Howard M, McShane, Fox, Jones R., Jones D, Poole, Calliste, Collett
Substitutes: Simpson, Marsh, Lawrence, Hogg (Collett)

**MONDAY 17 JANUARY 2005**
BOLTON WANDERERS (Away, Lancashire County FA Ground, Leyland)
W 2-1 (Timm, Poole)
Heaton, Picken, Eckersley, Evans J, Hogg, Jones R, Poole, Martin, Cooper, Timm, Collett
Substitutes: Neumayr (Martin), Crockett, Marsh, Calliste (Timm), Campbell (Cooper)

**THURSDAY 3 FEBRUARY**
MANCHESTER CITY (Home, Moss Lane) L 1-5 (Rossi)
Howard, Picken, Eckersley, Hogg, Spector, Ngalula, Bellion, Jones D., Ebanks-Blake, Rossi, Poole
Substitutes: Collett, Heaton, Martin (Poole), Timm, Campbell

**MONDAY 9 MAY**
**FINAL**
MANCHESTER CITY (Away)
L 2-3 (Rossi pen, Bellion)
Heaton, Picken, Lawrence, Piqué, McShane, Fox, Bellion, Ngalula, Heath, Rossi, Martin
Substitutes: Bardsley (Lawrence), Lee T, Jones R, Eagles (Martin), Neumayr

# PONTIN'S RESERVES

**BARCLAYS RESERVES STATS 2004/05**

| | Apps | Goals |
|---|---|---|
| Phil Bardsley | 1(2) | |
| David Bellion | 11 | 6 |
| Wes Brown | 1 | |
| Ramon Calliste | 3(3) | |
| Fraizer Campbell | 0(1) | |
| Roy Carroll | 3 | |
| Ben Collett | 1(5) | |
| Kenny Cooper | 1(2) | 1 |
| Lee Crockett | 0(1) | |
| Bojan Djordjic | 6 | |
| Chris Eagles | 11(1) | 4 |
| Sylvan Ebanks-Blake | 12(1) | 11 |
| Adam Eckersley | 12(1) | |
| Jonathan Evans | 1 | |
| Darren Fletcher | 1 | |
| David Fox | 14(3) | 1 |
| David Gray | 0(1) | |
| Colin Heath | 15(3) | 4 |
| Tom Heaton | 18 | |
| Steven Hogg | 1(2) | |
| Mark Howard | 9 | |
| David Jones | 24(2) | 7 |
| Ritchie Jones | 1(4) | |
| Kleberson | 2 | 1 |
| Lee Lawrence | 11(1) | |
| Paul McShane | 15(1) | 1 |
| Phil Marsh | 1(6) | 1 |
| Lee Martin | 11(2) | 4 |
| Liam Miller | 6 | 2 |
| Jamie Mullan | 0(1) | |
| Markus Neumayr | 1(1) | |
| Phil Neville | 1 | |
| Floribert Ngalula | 11(1) | 1 |
| Phil Picken | 23(3) | |
| Gerard Piqué | 16 | 1 |
| David Poole | 11(8) | 6 |
| Ricardo | 7 | |
| Kieran Richardson | 8 | 4 |
| Giuseppe Rossi | 20(3) | 16 |
| Louis Saha | 2 | |
| Alan Smith | 1 | |
| Jonathan Spector | 18 | |
| Luke Steele | 1 | |
| Paul Tierney | 5 | |
| Mads Timm | 2(5) | |
| Eddy Bosnar | | 1og |

**BARCLAYS ENGLISH PREMIER LEAGUE**

**BARCLAYS PREMIERSHIP RESERVE LEAGUE NORTH**

| | P | W | D | L | F | A | Pts |
|---|---|---|---|---|---|---|---|
| Manchester United | 28 | 19 | 6 | 3 | 68 | 23 | 63 |
| Aston Villa | 28 | 16 | 6 | 6 | 62 | 38 | 54 |
| Manchester City | 28 | 16 | 6 | 6 | 55 | 32 | 54 |
| Blackburn Rovers | 28 | 11 | 12 | 5 | 45 | 28 | 45 |
| Birmingham City | 28 | 12 | 7 | 9 | 37 | 36 | 43 |
| Wolverhampton W | 28 | 9 | 9 | 10 | 32 | 32 | 36 |
| Middlesbrough | 28 | 10 | 6 | 12 | 41 | 42 | 36 |
| Everton | 28 | 8 | 11 | 9 | 23 | 34 | 35 |
| Sunderland | 28 | 8 | 9 | 11 | 38 | 44 | 33 |
| Bolton Wanderers | 28 | 8 | 9 | 11 | 32 | 41 | 33 |
| West Bromwich Albion | 28 | 6 | 13 | 9 | 29 | 36 | 31 |
| Newcastle United | 28 | 8 | 7 | 13 | 30 | 41 | 31 |
| Leeds United | 28 | 7 | 7 | 14 | 31 | 52 | 28 |
| Liverpool | 28 | 6 | 8 | 14 | 27 | 47 | 26 |
| Nottingham Forest | 28 | 5 | 6 | 17 | 21 | 45 | 21 |

Front runner: David Bellion leads the way

Brian McClair's Midas touch shows no sign of abating as his Pontin's Reserves stormed to a League and Cup double. McClair juggled responsibility for the Reds' twin reserve sides with Ricky Sbragia during 2004/05 – and judging by results – the partnership is a dream ticket.

Just like their Barclays counterparts, United's Pontin's League challengers were firmly in the title running from the off and rarely slowed the pace. The Reds topped the table early on and stayed there while the contenders fell by the wayside. Blackpool were the only side to stay the course, but the Seasiders ultimately stumbled to leave United out front alone.

The League Cup offered a nice diversion from the normal programme, the 3-1 success in the final against Sheffield Wednesday giving some of the club's younger players a rare opportunity to play at Old Trafford.

Sadly, United will not be in a position to defend either of the Pontin's trophies next term, for the venture into the competitions was for just one season.

This was the fourth year since McClair returned to the club and each time he's ended the season with something to show for his efforts. Four seasons ago it was the Reserve League championship, the following year he masterminded the FA Youth Cup victory, and last term the prestigious Blue Stars Youth Tournament which, incidentally, was retained in May with a 2-0 victory over AIK Solna of Sweden.

**PONTIN'S HOLIDAYS LEAGUE DIVISION ONE (WEST)**

**WEDNESDAY 18 AUGUST 2004**
WREXHAM (Away, Racecourse Ground)
W 4-1 (Poole 2, McShane, Collett)
Heaton, Picken, Lawrence, Howard, McShane, Ngalula, Neumayr, Jones R, Ebanks-Blake, Poole, Collett
Substitutes: Shawcross (McShane), Lee, Fox, Jones D (Collett), Martin (Ngalula)

**WEDNESDAY 1 SEPTEMBER**
ROCHDALE (Home, Ewen Fields, Hyde)
W 3-1 (Eagles, Rossi, Richardson)
Steele, Picken, Tierney, McShane, Howard, Ngalula, Eagles, Jones R, Heath, Rossi, Richardson
Substitutes: Collett, Heaton, Piqué (McShane), Martin (Richardson), Neumayr (Rossi)

**WEDNESDAY 8 SEPTEMBER**
CARLISLE UNITED (Away, Brunton Park)
W 2-1 (Ebanks-Blake 2)
Ricardo, Simpson, Collett, Ngalula, Piqué Martin, Eagles, Neumayr, Ebanks-Blake, Calliste, Richardson
Substitutes: Shawcross (Ngalula), Lee, Lea, Evans S (Calliste)

**WEDNESDAY 15 SEPTEMBER**
v SHREWSBURY TOWN (Away, Gay Meadow)
W 5-2 (Piqué, Heath 2, Calliste, Timm)
Heaton, Poole, Eckersley, McShane, Piqué, Ngalula, Calliste, Jones R, Heath, Timm, Collett
Substitutes: Martin, Crockett, Neumayr, Howard

**MONDAY 4 OCTOBER**
v BURNLEY (Home, Ewen Fields, Hyde)
D 1-1 (Rossi)
Ricardo, Picken, Collett, Spector, Piqué, Ngalula, Eagles, Neumayr, Rossi, Bellion, Richardson
Substitutes: Heath (Rossi), Crockett, Hogg (Neumayr), Eckersley

**WEDNESDAY 13 OCTOBER**
CHESTER CITY (Home, Ewen Fields)
W 4-1 (Heath pen, Ebanks-Blake, Rossi 2)
Heaton, Picken, Eckersley, Lawrence, Piqué, Ngalula, Poole, Hogg, Heath, Ebanks-Blake, Collett
Substitutes: Rossi (Collett), McShane, Gibson (Eckersley), Neumayr

**WEDNESDAY 10 NOVEMBER**
MACCLESFIELD TOWN (Away, Moss Rose)
W 4-1 (Martin, Jones R pen, Fox, Neumayr pen)
Heaton, Fox, Eckersley, Tierney, Howard, Jones R, Neumayr, Timm, Calliste, Martin, Djordjic
Substitutes: Piqué, Crockett, Hogg, Gibson

**WEDNESDAY 1 DECEMBER**
BURY (Away)
D 1-1 (Hogg)
Ruddy, Simpson, Eckersley, Howard, Hogg, Fox, Jones R., Gibson, Calliste, Timm, Campbell
Substitutes: Shawcross, Crockett, Evans S (Gibson), Rose, Marsh (Timm)

**WEDNESDAY 8 DECEMBER**
OLDHAM ATHLETIC (Home, Ewen Fields)
L 3-5 (Campbell, Rossi, Puustinen)
Crockett, Simpson, Lea, Evans J, Jones R, Gibson, Gray, Martin, Campbell, Rossi, Evans S
Substitutes: Marsh, Heaton, Rose (Evans S), Mullan (Gray), Puustinen (Campbell)

**MONDAY 10 JANUARY 2005**
SHREWSBURY TOWN (Home, Ewen Fields)
W 3-0 (Calliste, Ebanks-Blake pen, Fox)
Heaton, Picken, Eckersley, Lawrence, Howard, Fox, Neumayr, Hogg, Calliste, Timm, Collett
Substitutes: Poole, Ebanks-Blake (Calliste), Rossi, Ngalula

**MONDAY 24 JANUARY**
STOCKPORT COUNTY (Home, Ewen Fields)
D 1-1 (Martin)
Heaton, Simpson, Collett, Hogg, Shawcross, Jones R, Calliste, Martin, Cooper, Timm, Evans S
Substitutes: Neumayr, Crockett, Marsh, Lea, Campbell (Evans S)

**WEDNESDAY 2 FEBRUARY**
CHESTER CITY (Away, Deva Stadium)
W 1-0 (Timm)
Heaton, Fox, Collett, Piqué, Evans J, Jones R, Neumayr, Martin, Heath, Timm, Calliste
Substitutes: Gibson, Crockett, Simpson, Campbell

**WEDNESDAY 9 FEBRUARY**
BLACKPOOL (Away, Bloomfield Road)
D 1-1 (Heath)
Crockett, Bardsley, Simpson, Evans J, Howard M, Hogg, Neumayr, Martin, Heath, Marsh, Mullan
Substitutes: Gray (Evans J), Moran (Simpson), Burns, Puustinen (Neumayr)

**TUESDAY 15 FEBRUARY**
MACCLESFIELD TOWN (Home, Ewen Fields)
W 3-1 (Neumayr, Timm, Bellion)
Howard T, Gray, Simpson, Howard M, Evans J, Jones R, Neumayr, Gibson, Bellion, Timm, Calliste
Substitutes: Marsh (Timm), Crockett, Moran (Neumayr), Mullan

**MONDAY 21 FEBRUARY**
BURNLEY (Away, Crown Ground, Accrington)
W 2-1 (Jones D, Calliste)
Heaton, Ngalula, Lea, Bardsley, Howard M, Jones D, Marsh, Neumayr, Calliste, Timm, Collett
Substitutes: Moran (Marsh), Crockett, Gray (Neumayr), Burns, Evans S (Calliste)

**WEDNESDAY 2 MARCH**
OLDHAM ATHLETIC (Away, Boundary Park)
W 2-1 (Ngalula, Timm)
Heaton, Simpson, Lawrence, McShane, Shawcross, Ngalula, Neumayr, Gibson, Marsh, Timm, Calliste
Substitutes: Moran (Neumayr), Crockett, Puustinen (Timm), Lea (Shawcross)

**MONDAY 7 MARCH**
BURY (Home, Ewen Fields)
W 3-1 (Heath 2, Marsh)
Heaton, Picken, Lawrence, Ngalula, McShane, Hogg, Neumayr, Jones R. Heath, Marsh, Collett
Substitutes: Eckersley, Lee T (Heaton), Piqué, Jones D, Martin (Hogg)

**TUESDAY 22 MARCH**
STOCKPORT COUNTY (Away, Edgeley Park)
L 1-2 (Bellion)
Heaton, Picken, Lawrence, Ngalula, Piqué, Jones D, Neumayr, Heath, Poole, Kleberson, Collett
Substitutes: Spector (Ngalula), Eckersley, Fox (Jones D), Bellion (Kleberson), Rossi

**TUESDAY 29 MARCH**
WREXHAM (Home, Ewen Fields)
W 3-2 (Bellion pen, Marsh 2)
Lee T, Fox, Lawrence, Shawcross, McShane, Hogg, Bellion, Marsh, Campbell, Kleberson, Gibson
Substitutes: Spector (Shawcross), Burns, Heath, Lea, Poole (Fox)

**WEDNESDAY 6 APRIL**
BLACKPOOL (Home, Ewen Fields)
W 1-0 (Bellion)
Heaton, Bardsley, Eckersley, McShane, Ngalula, Fox, Jones R, Jones D, Saha, Bellion, Martin
Substitutes: Marsh (Jones D.), Lee T, Rossi (Saha), Spector (Bardsley), Calliste

**WEDNESDAY 20 APRIL**
ROCHDALE (Away, Spotland)
D 0-0
Lee T, Picken, Lawrence, Bardsley, Ngalula, Fox, Jones R, Neumayr, Marsh, Brandy, Collett
Substitutes: Jones D, Heaton, Heath, McShane (Bardsley), Rossi (Brandy)

**MONDAY 25 APRIL**
CARLISLE UNITED (Home, Ewen Fields)
L 1-4 (Neumayr)
Lee T, Bardsley, Picken, Ngalula, Piqué, Fox, Neumayr, Hogg, Cooper, Marsh, Martin
Substitutes: Rossi (Martin), Heaton, Heath (Marsh), Eagles (Ngalula), Jones R

**PONTIN'S LEAGUE CUP GROUP FIVE**

**WEDNESDAY 22 SEPTEMBER 2004**
MACCLESFIELD TOWN (Away)
W 3-1 (Timm, Jones D, Calliste)
Heaton, Picken, Collett, McShane, Piqué, Ngalula, Neumayr, Jones D., Poole, Timm, Calliste
Substitutes: Howard, Crockett, Fox, Rossi (Timm)

**GROUP FIVE**
**WEDNESDAY 24 NOVEMBER**
TRANMERE ROVERS (Home, Ewen Fields)
W 4-2 (Evans S, Campbell, Gibson (2pens)
Crockett, Evans J, Piqué, Shawcross, Simpson, Gibson, Marsh, Martin, Campbell, Rossi, Evans S
Substitutes: Jones R (Simpson), Heaton, Rose (Evans S), Lea, Gray (Marsh)

**QUARTER-FINAL**
**TUESDAY 15 MARCH**
GRIMSBY TOWN (Home, Ewen Fields)
W 2-0 (Heath, Jones R)
Heaton, Ngalula, Lawrence, Howard M, Fox, Neumayr, Jones R, Heath, Calliste, Collett
Substitutes: Evans J (Howard M), Lee T, Mullan (Calliste), Moran, Marsh (Heath)

**SEMI-FINAL**
**MONDAY 11 APRIL**
SHREWSBURY TOWN (Home, Ewen Fields)
W 2-1 (Bellion, Jones R)
Lee T, Picken, Lawrence, Bardsley, Ngalula, Hogg, Jones R, Miller, Calliste, Bellion, Collett
Substitutes: McShane (Bardsley), Heaton, Marsh (Calliste), Neumayr, Spector (Picken)

**FINAL**
**MONDAY 2 MAY**
SHEFFIELD WEDNESDAY (Home, Old Trafford)
W 3-1 (Saha, Fox, Jones D)
Ricardo; Ngalula, Lawrence, Bardsley, McShane, Fox, Poole, Miller, Saha, Bellion, Collett
Substitutes: Neumayr, Lee T, Jones D (Poole), Jones R, Calliste (Collett)

# UNDER 18s

## PONTIN'S RESERVES STATS 2004/05

| | Apps | Goals |
|---|---|---|
| Phil Bardsley | 5 | |
| David Bellion | 4(1) | 4 |
| Fabien Brandy | 1 | |
| Ramon Calliste | 10 | 3 |
| Fraizer Campbell | 3(1) | 1 |
| Ben Collett | 12 | 1 |
| Kenny Cooper | 2 | |
| Lee Crockett | 2 | |
| Bojan Djordjic | 1 | |
| Chris Eagles | 3(1) | 1 |
| Sylvan Ebanks-Blake | 3(1) | 4 |
| Adam Eckersley | 6 | |
| Jonathan Evans | 4 | |
| Sean Evans | 2(3) | |
| David Fox | 8(1) | 2 |
| Darron Gibson | 5(1) | |
| David Gray | 2(2) | |
| Colin Heath | 7(2) | 6 |
| Tom Heaton | 12 | |
| Steven Hogg | 8(1) | 1 |
| Mark Howard | 8 | |
| Tim Howard | 1 | |
| David Jones | 3(1) | 1 |
| Ritchie Jones | 12 | 1 |
| Kleberson | 2 | |
| Lee Lawrence | 8 | |
| Michael Lea | 2(1) | |
| Tommy Lee | 3(1) | |
| Paul McShane | 7(1) | 1 |
| Phil Marsh | 7(3) | 3 |
| Lee Martin | 8(3) | 2 |
| Kyle Moran | 0(4) | |
| Jamie Mullan | 1(1) | |
| Markus Neumayr | 14(3) | 3 |
| Floribert Ngalula | 13 | 1 |
| Phil Picken | 9 | |
| Gerard Piqué | 7(1) | 1 |
| David Poole | 4(1) | 2 |
| Jami Puustinen | 0(3) | 1 |
| Ricardo | 2 | |
| Kieran Richardson | 3 | 1 |
| Danny Rose | 0(1) | |
| Giuseppe Rossi | 3(4) | 5 |
| John Ruddy | 1 | |
| Louis Saha | 1 | |
| Ryan Shawcross | 3(2) | |
| Danny Simpson | 7 | |
| Jonathan Spector | 1(3) | |

## PONTIN'S HOLIDAY LEAGUE DIV ONE (WEST)

| | P | W | D | L | F | A | Pts |
|---|---|---|---|---|---|---|---|
| Manchester United | 22 | 14 | 5 | 3 | 48 | 28 | 47 |
| Carlisle United | 22 | 13 | 3 | 6 | 43 | 36 | 42 |
| Blackpool | 22 | 12 | 4 | 6 | 34 | 21 | 40 |
| Oldham Athletic | 22 | 12 | 3 | 7 | 48 | 34 | 39 |
| Bury | 22 | 10 | 7 | 5 | 30 | 23 | 37 |
| Macclesfield Town | 22 | 8 | 7 | 7 | 31 | 27 | 31 |
| Burnley | 22 | 5 | 11 | 6 | 24 | 21 | 26 |
| Chester City | 22 | 7 | 3 | 12 | 25 | 37 | 24 |
| Stockport County | 22 | 5 | 7 | 10 | 28 | 37 | 22 |
| Shrewsbury Town | 22 | 5 | 6 | 11 | 25 | 31 | 21 |
| Rochdale | 22 | 4 | 6 | 12 | 23 | 38 | 18 |
| Wrexham | 22 | 6 | 0 | 16 | 27 | 54 | 18 |

The U18s: Could soon be household names

Francisco Filho's final season at United's Academy very nearly ended on a high note as his youngsters pushed all the way in pursuit of the U18 group title – but ultimately had to be content with runners-up spot behind Blackburn Rovers.

Rovers won the overall Academy title after defeating Coventry City 4-3 in the play-off final, but there was a stage when it looked like the Reds were mounting a serious challenge for top spot. The teams met in a proverbial six-pointer at Blackburn's Brockhall training complex in February; United winning a sensational game 3-2, having trailed 2-1 and been reduced to nine players. As a result, the Reds leapfrogged Rovers to go clear.

Filho's team had nine games remaining to consolidate pole position, but events after that terrific result didn't go to plan. Although the run-in saw just a solitary defeat – a 1-0 reverse at Sheffield Wednesday – drawn matches in the final two months of the season with Wolves, Manchester City, Newcastle and Barnsley effectively put paid to any real hopes of snatching the title. At least Filho's time at the club ended on a winning note as the lads closed the campaign with 2-1 wins over Derby County and Huddersfield Town respectively.

Fraizer Campbell completed the season as the under-18s' top marksmen with 14 goals to his name.

Sadly, there was to be no glory in the FA Youth Cup after the youngsters fell at the first hurdle, losing 1-0 against Stoke City at Ewen Fields, Hyde. Still, there's always next year...

**FA PREMIER ACADEMY LEAGUE U18**

SATURDAY 21 AUGUST 2004
FULHAM (Away)
W 3-1 (Martin, Rossi, Campbell)
Crockett, Simpson, Lea, Evans J, Shawcross, Lee K, Campbell, Gibson, Puustinen, Rossi, Martin
Substitutes: Rose, Backhouse, Mullan (Campbell), Burns (Puustinen), Evans S

SATURDAY 28 AUGUST
WEST HAM UNITED (Home, Carrington)
W 3-2 (Rossi 2, Evans S)
Crockett, Simpson, Lea, Evans J, Shawcross, Rose, Martin, Gibson, Campbell, Rossi, Evans S
Substitutes: Mullan (Evans S.), Backhouse, Puustinen (Shawcross), Burns, Moran (Campbell)

SATURDAY 4 SEPTEMBER
NEWCASTLE UNITED (Home)
L 1-4 (Rossi)
Crockett, Simpson, Lea, Evans J, Shawcross, Piqué, Martin, Gibson, Puustinen, Campbell, Lee K
Substitutes: Rossi (Puustinen), Rose (Evans J), Moran, Evans S, Mullan (Martin)

SATURDAY 11 SEPTEMBER
NOTTINGHAM FOREST (Away)
L 1-2 (Mullan)
Crockett, Simpson, Lea, Evans J, Shawcross, Rose, Mullan, Martin, Moran, Burns, Evans S
Substitutes: Campbell (Moran), Lee K (Martin), Gray (Burns), Marsh

SATURDAY 18 SEPTEMBER
SHEFFIELD UNITED (Home)
W 4-3 (Campbell 2, Mullan, Law og)
Crockett, Simpson, Lea, Gibson, Shawcross, Rose, Mullan, Martin, Moran, Campbell, Lee K
Substitutes: Puustinen, Heaton, Burns (Campbell), Marsh (Martin), Gray (Moran)

SATURDAY 25 SEPTEMBER
SUNDERLAND (Away)
W 3-1 (Gibson, Moran, Burns)
Crockett, Lee K, Lea, Evans J, Shawcross, Rose, Mullan, Gibson, Puustinen, Burns, Martin
Substitutes: Campbell (Burns), Backhouse, Moran (Martin), Marsh (Puustinen), Gray

SATURDAY 2 OCTOBER
WOLVERHAMPTON WANDERERS (Away)
W 2-0 (Moran, Marsh)
Crockett, Lee K, Lea, Evans, Shawcross, Rose, Gray, Gibson, Moran, Campbell, Mullan
Substitutes: Martin, Marsh (Gray), Puustinen, Burns

SATURDAY 9 OCTOBER
EVERTON (Home)
D 2-2 (Campbell 2)
Heaton, Simpson, Lea, Piqué, Shawcross, Rose, Marsh, Gibson, Moran, Campbell, Martin
Substitutes: Lee K. (Campbell), Burns (Moran), Gray (Marsh), Puustinen

SATURDAY 16 OCTOBER
BOLTON WANDERERS (Away)
W 3-2 (Marsh, Campbell, Puustinen)
Crockett, Simpson, Lee K, Evans J, Lea, Rose, Gray, Gibson, Burns, Campbell, Marsh
Substitutes: Puustinen (Burns), Heaton, Evans S (Campbell), Moran (Gray)

SATURDAY 23 OCTOBER
STOKE CITY (Home)
L 3-4 (Martin, Campbell, Puustinen)
Crockett, Simpson, Lee K, Howard, Lea, Rose, Marsh, Gibson, Puustinen, Campbell, Martin
Substitutes: Mullan (Marsh), Backhouse (Crockett), Evans S, Burns (Campbell), Moran

SATURDAY 30 OCTOBER
MANCHESTER CITY (Away)
W 2-1 (Rose, Ngalula)
Crockett, Simpson, Lea, Piqué, McShane, Ngalula, Martin, Gibson, Campbell, Jones R, Rose
Substitutes: Mullan (Rose), Heaton, Marsh (Piqué), Puustinen, Evans S (Martin)

SATURDAY 6 NOVEMBER
CREWE ALEXANDRA (Away)
D 3-3 (Gibson pen, Evans S, Campbell)
Crockett, Simpson, Lea, Evans J, Shawcross, Rose, Gray, Gibson, Moran, Campbell, Marsh
Substitutes: Evans S. (Moran), Heaton, Lee K (Shawcross), Burns, Puustinen (Gray)

SATURDAY 20 NOVEMBER
LIVERPOOL (Away)
W 2-1 (Gibson, Piqué)
Crockett, Simpson, Lea, Shawcross, Evans J, Piqué, Gray, Gibson, Burns, Rose, Evans S
Substitutes: Marsh, Puustinen, Mullan (Evans S), Lee K (Burns)

SATURDAY 4 DECEMBER
BLACKBURN ROVERS (Home)
L 1-2 (Evans J)
Crockett, Simpson, Lee K., Shawcross, Evans J, Rose, Mullan, Gibson, Moran, Burns, Martin
Substitutes: Puustinen (Moran), Heaton, Lea, Evans S. (Burns), Gray (Mullan)

SATURDAY 11 DECEMBER
STOKE CITY (Away, Lyme Valley Stadium, Newcastle-under-Lyme)
W 4-2 (Marsh 2 (1 pen), Puustinen 2)
Heaton, Simpson, Lea, Shawcross, McShane, Ngalula, Mullan, Lee K., Burns, Puustinen, Marsh
Substitutes: Gray, Crockett, Rose (Ngalula), Evans S, Moran

SATURDAY 8 JANUARY 2005
MANCHESTER CITY (Home)
W 2-1 (Gibson, Rose)
Heaton, Simpson, Lea, Shawcross, Evans J, Rose, Marsh, Gibson, Jones R., Campbell, Evans S
Substitutes: Puustinen, Amos, Burns, Moran, Lee K

SATURDAY 15 JANUARY
CREWE ALEXANDRA (Home)
W 5-0 (Evans S 2, Lee K, Gibson pen, Evans J)
Crockett, Simpson, Lea, Shawcross, Evans J, Rose, Mullan, Gibson, Puustinen, Lee K, Evans S
Substitutes: Burns (Puustinen), Heaton, Campbell, Marsh (Evans S), Moran (Mullan)

SATURDAY 5 FEBRUARY
LIVERPOOL (Home)
W 1-0 (Campbell)
Crockett, Simpson, Lee K., Shawcross, Evans J, Rose, Marsh, Gibson, Gray, Campbell, Evans S
Substitutes: Puustinen (Gray), Heaton, Burns, Mullan (Marsh), Moran (Campbell)

SATURDAY 12 FEBRUARY
BLACKBURN ROVERS (Away)
W 3-2 (Rose, Evans S 2)
Crockett, Gray, Lee K, Evans J. Simpson, Rose, Marsh, Jones R, Burns, Campbell, Evans S
Substitutes: Puustinen, Heaton, Mullan (Marsh), Moran (Evans S)

SATURDAY 18 FEBRUARY
WOLVERHAMPTON WANDERERS (Home)
D 1-1 (Mullan)
Crockett, Gray, Lee K, Jones R, Simpson, Rose, Mullan, Gibson, Moran, Campbell, Evans S
Substitutes: Puustinen, Heaton, Marsh, Lea, Burns (Moran)

SATURDAY 26 FEBRUARY
MANCHESTER CITY (Away)
D 1-1 (Campbell)
Crockett, Gray, Lee K, Lea, Simpson, Rose, Mullan, Gibson, Campbell, Burns, Evans S
Substitutes: Marsh (Burns), Heaton, Moran, Puustinen

SATURDAY 5 MARCH
EVERTON (Away)
W 3-0 (Shawcross, Gray, Campbell)
Crockett, Simpson, Lee K, Shawcross, Lea, Rose, Gray, Gibson, Campbell, Burns, Mullan
Substitutes: Marsh, Heaton, Puustinen (Burns), Jones R (Mullan)

SATURDAY 12 MARCH
BOLTON WANDERERS (Home)
W 1-0 (Campbell)
Crockett, Simpson, Lee K, Shawcross, Lea, Rose, Gray, Gibson, Puustinen, Campbell, Burns
Substitutes: Evans J, Lee T. (Crockett), Moran (Puustinen), Mullan, Marsh (Gray)

SATURDAY 19 MARCH
NEWCASTLE UNITED (Home)
D 1-1 (Campbell)
Lee T, Lee K, Lea M, Shawcross, Evans J, Rose, Simpson, Gibson, Burns, Campbell, Mullan
Substitutes: Marsh (Gibson), Crockett, Puustinen (Burns), Moran (Mullan), Hewson

SATURDAY 2 APRIL
SHEFFIELD WEDNESDAY (Away)
L 0-1
Lee T, Gray, Lee K, Lea M, Shawcross, Rose, Hewson, Gibson, Burns, Campbell, Evans S
Substitutes: Puustinen (Burns), Crockett, Mullan (Hewson), Moran (Gray)

SATURDAY 9 APRIL
BARNSLEY (Home)
D 2-2 (Campbell, Simpson)
Crockett, Simpson, Lee K, Lea M, Jones R, Rose, Mullan, Gibson, Moran, Campbell, Burns
Substitutes: Evans S (Burns), Lee T, Puustinen, Shawcross

SATURDAY 16 APRIL
DERBY COUNTY (Home)
W 2-1 (Gibson, Burns)
Crockett, Simpson, Lea M, Evans J, Shawcross, Rose, Mullan, Gibson, Burns, Campbell, Lee K
Substitutes: Puustinen (Mullan), Lee T, Evans S, Moran (Campbell)

SATURDAY 24 APRIL
HUDDERSFIELD TOWN (Away)
W 2-1 (Burns 2)
Crockett, Simpson, Lea M., Moran, Shawcross, Rose, Mullan, Lee K, Burns, Campbell, Evans S
Substitutes: Puustinen (Mullan), Lee T

**FA YOUTH CUP THIRD ROUND**

THURSDAY 16 DECEMBER 2004
STOKE CITY (Home, Ewen Fields, Hyde)
L 0-1
Crockett, Evans J, Shawcross, Jones R, Piqué, Gibson, Martin, Marsh, Puustinen, Rossi, Mullan
Substitutes: Gray, Amos, Evans S (Puustinen), Simpson (Piqué), Campbell (Marsh)

# TROPHY TIME

**APPEARANCES: ACADEMY UNDER-18**

| | Apps | Goals |
|---|---|---|
| Chris Backhouse | 0 (1) | |
| Aaron Burns | 15 (6) | 4 |
| Fraizer Campbell | 22 (2) | 14 |
| Lee Crockett | 23 | |
| Jonathan Evans | 16 | 2 |
| Sean Evans | 11 (5) | 6 |
| Darron Gibson | 24 | 6 |
| David Gray | 11 (4) | 1 |
| Tom Heaton | 3 | |
| Sam Hewson | 1 | |
| Mark Howard | 1 | |
| Ritchie Jones | 5 (1) | |
| Michael Lea | 24 | |
| Kieran Lee | 21 (4) | 1 |
| Tommy Lee | 2 (1) | |
| Paul McShane | 2 | |
| Phil Marsh | 8 (8) | 4 |
| Lee Martin | 10 | 2 |
| Kyle Moran | 9 (10) | 2 |
| Jamie Mullan | 14 (9) | 3 |
| Floribert Ngalula | 2 | 1 |
| Gerard Piqué | 4 | 1 |
| Jami Puustinen | 7 (10) | 4 |
| Danny Rose | 25 (2) | 3 |
| Giuseppe Rossi | 2 (1) | 4 |
| Ryan Shawcross | 21 | 1 |
| Danny Simpson | 25 | 1 |
| Nicky Law (Sheffield United) | | 1og |

**FA PREMIER ACADEMY LEAGUE – UNDER-18 (GROUP C)**

| | P | W | D | L | F | A | Pts |
|---|---|---|---|---|---|---|---|
| Blackburn Rovers | 28 | 19 | 4 | 5 | 57 | 24 | 61 |
| Manchester United | 28 | 17 | 6 | 5 | 61 | 41 | 57 |
| Everton | 28 | 14 | 9 | 5 | 46 | 34 | 51 |
| Manchester City | 28 | 13 | 10 | 5 | 66 | 37 | 49 |
| Crewe Alexandra | 28 | 13 | 6 | 9 | 53 | 44 | 45 |
| Stoke City | 28 | 10 | 9 | 9 | 39 | 46 | 39 |
| Wolverhampton Wanderers | 28 | 8 | 13 | 7 | 38 | 39 | 37 |
| Bolton Wanderers | 28 | 6 | 7 | 15 | 38 | 53 | 25 |
| Liverpool | 28 | 5 | 7 | 16 | 24 | 52 | 22 |

David Jones lifts the FAPRL shield after the Reds' 4-2 win over Charlton Athletic

Celebrating the FA Premier Reserve League play-off win at The Valley

The Pontin's League champions enjoy the moment

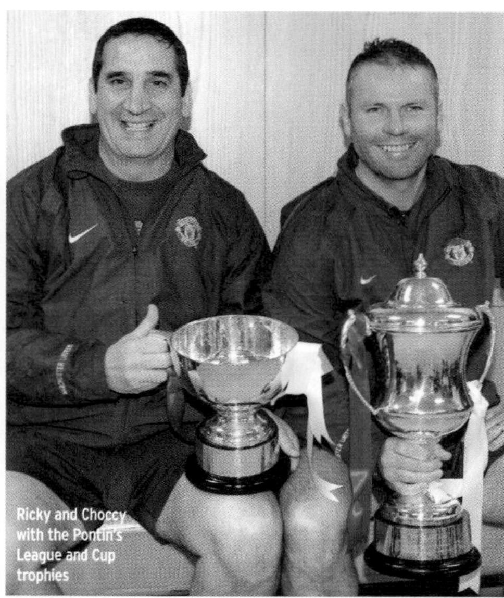
Ricky and Choccy with the Pontin's League and Cup trophies

The Reds pick up the Barclays FA Premier Reserve League trophy

# YOUNG PROFESSIONALS

COLIN HEATH

**Position** Forward
**Birthdate** 31 December 1983
**Birthplace** Chesterfield
**Signed** trainee 3 July 2000
Signed professional 31 December 2000

MARK HOWARD

**Position** Defender
**Birthdate** 29 January 1986
**Birthplace** Salford
**Signed** non-contract 8 July 2002

ADAM ECKERSLEY

**Position** Defender
**Birthdate** 7 September 1985
**Birthplace** Manchester
**Signed** non-contract 8 July 2002
Signed professional 1 July 2004

PHIL BARDSLEY

**Position** Defender
**Birthdate** 28 June 1985
**Birthplace** Salford
**Signed** non-contract 1 July 2001
Signed professional 1 July 2003

KENNY COOPER

**Position** Forward
**Birthdate** 21 October 1984
**Birthplace** Baltimore, USA
**Signed** non-contract 6 October 2003
Signed professional 1 January 2004

PAUL McSHANE

**Position** Defender
**Birthdate** 6 January 1986
**Birthplace** Kilpedder, County Wicklow
**Signed** non-contract 8 July 2002
Signed professional 6 January 2003

DAVID FOX

**Position** Midfielder
**Birthdate** 13 December 1983
**Birthplace** Stoke-on-Trent
**Signed** trainee 3 July 1999
Signed professional 31 December 2000

FLORIBERT NGALULA

**Position** Defender
**Birthdate** 7 March 1987
**Birthplace** Brussels, Belgium
**Signed** non-contract 7 July 2003
Signed professional 7 March 2005

PHIL PICKEN

**Position** Defender
**Birthdate** 12 November 1985
**Birthplace** Manchester
**Signed** non-contract 8 July 2002
Signed professional 1 July 2004

MARKUS NEUMAYR

**Position** Midfielder
**Birthdate** 26 March 1986
**Birthplace** Hosbach, Germany
**Signed** non-contract 1 July 2003
Signed professional 16 May 2003

LUKE STEELE

**Position** Goalkeeper
**Birthdate** 24 September 1984
**Birthplace** Peterborough
**Signed** 13 May 2002
transferred from Peterborough United

TOM HEATON

**Position** Goalkeeper
**Birthdate** 15 April 1986
**Birthplace** Chester
**Signed** non-contract 8 July 2002
Signed professional 1 July 2003

# ACADEMY ROLL CALL

United's Academy is where the next batch of talented youngsters are planning their break into the big time

## FIRST YEARS

| Name | Position | Birthdate | Birthplace | Date signed |
|---|---|---|---|---|
| **Febian Brandy** | Forward | 04/02/1989 | Manchester | July 2005 |
| **Craig Cathcart** | Centre back | 06/02/1989 | Belfast | July 2005 |
| **James Chester** | Centre back | 23/01/1989 | Warrington | July 2005 |
| **Richard Eckersley** | Right back | 12/03/1989 | Salford | July 2005 |
| **Christopher Fagan** | Forward | 11/05/1989 | Dublin | July 2005 |
| **Sam Hewson** | Midfielder | 28/11/1988 | Bolton | July 2005 |
| **Ron-Robert Zieler** | Goalkeeper | 12/02/1989 | Cologne, Germany | July 2005 |

## SECOND YEAR

| Name | Position | Birthdate | Birthplace | Date signed |
|---|---|---|---|---|
| **Aaron Burns** | Forward | 08/11/1987 | Manchester | July 2004 |
| **Fraizer Campbell** | Forward | 13/09/1987 | Huddersfield | July 2004 |
| **Lee Crockett** | Goalkeeper | 04/10/1987 | Peterborough | July 2004 |
| **Jonathan Evans** | Midfielder | 03/01/1988 | Belfast | July 2004 |
| **Sean Evans** | Defender | 25/09/1987 | Ludlow | July 2004 |
| **Darron Gibson** | Midfielder | 25/10/1987 | Londonderry | July 2004 |
| **Michael Lea** | Defender | 04/11/1987 | Leigh | July 2004 |
| **David Gray** | Forward | 04/05/1988 | Edinburgh | July 2004 |
| **Kieran Lee** | Midfielder | 22/06/1988 | Stalybridge | July 2004 |
| **Jamie Mullan** | Midfielder | 10/02/1988 | Nottingham | July 2004 |
| **Daniel Rose** | Midfielder | 21/02/1988 | Bristol | July 2004 |
| **Ryan Shawcross** | Midfielder | 04/10/1987 | Chester | July 2004 |

## THIRD YEAR

| Name | Position | Birthdate | Birthplace | Date signed |
|---|---|---|---|---|
| **Richard Jones** | Midfielder | 26/09/1986 | Manchester | 7 July 2003 |
| **Philip Marsh** | Forward | 15/11/1986 | St Helens | 7 July 2003 |
| **Kyle Moran** | Forward | 07/06/1987 | Dundalk | 7 July 2003 |
| **Floribert Ngalula** | Defender | 07/03/1987 | Brussels, Belgium | 7 July 2003 |
| **Daniel Simpson** | Defender | 04/01/1987 | Salford | 7 July 2003 |
| **Jami Puustinen** | Forward | 09/01/1987 | Espoo, Finland | 29 Sep 2003 |
| **Lee Martin** | Midfielder | 09/02/1987 | Taunton | 15 Dec 2003 |

## SUPPORTERS' CLUB BRANCHES

A list of all official branches of the supporters' club can be found on the following pages.

## AWAY TRAVEL

**Domestic games:** All club members, which includes Private Box holders, Executive Suite & Club Class members and Season Ticket and League Match Ticket Book holders, are automatically enrolled in our Away Travel Club and, as such, are entitled to book coach travel from Old Trafford to all Premiership venues. Full details can be found on this page.

**How to make a booking:** You can book a place on a coach, subject to availability, upon personal application at the Ticketing & Membership Services office, in which case you must quote your MUFC membership number. Alternatively, you can make a postal application by submitting the relevant payment, a stamped addressed envelope and a covering letter quoting your MUFC membership number. Telephone reservations are also acceptable during normal office hours on 0870 442 1994 if making payment by credit/debit card. Cancellations must be made in advance of the day of the game. It should be noted that this season all coaches will be of an Executive standard, ie. toilet facilities, video entertainment and refreshment availability. Car park attendants will be on duty should you wish to park your car on one of our car parks before travelling to an away game. This service is offered at no extra charge but we wish to point out that the club will not be held responsible for any damage or theft from your vehicle. Members are advised to check match ticket availability before booking a place on a coach. Details can be obtained by telephoning our Ticket & Match Information line on 0870 442 1968.

**European travel:** Ticketing & Membership Services is also responsible for organising members' travel and distribution of match tickets for our European away games. Details will be made known when available, via usual channels.

### MEMBERS' TRAVEL

| | Return fare | *Departure time | **Estimated return time to OT |
|---|---|---|---|
| Arsenal | £25.00 | 8.30am | 9.30pm |
| Aston Villa | £18.00 | 11.30am | 7.30pm |
| Birmingham City | £18.00 | 11.30am | 7.30pm |
| Blackburn Rovers | £15.00 | 1.00pm | 6.15pm |
| Bolton Wanderers | £12.00 | 1.00pm | 6.15pm |
| Charlton Athletic | £25.00 | 8.00am | 10.00pm |
| Chelsea | £25.00 | 8.30am | 9.30pm |
| Everton | £15.00 | 1.00pm | 6.15pm |
| Fulham | £25.00 | 8.30am | 9.30pm |
| Liverpool | £15.00 | 1.00pm | 6.15pm |
| Middlesbrough | £18.00 | 11.00am | 8.00pm |
| Newcastle United | £18.00 | 10.30am | 8.30pm |
| Portsmouth | £25.00 | 8.30am | 10.00pm |
| Sunderland | £18.00 | 11.00am | 8.00pm |
| Tottenham Hotspur | £25.00 | 8.30am | 9.30pm |
| West Bromwich Albion | £18.00 | 11.30am | 7.30pm |
| West Ham United | £25.00 | 8.30am | 9.30pm |
| Wigan Athletic | £12.00 | 1.00am | 6.15pm |
| Wembley Stadium | £25.00 | 7.00am | 11.00pm |

All times based on games with a 3.00 pm kick-off

* Departure times are subject to change and it is vital to check the actual time when making your booking

** Return times shown are only estimated and are subject to traffic congestion

If you have any query or require further information regarding membership, domestic away travel, European away games, personal insurance or branches of the supporters' club, please write to this address: Manchester United Football Club, Ticketing & Membership Services, Department M, Old Trafford, Manchester M16 0RA. Or, if you prefer, you can telephone the office on 0870 442 1994 or send a fax on 0161 868 8837. R.N.I.D. Textphone 0161 868 8668

# SUPPORTERS' INFORMATION

ENGLAND, SCOTLAND & WALES

**ABERDEEN** Branch Secretary: **Michael Stewart**, 26 Dubford Crescent, Bridge of Don, Aberdeen, AB23 8FT. Tel: 01224 822826 (after 7.00pm); Mobile: 07740 980967; Email: stewart_m@btinternet.com.
Departure points (excluding early kick-offs): Guild Street, Aberdeen 6.00am; Forfar Bypass 6.45am; The Kingsway, Dundee 7.00am; Stirling Services 8.15am (coach for home games only). New members welcome - contact Branch Secretary for further information.

**ABERGELE AND COAST** Branch Secretary: **Eddie Williams**, 14 Maes-y-Dre, Abergele, Clwyd, North Wales, LL22 7HW. Tel: 01745 823694.
Departure points: Aber; Llanfairfechen; Penmaen Mawr; Conwy; Llandudno Junction; Colwyn Bay; Abergele; Rhyl; Rhuddlan; Dyserth; Prestatyn; Mostyn; Holywell; Flint; Deeside.

**ABERYSTWYTH AND DISTRICT** Branch Chairman: **A Howe**.
Tel: 01970 615757.
Departure points: please contact Branch Chairman.

**ASHBOURNE** Branch Secretary: **Diane O'Connell**, 1 Milldale Court, Ashbourne, Derbyshire, DE6 1SN. Tel: 01335 346105.
Departure points: The Maypole, Bridge Street, Derby, three-and-a-half hours before kick-off; McDonald's, Markeaton Roundabout, Derby, three-and-a-half hours before kick-off; Hanover Hotel, Ashbourne, three hours before kick-off; Ashbourne Bus Station, three hours before kick-off. Contact Branch Secretary for details of travel to away fixtures.

**AYRSHIRE** Branch Secretary: **Mr Peter Howe**. Tel: 01292 318128 (after 7.00pm); Email: peter@howe.fslife.co.uk.
Branch Chairman: **Mr Ward Shields**. Tel: 01292 316232; Branch Treasurer: **Mr David Emmett**. Tel: 01292 311831. Match Secretary: **Mr Brian Grey**. Tel: 01292 318380.

**BARNSLEY** Branch Secretary: **Miss Ann-Marie Self**, 87 Snydale Road, Cudworth, Barnsley, S72 8LH. Tel: 01226 717 274; Mobile: 07767 870855.
Departure points: 12.30pm (5.30pm), Locke Park Working Men's Club, Park Road, Barnsley via A628. Or two-and-a-half hours before any other kick-off times. Times in brackets refer to evening fixtures.

**BARROW-IN-FURNESS** Branch Secretary: **Robert Bayliff**, 183 Chapel Street, Dalton-in-Furness, Cumbria, LA15 8SL. Mobile: 07788 762936.
Departure points: Barrow, Ramsden Square, 9.30am (4.00pm); Dalton 9.45am (4.15pm); Ulverston 10.00am (4.30pm). A590 route to M6. Times in brackets refer to evening fixtures.

**BEDFORDSHIRE** Branch Secretary: **Craig Dilley**, 89 Dells Lane, Biggleswade, Bedfordshire, SG18 8LH. Mobile: 07977 501133 (up to 9.00pm only); Email: mufcbedfordbranch@hotmail.co.uk.
Departure points: Bedford Bus Station; 'Coachways', Junction 14, M1.

**BERWICK-UPON-TWEED** Branch Secretary: **Margaret Walker**, 17 Lords Mount, Berwick-upon-Tweed, Northumberland, TD15 1LY. Branch Chairman: **Raymond Dixon**, 92 Shielfield Terrace, Berwick-upon-Tweed. Tel: 01289 308671. SAE for all enquiries please.
Departure points: Berwick; Belford; Alnwick; Stannington; Washington; Scotch Corner; Leeming Bar; and anywhere on the main A1 by arrangement.

**BIRMINGHAM** Branch Secretary: **Paul Evans**, 179 Longbridge Lane, Longbridge, Birmingham B31 4LA. Tel: 0121 604 1385 (6.30pm-9.00pm).
Coaches operate to all home games. For times and additional information please telephone or send a stamped addressed envelope. Departure points: Birmingham City Centre; Perry Barr; Junction 7, M6.

**BLACK COUNTRY** Branch Secretary: **Ade Steventon**. Tel: 0121 531 0826 (6.30pm-9.00pm). Mobile: 0784 3578763.
The branch operates to all home games. Departure points: Talk of the Town, Darlaston, 11.00am (4.00pm); Woden Public House, Wednesbury, 11.10am (4.10pm); Friendly Lodge Hotel, J10, M6 11.20am (4.20pm); The Chase Gate Public House, off J11, M6, 11.30am (4.30pm). For further information please contact the Branch Secretary. Please phone well in advance to book coach places. All queries between 6.30pm-8.30pm weekdays only.
Times in brackets refer to evening fixtures.

**BLACKPOOL, PRESTON AND FYLDE** Branch Chairman: **Martin Day**. Tel: 07971 963264; Email: martin@melday.fsnet.co.uk. Coach Travel: **Jean**

**Halliday**. Tel: 01772 635887. Branch Membership Secretary: **Sharon Randall**. Tel: 07879 683744. Social Secretary: **Tony Nicholson**. Tel: 07760 226893. Pick-up points: Bispham; Blackpool; St Annes; Lytham; Freckleton; Preston. Away travel to Blackburn, Bolton, City, Leeds, Liverpool, Everton and other north-west clubs in Cup competitions. Out-of-town Reds are welcome to travel with branch.
**BRADFORD AND LEEDS** Branch Secretary: **Sally Hampshire**, PO Box 87, Cleckheaton, West Yorkshire, BD19 6YN. Tel: 07973 904554; Email: ian.Hampshire@btinternet.com. Website: www.bradfordreds.co.uk.
**BRIDGNORTH AND DISTRICT** Branch Secretary: **Ann Saxby**, 30 Pitchford Road, Albrighton, Near Wolverhampton, WV7 3LS. Tel: 01902 373260.
**BRIDGWATER AND SOUTH WEST** Branch Secretary: **Ray White**, 4 Spencer Close, Bridgwater, Somerset, TA6 5SP. Tel: 01278 452186; Mobile: 07850 950750; Email: raywhite@bridgwater-reds.co.uk. Website: www.bridgwater-reds.co.uk.
Departure points: Taunton; Bridgwater; Weston-Super-Mare; Clevedon, Aztec West (Bristol).
**BRIGHTON** Branch Secretary: **Colin Singers**. Tel: 01903 761679 (after 6pm); Mobile: 07793 837595. For any information, contact Colin.
**BRISTOL, BATH AND DISTRICT** Branch Chairman: **Mr Ashley Powell,** 70 Cainscross Road, Stroud, Glos, GL5 4HB. Tel: 07976 516312; Email ash@muscbb.co.uk. Branch Secretary: **Miss Eve Berry**, 9 Whitestone Road, Frome, Somerset, BA11 2DN. Tel/Fax: 01373 467309; Mobile: 07973 816190. Branch Administrator: **Mr Les Purnell**. Email: les@muscbb.co.uk. Website: www.muscbb.co.uk.
Departure points: Bath Railway Station (by bus stop), 8.05am (12.45pm); Keynsham (opposite church), 8.20am (1.05pm); Bristol Temple Meads (outside Reckless Engineer Pub), 8.40am (1.20pm); Bradley Stoke (bus stop opposite Hilton Hotel), 9.00am (1.40pm); J13, M5, Stroud (Travelodge), 9.15am (1.55pm). Times given are for 3pm kick-offs. Times in brackets refer to evening kick-offs. Departure times for 12.00/12.45pm kick-offs are two hours earlier; for 16:05/17:15 kick-offs the departure time is one hour later from each point.
**BURTON-ON-TRENT** Branch Secretary: **Mrs Pat Wright**, 45 Foston Avenue, Burton-on-Trent, Staffordshire, DE13 0PL. Tel: 01283 532534; Mobile 07821 610942.
Departure points: Moira (garage); Swadlincote; Burton (B&Q Lichfield Street); Stoke area.
**CARLISLE AND DISTRICT** Branch Secretary: **Arnold Heard,** 28 Kentmere Grove, Morton Park, Carlisle, Cumbria, CA2 6JD. Tel/Fax: 01228 538262.
Departure points: for times and details, please contact the Branch Secretary.
**CENTRAL POWYS** Branch Secretary: **Bryn Thomas**, 10 Well Lane, Bungalows, Llanidloes, Powys, SY18 6BA. Tel: 01686 412391 (home), 01686 413200 (work).
Departure points: Crossgates, 10.30am; Rhayader, 10.45am; Llanidloes, 11.05am; Newtown, 11.25am.
**CHEPSTOW AND DISTRICT** Branch Secretary: **Anthony Parsons**, 56 Treowen Road, Newbridge, Newport, Gwent, NP11 3DN. Tel: 01495 246253.
Departure points: Newbridge; Pontypool; Cwmbran Bus Station; Malpas; Langstone Coldra; Chepstow. For departure times and further details contact the Branch Secretary
**CHESTER AND NORTH WALES** Branch Chairman: **Eddie Mansell,** 45 Overlea Drive, Hawarden, Deeside, Flintshire, CH5 3HR. Tel: 01244 520332. Branch Secretary: **Mrs Kate Reynolds**, 139 Park Avenue, Bryn-Y-Baal, Mold, Flintshire, CH7 6TR. Tel: 01352 753962. Branch Membership Secretary: **Mrs Irene Keidel**, 3 Springfield Drive, Buckley, Flintshire, CH7 2PH. Tel: 01244 550943.
Departure points: Oswestry; Ellesmere; Wrexham; Chester (Northgate Street); Rhyl; Greenfield; Flint; Queensferry (ASDA Store); Whitby (Woodlands); Ellesmere Port (Bus Station); Frodsham.
**CLEVELAND** Branch Chairman: **Paul McClaren**. Mobile: 07867 563757. Branch Secretary: **Brian Tose**, 36 Staithes Lane, Staithes, Saltburn by Sea, Cleveland, TS13 5AD. Mobile: 07811 612949.
Departure points: please contact the Branch Secretary for details.
**COLWYN BAY AND DISTRICT** Branch Secretary: **Clive Allen**, 62 Church Road, Rhos-on-Sea, Colwyn Bay, North Wales, LL28 4YS. Tel: 01492 546400; Mobile: 07831 403860; Email: clive.allen8@btinternet.com. Branch Chairman: **Bill Griffith**, 'Whitefield', 60 Church Road, Rhos-on-Sea, Colwyn Bay, North Wales, LL28 4YS. Tel: 01492 540240.
Departure points: bus stop, Mostyn Broadway (adjacent to car park), 10.45am (3.45pm); bus stop opposite Llandudno Junction Railway Station, 11.00am (4.00pm); bus stop, Mochdre, 11.00am (4.00pm); Church Road, Rhos-on-sea, 11.15 am (4.15pm); Guy's Newsagents, Conway Road, Colwyn Bay, 11.30am (4.30pm); Plough Hotel, Aston Hill, Queensferry 12.45pm (5.45pm). Times in brackets refer to evening fixtures.
**CORBY AND KETTERING** Branch Secretary: **Andrew Lindner**, 54 Walsingham Avenue, Kettering, Northants, NN15 5ER. Tel: 01536 519625. Branch Meetings: first Sunday of the month, 7.15pm, alternately at the Wayfarers, London Road, Kettering and the following month at the Corby Rugby Club, Rockingham Road, Corby.
Departure points: Co-op Extra Store, Alexander Road, Corby, 8.30am (1.30pm); Co-op Extra Superstore, Northfield Avenue, Kettering, 8.40am (1.40pm). Times in brackets refer to evening fixtures.
**CRAWLEY** Branch Secretary: **Robert Tweddle**, 206 Gossops Drive, Crawley, West Sussex, RH11 8LJ. Mobile: 07986 115832.
**CREWE AND NANTWICH** Branch Secretary: **Andy Ridgway**, 38 Murrayfield Drive, Willaston, Nantwich, Cheshire, CW5 6QF. Tel: 01270 568418; Website: www.mufccn.co.uk.
Departure points: Nantwich Barony, 12.30pm (5.00pm); Earl of Crewe, 12.40pm (5.10pm); Cross Keys, 12.50pm (5.20pm). Away travel subject to demand. Times in brackets refer to evening fixtures.
**DONCASTER AND DISTRICT:** Branch Secretary: **Albert Thompson**, 89 Anchorage Lane, Sprotboro, Doncaster, South Yorkshire, DN5 8EB. Tel: 01302 782964. Branch Treasurer: Sue Moyles, 217 Warningtongue Lane, Cantley. Tel: 01302 530422; Mobile: 07740 699824; Fax: 01302 349203; Email: sfmoyles@hotmail.com. Branch Chairman: Paul Kelly, 58 Oak Grove, Conisbrough, DN12 2HN. Tel: 01709 324058. Branch Membership Secretary: Mrs L Sudbury, 8 Parkway, Armthorpe, Doncaster. Tel: 01302 834323. Meetings are held on the first Monday of every month (unless there is a home match) in the Co-op Social Club (at the back of The Range) at 7.30pm.
Departure points: Broadway Hotel, Dunscroft, 10.30am (4.30pm); Edenthorpe, 10.40am (4.40pm); Waterdale (opposite main library), 10.45am (4.45pm); The Highwayman, Woodlands, 11.00am (5.00pm). Times in brackets refer to 8.00pm kick-offs.
**DORSET** Branch Secretary: **Mark Pattison,** 89 Parkstone Road, Poole, Dorset, BH15 2NZ. Tel: 01202 744348.
Departure points: Poole Train Station, 6.15am (10.30am); Branksome (Courts), 6.20am (10.35am); Bournemouth, 6.30am (10.45am); Ringwood, 7.00am (11.15am); Rownham Services, 7.15am (11.30am); Chieveley Services, 8.30am (12.30pm). Times in brackets refer to evening fixtures.
**DUKINFIELD AND HYDE** Branch Secretary: **Marilyn Chadderton,** 12 Brownville Grove, Dukinfield, Cheshire, SK16 5AS. Transport Secretary: **Gareth Chadderton**. Tel: 0161 366 8165.
Departure points: Details of meetings and travel are available from the above or S Jones, Tel: 0161 343 5260.
**EAST ANGLIA** Branch Secretary: **Mark Donovan**, 55 The Street, Holywell Row, Bury St Edmunds, Suffolk, IP28 8LT. Tel: 01638 717075. (9.00am-6.00pm); Email: manutdeastanglia@aol.com.
Executive coaches operated to all home fixtures via the following routes - Service No 1: Clacton, Colchester, Braintree, Gt Dunmow, Bishop's Stortford. Service No 2: Felixstowe, Nacton, Ipswich, Stowmarket, Bury St Edmunds. Service No 3: Thetford, Mildenhall, Newmarket, Cambridge, Huntingdon. Service No 4: Gt Yarmouth, Norwich, Dereham, Swaffham, Kings Lynn. We also operate coaches to all away games; departure details are dependent on demand and match ticket availability. Further information about our club together with details of your local representative can be obtained by contacting the above telephone no or email address.
**EAST MANCHESTER** Branch Secretary: **Tony McAllister**, 10 Walmer Street, Abbey Hey, Gorton, Manchester, M18 8QP. Tel: 0161 230 7098; Mobile: 07786 222596; Email: anthony.mcallister22000@yahoo.co.uk. Branch meetings are held on the last Thursday of each month (8.00pm) at Gorton Sport and Social Club, Ashkirk Street, Gorton, Manchester.
**EAST YORKSHIRE** Branch Secretary: **Ian Baxter**, 14 Old Road, Holme Moor, York, YO43 4AD. Mobile: 07768 821844. Hull Administrator: **Fred Helas**. Mobile: 07774 775 078.

Departure points: Hull Coach - Hull Marina, 10.30am (3.30pm); Howden Coach - Bay Horse, Market Weighton, 10.30am (3.30pm); Redbrick Café, Howden, 11.00am (4.00pm). Times in brackets refer to evening fixtures.
**ECCLES** Branch Secretary: **Gareth Morris**, 11 Brentwood Drive, Monton, Eccles, Manchester, M30 9LP. Tel: 0161 281 9435.
Departure point (away games only): Rock House Hotel, Peel Green Road, Peel Green, Eccles. For departure times please contact the Branch Secretary.
**EDINBURGH** Branch Chairman: **Paul Shaw**, 59/12 Watson Crescent, Edinburgh, EH11 1EW. Tel: 0131 478 3536 (after 6pm); Mobile: 07762 772637; Email: paul_shaw_musc@yahoo.co.uk. Branch Secretary: **Neil Coulter**, 24 Silverknowes, Eastway, Edinburgh, EH4 5NE. Mobile: 07958 533652. Branch Treasurer: **Ritchie McRobbie**. Committee Members: **Willie Bortwick**, **John Carse**. Committee meetings are held once a month and general meetings are held when necessary. New members are always welcome.
Departure points: for departure times and details, please contact the branch secretary.
**FEATHERSTONE AND DISTRICT** Branch Secretary: **Paul Kingsbury**, 11 Hardwick Road, Featherstone, W Yorks, WF7 5JA. Tel: 01977 793910; Mobile: 07789 040536 (matchdays only). Branch Treasurer: **Andy Yates**, 55 Camp Mount, Pontefract, West Yorkshire, WF8 4BX. Tel: 01977 798995; Email: andy.yates@hansonplc.com. Meetings are held every fortnight (Mondays) at the Girnhill Lane WMC, Girnhill Lane, Featherstone.
Departure points: Pontefract Sorting Office, 10.30am (3.30pm); Corner Pocket, Featherstone, 10.40am (3.40pm); Green Lane, Featherstone, 10.45am (3.45pm); Castleford Bus Station, 10.55am (3.55pm). Times in brackets refer to evening fixtures.
**FLEETWOOD** Branch Secretary: **Stuart Gill**. Tel: 01253 865450; Email: fleetwoodreds@eudoramail.com. For details contact the Branch Secretary or **Brian Houten**, tel: 01253 875876.
**GLAMORGAN AND GWENT** Branch Secretary: **Neil Chambers**, 201 Malpas Road, Newport, South Wales, NP20 5PP. Branch Chairman: **Cameron Erskine**. Tel: 02920 318287 (10.00am-1.00pm Monday-Friday; answerphone at other times); Mobile: 07885 615546; Email: c.erskine@ntlworld.co.uk.
Departure points: Skewen; Port Talbot; Bridgend; Cardiff; Newport.
**GLASGOW** Branch Secretary: **David Sharkey**, 45 Lavender Drive, Greenhills, East Kilbride, G75 9JH. Tel: 01355 902592 (7.00pm-11.00pm).
Departure points: George Square, 8.15am (1.00pm); The Angel, Uddingston, 8.30am (1.15pm); any M74 service stations. A coach runs to all home games. Times in brackets refer to evening fixtures.
**GLOUCESTER AND CHELTENHAM** Branch Secretary: **Paul Brown**, 59 Katherine Close, Churchdown, Gloucester, GL3 1PB. Tel: 01452 859553; Mobile: 07801 802593; Email: muscglos@aol.com.
Departure points: Bennetts Yard, Eastern Ave, Glos, 8.45am (1.45pm); Station Road, Gloucester 9.00am (2.00pm); Cheltenham Railway Station (outside Midland Hotel), 9.10am (2.10pm); Cheltenham Gas Works Corner, 9.15am (2.15pm). Times in brackets refer to evening fixtures.
**GRIMSBY AND DISTRICT** Branch Secretary: **Bob England**, 5 George Butler Close, Laceby, Grimsby, DN37 7WA. Tel: 01472 752130; Email: secretary@manutdgrimsby.com. Travel Arrangements: **Craig Collins** (Branch Chairman). Tel: 01472 314273; Website www.manutdgrimsby.com.
**GUERNSEY** Branch Secretary: **Harry Dick-Cleland**, Sand Dollar, 16 Les Grands Loriers, Vale Guernsey, Channel Islands, GY3 5HW. Tel: 01481 245877; Email: harrydc@cleland.gg.
**GUIDE BRIDGE AND DISTRICT** Branch Secretary: **Mike Parkinson**. Mobile: 07971 117337; Email: mike.parkinson@talk21.com. Branch meetings are held monthly - new members are welcome. The branch is based at the Corporation Arms at Guide Bridge in Tameside. Further details on www.manutd.com/supportersunited.
Transport to all home games leaves an hour before kick-off. Please arrive 30 minutes before departure. Away travel is organised according to destination and kick-off time.
**GWYNEDD** Branch Secretary: **Gwyn Hughes,** Sibrwd y Don, Tan y Cefn, Llanwnda, Caernarfon, Gwynedd, LL54 7YB. Tel: 07050 380804; Email: MUSCGwynedd@hotmail.co.uk. Ticket Secretary: **Stephen Jones**, Gwynant, Carmel, Caernarfon, Gwynedd, LL54 7AA. Tel: 07747 614923.
Departure points: Pwllheli; Llanwnda; Caernarfon; Bangor. For departure times, please contact the Branch Secretary.
**HAMPSHIRE** Ticket and travel secretary: **Angela Hebberd**, 41 Oak Hill, Alresford, Hampshire, SO24 9JZ. Tel/Fax: 01962 734631. General Secretary: **Roy Debenham**, 11 Lindley Gardens, Alresford, Hampshire, SO24 9PU. Tel/Fax: 01962 734420.
Departure points: (1) King George V Playing Fields, Northern Road, Cosham 7.00am (12.00 noon); (2) Hedge End 7.20am (12.20pm); (3) Bullington Cross Inn, Junction off A34 & A303, 7.50am (12.50pm); (4) Tot Hill Services (A34), just south of Newbury, 8.10am (1.10pm). Times in brackets refer to evening fixtures.
**HARROGATE AND DISTRICT** Branch Secretary: **Michael Heaton**, Railway Cottage, Grange Road, Dacre Banks, Harrogate, N Yorks, HG3 4EF. Tel & Fax: 01423 780679; Mobile: 07790 798328; Website: www.heatonsheroes.co.uk. Send s.a.e for membership details. Meetings are held every third Thursday in each month at the Dacre Banks Memorial Hall.
Departure points include: Nidderdale; Rippon; Northallerton; Leyburn; Harrogate; Skipton; and Earby areas. Coaches also operate to all away games, including European matches. For further information contact the Branch Secretary.
**HASTINGS** Branch Secretary: **Tim Martin**, 94 Gillsmans Hill, St Leonards-on-Sea, East Sussex, TN38 0SL (*no personal callers please*). Tel: 01424 442073 (6.00pm-8.00pm); Mobile: 07973 656716 (daytime); Email: martin@silvan.fsnet.co.uk.
Departure points: Eastbourne, Tesco roundabout, 5.40am; Bexhill, Viking chip shop, 6.00am; Silverhill, traffic lights, 6.15am; Hurst Green, George Pub, 6.40am; Pembury, Camden Arms Pub, 7.00am. All these times are for 3pm or 4pm kick-offs. For match bookings, or for details of travel to away games, please contact the Branch Secretary.
**HEREFORD** Branch Secretary: **Norman Elliss**, 40 Chichester Close, Abbeyfields, Belmont, Hereford, HR2 7YU. Tel: 01432 359923; Fax: 01432 342880; Mobile: 07903 652218.
Midweek match route - minibus provided, pick-up Worcester, Manor House Farm Pub, 1.45pm; Malvern Link, BP station, 2.00pm; Ledbury, Market House, 2.15pm. Main coach to leave Hereford, Bulmers Car Park (Whitecross Road), 3.00pm. Weekend Match Route - the coach will depart from Hereford, Bulmers Car Park (Whitecross Road), 9.00am for Saturday matches, 10.00am for Sunday matches, picking up en route as follows: Ledbury, 9.30am (Saturday matches), 10.00am (Sunday matches); Malvern Link, BP Station, 9.45am (Saturday), 10.45am (Sunday); Worcester, Manor Farm, 10.00am (Saturday), 11.00am (Sunday). Please note that for some matches, times will change due to Sky television coverage, so please confirm when you book your seat.
**HERTFORDSHIRE** Correspondence to: **Steve Bocking**, 64 Westmill Road, Hitchin, Herts, SG5 2SD. Tel: 01462 622076. Membership - contact Mick Slack. Tel: 01462 622451.
Organised travel to home and some away games. Pick-up points at Hertford; Welwyn; Stevenage; Hitchin; and Luton. For travel arrangements, contact Mick Prior, tel: 01438 361900.
**HEYWOOD** Branch Secretary: **Jacqui Sugden**. Tel: 07956 664630; Email: Jacqui@rhinorecruitment.co.uk. Branch Treasurer: **Jack Sykes**. Tel: 01706 369353. For information re. match travel etc, see the Branch Website: www.heywoodreds.co.uk.
**HIGHLANDS AND ISLANDS** Branch Secretary: **Ronnie McKay**, Creag Ard House, 5 Longrigg Road, Strontian, Argyll, PH36 4HY. Tel/Fax: 01967 402012; Mobile: 07818 243284; Email: Ronniemckay@btinternet.com; Website: www.creagardhouse.co.uk. New members welcome; contact the Branch Secretary for further details.
Departure points: Buckie; Elgin; Nairn; Inverness; A9 Perth and Sterling Services; or any service stations on the M74.
**HIGH PEAK** Branch Chairman: **Dave Rhodes**, 21 Park Road, Whaley Bridge, High Peak, SK23 7DJ. Tel: 01663 732484. Branch Secretary: **Keith Udale**, 101 Station Road, Marple, Stockport, SK6 6PA. Tel: 0161 427 1805; Mobile: 07810 567953; Email: k.udale@rds.co.uk; Fax: 0208 543 7330. Branch Treasurer: **Lise Udale**. Tel: 0161 427 1805. The Branch holds meetings on the last Thursday in the month at the The Memorial Club in Chapel-en-le Frith, The Jodrell Arms at Whaley Bridge and The Navigation Marple.
Departure Points: Memorial Club, Chapel; Jodrell Arms, Whaley Bridge; Bus Station, New Mills; Navigation, Marple.
**HYNDBURN AND PENDLE** Branch Secretary: **Alan Haslam**, 97 Crabtree Avenue, Edgeside, Waterfoot, Rossendale, BB4 9TB. Tel: 01706 831736.
Departure points: Barnoldswick, 11.15am (4.45pm); Nelson, 11.30am (5.00pm); Burnley, 11.45am (5.15pm); Accrington, 12.15pm (5.45pm); Haslingden, 12.20pm (5.50pm); Rawtenstall, 12.30pm (6.00pm). Times in brackets refer to evening fixtures.
**INVICTA REDS (KENT)** Branch Secretary: **Vic Hatherly**, Mobile: 0773 668 6962. Tickets and Travel: Shaun Rogers. Tel: 01622 721344 (not after 9.00pm). Correspondence: **Invicta Reds (Kent)**, 19 Tarragon Road, Maidstone, Kent, ME16 0UR. Email: invicta.reds@ntlworl.com; Website: www.invictareds.org.uk.
Departure points: Ramsgate; Herne Bay; Magistrates Court, Canterbury; M2, Medway Services; M2, Junction 3, Chatham; Little Chef Services, Cobham; Dartford Tunnel; M25, Junction 28, A10;
M25, Junction 26, Waltham Abbey.
**ISLE OF MAN** Branch Secretary: **Gill Keown,** 5 King Williams Way, Castletown, Isle of Man, IM9 1DH. Tel: 01624 823143; Mobile: 07624 497160; Email: reddevil@manx.net. Branch Chairman: **Lee Watson**, 22a Duke Street, Douglas, Isle Of Man, IM1 2AY. Tel: 07624 497364; Email: lee@extreme-ag.com.
**JERSEY** Branch Secretary: **Mark Jones**, 5 Rosemount Cottages, James Road, St. Saviour, Jersey, Channel Islands, JE2 7RR. Tel: 01534 734786 (home), 01534 885885 (work); Email: mark.jones@gtlsi.com; Website: mujersey.com. Should any members be in Jersey during the football season, the branch shows television games in a private club. Free food

provided, everybody welcome, including children. Contact the Branch Secretary for details.
**KEIGHLEY** Branch Secretary: **Mick Bugeja**, 1 Carlby Grove, Fell Lane, Keighley, W Yorks, BD22 6DZ. Tel: 01535 681055; Mobile: 07808 943423; Email: mjbugeja@fsmail.net.
Departure points: coach leaves Keighley from Keighley Technical College in Cavendish Street, then travels to Colne and joins M65 & 66 to Manchester. Contact the Branch Secretary for membership details and match bookings.
**KNUTSFORD** Branch Secretary: **John Butler**, 4 Hollingford Place, Knutsford, WA16 9DP. Tel: 01565 651360; Fax: 01565 634792; Email: johnmbutler@onetel.com. Branch Treasurer: **John Aston**. Branch Chairman: **Angus Campbell**. Please contact the Branch Secretary for details of meetings (usually weekly) at The White Bear.
**LANCASTER AND DISTRICT** Branch Secretary: **Andy Baker**, 78 Highland Brow, Galgate, Nr Lancaster, LA2 0NB. Mobile: 07808 395488; Email: a.baker@lancaster.ac.uk.
Departure points: Carnforth, Ex-Servicemens, 11.45am (4.45pm); Morecambe, Shrimp roundabout, 12.00pm (5.00pm); Lancaster, Dalton Square, 12.20pm (5.20pm), University Gates, 12.30pm (5.30pm); then A6 route to Broughton roundabout for M6-M61. Times in brackets refer to evening fixtures.
**LEAMINGTON SPA** Branch Secretary: **Mrs Norma Worton**, 23 Cornhill Grove, Kenilworth, Warwickshire, CV8 2QP. Tel: 01926 859476. Email: norma.worton@virgin.net.
Departure points: Leamington Spa, Newbold Terrace; Kenilworth, Leyes Lane; Coventry, London Road.
**LINCOLN** Branch Secretary: **Steve Stone**, 154 Scorer Street, Lincoln, Lincolnshire, LN5 7SX. Tel: 01522 885671.
Departure points: Unity Square, 9.50am, Saturday games (3.00pm kick-off); Unity Square, 2.50pm, midweek matches.
**LONDON** Branch Secretary: **Ralph Mortimer**, 55 Boyne Avenue, Hendon, London, NW4 2JL.
Departure points: Semley Place, Victoria, 8.00pm (12.30pm); Staples Corner, 8.30am (1.15pm); Junction 11, M1, 9.00am (1.45pm). A coach will run to all away games subject to sufficient numbers/tickets. Email any enquiries to: mortijr@aol-com or telephone 0208 203 1213 after 6.00pm. Times in brackets refer to midweek games.
**LONDON ASSOCIATION** Branch Secretary: **Najib Armanazi**. Tel: 07941 124591; Email: najcantona@hotmail.com. Branch Membership Secretary: **Alison Watt**. Tel: 01322 558333 (7pm–9pm only). Travel Enquiries: **Amit Basu**. Email: mulatravel@btinternet.com.
**LONDON FAN CLUB** Branch Secretary: **Paul Molloy**, 65 Corbylands Road, Sidcup, Kent, DA15 8JQ. Tel/Fax: 020 8302 5826. Branch Travel Secretary: **Mike Dobbin**. Email: info@mulfc65.freeserve.co.uk.
Departure points: Euston Station by service train - meeting point at top of escalator from Tube. Cheap group travel to most home and away games.
**MANCHESTER UNITED DISABLED SUPPORTERS' ASSOCIATION (MUDSA)** Branch Secretary: **Phil Downs MBE**, MUDSA, PO Box 141, South D.O., Manchester, M20 5BA. Tel/Fax: 0845 2301989. Email: disability@manutd.co.uk; Website: www.mudsa.com & www.manutd.com/access.
**MANSFIELD** Branch Secretary: **Peggy Conheeney**, 48 West Bank Avenue, Mansfield, Nottinghamshire, NG19 7BP. Tel/Fax: 01623 625140.
Departure points: Butlers Garage, 10.00am (4.00pm); Northern Bridge, Sutton, 10.10am (4.10pm); Mansfield Shoe Co, 10.20am (4.20pm); Pegs Home, 10.25am (4.25pm); Young Vanish, Glapwell, 10.40am (4.40pm); Hipper Street School, Chesterfield, 10.55am (4.55pm). Away games are dependent on ticket availability - please contact the Branch Secretary. Times in brackets refer to evening fixtures.
**MID CHESHIRE** Branch Secretary: **Leo Lastowecki**, 5 Townfield Court, Barnton, Northwich, Cheshire, CW8 4UT. Tel: 01606 784790.
Departure points: please contact the Branch Secretary.
**MIDDLETON AND DISTRICT** Branch Secretary: **Kevin Booth**, 8 Wicken Bank, Hopwood, OL10 2LW. Tel: 01706 624196; Mobile: 07762 741438. Branch Chairman: **Mike Conroy**, 12 Lulworth Road, Middleton, Manchester 24. Tel: 0161 653 5696.
Home Games: coaches depart from Crown Inn, Middleton, one hour prior to kick-off. For details of away games, please contact the Branch Secretary.
**MILLOM AND DISTRICT** Branch Secretary: **Edward Pattinson**, 8 Queens Park, Millom, Cumbria, LA18 5DY. Tel: 01229 772468.
**NEWTON-LE-WILLOWS** Branch Chairman: **Mark Coleman**, Email: mark.coleman6@tiscali.co.uk. Assistant Branch Ticket Secretary: **Margaret Shannon**. Mobile: 07974 187421. Branch Ticket Secretary: **Anthony Hatch**. Mobile: 0777 169 332. **Mrs Joan Collins**, 37 Birley Street, Newton-le-Willows. Honorary President: Sir Alex Ferguson. Meetings are held on the first Thursday of every month at the Kirkfield Hotel, High Street, Newton-le-Willows. There is selected home and away match travel.
**NORTH DEVON** Branch Secretary: **Dave Rogan**, Leys Cottage, Hilltop, Fremington, Nr Barnstaple, EX31 3BL. Tel/Fax: 01271 328280; Mobile: 07967 682167; Email: daveroganuk@yahoo.co.uk.
Departure points: Please contact the Branch Secretary.
**NORTH EAST** Branch Secretary: **John Burgess**, 10 Streatlam Close, Stainton, Barnard Castle, Co Durham, DL12 8RQ. Tel: 01833 695200.
Departure points: Newcastle Central Station, 8.30am (1.00pm); A19/A690 roundabout, 8.50am (1.20pm); Peterlee, A19-B1320 slip road, southbound, 9.00am (1.30pm); Hartlepool Baths, 9.15am (1.45pm); Hartlepool, Owton Lodge, 9.20am (1.50pm); Hartlepool, Sappers Corner, 9.25am (1.55pm); Billingham, The Swan Pub, 9.30am (2.00pm); Darlington, Feethams on dual carriageway, 10.00am (2.30pm); Scotch Corner, 10.10am (2.40pm); Leeming Bar Services, A1, 10.20am (2.50pm).
**NORTH MANCHESTER** Branch Secretary: **Graham May**. Tel: 07931 505488. Coaches to all home and away games from the Sun Inn. For all home coach details contact Branch Treasurer **Garry Chapman**, tel: 07748 970225.
**NORTH POWYS** Branch Secretary: **Glyn T Davies**, 7 Tan-y-Mur, Montgomery, Powys, SY15 6PR. Tel: 01686 668841 (24hr answerphone) For all enquiries about tickets, matches and coach travel, please contact the Branch Secretary. Branch meetings are held every eight weeks; for all membership enquires, please contact the Branch Secretary.
Coaches depart as follows: Saturdays - early kick-offs, 8.30am/3.00pm kick-offs, 10.30am; evening games, 4.00pm. Coaches leave Back Lane Coach Park, Newtown, calling in at Abermule (Waterloo Hotel), Welshpool (Spar Car Park) Four Crosses and Mile End Service Station. If Secretary is unavailable, please contact **Mr Raymond Davies**, tel: 01547 528318.
**NORTH STAFFORDSHIRE** Branch Secretary: **Peter Hall**, Cheddleton Heath House, Cheddleton Heath Road, Leek ST13 7DX. Tel: 01538 360364. Departure points: Leek Bus Station, 12.30pm (5.15pm). Times in brackets refer to evening fixtures.
**NORTH YORKSHIRE** Branch Secretary: **Andy Kirk**, 80 Trafalgar Road, Scarborough, YO12 7QR. Tel/Fax: 01723 372876; Mobile: 07766 338164; Email: andykirk25@yahoo.co.uk.
Departure points: Executive coaches to all home games from Whitby, Scarborough, Malton and York; booking in advance is required. Please phone the Branch Secretary for further details.
**NOTTINGHAM** Branch Secretary: **Lindsay Roe**, 3 Victoria Street, Ilkeston, Derbyshire, DE7 8JQ. Tel/Fax: 0115 9301788; Mobile: 07900 128306; Email: lindsayroe@tiscali.co.uk.
Departure points: Nottingham, Derby Road, 9.30am (3.00pm); Ilkeston, Notts Road, 9.45am (3.15pm); Eastwood, Safeway, 10.00am (3.30pm); Junction 28, M1, 10.15am (3.45pm). Times in brackets refer to evening fixtures.
**OLDHAM** Branch Secretary: **Dave Cone**, 20 Gilderdale Close, Shaw, Oldham, Lancashire, OL2 7UN. Tel: 01706 665588; Mobile: 07760 203258; Email; cosman@ntlworld.com. Branch Chairman: **Martyn Lucas**, 5 Rose Close, Clayton-Le-Woods, Leyland, PR25 5TQ. Tel: 01772 459521; Mobile: 07711 353857; Email: martyn711@aol.com. Travel: **Les Watson**. Mobile: 07940 081891. Website: www.oldhamreds.org.uk. Meetings are held at The Horton Arms, 1 Ward Street, off Middleton Road, Chadderton, Oldham.
Departure points: Horton Arms two hours prior to kick-off. Away travel subject to receiving tickets.
**OXFORD, BANBURY AND DISTRICT** Branch Secretary: **Mick Thorne**, "The Paddock", 111 Eynsham Road, Botley, Oxford, OX2 9BY. Tel/Fax: 01865 864924; Email: mickthorne@tinyworld.co.uk.
Departure points: McLeans Coach Yard, Witney, 6.30am for 12.00-1.00pm kick-offs, 8.00am for 3.00pm-4.00pm kick-offs, 1.30pm for evening kick-offs; Botley Road Park 'n' Ride, Oxford, 7.00am for 12.00-1.00pm kick-offs, 8.30am for 3.00pm-4.00pm kick-offs, 2.00pm for evening kick-offs; Plough Inn, Bicester, 7.15am for 12.00-1.00pm kick-offs, 8.45am for 3.00pm-4.00pm kick-offs, 2.15pm for evening kick-offs; Bus Station, Banbury, 7.30am for 12.00-1.00pm kick-offs, 9.00am for 3.00pm-4.00pm kick-offs, 2.30pm for evening kick-offs. Coach fares for all home games - adults £15.00, Junior & OAPs £10.00. All coach seats must be booked in advance. Coaches are non-smoking & no alcohol is allowed on the coaches. Away match coaches are subject to demand. European away trips are subject to match tickets; itineraries available after the draw. Please send sae or email for full details.
**PETERBOROUGH AND DISTRICT** Branch Secretary: **Andrew Dobney**, MUSC Peterborough, PO Box 1127, Spalding, Lincs, PE11 9AA. Tel: 07821 396131 (7.30pm-9.00pm only).
Departure points: Spalding Bus Station, 8.30am (1.15pm); Peterborough, Key Theatre, 9.15am (2.00pm); Grantham, Foston Services, 10.00am (2.45pm). Times in brackets refer to evening fixtures.
**PLYMOUTH** Branch Secretary: **Dave Price**, 34 Princess Avenue, Plymstock, Plymouth, PL9 9EP. Tel: 01752 482049; Email: D.J.Price@plymouth.ac.uk. Departure points: Tamar Bridge, 6.30am (4.00am); Plymouth city centre, Exeter Street, 6.45am (4.15am); Plympton 7.00am (4.30am); Ivybridge 7.10am (4.40am); Exeter Services 7.45am (5.15am). Times are for 3:00pm kick-offs; times in brackets refer to midday kick-offs. Midweek games depart Tamar Bridge at 10.30 and the other pick-up points at the time intervals shown above. There is a regular coach service to most home games. Non-Branch members are welcome to travel with us.
**PONTYPRIDD** Branch Secretary: **Lawrence Badman**, 11 Laura Street, Treforest, Pontypridd, Mid Glamorgan, South Wales, CF37 1NW. Tel: 01443 406894; Mobile: 07966 144282; Email: lawrence@pmusc.fsnet.co.uk. Phone

calls 5.00pm-7.00pm only; answerphone at other times. Branch Away Travel Secretary: **Gareth Williams**. Mobile: 07879 036206. Branch Chairman: **Steve Pember**. Tel: 01291 431720; Mobile: 07989 441683; Email: spember@tiscali.co.uk.
Departure points: Treorchy; Porth; Pontypridd; Caerphilly; Newport.
**REDDITCH** Branch Secretary: **Mark Richardson**, 90 Alcester Road, Hollywood, Worcestershire, B47 5NS. Tel/Fax: 0121 246 0237.
Departure points: Redditch; Bromsgrove.
**ROSSENDALE** Branch Secretary: **Ian Boswell**, 44 Cutler Lane, Stacksteads, Bacup, Lancs, OL13 0HW. Tel: 01706 874764; Mobile: 07802 502356 (all enquiries). Meetings are at The Royal Hotel, Waterfoot - see local press or email ROYALREDS@theroyal-hotel.co.uk.
Coach travel arrangements: contact Paul Stannard, tel: 01706 214493, fax: 01706 215371 or email Paul@theroyal-hotel.co.uk.
**RUGBY AND NUNEATON** Branch Secretary: **Greg Pugh**, 67 Fisher Avenue, Rugby, Warwickshire, CV22 5HW. Tel: 01788 567900. Phone calls 7.30pm-8.30pm. Branch Chairman: **Mick Moore**, 143 Marston Lane, Attleborough, Nuneaton, Warwickshire. Tel: 01203 343 868. Phone calls 6.00pm-7.30pm.
Departure points: Ashlawn School, Rugby, 8.45am; St Thomas Cross Inn, 9.00am; McDonald's, Junction 2, M6, 9.15am; Coton Road, Nuneaton 9.30am; Corley Services, M6, 9.45am. Please ring for midweek and other start times.
**RUNCORN AND WIDNES** Branch Secretary: **Elizabeth Scott**, 39 Park Road, Runcorn, Cheshire, WA7 4SS. Tel: 01928 591168.
**SCUNTHORPE** Branch Secretary: **Pat Davies**. Tel: 01724 851359. Branch Chairman: **Guy Davies**. Tel: 01724 851359. Transport: Tel: 01724 851359.
**SHEFFIELD AND ROTHERHAM** Branch Secretary: **Terry Watson**, 103 West Hill, Kimberworth, Rotherham, S61 2EX. Tel: 01709 557589. Coach travel available to all home games.
Departure points: midweek games - Conisboro, Star Inn, 4.00pm; Rotherham, Nellie Denes, 4.15pm; Meadowhall Coach Park, 4.30pm. For weekend games, departure times - from Conisboro, Star Inn/Rotherham, Nellie Denes/Sheffield, Midland Station - depend on Sky television; phone the Branch Secretary for confirmation of departure times for weekend games.
**SHOEBURYNESS, SOUTHEND AND DISTRICT** Branch Secretary: **Bob Lambert**, 23 Royal Oak Drive, Wickford, Essex, SS11 8NT. Tel: 01268 560168. Branch Chairmain: **Gary Black**. Tel: 01702 219072.
Departure points: Shoeburyness, Cambridge Hotel, 7.00am; Bell Public House, A127, 7.15am; Rayleigh Weir, 7.20am; McDonald's, A127, 7.30am; Fortune of War Public House, A127, 7.40am; Brentwood High Street, 8.00am; Little Chef, Brentwood bypass, 8.05am. Additional pick-ups by arrangement with the Branch Secretary. All coach seats should be booked in advance. Ring for details of midweek fixtures.
**SHREWSBURY** Branch Secretary: **Martyn Hunt**, 50 Whitehart, Reabrook, Shrewsbury, SY3 7TE. Tel: 01743 350397.
Departure points: Reabrook Island; Abbey Church; Monkmoor Inn; Heathgates Island; Harlescott Inn. For 3.00pm & 4.00pm kick-offs, depart Reabrook at 10.30am; for 7.30pm & 8.00pm kick-offs, depart Reabrook at 3.00pm.
**SOUTH ELMSALL AND DISTRICT** Branch Secretary: **Bill Fieldsend**, 72 Cambridge St, Moorthorpe, South Elmsall, Pontefract, West Yorkshire, WF9 2AR. Tel: 01977 648358; Mobile: 07818 245954. Branch Treasurer: **Mark Bossons**. Tel: 01977 650316. Meetings are on the first Tuesday of every month at The Old Scout Hall, End of Beech Street, South Elmsall.
Departure points: Cudworth Library, 11.30am (4.30pm); Bus Station, 11.45am (4.45pm); Mill Lane, 11.50am (4.50pm); Pretoria WMC, 12.00 (5.00pm). Times in brackets refer to evening fixtures.
**SOUTHPORT** Branch Secretary: **Mr B Budworth**, 51 Dawlish Drive, Marshside, Southport, PR9 9RB. Tel: 01704 211361. Branch Chairman: **Mr J Mason**, 57 Claremont Road, Birkdale, Southport. Tel: 01704 565466; Branch Treasurer: **Mr JA Johnson**, 129 Hart St, Southport, PR8 6DY. Tel: 01704 530814; Email: joseph.johnson1@btinternet.com; Branch Membership Secretary: **Mr David Cormack**, 24 Fleetwood Road, Churchtown, Southport. Tel: 01704 510330; Branch Transport Secretary: **Mr N Rimmer**, 41 Everton Road, Birkdale, Southport PR8 4BT. Tel: 01704 563239.
**STALYBRIDGE** Branch Secretary: **Walt Petrenko**. Mobile: 07980 698964. Branch Chairman: **S Hepburn**. Tel: 0161 344 2328. Branch Treasurer: **R A Wild**. Tel: 0161 338 7277. Branch Membership Secretary: **A Baxter**. Tel: 07885 809777. Away Travel: **Nigel Barrett**. Mobile: 07802 799482. Home Travel: **B Williamson**. Tel: 0161 338 6832.
Departure point: Pineapple, Stalybridge; tel: 0161 338 2542. Home coach leaves between one and one-and-a-half hours before kick-off. Away coaches are arranged when applicable per game - coaches run to most games depending on ticket allocation.
**STOKE-ON-TRENT** Branch Secretary: **Geoff Boughey**, 63 Shrewsbury Drive, Newcastle, Staffordshire, ST5 7RQ. Tel/Fax: 01782 561680 (home); Mobile: 07768 561680; Email: geoff.boughey@btinternet.com. Branch meetings are held every Monday night. Contact the Branch Secretary for details.
Departure points: Hanley Bus Station, 12.00noon (5.00pm); School Street, Newcastle, 12.10pm (5.10pm); Little Chef, A34, 12.15pm (5.15pm); The Millstone Pub, Butt Lane, 12.30pm (5.30pm). Times in brackets refer to evening fixtures.
**STOURBRIDGE AND KIDDERMINSTER** Branch Secretary, **Robert Banks**, 7 Croftwood Road, Wollescote, Stourbridge, West Midlands, DY9 7EU. Tel: 01384 826636.
Departure points: Please contact the Branch Secretary for departure points and times.
**SURREY** Branch Membership Secretary: **Mrs Maureen Asker**, 80 Cheam Road, Ewell, Surrey, KT17 1QF. Tel: 0208 393 4763. Home League Games Co-ordinator: **John Ramsden**, 22 Pound Lane, Godalming, Surrey. Tel: 01483 420909; Mobile: 07841 634540.
**SWANSEA** Branch Secretary: **Dave Squibb**, 156 Cecil Street, Mansleton, Swansea, SA5 8QJ. Tel: 01792 641981 (between 4.00pm-8.00pm); Email: davesquibb@ntlworld.com.
Departure points: Swansea (via Heads of Valleys Road); Neath; Hirwaun; Merthyr; Tredegar; Ebbw Vale; Brynmawr; Abergavenny; Monmouth.
**SWINDON** Branch Secretary: **Martin Rendle**, 19 Cornfield Road, Devizes, Wiltshire, SN10 3BA. Tel: 01380 728358 (between 8.00pm-10.00pm, Monday to Friday).
Departure points: Kingsdown Inn; Stratton St Margaret; Swindon.
**SWINTON** Branch Secretary: **Hugh Rotherham**, 61 Worsley Road, Clifton, Swinton, M27 5SP. Mobile: 07957 716982; Email: ue.rotherham@ntlworld.com. Meetings take place on the last Thursday of each month at the Royal British Legion, Bolton Road, Pendlebury, Salford, at 8pm.
**TELFORD** Branch Secretary: **Sal Laher**, 4 Hollyoak Grove, Lakeside, Priorslee, Telford, TF2 9GE. Tel: 01952 299224; Email: sal.laher@btinternet.com.
Departure points: Saturday (3.00pm kick-offs) - Cuckoo Oak, Madeley, 10.30am; Heath Hill, Dawley, 10.40am; Bucks Head, Wellington, 10.50am; Oakengates, 11.00am; Bridge, Donnington, 11.10am; Newport, 11.20am. Midweek departures (for 8.00pm kick-offs) start at 4.30pm, and depart from each of the subsequent locations at 10-minute intervals, as above. Contact the Branch Secretary for membership and further details.
**TORBAY** Branch Secretary: **Vernon Savage**, 5 Courtland Road, Shiphay, Torquay, Devon, TQ2 6JU. Tel: 01803 616139 (answerphone); Mobile: 07765 394238.
Departure points: Upper Cockington Lane, Torquay; Newton Abbot Railway Station; The Avenue, Newton Abbot; Willcocks Garage, Kingsteignton; Countess Wear Roundabout, Exeter; Junction 25, M5, Taunton. All departure times will be confirmed by the Branch Secretary dependant on the match kick-off time; additional departure points en route can be arranged via the Branch Secretary. The branch runs a coach to all weekend Premiership & Cup games at Old Trafford, plus selected midweek European fixtures. The branch does not organise coach travel to away fixtures. The branch produces four editions of its newsletter every season, which culminates in the AGM at The Jolly Abbot, East Street, Newton Abbot. Full details from the Branch Secretary to whom all enquiries should be directed. All branch members must be registered with Old Trafford.
**UTTOXETER AND DISTRICT** Branch Secretary: **Mrs TA Bloor**, 63 Carter Street, Uttoxeter, Staffordshire, ST14 8EY. Branch Chairman: **Mr P Adams**. Branch Treasurer: **Mr A Whitworth**. Tel: 01885 566481.
Travel to matches: leaving White Hart Hotel, Carter Street, Uttoxeter, at 11.30am on Saturdays, 4.30pm for night games.
**WALSALL** Branch Secretary: **Graham Sleigh**, 36 Sharon Way, Hednesford, Cannock, Staffs, WS12 2NF. Tel: 01543 871631.
Departure points: Junction 9, M6, 10.50am (3.50pm); Bell Pub, Bloxwich, 11.15am (4.15pm); Roman Way Hotel, A5, Cannock, 11.30am (4.30pm); Shire Horse Pub, Stafford, 11.50am (4.50pm). Times in brackets refer to evening fixtures.
**WARRINGTON** Branch Secretary: **Su Buckley**, 4 Vaudrey Drive, Woolston, Warrington, Cheshire, WA1 4HG. Tel: 01925 816966.
Departure points: Blackburn Arms two hours before kick-off, then Last Orders, Chevvies and Rope 'n' Anchor.
**WELLINGBOROUGH** Branch Secretary: **Phil Walpole**, 7 Cowgill Close, Cherry Lodge, Northampton NN3 8PB. Tel/Fax: 01604 787612; Email: cockneyred@btinternet.com.
Departure points: Shoe Factory, Irchester Road, Rushden, 8.30am (1.30pm); Doc Martins Shoe Factory, Irchester, 8.35am (1.35pm); The Cuckoo Public House, Woolaston, 8.45am (1.45pm); Police Station, Wellingborough, 8.55am (1.55pm); Trumpet Public House, Northampton, 9.10am (2.10pm); Abington Park bus stop, Northampton, 9.15 am (2.15pm); Campbell Square, Northampton, 9.20am (2.20pm); Mill Lane layby (opposite Cock Hotel Public House), Kingsthorpe, 9.25am (2.25pm); top of Bants Lane (opposite Timken), Dugton, 9.30am (2.30pm). Times in brackets refer to evening fixtures.
**WEST CUMBRIA** Branch Secretary: **Anthony Penn**, 38 Thorncroft Gardens, Workington, Cumbria, CA14 4DP. Tel: 01900 66499; Mobile: 07742 530970.
Departure points: Coach 1 departs - Egremont, 9.45am (3.15pm); Cleator Moor, 10am (3.30pm); Whitehaven, 10.15am (3.45pm); Cockermouth, 10.35am (4.05pm). Coach 2 departs: Distington, 9.40am (2.40pm); Harrington, 9.45am (2.45pm); Moss Bay, 9.50am (2.50pm); Workington, 10am (3.00pm); Flimby, 10.10am (3.10pm); Netherton, 10.15am (3.15pm); Dearham, 10.20am (3.20pm). Times in brackets refer to 7.45pm or 8.00pm

kick-offs - contact the Branch Secretary for other kick-off times.
**WEST DEVON** Branch Secretary: **Mrs R M Bolt**, 16 Moorview, North Tawton, Devon, EX20 2HW. Tel: 01837 82682 (all enquiries).
Departure points: North Tawton; Crediton; Exeter.
**WESTMORLAND** Branch Secretary: **Dennis Alderson**, 71 Calder Drive, Kendal, Cumbria, LA9 6LR. Tel: 01539 728248; Mobile: 07973 965373.
Departure points: Ambleside; Windermere; Staveley, Kendal and Forton Services. For departure times and further details, please contact the Branch Secretary.
**WORKSOP** Branch Secretary: **Mick Askew**, 20 Park Street, Worksop, Nottinghamshire. Tel: 01909 486194; Mobile 07976 894 890.
**WYTHENSHAWE** Branch Secretary: **Stuart Murphy**, 8 Comrie Walk, Wythenshawe, M23 2QF. Mobile: 07946 004045; Fax: 0161 998 3003; Email: wythenshawereds@yahoo.co.uk. Contact the Branch Secretary for more information.
**YEOVIL** Branch Secretary: **Richard Cox**, Hozen Cottage, 59 Water Street, Martock, Somerset, TA12 6JP. Mobile: 07930 505349; Email: richard.chapmancox@btinternet.com.
Departure points: Yeovil; Taunton. Please contact the Branch Secretary for departure times. Transport is available to non-branch members.

## NORTHERN IRELAND & THE REPUBLIC OF IRELAND

**ABBEYFEALE AND DISTRICT** Branch Secretary: **Denis O'Sullivan**. Tel: 068 32525 or 086 8157146. Branch Chairman: **Denis Daly**. Tel: 068 31712 or 087 9880015. Branch Vice-Chairman: **Gerard Foley**. Tel: 068 32979 or 087 4125748. Branch Treasurer: **Paddy Finucane**. Tel: 068 32036. Youth Officer: **Richard O'Mahony**. Tel: 068 32305 or 087 2055031. Public Relations Officer: **Tomas Mann**. Tel: 068 31025 or 087 9130180. Regular meetings are held at Donal and Ann's Bar, Abbeyfeale - contact the Branch Secretary for more details.
**ANTRIM TOWN** Branch Secretary: **Brendan O'Neill**, 86 Ballycraigy Road, Glengormley, Co Antrim, BT36 4SX. Tel: 028 90 842929. Branch Chairman: **William Cameron**, 92 Donegore Drive, Parkhall, Antrim, N Ireland. Tel: 02894 461634. Club meetings are held every other Thursday in the 'Top of the Town Bar', Antrim. All members must be registered with Manchester United's official membership scheme.
**ARKLOW AND SOUTH LEINSTER** Branch Secretary: **James Cullen**, 52 South Green, Arklow, Co Wicklow, Eire. Tel: 086 2327859 or 0402 39816; Email: cullenmichelle@hotmail.com.
All trips are arranged via local committee members with pick-ups from Waterford to Dublin. If anyone is interested in joining, please contact the Branch Secretary.
**BALLYCASTLE** Branch Chairman: **Donald McAuley**. Branch Vice-Chairman: **Aiden McCarry**. Branch Secretary/Treasurer: **Patricia McKendry**, 20 Carnduff Park, Ballycastle, Co Antrim, N Ireland, BT54 6LN. Tel: 028 207 69269.
**BALLYMENA** Branch Chairman: **Martin Etherson**, Greenview, 91 Rankinstown Road, Ballymena BT42 3HR. Tel: 07710 663 250; Email unitedexecutive@btconect.com. Branch Secretary: Ronan McLaughlin, 94 Galgorm Road, Ballymena, BT42 1AA. Tel: 07703 360447. Monthly meetings are held at Ballymena Showground's Social Club on the first Monday of each month.
**BALLYMONEY** Branch Secretary: **Malachy McAleese**, 8 Riverview Park, Ballymoney, Co Antrim, Northern Ireland, BT53 7QS. Tel: 028 276 67623. Branch Chairman: **Gerry McAleese**, 11 Greenville Avenue, Ballymoney, Co Antrim, Northern Ireland. Tel: 028 276 65446. Meetings are held on the last Thursday of every month at Ballymoney United Social Club, 35 Castle Street, Ballymoney; new members always welcome. Tel: 028 276 66054; Email: info@musc-ballymoney.co.uk; Website: www.musc-ballymoney.co.uk.
Departure points: Ballymoney United Social Club, Grove Road, Ballymena; Belfast Harbour; Belfast International Airport;
**BANBRIDGE** Branch Secretary: **James Loney**, 83 McGreavy Park, Derrymacash, Lurgan, Northern Ireland, BT66 6LR. Tel: 028 38 345058; Mobile: 07901 833076; Email: james@mcgreavy4027freeserve.co.uk.
Branch Chairman: **Kevin Nelson**, 10 Ballynamoney Park, Derrymacash, Lurgan, N Ireland. Mobile: 07743 191418.
Departure points: Corner House, Derrymacash; Lurgan Town Centre; Newry Road, Banbridge.
**BANGOR** Branch Secretary: **Ray McElrath**, 3 Brooklands Manor, Bangor, Co Down, BT20 5LJ. Email: ray@mcelrath.fsnet.co.uk.
Branch meetings are held every other Monday, at 8.00pm, at the Imperial Bar, Central Avenue, Bangor.
**BELFAST REDS** Branch Secretary: **John Bond**, 53 Hillhead Crescent, Belfast, Northern Ireland, BT11 9FS. Tel: 028 90 627861.
**BRAY** Branch Secretary: **Ravi Antour**, c/o Lower Dargle Road, Bray. Tel: 028 60477. Branch Chairman: **Noel Ryder**, 3 Avondale Court, Kerry Road, Bray, Co Wicklow. Tel: 205 0578.
**BUNDORAN** Branch Secretary: **Rory O'Donnell**, Doonan Court, Donegal Town, Co Donegal. Tel: 073 23629; Mobile: 087 245 6994.
Departure points: Rory's Autospares, Donegal Town and The Chasing Bull, Bundoran. All bookings to be made through the Branch Secretary only. Bookings should be made early to avoid disappointment. New members always welcome.
**CARLINGFORD LOUTH** Branch Secretary: **Harry Harold**, Mountain Park, Carlingford, Co Louth, Ireland. Tel: 00 353 42 9373379.
**CARLOW** Branch Secretary: **Simon Racklett**. Tel: 00 353 87673 4545; Email: manutdsccarlow@eircom.net. Branch Chairman: **Seamie Payne**. Branch Treasurer: **Sean Lawlor**. Regular meetings are held at McHughs Hotel, Dublin St, Carlow. Contact the Branch Secretary for more details.
**CARRICKFERGUS** Branch Secretary: **Gary Callaghan**, 3 Red Fort Park, Carrickfergus, Co Antrim, Northern Ireland, BT38 9EW. Tel: 028 93 355362; Fax: 028 93 360422; Email: gary@carrickmusc.co.uk; Website: carrickmusc.co.uk. Branch Chairman: **Billy Manderson**. Tel: 028 9336 5920. Branch Vice-Chairman: **Alan Jackson**. Tel: 028 9336 7019. The branch holds its meetings fortnightly on a Monday evening at 8.00pm in the Quality Hotel, Carrickfergus. New members are welcome, especially family and juniors. The branch presently has a membership of 165 and organises trips to Old Trafford for all home games. It also travels to away matches including European ties whenever possible.
**CARRYDUFF** Branch Secretary: **John White**, 'Stretford End', 4 Baronscourt Glen, Carryduff, Co Down, Northern Ireland, BT8 8RF. Tel: 028 90 812377; Email: jw@carryduffmusc.com. Branch Chairman: **John Dempsey**, 16 Baronscourt Glen, Carryduff, BT8 8RF. Tel/Fax: 028 90 814823 (7.00pm-9.00pm urgent business only); Email: jd@carryduffmusc.com.
Branch Treasurer: **Damien Friel**. Tel: 07802 929361; Email: bigdee@carryduffmusc.com; Website: www.carryduffmusc.com. Branch meetings are held every week. New members, particularly juniors, are always welcome as the branch has a strong family and cross community ethos. *All* members must be registered with Manchester United's official membership scheme.
Departure points: the branch organises coach trips to Old Trafford for every home game from The Royal Ascot, Carryduff and The Grand Opera House, Belfast. No alcohol and no other club colours are permitted on the coach.
**CASTLEDAWSON** Branch Secretary: **Niall Wright**, 22 Park View, Castledawson, Co Londonderry, Northern Ireland. Tel: 028 79 468779.
**CASTLEPOLLARD** Branch Secretary: **Anne Foley**, Coole, Mullingar, Co Westmeath, Ireland. Tel/Fax: 00 353 44 61613; Email: muscpollard@hotmail.com. Branch meetings are held on the third Monday of every month; there is notification of additional meetings by 'newsletter'.
Departure points: The Square, Castlepollard; additional pick-up points by arrangement with the Branch Secretary.
**CASTLEWELLAN** Branch Secretary: **John Hydns**, 7 Bay Rock Ave, Ardglass, Co Down, BT30 7TN. Tel: 028 44 842411. Branch Chairperson: **Mr Peter O'Shea**, 17 Phennick Way, Ardglass, Co Down, BT30 7UX. Tel: 028 44 842418. Branch Treasurer: **Gareth Henvey**, 11 Phennick Way, Adglass, Co Down, BT30 7UX. Tel: 028 44 841297.
**CAVEHILL** Branch Secretary: **Dennis Corry**. Tel: 02890 803333; Mobile: 07802 188592; Email: dennis.corry@ntlworld.com. Branch Treasurers: Ronald Black & Stanley Black. Club Website: www.cavehillmusc.org. Meetings are at Ligoniel pigeon club at 1pm every other Sunday; new members are welcome.

**CITY OF DERRY** Branch Secretary: **Mark Thompson**, 210 Hillcrest, Kilfennan, Londonderry, BT47 6GF. Tel: 028 71 34 6537; Mobile: 07841 373795; Email: secretary@cityofderrymusc.com; Website: www.cityofderrymusc.com. Meetings are held on the first Tuesday of every month at the Gallery Bar, Dungiven Road, Londonderry, at 8.30pm.
**CLARA** Branch Secretary: **Michael Kenny**, River Street, Clara, Co Offaly, Ireland.
**CLONMEL** Branch Secretary: **Anthony O'Sullivan**, No. 41 Honeyview Estate, Clonmel, Co Tipperary, Ireland. Tel: 052 26596 (home); Mobile: 086 837 9836. Branch Treasurer: **Hughie O'Meara**. Tel: 086 3120422. Branch Chairperson: **John Conran**. Tel: 086 2535620. Club Branch Mobile: 086 0553469. There are regular meetings at Gleeson's Bar, Clonmel. For further information contact the Branch Secretary.
**COLERAINE** Branch Secretary: **Maud Doherty**, 12 Blackthorn Court, Coleraine, Co Derry, Northern Ireland. Tel: 028 703 54773.
**COMBER** Branch Secretary: **Derek Hume**, 14 Carnesure Hts, Comber, Co Down. Tel: 028 91 872608. Branch Chairman: **Stephen Irvine**. Branch Email: Comberbranch@onetel.net.uk. Branch meetings are held on various Tuesdays; details of these meetings are printed in *The Newtownards Chronicle* newspaper and are also available to view on the website: www.propertysnaps.co.uk/CD.
**COOKSTOWN** Branch Secretary: **Geoffrey Wilson**, 10 Cookstown Road, Moneymore, Co Londonderry, Northern Ireland, BT45 7QF. Tel: 028 86748625; Mobile: 07855 760981; Email: gwilson@telco4u.net. Meetings are on the first Monday of every month at the Royal Hotel, Cookstown, 9.00pm sharp. New members are welcome, however all members must be registered with Manchester United's official membership scheme.
**CORK AREA** Branch Chairman: **Martin O'Neill**, Across the Tracks, The Highlands, Glounthaune, Co Cork. Tel: 087 2645066. Branch Treasurer: **Brendan Murphy**, Muskerry Est, Ballincollig, Co Cork.
**COUNTY CAVAN** Chairman: **Owen Farrelly**. Tel: 046 42184. Secretary: **Gerry Heery**. Tel: 087 6181295. Assistant Secretary: **Jimmy Murray**. Tel: 086 8289504. Branch Email: co.cavanbranch@eircom.net; Website: www.cocavanbranch.homestead.com. Meetings are held on the third Monday of each month in Tyrrells, Main St, Mullagh, Co Cavan.
**COUNTY LONGFORD** Branch Secretary: **Seamus Gill**, 17 Springlawn, Longford, Republic of Ireland. Tel: 00353 86 8341918; Fax: 00353 43 47848; Email: seamusgill2002@eircom.net. Branch Chairman: **Harry Ryan**, 58 Teffia Park, Longford, Co Longford. Branch Treasurer: **Nicola King**, 18 Harbour Row, Longford, Co Longford.
**COUNTY MONAGHAN** Branch Chairman: **Peter O'Reilly**. Branch Secretary: **Seamus Gallagher**. Tel: 047 83265/81577 (home) or 0868 307689; Email: seamusgallagh16@hotmail.com. Assistant Branch Secretary: **John Hughes**. Branch Treasurers: **Ann Devine** & **Jane Flynn**. Meetings are held fortnightly on Thursdays throughout the season at Poc Fada , North Road, Monaghan Town.
**COUNTY ROSCOMMON** Branch Chairman: **Noel Scally**, Cashel, Boyle, Co Roscommon, Ireland. Tel: 00353 872228466; Email: mandnscally@eircom.net. Branch Secretary: **Mr Padraig McCrann**. Email: padraigmccrann@eircom.net. Branch President: **George Tiernan**. Branch Treasurer: **Mr Francis Dwyer**. Tel: 00353 8723 77203.
**COUNTY TIPPERARY** Branch Secretary: **Mrs Kathleen Hogan**, 45 Canon Hayes Park, Tipperary, Republic of Ireland. Tel: 062 51042.
**COUNTY WATERFORD** Branch Secretary: **Kevin Moore**. Tel: 086 3925677. Branch Chairman: **Pat Grant Snr**. Tel: 087 6234573. Branch Treasurer: **Teresa Fraher**. Tel: 058 44576. Branch President: **John O'Shea**. Branch meetings are held in Lawlors Hotel, Dungarvan. Manchester United match members meet in John Keane's Pub, Mary Street, Dungarvan, Co Waterford. New members are always welcome - contact any of the above numbers or email moorek70@yahoo.co.uk.
**CRAIGAVON** Branch Secretary: **Eamon Atkinson**, 8 Rowan Park, Tullygally Road, Craigavon, Co Armagh, Northern Ireland, BT65 5AY. Tel: 028 38 343870. Branch Chairperson: **Conor McCorry**. Branch Treasurer: **Susan Atkinson**, 8 Rowan Park, Craigavon BT65 5AY. Tel: 028 38 343870. Assistant Branch Secretary: **Karen McConville**. Meetings are held on the first Tuesday of each month at the Goodyear Sports & Social Club, Silverwood, Craigavon. Departure points: Lurgan; Craigavon; Portadown; Tandragee; Dundalk; Dublin Port.
**DONEGAL** Branch Chairman: **Willie Diver**. Tel: 00353 8727 599192. Branch Secretary: **Liam Friel**, Kiltoal, Convoy, Co Donegal, Ireland. Mobile: 00 353 87 6736967. Branch Treasurer: **Paddy Delap**. Tel: 00 353 74 912 2240. Branch Travel Organiser: **Tony Murray**. Tel: 00 353 72 912 4111. Branch Public Relations Officer: **Donna Friel**. Tel: 00353 749125220. Club meetings are held in Dry Arch Inn, Port Road, Letterkenny, Donegal.
**DOWNPATRICK** Branch Secretary: **Terry Holland**, 137 Ballyhornan Road, Downpatrick, Co Down, Northern Ireland. Tel/Fax: 028 44 842550; Mobile: 07712 622242; Website: www.dpmusc.co.uk. Branch meetings are held fortnightly on Monday evenings at 8.00pm at 'Hogans Bar', Market Street, Downpatrick.
**DUNDALK** Branch Chairman: **Michael McCourt**. Branch Secretary: **Catherine Kieran**. Branch Treasurer: **Ailish Kelly**. Ticket & Travel: **Dickie O'Hanrahan**. Tel: 00353 86 1658385. Committee Members: **D Kelly**, **G Dullaghan**, **S Kelly**.
**DUNGANNON** Branch Secretary: **Ian Hall**, 'Silveridge', 229 Killyman Road, Dungannon, Co Tyrone, Northern Ireland, BT71 6RS. Tel/Fax: 028 87 723085 (home), 028 87 752255 (work); Mobile: 07787 124765. Email: burroweshall@clara.co.uk. Meetings are held every two weeks (all year) at Cobbles Bar, Church Street, Dungannon. For details on membership meetings, trips etc, contact the Branch Secretary or Keith Houston, tel: 028 87 722735 (mobile: 07813 208925) or Sean Campbell, tel: 07810 416080.
**EAST BELFAST** Branch Secretary: **Girvin Miskimmin**, 39 The Brambles, Lisburn, Northern Ireland, BT28 2XY. Tel: 028 92 604527; Email: g.miskimmin@bt282xy.fsnet.co.uk; Website: www.ebmufc.co.uk.
Meetings are held at The Ulster Maple Leaf Club on match nights and/or fortnightly. All members must be registered with the Manchester United Official Membership Scheme and must participate in Manchester United Development Association's Super Pools Scheme.
**ENNIS** Branch Secretary: **Seamus Hughes**, 'Old Trafford', Quin, Ennis, Co Clare, Republic of Ireland. Tel: 065 68 20282; Mobile: 086 239 3975. Branch Chairman: **Eamon Murphy**, Knockboy, Ballynacally, Co Clare, Ireland. Tel: 065 68 28105.
**FERMANAGH** Branch Secretary: **Gabriel Maguire**, 80 Glenwood Gardens, Enniskillen, BT74 5LU. Tel: 028 66 325 950; Mobile: 07788 421739. Branch Chairman: **Eric Brown**, 166 Main Street, Lisnaskea. Branch Treasurer: **Mr D Humes**, 28 Main Street, Rosscolban, BT93 1TF. Meetings are held in Charlie's Lounge, Enniskillen.
**FIRST BALLYCLARE** Branch Secretary: **Alan Munce**, 7 Merion Park, Ballyclare, Co Antrim, Northern Ireland, BT39 9XD. Tel: 028 93 324126; Mobile: 07970 459529; Email: munceasj@supanet.com. Meetings held at Five Corners Guest Inn, Ballyclare, on the first Monday of the month, at 7.30pm.
**FIRST NORTH DOWN (BANGOR)** Branch Secretary: **Robert Quee**, "Stretford End", 67 Springhill Road, Bangor West, Co Down, BT20 3PD. Tel: 028 91 453094; Mobile: 07790 761828; Email: Robert_quee@hotmail.com. Branch Chairman: **Walter Geary**, 25 Beaumont Drive, Bangor, BT19 6WH. Tel: 028 91 462732; Mobile: 07803 109429. First North Down supporters meet on alternative Thursdays evenings at 8.00pm at Hamilton House, Hamilton Road, Bangor. New members are always welcome. The branch operates a "Family Package Membership"; for further details please contact the Branch Secretary or Branch Chairman.
**FOYLE** Branch Secretary: **Martin Harkin**, 2 Harvest Meadows, Dunlade Road, Greysteel, Co Derry, Northern Ireland, BT47 3BG. Tel: 07816 213522. Meetings are held at AOH club, Foyle Street, Derry, on consecutive Thursdays at 9.30 pm.
Travel arrangements are varied due to the time constraints of boat departures. The majority of trips consist of bus and ferry plus hotel accommodation, but a decision was taken for the 2005/06 season to fly to certain games.
**GALWAY** Branch Secretary: **Patsy Devlin**, 153 Baile an Choiste, Castlegar, Galway, Ireland. Mobile: 00 353 87 2530366; Fax: 00 353 91 770998; Email: devlinpatsy@hotmail.com.
Meetings are held monthly (check local press and local radio). Members attend all home games. Membership is open all year round; for details, please contact the Branch Secretary.
**GLENOWEN** Branch Secretary: **Jim Turner**, 4 Dermot Hill Drive, Belfast, Northern Ireland, BT12 7GG. Tel: 02890 242682; Mobile: 07990 848 961 (daytime); Email: musc.glenowen@ntlworld.com.
Meetings are held every week on Wednesday evening in 'Biddy Duffys Bar', Andersonstown Road, Belfast. Contact the Branch Secretary for further details.
**HILLTOWN** Branch Secretary: **Gery Durkin**, 14 Meadowlands Avenue, Warrenpoint, Co Down, Northern Ireland, BT34 3FY. Mobile: 07742 198217 159.
**IVEAGH YOUTH** Branch Secretary: **Russell Allen**, 2 Iveagh Crescent, Belfast, Northern Ireland, BT12 6AW. Tel: 028 90 329631. Assistant Branch Secretary: **Brendan McBride**, 3 Gransha Park, Belfast, BT11 8AT. Tel: 028 90 203171.
**IRELAND (DUBLIN)** Founded 1969. Branch Secretary: **Eddie Gibbons**, 19 Cherry Orchard Crescent, Ballyfermont, Dublin, 10. Tel: 01 626 9759; Fax: 01 6236388; Mobile: 087 2482950. Email: muscirlbranch@hotmail.com. Branch Membership Secretary: Michael O'Toole, 49 Briarwood Lawn, Mulmuddart, Dublin 15. Tel: 01 821 5702.
The committee meets every Monday night in The INTO, Teachers Club, 36 Parnell Square from 6.30pm-8.00pm for bookings/membership etc, except when United play live on TV, or Bank Holidays, when the branch meets on Tuesday night.
**KILKENNY** Branch Secretary: **John Joe Ryan**, Priory Lodge, John's Quay, Kilkenny. Tel: 056 65827 (daytime), 056 65136 (after 6.00pm); Fax: 056 64043. Branch Chairman: **Joe Fitzpatrick**. Assistant Branch Secretary: **Miss Elaina Ryan**. Committee members: **P J Hogan**, **Tom Kenny**, **Peter Morgan**, **Brendan Kennedy**.
**KILLALOE AND ROSCREA** Branch Secretary: **Michael Flynn**, 611 Cross Roads, Killaloe, Co Clare, Ireland. Tel: 061 376031. Branch Chairman:

**Seamus Doran**, 7 Limerick Street, Roscrea. Tel: 0505 23194.
**KILLARNEY** Branch Secretary: **John G Nagle**. Tel: 00353 876707740. Branch Chairman: **Bill Keefe**. Branch Treasurer: **Denis Spillane**. Branch Vice-Treasurer: **Frank Roberts**, St Margarets Road, Killarney. Tel: 00353 87 9451503. Meetings are held on the first Wednesday of every month, rotating between three bars - Darby O'Gills, Killarney; Dennehy's Corner, Rathmore; Murphy's, Boherbue - at which future trips are organised.
**KILLMALLOCK** Branch Secretary: **Kim O'Connell**, Fanstown, Kilmallock, Co Limerick. Tel: 00 353 63 98372 (home); Mobile: 00 353 87 2876498; Branch Chairman: **John Manning**. Tel: 00 353 87 2675516. Branch Treasurer: **Ivan Whitley**. Tel: 00 353 87 274952. Branch Public Relations Officer: **John Connell**. Tel: 00 353 87 6291309. Monthly meetings are on the second Monday of each month in Ivans Bar, Kilmallock, Co Limerick. Contact the Branch Secretary for more details.
**LAGAN** Branch Secretary: **William Thompson**, 5 Church Drive, Glengormley, Newtownabbey, BT36 6EX. Tel: 02890 587087. Mobile: 07900 957461.
**LAOIS** Branch Secretary: **Christy Dunne**, Canal Road, Portarlington, Co Laois, Ireland. Tel: 0502 23604. Mobile: 087 9171770.
**LARNE** Branch Secretary: **Brian Haveron**. Mobile: 07785 388959; Email bhaveron@fgwilson.com. Branch Chairman: **John Hylands**. Tel: 02828 277888. Branch meetings are held every Monday night at 8.00pm at St John's Masonic Club Rooms, Mill Brae, Larne. New members are welcome to this family orientated club.
**LIMAVADY** Branch Chairman: **Harry Lyness**. Tel: 077409 86937. Branch Treasurer: **Liam McNally**. Tel: 028 77764415. Meetings are held in the Thatch Bar, Limavady, on the first Monday of every month at 8.00pm.
**LIMERICK** Branch Secretary: **Dennis O'Sullivan**, 14 Rossa Avenue, Mulgrave Street, Limerick, Republic of Ireland. Tel: 061 411763; Mobile: 086 8435828.
**LISBURN** Branch Secretary: **Mark Hutton**, 46 Lyndhurst Parade, Belfast, BT13 3PB. Tel: 02890 717242; Mobile: 07732 921257; Email janet.hutton@fsmail.net.
**LISTOWEL** Branch Secretary: **Aiden O'Connor**, Gurtinard, Listowel, Co Kerry, Ireland. Tel: 00353 6821741. Assistant Branch Secretary: **David O'Brien**, Bedford, Listowel, Co Kerry, Ireland. Tel: 068 22250.
**LURGAN** Branch Secretary: **John Furphy**, 123 Drumbeg North, Craigavon, Co Armagh, N Ireland, BT65 5AE. Tel: 028 38 341842.
**MAYO** Branch Secretary: **Seamus Moran**, Belclare, Westport, Co Mayo, Ireland. Tel: 00 353 982 7533 (home), 00 353 985 5202 (away); Mobile: 00 353 872 417966; Email: moran_seamus@allergan.com. Branch Chairperson: **Liam Connell**. Email: liam.connell@whb.ie. Branch Treasurer: **T J Gannon**. Email: gannon_tommy@allergan.com. PRO: **Kieran Mongey**, Blackfort, Castlebar, Co Mayo, Ireland. Meetings take place every four weeks on Wednesdays in the Welcome Inn Hotel in Castlebar at 9.30 pm. All are welcome.
**MEATH** Branch Secretary: **Colm McManus**, 46 Beechlawn, Kells, Co Meath, Republic of Ireland. Tel: 046 49831.
Pick-up points for travel to Old Trafford: Jack's Railway Bar, Kells; Fairgreen, Naven.
**MOURNE** Branch Secretary: **Michael Peacock**, 3 Meadowlands, Kilkeel, Co Down, Northern Ireland, BT34 4YD. Tel: 028 417 63409. Branch Chairman: **Liam McCartan**, 48 Leestone Road, Kilkeel, Co Down, BT34 4NW. Tel: 028 417 64175. Branch Treasurer: **John Charleton**, 47 Mountain Road, Kilkeel, Co Down, BT34 4BB. Tel: 028 417 63724. Meetings for members are held on the first Monday of each month (August to April) at 8.00 pm in the Kilmorey Hotel, Kilkeel. New members welcome.
**MUCKAMORE ABBEY** Branch Secretary: **Alastair Bell**. Tel: 028 94 432677; Email: Alistair@bell179.freeserve.co.uk or muckamorereds@hotmail.co.uk. Branch Chairman: **Desi Lundy**. Tel: 028 94466896. Branch Treasurer: **Bert Lewis**. Tel: 078 10568996; Email bert@lewis10.fsnet.co.uk. Branch Website: www.muckamorereds.co.uk. Branch meetings are on the last Monday of every month in the recreation hall, Muckamore Hospital, at 8.30pm.
**NEWRY** Branch Secretary: **Brendan McConville**, 14 Willow Grove, Newry, Co Down, BT34 1JH. Tel: 028 3026 6996; Mobile: 07786 070254; Email: manubrendan@triscali.co.uk. Branch Chairman: **Jeffrey Clements**. Tel: 028 3026 7158. Meetings are on the first Tuesday of each month at The Cue Club, Newry. Tel: 028 3026 6066.
**NEWTOWNARDS** Branch Secretary: **Joe Tully**, 10 Stanvilla Road, Newtownards, Co Down, BT23 8HE. Mobile: 07710 090857.
**NIAS** Branch Secretary: **Eddie Murphy**, 121 Colinmill, Dunmurry, BT17 0AS. Mobile: 07887 588508; Email: emurphy@niamb.co.uk. Branch Chairman: **Terry Gorman**, 6 Sinclair Park, Bangor, BT19 1PG. Mobile: 07909 908071; Email: tgorman@niamb.co.uk.
**NORTH BELFAST** Branch Secretary: **Robert Savage**, 47 Mayfield Road, Newtownabbey, Northern Ireland, BT36 7WD. Tel: 028 90 847237. Meetings are held every month. Please contact the Branch Secretary if you require additional information.
**OMAGH** Branch Secretary: **Brendan McLaughlin**, 4 Pinefield Court, Killyclougher, Omagh, Co Tyrone, Northern Ireland, BT79 7YT. Tel: 028 82 250025; Mobile: 077 125 76708; Email: brendan.mclaughlin@btinternet.com. Branch Chairman: **Mervin King**, 92 Drumlegagh Road, South Omagh, BT78 4TW. Tel: 0288 224 1498. Branch Treasurer: **Brian Mellon**, 22 Killyclogher Road, Omagh, Co Tyrone, BT79 0AX.
**PORTADOWN** Branch Secretary: **Harold Beck**, 23 Kernan Grove, Portadown, Co Armagh, BT63 5RX. Tel: 028 3 833 6877; Mobile: 07703 360423; Email: harrybeck@mail.com. Branch Treasurer: Harold Blevins, 47 Creenagh Road, Loughgall, Co Armagh, BT61 8JL. Tel: 028 38 891103; Mobile: 07753 640714. Meetings are held on the third Monday of each month at Gary's Lounge, Bridge Street, Portadown.
Pick-up points: Loughgall; Portadown; Lurgan; Lisburn; Moira; Banbridge.
**PORTAFERRY** Branch Secretary: **Aiden Hughes**, Mermaid Bar, Kirkcubbin, Co Down, Northern Ireland. Tel: 028 427 38215. Branch Chair: **Tony Cleary**. Branch Treasurer: **Hugh Conlon**. Branch meetings are held on the first Tuesday of every month @9.00pm at McNamara's, High Street, Portaferry.
**PORTAVOGIE** Branch Secretary: **Robert McMaster**, 2 Westlea Gardens, Portavogie, Co Down, BT22 1EG. Tel: 028 427 71935.
**PORTRUSH** Chairman: **Mr Gary Ramsey**. Mobile: 07742 039451. Branch Treasurer: **Mr Peter Boreland**. Branch Secretary: **Julie Ramsey**, 29 Hopefield Park, Portrush, N Ireland, BT52 8SW.
**PORTSTEWART** Branch Secretary: **Richard McDermott**. Tel: 028 70822373 (home); Mobile: 0776 7884400; Email: r_mcdermott@btconnect.com. Club meetings are held on the first Tuesday of each month, July to April, at Cromore Halt, Portstewart.
**ROSTREVOR** Branch Chairman: **John Parr**, 16 Drumreagh Park, Rostrevor, BT34 3DU. Tel: 028 417 39797. Branch Secretary: **Roger Morgan**, 23 Ardfield Crescent, Warrenpoint, Co Down, Northern Ireland. Tel: 028 417 54783. Branch Treasurer: **John Franklin**, 14 Rosswood Park, Rostrevor, Co Down, BT34 3DZ. Tel: 028 417 38906. Assistant Branch Secretary: **M Rea**, 8 The Square, Rostrevor, Co Down. Tel: 028 417 39808. Club President: **Paul Braham**.
**SION MILLS** Branch Secretary: **Jim Hunter**, 122 Melmount Road, Sion Mills, Co Tyrone, Northern Ireland, BT82 9EU. Tel/Fax: 028816 58226 (home); Mobile: 07752 658808. Meetings are held on the first Monday of each month during the season; all meetings are held in Marshalls Bar, Sion Mills New members always welcome.
**SLIGO** Branch Chairman: **Eddie Gray**, 27 Cartron Heights, Sligo, Republic of Ireland. Tel: 00 353 7191 44387; Mobile: 086 607 5855. Branch Secretary: **Martin Feeney**, 7 Cartron Bay, Sligo, Republic of Ireland. Tel: 00 353 71 9153838; Mobile: 086 0795137. Monthly meetings are held in the Embassy Rooms, Sligo.
**SOUTH BELFAST** Branch Secretary: **James Copeland**, 17 Oakhurst Avenue, Blacks Road, Belfast, BT10 0PD. Tel: 028 90 615184; Mobile: 07769 594875. Branch Chairman: **Danny Nolan**. Branch Vice-Chairman: **Michael Murphy**. Branch Treasurer: **James McLaughlin**. Branch Fundraising Officers: **Simon Murray**, **Pól Mead**.
Departure point for all matches: Balmoral Hotel, Blacks Road.
**STEWARTSTOWN** Branch Secretary: **Stephen Coyle**, 8 Coolnafranky Park, Cookstown, Co Tyrone, Northern Ireland, BT80 8PN. Tel: 028 86 765511; Mobile: 07789 334366.
**STRABANE** Branch Secretary: **Gerry Donnelly**, 27 Dublin Road, Strabane, Co Tyrone, Northern Ireland, BT82 9EA. Tel: 02871 883376; Email gdonnelly27@hotmail.com.
**TALLAGHT** Branch Secretary: **Jimmy Pluck**, 32 Kilcarrig Cresent, Fettercairn, Tallaght, Co Dublin, 24, Republic of Ireland. Tel/Fax: 00 353 4049768 (home); Mobile: 087 1237471 (anytime).
**TIPPERARY TOWN** Branch Secretary: **John Ryan**, 35 O'Brien Street, Tipperary Town, Co Tipperary, Republic of Ireland. Mobile: 00 353 86 883 1456 (24-hours); Fax: 00 353 62 31598; Email: johncantona.ryanmbe@eircom.com.
**TOWER ARDS** Branch Secretary: **Stephen Rowley**, 27 Trasnagh Drive, Newtownards, Co Down, BT23 4PD. Tel: 028 91 810457 (home), 028 91 810457 (work); Email: Stephen.rowley8@btinternet.com. Assistant Branch Secretary; **Alan Rowley**. Email: alan.rowley1@btinternet.com. Meetings are held every second Sunday in the Tower Inn, Mill Street, Newtownards.
**TRALEE** Branch Secretary: **Johnny Switzer**, Dromtacker, Tralee, Co Kerry, Ireland. Tel: 00353 066 7124787. Branch Chairman: Francis Boyle, Clahane, Tralee, Co Kerry. Tel: 00353 876963822.
**WARRENPOINT** Branch Secretary: **Martin McGivern**, 15 Springmeadows, Warrenpoint, Co Down, BT34 3SU. Tel: 028 417 54355; Mobile: 07736 160845; Email: martin.mcgivern@btconnect.com. Branch Chairman: **John Bird**, 23 Greendale Crescent, Rostrevor, Co Down. Tel: 028 417 38376. Branch Treasurer: **Leo Tohill**, 46 Carmen Park, Warrenpoint, Co Down. Tel: 028 417 72453; mobile 07752 924705. Branch Website: www.muwp/manutd.htm. The club is based at The Square Peg, Warrenpoint, Co Down, N Ireland. Tel: 028 417 53429. The branch meets on the last Friday of every month at 8.00pm in the Square Peg Bar, Warrenpoint. Tel: 028 417 53429.
**WEST BELFAST** Branch Secretary: **John McAllister**, 25 Broadway, Belfast, BT12 6AS. Tel: 028 90 329423; Fax: 0871 242 0360; Email: hoyt@supanet.com. Branch Chairman: **George McCabe**, 21 Beechmount Street, Belfast, BT12 7NG. Branch Treasurer: **Gerald Burns**; Branch Committee: **Liam Curran**, **Hugh Kerr**, **Mr S Thompson**, **Mr J Webb**. Meetings are held fortnightly on Tuesday evenings in "The Red Devil Bar", Falls Road, Belfast. For information, contact the Branch Secretary.

OVERSEAS BRANCHES

**BELGIUM** Branch Secretary: **Peter Bauwens**, Baarsstraat 10 9940, Evergem, Belgium. Tel/Fax: 00 32 935 77789; Email: peter.bauwens@unilever.com.

**CANADA** Branch Secretary: **Kevin Kerr**, Manchester United Supporters Club, 2368 Yonge Street, Toronto, Ontario, Canada. Tel: 00 1 416 544 8070201; Website: www.muscc.com. For membership information, email: chairmanmuscc@rogers.com.

**CYPRUS** Branch Chairman: **Ronis Soteriades**, PO Box 51365, 3504 Limassol, Cyprus. Tel: 00 357 25337690; Fax: 00 357 25388652; Email: info@grammarschool.com.cy.

**HELLENIC SUPPORTERS CLUB** (Officially affiliated to the Cyprus Branch) Contact: **Themis Giannousis,** Sokratous 39, 41336 Larisa, Greece. Tel/Fax: 00 30 24 105 79591203.

**GERMAN FRIENDS** Branch President: **Gerhard Wachter**, Silberstein 37, 95179 Geroldsgrün, Germany. Tel: +49 9267 914725204.

**GERMAN REDS** Branch Chairman: Michael Gorka, Toepferstrasse 7a, D-19246, Zarrentin, Germany. Tel: 00 49 162 3007083; Email: manu@michaelgorka.de. Branch Secretary: Thomas Rochel. Tel: 0049 391 7338275; Fax: 0049 391 7313127; Email: th.rochel@arcor.de.

**GIBRALTAR** Branch Chairman: **Clive A Moberley**. Tel: 00 350 74391; Email: clivemob@gibnet.gi. Branch Membership Secretary: **Brian Cardona**. Tel: 00 350 76653; Email: cardman@gibtelecom.net. Branch Treasurer: **Dennis R Peralta**. Tel: 00 350 77165; Email: nugget@gibtelecom.net. Committee Members: **Anthony Barnett**, **Christabelle Barnett**, **Damian Cruz**, **Billy Lima**, **Malcolm Beanland**, **KevinTewkesbury**. Branch Address: PO Box 22, Gibraltar. Email: info@manutd-gibraltar.com; Website: www.manutd-gibraltar.com.

**HOLLAND** Branch Secretary: **Dennis van der Vin**. Branch Chairman: **Ron Snellen**, PO Box 33742, 2503 BA Den Haag, Holland. Tel: 00 31 70 329 8602; Fax: 00 31 70 367 2247; Email: d.van.der.vin@hccnet.nl; Website: www.dutch-mancunians.nl.

**HONG KONG** Branch Secretary/Treasurer: **Rick Adkinson**. Branch Chairman: **Mark Saunders**. Branch Vice-Chairman: **Clive Saffery**. Branch Address: 12B Shun Ho Tower, 24-30 Ice House Street, Central, Hong Kong. Tel: 00 852 2869 1993; Fax: 00 852 2869 4312; Email: muschkb@pacific.net.hk.

**ICELAND** Branch Secretary: **Bubbi Avesson**, Studningsmannaklubbur, Manchester United á Íslandi, PO Box 12170, 132 Reykjavik, Iceland.

**KREFELD REDS** Branch Secretary: **John McFadyen,** 13 Canberra Square, Waddington, Lincolnshire, LN5 9PJ. Tel: 0044 (0)1522 721243 (home); Email: djandboys@hotmail.com. Branch Chairman: **Stuart Dykes**, Grete-Schmitz 8, 47829 Krefeld, Germany. Tel: 00 49(0)2151 477917; Mobile: 00 49 (0)1723 985152; Email: stuart.dykes@t-online.de. Branch Treasurer: **Michael Renshaw**, Am Römerborn 5, 65307 Bad Schwalbach. Tel: 0049 (0)1624 724890; Mobile: 0049 (0)1726 110872; Email: michael.renshaw@sap.com. British Servicemen may apply for membership, providing they are resident in BFG at the time of enrolment. Continued membership will be permitted pending possible return to BFG. Contact the Branch Secretary for further details. All non-English correspondence is to be submitted via the Branch Chairman.

**LUXEMBOURG** Branch Secretary: **Steve Kaiser**. Tel: 00 352 4301 33073 (work), 00 352 340265 (home); Email: Kaisers@pt.lu.

**MALTA** (since 1959) Branch Secretary: **Joseph Tedesco**. Branch President: **James Bullock**. Branch Address: Quarries Square Street, Msida MSD 03, Malta. Tel: 00 356 21223531; Fax: 00 356 21231902; Email: musc@maltanet.net; Website: www.manutd-malta.com.

**MAURITIUS** Branch Secretary: **Yacoob Atchia**, Flamingo Pool House, Remeno Street, Rose Hill, Mauritius, Indian Ocean. Tel: 464 7382 or 454 7761 or 454 3570 or 464 7750; Fax: 454 7839; Email: abyss.manutd@intnet.mu. Branch Chairman: **Swallay Banhoo**. Tel: 464 4450 (home). Branch Treasurer: **Naniel Baichoo**. Tel: 454 3570 (work), 465 0387 (home).

**NEW SOUTH WALES** Manchester United Supporters Club of NSW (Australia). Branch Chairman: **Steve Griffiths**. Tel: 040 802 28766; Email: chairman@manutdnsw.com. Branch Vice-Chairman: **Tony Redman**; Branch Treasurer: **Sean Thompson**; Branch Secretary: **Mark O'Connor**. Founders: **Fred & Ann Pollitt**. Email: fredthered@muscuk.fsnet.co.uk. Branch Website: www.manutdnsw.com; Tel: (02) 46 485930. Club meetings are held on the second Monday of each month at Sutherland United Services Club, 7 East Parade, Sutherland NSW.

**NEW ZEALAND** Branch Chairman: **Brian Wood**, 55 Pine Street, Mount Eden, Auckland, New Zealand. Email: woody.utd@xtra.co.nz. Branch Secretary: **Gareth Goodinson**, 20 Sandown Road, Rothesay Bay, Auckland, New Zealand. Branch Treasurer: **Gillian Goodinson**.

**SCANDINAVIAN** Branch Secretary: **Per H Larsen**, PO Box 4003, Dreggen, N-5835 Bergan, Norway. Tel: +47 5530 2770 (8.00pm-4.00pm, Monday to Friday); Fax: +47 5596 2033; Email: muscsb@united.no.

**SOUTH AFRICA** Branch Chairman: **Gary Bailey**. Branch Secretary: Ethel Sleith, PO Box 13990, Witfield, 1467, Gauteng. Tel/Fax: (011) 615 0040; InfoLine: (011) 615 0047; Email: Ethelred@mweb.co.za; Website: www.manutd.co.za.

**SOUTH AUSTRALIA** Branch Secretary: **Mick Griffiths**. Tel: 08 82644499. Branch Chairman: **Chris Golder**. Tel: 08 82630602. Branch Vice-Chairman: **John Harrison**. Tel: 08 82603413. Branch Treasurer: **Charlie Kelly**. Tel: 08 82628245. Branch Address: PO Box 276, Ingle Farm, South Australia 5098. Fax: 08 82816731. Meetings are held at the Para Hills Soccer Club, Bridge Road, Para Hills, SA. The Manchester United Supporters Amateur League Soccer team train and play at Para Hills Soccer Club.

**SOUTH EAST ASIA** Manager: **Jeremy Goon**, 6-B Orange Grove Road, Singapore, 258332. Tel: 00 65 737 0677; Fax: 00 65 733 5073; Email: members@manutd-sea,com.sg.

**SWISS DEVILS** Branch Secretary: **Marc Tanner**, Dorfstrasse 30d, 5430 Wettingen, Switzerland. Tel: (00 41 56) 426 94 80. Branch Chairman: **Mario Kundert**, Landstrasse 36, 8754 Netstal, Switzerland. Tel: 004155 640 5610; Branch Website: www.swissdevils.ch; Email: info@swissdevils.ch.

**TOKYO** Branch Secretary: **Hiroki Miyaji**, 2-24-10 Minami-Ayoma, Minato-ku, Tokyo, Japan. Tel: +81 3 3470 3441. English information: **Stephen Ryan**. Tel: +81 3 3380 8441; Email: best-oz@kk.iij4u.or.jp.

**USA** Branch Secretary: **Peter Holland**, PO Box 4199, Huntington, NY 11743. Tel: 631 547 550 (daytime); Fax: 631 547 6800; Email: pholland@muscusa.com. Branch Membership Secretary: **Trevor Griffiths**, 14 Lo Glen Keith Road, Glen Cove, NY 11542. Tel: 718 381 5300 ext 23 (daytime), 516 759 8634 (evenings); Email: tgmufc@aol.com; Website: www.muscusa.com.

**VICTORIA, AUSTRALIA** Branch President: **Kieran Dunleavy**. Tel/Fax: (03) 9 850 8109. Branch Address: Manchester United Supporters Club of Victoria, PO Box 1199, Camberwell 3105, Australia. Website: www.vicmanutd.com; Email: muscovic@vicnet.net.au.

**WESTERN AUSTRALIA** Branch Chairman: **Graham Wyche**, 19 Frobisher Avenue, Sorrento 6020, Perth, Western Australia. Tel/Fax: (08) 9 447 1144; Mobile: 0417 903 101; Email: freobook@omen.com.au.